JIHAD AND ITS INTERPRETATIONS IN PRE-COLONIAL MOROCCO

State–society relations during the French conquest of Algeria

Amira K. Bennison

RoutledgeCurzon
Taylor & Francis Group
LONDON AND NEW YORK

First published 2002
by RoutledgeCurzon
11 New Fetter Lane, London EC4P 4EE

Simultaneously published in the USA and Canada
by RoutledgeCurzon
29 West 35th Street, New York, NY 10001

RoutledgeCurzon is an imprint of the Taylor & Francis Group

Typeset in 10/12 Times New Roman by
Newgen Imaging Systems (P) Ltd, Chennai, India
Printed and bound in Great Britain by
Antony Rowe Ltd, Chippenham, Wiltshire

British Library Cataloguing in Publication Data
A catalogue record for this book is available from the British Library

Library of Congress Cataloging in Publication Data
A catalog record for this book has been requested

ISBN 0-7007-1693-9

CONTENTS

ACKNOWLEDGEMENTS

Like all other academic works, this study is the fruit of numerous collaborations and generous assistance as well as personal endeavour. I would like to thank Basim Musallam for encouraging me to go to Harvard where my fascination with Moroccan history began. There, Susan Gilson Miller and Ahmed Taoufik gave me my first glimpses of the complexities of state–society relations in pre-colonial Morocco. My thanks to both of them for setting me on my path and graciously assisting along the way. However, I owe my greatest debt to Michael Brett for his guidance and support and for the many insights into Maghribi history which he has shared with me over the last decade, first as my doctoral supervisor and then as a colleague and friend. I am also very grateful to Lawrence Rosen for reading and commenting on the manuscript and offering much moral support. Several of my Cambridge colleagues and friends have also offered their comments, assistance and support. I would like to express my gratitude to James Montgomery and Tarif Khalidi in particular. My thanks are also due to the British Academy, whose award enabled me to undertake this project, and the Leverhulme Trust and Manchester University for granting me a post-doctoral fellowship which enabled me to convert my doctoral dissertation into a book. In Morocco, I am grateful to the staff of the Direction des Archives Royales, and especially to its head, the Royal Historian, Abdelwahab Ben Mansour, who offered me every assistance as well as kind hospitality. I am also indebted to the staffs of the Bibliotheque Royale, the Manuscript section of the Bibliotheque Nationale and the Université Mohammed V in Rabat, especially Abderrahman Moudden, for welcoming me to the History Department. Special thanks are due to the historians Fatima Harrak and Mohamed El Mansour for their help and to Latifa Laamiqi for her generous assistance. Over the years, many other scholars and friends have offered their advice, insights and encouragement, I would like to thank all of them, especially William Graham, Tarik Youssef, Ralph Smith, Katia Boissevain, Julia Clancy-Smith and Chris Wood. Finally, it goes without saying that any errors are my own.

LIST OF ABBREVIATIONS

AAE	Les Archives des Affaires Etrangères, Quai d'Orsay, Paris.
AHG	Les Archives Historiques de la Guerre, Chateau de Vincennes, Paris.
BG	Bibliotheque Generale (*al-Khizāna al-ᶜāmma*), Rabat.
BR	Bibliotheque Royale (*al-Khizāna al-ḥasaniyya*), Rabat.
CP	Correspondance Politique – Maroc, Archives des Affaires Etrangères, Paris.
DAR	Direction des Archives Royales (*Mudiriyyat al-wathā'iq al-malikiyya*), Rabat.
FO	Foreign Office Files, Public Record Office, Kew.
PRO	Public Record Office, Kew.
TA	al-Tartīb al-ᶜāmm (General Correspondence), Direction des Archives Royales, Rabat.

NOTE ON TRANSLITERATION

The transliteration of Maghribi Arabic and the rendering of proper nouns and place names for an English-speaking readership is complicated by the predominance of French spellings. To maximise the clarity of the text I have made various compromises. I have adopted an English transliteration system based on Hans Wehr's Dictionary of Modern Standard Arabic, with the exception that I have transliterated dhal using dh rather than ḍ. ^{c}Ayn is indicated by ^{c} and Hamza with a comma. With regard to place names, I have used the usual English spellings but modified them to reflect the Arabic spelling, for example, Marrakesh rather than Marrakech, Fes rather than Fez and Tanger rather than Tangiers. In the case of less well-known place names, I have used English transliteration, for example, Shafshawan rather than Chefchaouen and Wajda rather than Oudjda.

THE PRE-COLONIAL WESTERN MAGHRIB

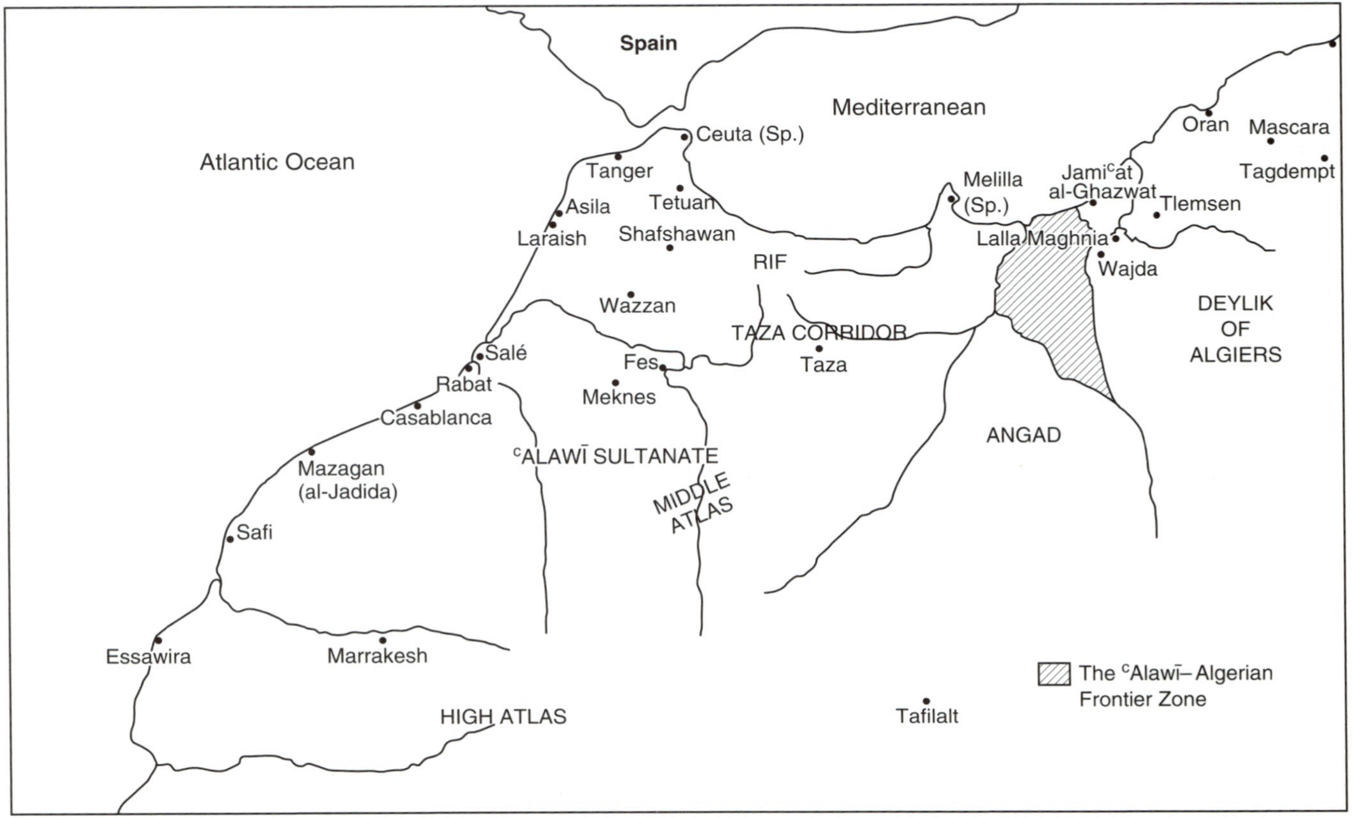

THE NORTHERN SULTANATE

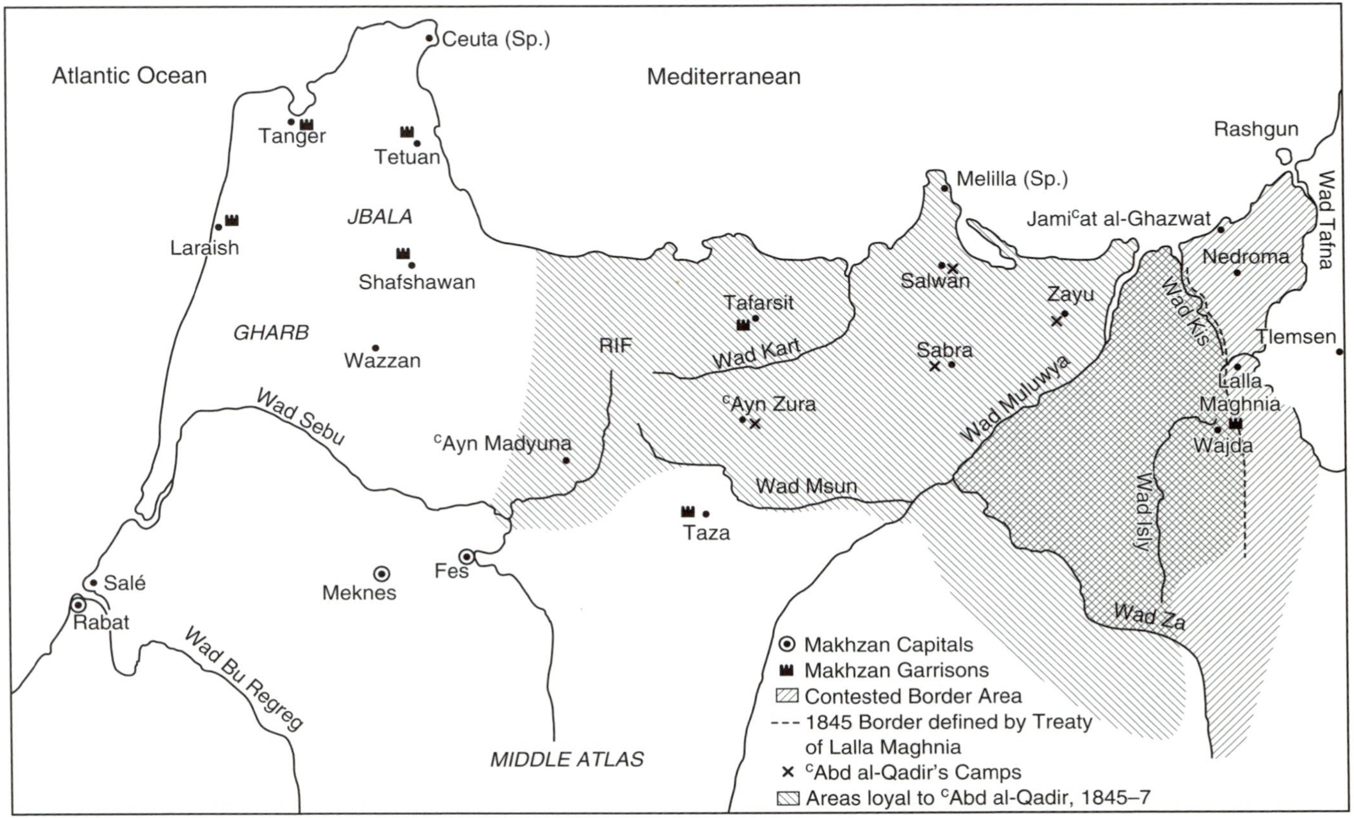

Atlantic Ocean
Mediterranean
Ceuta (Sp.)
Tanger
Tetuan
JBALA
Laraish
Shafshawan
GHARB
Wazzan
Wad Sebu
ᶜAyn Madyuna
RIF
Tafarsit
Wad Kart
ᶜAyn Zura
Wad Msun
Taza
Fes
Meknes
Salé
Rabat
Wad Bu Regreg
MIDDLE ATLAS
Melilla (Sp.)
Jamiᶜat al-Ghazwat
Salwan
Zayu
Sabra
Wad Muluwya
Rashgun
Wad Tafna
Nedroma
Wad Kis
Tlemsen
Lalla Maghnia
Wajda
Wad Isly
Wad Za
Makhzan Capitals
Makhzan Garrisons
Contested Border Area
1845 Border defined by Treaty of Lalla Maghnia
ᶜAbd al-Qadir's Camps
Areas loyal to ᶜAbd al-Qadir, 1845–7

THE TRIBES OF THE RIF

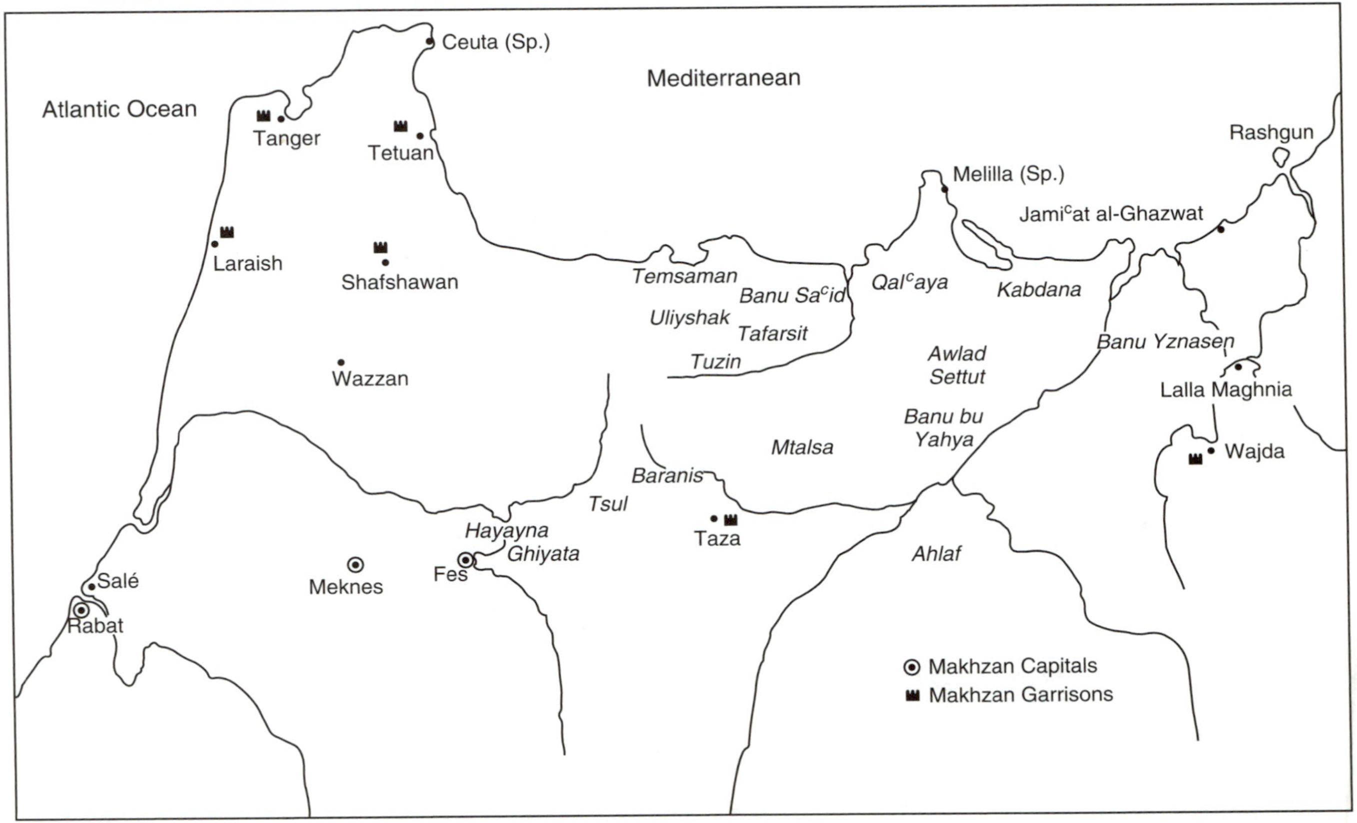

1

INTRODUCTION

This book is about Islamic statehood, an issue which looms large in the Islamic world today as secular and religious paradigms of government compete for legitimacy, generating tensions which frequently lead to violence. In the western media, clashes between western-supported regimes and their opponents are generally reduced to a simplistic formula: that of secular democracy versus Islamism. However, political players throughout the region, whatever their apparent orientation, combine secular, religious, national and Islamic elements in their ideologies of power. Secular revolutionary regimes in Iraq and Syria have made extensive use of Islamic rhetoric, whilst Islamist movements, such as the Muslim Brothers in Egypt or the Islamic revolutionaries in Iran exhibit clearly nationalist and democratic tendencies.

The multi-layered nature of contemporary Islamic political discourse is a product of the rich Islamic political tradition which makes myriad ideological positions available to those in power and those who oppose them. It is also a product of the implantation of western notions of government and nationhood in Islamic societies, where they have continuously interacted with older perceptions of statehood and identity. The roots of this interaction, with its often conflictual aspects, lie in the nineteenth century when the states of the Islamic world came face to face with the expansive imperialist powers of western Europe and the concepts of nationhood and government which they upheld. This produced dynamic syntheses such as Ottomanism and Islamic Modernism followed by the apparent replacement of traditional political concepts with western-inspired models. However the contemporary crises of legitimacy experienced by many Muslim regimes make it clear that older concepts of state and society were not actually replaced but temporarily submerged.

British and French colonial regimes and the secular nationalist and/or revolutionary regimes which succeeded them have tended to ignore the link between pre-colonial syntheses of 'tradition' and 'modernity', and colonial and post-colonial political identities. This link has nonetheless been brought to the fore by contemporary Islamist movements such as Hizb al-Tahrir, whose ahistorical view of a universal Muslim polity is based on late Ottoman caliphal ideology rather than the classical Islamic caliphate. The concept of holy war (jihad) has also achieved new prominence at the international and national levels as a way to legitimise attacks against non-Muslims and struggles against the 'un-Islamic' forces at work in Muslim societies. Although contemporary interpretations are different from those of earlier eras, current jihad concepts have clear antecedents in pre-colonial political discourse. Their resurrection makes little sense without an understanding of the political profile of the Islamic world in the early modern period, the role of religion in state–society relations at that time, and the complex effects which the colonial encounter had upon them.

These transformations have been the subject of much scholarship but their occurrance in Morocco, the focus of this book, is relatively understudied. Nonetheless, Morocco offers fresh perspectives on the character of pre-colonial Muslim polities, the interplay between traditional and modern political systems, and the role of religious concepts such as jihad in both. It is the only modern Middle Eastern or Maghribi state where the pre-colonial dynasty has continued in power and traditional religio-political notions have become key components of modern national identity and statehood. As such, it offers insight into state formation across the colonial divide and the mechanics of legitimation and contestation within one Islamic society in the modern period.

The Moroccan experience also adds an extra dimension to our understanding of patterns of religious renewal, anti-colonial resistance and modernisation in the Islamic world from 1750. As an independent sultanate with a long religio-political tradition, Morocco provides a comparison with larger states such as the Ottoman empire and Iran which were confronted with similar challenges of modernisation and adaptation to a European-dominated global economy in the eighteenth and nineteenth centuries. However, its relatively small size and location on the western edge of the Islamic world meant that its political discourse maintained a more explicitly religious and militant tone than that of the Ottomans. Whilst holy war represented only one strand in imperial Ottoman political legitimation, it secured a central position in Morocco as sultanic defence of the faith against both the ever-present foreign infidel and the domestic rebel.

The state's emphasis on the sultan's obligation to actively defend the faith by means of jihad generated a conceptual framework susceptible to appropriation by others. This became apparent when a wave of religious renewal swept across the Islamic world during the eighteenth century. While initiatives such as the Wahhabi movement in Arabia and the West African jihad movements drew their inspiration from scholarly circles, the mystics who led renewal in North Africa were able to adapt religious initiatives already taken by the Moroccan sultans.[1] These mystics had considerable impact across the Maghrib and the Middle East where their activist approach to social and political as well as religious issues greatly influenced the Islamic Modernists and Pan-Islamists of the late nineteenth and early twentieth centuries. The latter in turn contributed to the thought of the Egyptian Muslim Brothers, an important source of inspiration for modern Islamists and their vision of jihad.

The jihadist component in Moroccan state–society discourse also encouraged Moroccans to play a significant, but largely unrecognised, part in the first phase of Maghribi resistance to colonialism, ^{c}Abd al-Qādir's jihad against the French conquest of Algiers in the 1830s and 1840s. Finally, when armed resistance began to seem futile without technological and military parity, jihad ideology provided the sultanate with a means of legitimising modernisation, which began with the army and then spread to government. The debates which ensued about how to defend a Muslim society from imperial European penetration without sacrificing its identity add a distinctive Maghribi voice to the Egyptian and Ottoman voices which explored the same issues in the nineteenth century. The ^{c}Alawī sultanate of Morocco can be seen, therefore, as one significant piece in a much larger jigsaw encompassing the Muslim Mediterranean, Islamic Africa, and regions further afield at the dawn of the imperial age.

This approach challenges a tendency within Moroccan studies to view Moroccan state and society as a world apart and adapts the argument applied by Vincent Cornell in his study of Moroccan sainthood that, despite its specificities, Moroccan society shared the universal cultural framework engendered by Islam.[2] From this perspective, ethno-linguistic categorisation of the population as Arabs or Berbers seems less important than broader questions about religion and politics applicable to many Muslim tribal societies. Furthermore, Morocco's political separation from the Ottoman empire seems less crucial than social and economic 'overlaps' with neighbouring areas and shared elements in their political cultures.

This study's primary unit of analysis is therefore pre-colonial Morocco understood not as a closed unit of reference but as a regional Islamic society influencing and influenced by adjacent regions and located within the cultural nexus of the *dār al-islām* in its entirety. This society inhabited roughly the same space as the contemporary Moroccan state: the Atlantic plains, the surrounding arc of mountains composed of the Rif, Middle Atlas, High Atlas and Anti-Atlas ranges, and the desertic pre-Sahara. Like many Islamic societies, it was a composite of linguistic and ethnic elements – Berber and Arabic-speaking tribesmen, sub-Saharan Africans, and Arab or Arabised urbanites, a significant proportion of whom boasted Andalusī ancestry. The main sociological division lay between town and tribe, although the tribal ethos penetrated the city and vice-versa.

Only 5–10 per cent of the population resided in Morocco's towns, but they were vital centres of government, religion and commerce. The most important were Fes and Marrakesh both of which had served as dynastic capitals in the past. The existence of two key urban centres signalled a north–south divide which was often more important than the frequently cited divisions between Arab and Berber or lands of government (*makhzan*) and dissidence (*sība*). Europeans described Morocco as an 'empire' consisting of two 'kingdoms', Fes and Marrakesh, but the two cities actually represented overlapping cultural zones which can be characterised as Andalusī and Saharan.

In the north, the dominant culture was that of al-Andalus, carried across the Straits of Gibraltar during the centuries of the Reconquista. It was especially influential in Fes, Tetuan, Tanger and Rabat–Salé and connected them with a string of cities across the Ottoman Maghrib which had also received migrants from the Iberian peninsula. Andalusī culture within Morocco was characterised by nostalgia for al-Andalus and a receptivity to ideas of jihad against the 'infidel'. Trading patterns complemented this Mediterranean cultural orientation. Although Fes was an entrepot for trans-Saharan caravans coming up the Wad Ziz from the pre-Saharan oasis of Tafilalt, its most important function was to channel commodities along the great west–east land route to Egypt. It was also the starting point for the main Moroccan ḥajj caravan. For Marrakesh the Saharan and sub-Saharan worlds had greater significance and commerce with them created a culture distinct from that of the north. Marrakesh also possessed closer links to the Atlantic ports which traded with Europe from the fifteenth century. As a result the elite of Marrakesh frequently adopted a more liberal attitude towards the 'infidel' than the elite of Fes.

Outside the towns, Moroccan society was predominantly tribal.[3] In the Moroccan context the term 'tribe' indicated a kin group in the broadest sense. Most tribes, Arab and Berber, claimed descent from an eponymous ancestor but others were communities of place or even of function brought together by the agency of the state which took on the attributes of a tribe over time. The dominance of tribal structures indicated the importance of genealogy as an explanatory mode in Moroccan society, a fact which affected all spheres of life, including politics where alliances, submission and opposition were frequently influenced – and explained – by reference to kinship ties.

Other aspects of tribalism also had political implications. Most importantly, tribal society did not differentiate military from civilian roles and every tribesman was a warrior as well as a farmer or herder. As in other parts of the Maghrib and the Middle East, this presented states with major problems of control and impelled them to supplement their military resources – which were often unequal to dealing with the tribes – with other methods of control. The situation was exacerbated by the inherent mobility of tribal societies. In Morocco, Berber and Arab tribes of the less fertile desert fringe had pushed steadily north and west through the mountain ranges to the fertile Atlantic plains over the centuries, making and remaking the tribal map of the region.

Despite constant modification by tribal movements, a north–south divide was also evident in the countryside. In the north, the proximity of the Iberian peninsula and the Mediterranean and links with the Ottoman Maghrib affected rural as well as urban life. Many Andalusī Muslims had sought refuge in the Rif mountains founding enclaves like Shafshawan and propagated jihadist sentiments among the tribes. As a result many Rif tribes considered themselves holy warriors (*mujāhidūn*) defending the frontier, a duty they discharged by harassing the Spanish enclaves of Ceuta and Melilla and by small-scale piracy along the Rif coast.[4] This fostered a black market economy which supplemented the meagre products of Rif agriculture and stock-keeping.

Two main routes bisected the north, the Taza corridor running between the Rif and Middle Atlas from Fes to Tlemsen and the passage east of the Middle Atlas from the Sahara to the Mediterranean. Both fostered interaction between the rural northeast and the neighbouring deylik of Algiers. The Taza corridor was the main channel for commercial and religious traffic to and from Fes while the eastern Middle Atlas was a migratory path, a trade route and the frontier between the sultanate and the deylik of Algiers. Several tribes such as the Berber Banū Yznāsen of the Rif, the Arab tribes of the Angad, the Awlād Sīdī al-Shaykh and Dhū'l-Manī^{c} Arabs of the pre-Sahara straddled the entire border zone generating myriad socio-economic links which transcended the political boundary.[5]

A vital component in Moroccan society, urban and rural, was Islam. Moroccan cities harboured *^{c}ulamā'* elites, comparable to those of other Maghribi cities, who propagated a text-based form of Islam based on the Qur'ān and the letter of the Mālikī school of law. Rural Islam was mediated through persons rather than texts in the form of holy men who fulfilled religious and social functions. This did not mean that it was necessarily less orthodox than urban Islam, although it was often considered so from the perspective of the city, but that religion, in the form of innate holiness (*baraka*), was seen to reside in individuals.

Such attitudes reflected the fact that charismatic preachers, scholars and Sufi mystics, known generically as marabouts (*murābiṭ, murābiṭūn*), had directed rural islamisation from earliest times. Some were descended from the Prophet (*sharīf, shurafā'*) while such ancestry was assumed for others, thereby creating a broad overlap between the categories of marabout and *sharīf*. It was also assumed that marabouts and *shurafā'* could pass on their powers to their descendants. Both, therefore, established rural religious lineages recognised by the tribes among whom they lived as repositories of the faith in the form of *baraka*.

The difference between marabouts and *shurafā'* was the source of their *baraka*: in the case of marabouts their personal spiritual powers indicated their possession of *baraka*, whilst the *shurafā'* possessed inherent genealogical *baraka* regardless of their personal qualities.[6] This distinction affected their respective functions. Marabouts and maraboutic lineages, large and small, performed the religious, pacific roles of educators, mediators and guarantors of safe passage through the territories of the tribe or tribes subject to their influence. Their authority rested on the efficacy of their religious sanctions which in turn rested upon tribal recognition of the potency of their *baraka*. At different times the authority of maraboutic lineages such as the marabouts of Iligh in the Sus or of Dila' in the Middle Atlas was so widely recognised that they attempted to convert it to political power but then faced the difficulty of transforming religious authority based on pacifism into power based on force. The Nāṣiriyya religious brotherhood of Tamgrut in the Dar^{c}a valley was similarly powerful but maintained its influence by avoiding direct bids for political power.

The *shurafā'* did not face such constraints even when they performed similar functions to marabouts because their genealogy enabled them to claim a religio-political role in the tradition of their ancestor, the Prophet. It was this aspect of sharifism, the potential to cross the line between the pacific/religious and military/political spheres which enabled sharifian lineages to emerge as the main contenders for power in Morocco after 1500. Their genealogical prestige enabled them to overcome tribal divisions and, since their veneration was common to all parts of the western Maghrib, they could also partially surmount the cultural differences between the north and south. The sultanate created by these sharifian lineages was contemporary with the Ottoman sultanate but outlived it, surviving the colonial era from 1912 to 1956 to re-emerge as the present Moroccan monarchy.

Studies of the pre-colonial sharifian sultanate often view it in isolation but the significance of Moroccan pre-colonial political culture only really emerges through its contextualisation within the wider Islamic world. The sultanate was one of several Islamic states formed after 1500 in which ruling dynasties with absolutist pretensions used military elites recruited from socially marginal or alien groups to extract taxes from predominantly rural societies. They justified and legitimised their imposition of hierarchical politico-military structures on society by reference to Islam. In the majority of cases this entailed interpreting the dynasty and the state it headed as vital to the maintenance of Islam as a faith through the preservation of societal order. In the Ottoman empire, the largest Islamic state of the time, the sultans ruled as defenders of the frontier between the Muslim and non-Muslim worlds, the *dār al-islām* and *dār al-ḥarb*, and protectors of the Sharīᶜa. The Ottomans based their extraction of wealth from their subjects, the flock, upon the circle of equity, a formula of government dating from antiquity and incorporated into Islamic ethics, which they reworked as an adjunct to military absolutism.[7] In its Ottoman form the circle of equity stated:

> There can be no royal authority without the military.
> There can be no military without wealth.
> The subjects produce the wealth.
> Justice preserves the subjects' loyalty to the sovereign.
> Justice requires harmony in the world.
> The world is a garden, its walls are the state.
> The Shari'a orders the state.
> There is no support for the Shari'a except through royal authority.[8]

It envisaged a static society of four estates, men of the sword, men of the pen, merchants and peasants, regulated by the agency of the sultan and his army. The sultan had the right to gather taxes because he had to support his army, but also a responsibility to ensure that they were collected in a just way. The circle of equity expressed an ideal rather than political reality and it was most often cited when socio-political and economic change blurred the relations it defined.[9] Its principles nonetheless legitimised what Gellner called the 'Mamluk' option in Middle Eastern government, the institutionalised use of a military slave elite to support a dynasty.[10]

Most of the Maghrib became part of the Ottoman empire during the sixteenth century as the Ottomans and Habsburgs struggled for Mediterranean hegemony. By the end of the century the Ottomans had super-imposed the 'Mamluk' or Ottoman option of government over earlier tribal forms of Maghribi statehood described by the fourteenth century historian, Ibn Khaldūn. According to the Khaldunian model, Maghribi political history was cyclical: at the start of each cycle a well-organised and militant tribal group from the periphery, united by kin solidarity (*ᶜaṣabiyya*) and often a religious programme, assumed power over the cities of its predecessor, thereby establishing a new urban-based regime which would be replaced in time by a new generation of tribesmen from the fringe.[11] Polities which began in this way as tribal chieftaincies possessed greater longevity if the paramount chief and his lineage managed to use religion to justify the replacement of power-sharing between collateral lineages with a political hierarchy headed by themselves.

The sixteenth century fusion between tribal and Ottoman patterns in the Maghrib produced a cluster of political systems in which the apparatus of government was known as the *makhzan* or storehouse, a word well-suited to the idea of government as an extractive machine. These political systems were supported by professional slave armies of the Janissary type and allied tribes, known as *makhzan* (government) or *jaysh* (army) tribes, who served the state in return for tax exemptions and other privileges. Although peripatetic for at least part of the year, rulers resided in cities and required the support of their commercial and religious elites. They also required the support of the rural tribal population known along with their urban counterparts as the *raᶜāyā*, (Turkish: *reaya*), a term more appropriate to the usually unarmed sedentary populations of the Fertile Crescent and Egypt than to the predominantly armed tribal subjects of Maghribi states. As a result these states confronted the problem that, although Ottoman absolutism posited a strict separation between an arms-bearing military elite and a weaponless subject population, this ideal conflicted with the norms of tribal society in which every man had a military as well as civilian role.

The rulers of the autonomous provinces of the Ottoman Maghrib – Tripoli, Tunis and Algiers – legitimised themselves in their capital cities as delegates appointed by the Ottoman sultan to fulfil his duty to defend the frontier and maintain the Islamic way of life. Although not indigenous, their patronage of religion, law, public order and commerce persuaded indigenous urban elites to accept their rule. Some diffusion of power from imported to local ruling elites in the form of the *kulogullari*, sons of Turks by indigenous women, facilitated this process. In the countryside, they tackled the problem of handling an armed tribal *raᶜāyā* using tactics of coercion and co-optation. Recruitment of *makhzan* tribes, alliances and sporadic shows of force secured conditional tribal acquiescence to their rule.

The reasons why the expanding Ottoman empire did not conquer Morocco during the sixteenth century have not been fully researched but may reflect the difficulties they envisaged in subduing a heterogeneous tribal population as well as the strategic value of leaving a buffer state between their domains and those of the Habsburgs.[12] Instead, southern Ḥasanī lineages of *shurafā'*, the Saᶜdī and ᶜAlawī dynasties, emerged to partially implement the Ottoman option of government in

Morocco. Although independent of Istanbul both were influenced by Ottoman government. This tendency started with the Sa^{c}dī sultans but became more pronounced during the subsequent ^{c}Alawī era when the sultanate came to resemble its Ottoman neighbours in the Maghrib in structure and adopted elements of imperial Ottoman political theory.

As indigenous tribal lineages, the emergence of these dynasties followed the Khaldunian trajectory. Like their predecessors, they came from the tribal fringe, relying upon their religious status as descendants of the Prophet to raise themselves above competitors for power. They had to capture key cities, consolidate their power and authority and extend it over the tribal periphery from which they themselves had come. To do this they had to resolve the tensions between sociopolitical equality and hierarchy, between power sharing and its monopolisation, generated by the imposition of a hierarchical state of tribal origin upon a tribal population among whom leadership was either shared by groups of elders or assumed by chiefs who had proven their worth.[13]

The sharifian dynasties' solution was to adapt the tools developed by the Habsburgs and Ottomans, gunpowder weaponry and a professional army, composed of slaves in the Islamic case. The Sa^{c}dī dynasty put together an army of Ottoman mercenaries, Spanish renegade artillerymen, black slaves and military tribes which was never more than the sum of its parts. Their ^{c}Alawī successors learned the lesson and formed a black slave army, the ^{c}Abīd al-Bukhārī, modelled on the Janissaries and supplemented by indigenous tax-exempt *jaysh* tribes. They tackled the problem of an armed tribal *ra^{c}āyā* by using the coercive power of the ^{c}Abīd to secure their monopoly of power, invoking religion to justify it. The religious justifications they developed gave pre-colonial Moroccan religio-political discourse its richness.

Like the Ottomans, the sharifian sultans presented their state as a continuation of the caliphal paradigm of government and legitimised their rule in terms of defence of the faith at home and abroad by means of jihad.[14] The ^{c}Alawī sultan was caliph/imam of the *umma*, the universal Muslim community, the physical replacement of the Prophet Muḥammad, and God's deputy on earth.[15] His position was, therefore, a religio-political one essential to the welfare of the *umma*, whose justification lay in the revelation of Islam itself. Sharifism was intrinsic to the dynasty's claim to caliphal status, not only adding a vital genealogical component to Islamic statehood but promising the entire community the benefit of sharifian *baraka*. The eighteenth century historian, al-Ḍu^{c}ayyif, conveys this in his account of the oath of allegiance to Mawlay Ismā^{c}īl, second sultan of the ^{c}Alawī dynasty:

> He [Mawlay Ismā^{c}īl] nurtured with the *baraka* of his life a proliferation of offspring. He granted life to the valleys and plains and civilisation flourished. In his days, the people renewed the sciences and exchanges of knowledge thrived. The stars in his orbit shone brightly and the poor and orphans found sustenance.[16]

This distinguished ᶜAlawī absolutism from its Ottoman counterpart: whereas the Ottoman sultan was the embodiment of justice, the ᶜAlawī sultan was the embodiment of *baraka*. By defining the ruler in such terms the dynasty consolidated its religious status. In a society containing numerous lineages of *shurafā'*, however, sharifism alone could not guarantee legitimacy. The Saᶜdī and ᶜAlawī sultans, therefore, promoted the concept that the state existed to wage the jihad as the principal sign of their right to rule. This paved the way for the development of the jihadist strand in Moroccan political culture which is the topic of this study.

The religious dimensions of political legitimacy, whether rooted in justice or *baraka*, made Islamic states vulnerable to religious opposition and in the mid-eighteenth century a spate of religio-political movements questioned their ability to nurture the Islamic way of life using the idiom of jihad. In Arabia, Muḥammad b. ᶜAbd al-Wahhāb launched a jihad to reinstate Islam in its pristine form in reaction to what he believed was the degradation of the faith by the tribesmen of the Najd and the Ottoman *ᶜulamā'*. In West Africa, Muslim religious leaders rejected traditional accommodations with African animist religions and launched jihad movements to establish new Muslim states which outlawed syncretic practices.[17] In the Maghrib, scholarly mystics from the ᶜAlawī sultanate and the western part of the deylik of Algiers founded new religious brotherhoods or remodelled existing ones. These brotherhoods were more tightly organised than those which preceded them and possessed a socially and politically activist approach expressed in their provision of rural religious education and open criticism of Maghribi rulers and urban *ᶜulamā'*. In several cases verbal criticism from Sufi shaykhs preceded brotherhood rebellions conceptualised as holy wars (jihad) against corruption (*fasād*) by those who waged them.

Studies over the last decade have revealed the impact which Moroccan religio-political thought had on the Maghribi version of eighteenth century religious renewal.[18] Several Sufi reformers appear to have been influenced by the reformist ideas of the ᶜAlawī sultan, Sidi Muḥammad, and borrowed their jihadist rhetoric from ᶜAlawī religio-political discourse. This forced the dynasty to counter such oppositional religious constructs by characterising brotherhood 'jihads' as 'revolts' against legitimate Islamic authority. This initiated a fertile period of state–society debate about the meaning of jihad which intersected with the beginnings of European imperial pressure upon the Maghrib.

This was a crucial juncture. Under the growing impact of European imperialism, western Maghribi jihad dialectics gained heightened significance, and efforts to reform the Islamic state and society became part and parcel of the struggle to resist infidel conquests which began in the 1830s. The foremost proponents of a jihad against internal decadence and imperial takeover were Mawlay ᶜAbd al-Raḥmān, sultan of Morocco, and the west Algerian Qādirī Sufis, Muḥyī al-Dīn and his son, ᶜAbd al-Qādir al-Jazā'irī. When the French conquered Algiers in 1830, the Moroccans responded most vigorously and proved keenest to launch a jihad to reinstate Islamic government and defend the *dār al-islām* from the French. Two years later, ᶜAbd al-Qādir took the initiative and launched an independent jihad in alliance with the Moroccans to institute a hegemonic reformist Islamic political order in Algeria and prevent its takeover by the French.

ᶜAbd al-Qādir has, of course, been the subject of numerous studies which have analysed him and interpreted his actions from several different perspectives. The earliest, written by French military commanders, catalogue the evolution of French imperial attitudes in response to the resistance offered by ᶜAbd al-Qādir and others.[19] They, therefore, focused upon him as a representative of a backward and fanatical culture in need of the French *mission civilisatrice*, but also made him the epitome of French nostalgia for the chivalric past. In nineteenth and twentieth century British historiography he also played a heroic role as warrior leader of the Arabs, a people who had the potential to act as British allies in their struggle for imperial dominion.[20] His identification as representative of the Arabs paved the way for his appropriation by Algerian nationalists as the personification of Algerian nationhood on the eve of the colonial onslaught. Since independence, other dimensions of his history such as his religiosity, his spirituality, and his location in the scholarly west Algerian milieu have been addressed.[21] However, the alliance between his lineage and the ᶜAlawī sultanate remains uncharted and the multiple ideological and material connections between the northern sultanate and west Algeria in this crucial period downplayed.

The colonial period not only obscured the link between ᶜAbd al-Qādir and the ᶜAlawī sultanate, but also subverted the sultanate's pre-colonial profile in other ways. The dominant French colonial discourse dismissed the sultanate as a failure in the world of nation-states because, judged by European criteria, the ᶜAlawī sultans had not involved their subjects in the political process and did not represent them. They saw Moroccan government as purely coercive and the sultanate as divided into two parts, the lands of government, *bilād al-makhzan*, where the sultans could enforce obedience and the lands of dissidence, *bilād al-sība*, where they could not. In the colonial view, the division between 'government' and 'dissidence' corresponded to an ethnic division between incursive Arab conquerors and indigenous Berbers, and a religio-cultural division between the orthodox 'Arab' Islam of the cities and the popular 'Berber' Islam of the countryside.[22] Although early French observers realised that such an analysis was too simplistic, it became the basis for the 'colonial vulgate' which perceived Moroccan history during the Islamic period as a series of failed attempts by Berbers and Arabs alike to create a united state, or for a single Moroccan nation to emerge.[23] The thrust of this discourse was to place the French colonial authorities in the position of having taken up the political challenge to create a single unified state and succeeded where indigenous Berber rulers and Arab imperialists from the Orient had failed.[24]

The distinction between *bilād al-makhzan* and *bilād al-sība* which the French identified certainly existed but did not necessarily have the meaning with which they invested it. The words themselves, *makhzan* (storehouse/government) and *sība* (that which goes to waste) suggest material rather than political categories: areas where tax was collected and areas where it was not. Neither of these areas had fixed boundaries nor were they necessarily related to language, culture or interpretations of Islam. It was true that over the centuries since the Arab conquest the Rif and Atlas mountains encircling the Moroccan plains had become bastions of different Berber languages and cultures against the spread of Arabic outwards from the cities and across the desert, and that mountain areas more successfully resisted state tax-gathering than lowland areas. However, Berbers served the state at different times and Arab tribes could resist state tax gathering as strenuously as their Berber neighbours.

Another problem with viewing the pre-colonial period through a colonial or post-colonial prism is that it perpetuates the false impression of the Moroccan sultanate's isolation from the Ottoman Maghrib and the Islamic east. French colonial authorities endeavoured to protect the colony of Algeria by delineating and closing its borders with Ḥusaynid Tunis and the ᶜAlawī sultanate. These borders, which outlined the post-colonial states of Morocco, Algeria and Tunisia, coincided to an extent with earlier borders but differed greatly from them in character. Before the arrival of the French, marcher areas predominated and neighbouring regimes more usually commanded the allegiance of towns and tribes than possessed land *per se*. Where specific territorial claims existed they were frequently notional without physical representation on the ground. The fluid nature of such boundaries allowed considerable human movement from one state to another for education, trade, and seasonal migration. Morocco was therefore by no means as isolated from the neighbouring deylik of Algiers as the colonial and post-colonial phases suggest. This can be seen in the similarities between the structures of government in each, and, more importantly, in the demonstrable sense of cultural community between the northeastern sultanate and the western deylik of Algiers mentioned above. The openness of the pre-colonial border explains why Morocco should have been involved in west Algerian resistance to the French conquest and why ᶜAbd al-Qādir's jihad was a Moroccan as well as Algerian affair.

With respect to domestic politics, scholars are now moving away from analyses based on colonial interpretations of *makhzan* and *sība* to re-investigate both the tenets of pre-colonial political discourse and their perpetuation into the post-colonial era. A recent volume edited by Rahma Bourquia and Susan Gilson Miller, *In the Shadow of the Sultan: Culture, Power and Politics in Morocco*, attempts this very task.[25] Another study of the durability of traditional religio-political modes of interaction is Abdellah Hammoudi's, *Master and Disciple*, which asserts that social and political relations in contemporary Morocco draw extensively on the medieval relationship between a Sufi master and his disciple.[26] These and other studies stress the importance of communal religio-cultural values in political legitimation and the fact that dynastic legitimacy had to be constantly adjusted and proved to society. They highlight, in particular, different Moroccan dynasties' use of jihad in state formation and maintenance and their use of descent from the Prophet to legitimise themselves.

The aim of this study is to pick up some of these threads and explore the part which sharifism and jihad played in pre-colonial Moroccan statehood, the spread of such ideas eastwards into the deylik of Algiers, and their interaction with French imperialism and trends of Muslim modernisation emanating from the Ottoman east. It begins by investigating the development of sharifism and jihad as political ideologies in the Islamic west over several centuries. It then identifies how they were used by Mawlay ^{c}Abd al-Raḥmān, sultan of Morocco, and ^{c}Abd al-Qādir, the best known leader of resistance during the watershed decades of the 1830s and 1840s when the French established themselves as colonial masters of Algeria.

An aspect of ^{c}Alawī jihad ideology I wish to highlight is the evolving relationship between dynastic concepts of jihad against the European infidel and jihad against dissidence, rebellion and challenges for power, collectively described as 'corruption' (*fasād*) in the early modern period. Although such ideas began as dynastic constructs, the ^{c}Alawī dynasty could not maintain a monopoly over them: both the ideas of jihad against the infidel and jihad against internal corruption could be, and were, utilised by competing centres of power, initiating complex debates on the legitimacy of rival 'holy wars' and 'rebellions'. Such discourses and counter-discourses offer an alternative perspective on Moroccan state–society interaction to the *makhzan–sība* model.

Debate between the sultan and his subjects as to what constituted holy war and what constituted rebellion was heightened at moments of crisis. The French conquest of Algiers in 1830 triggered such a crisis by presenting a regime which used its jihad credentials to legitimate its existence with a real infidel threat to fight. I hope to demonstrate that, contrary to colonial French notions, the pre-colonial Moroccan political system possessed considerable moral resources as a result of its use of sharifism in conjunction with jihadist ideologies, and was able to use the latter to respond dynamically to the challenges and opportunities presented by French expansion into the Maghrib in the decades after they captured Algiers.

In analysing the formative decades of the 1830s and 1840s, I also hope to demonstrate that early resistance to colonialism in Algeria was not driven by proto-nationalist sentiments but by principles of sharifism and jihad inspired by the ^{c}Alawī model, common throughout the western Maghrib. Resistance thus involved not only ^{c}Abd al-Qādir and the population of the Ottoman province of Algiers but also the ^{c}Alawī sultan and his subjects, belying the 'Moroccan' or 'Algerian' frameworks used by colonial and nationalist discourses. Such categories started to impinge upon Maghribi consciousness in the later 1840s when the French implanted their concept of territorial statehood in the Maghrib by establishing the borders of *l'Algérie française* in 1845.

Their definition of a new type of border between the sultanate and Algeria initiated a period of ^{c}Alawī military and governmental modernisation comparable to and contemporary with the *niẓām-i cedīd* and Tanzimat phases in the Ottoman empire. It also prompted a series of domestic political crises symptomatic of the confrontation between indigenous and European political concepts as the Moroccan sultan, ^{c}Abd al-Qādir and the population of the region debated the religiously acceptable response to the border laid down in the 1845 treaty of Lalla

Maghnia. The rhetoric of these crises revolved around competing interpretations of holy war and, by extension, rebellion. I hope to demonstrate that such crises, although they ultimately facilitated colonial penetration, also allowed constant renegotiation of the principles of Moroccan statehood during the nineteenth century. Such renegotiation consolidated proto-national Moroccan identity and laid the foundations for the layering of traditional and modern elements which still characterises Moroccan statehood today.

The study is divided into seven chapters. The next chapter, Chapter 2, surveys the evolution of the sharifian jihad model of statehood in the northwest Maghrib and the contribution of different dynasties and rulers to its formulation up to 1830. It also identifies the gradual spread of ᶜAlawī dynastic theory out from the centre to society itself and its geographical extension into the western province of the deylik of Algiers, creating a religious and cultural zone of ᶜAlawī influence larger than the sultanate. This involves an analysis of ᶜAlawī theories of holy war against the infidel and holy war against rebellion/corruption, and their appropriation by different groups in society, including scholarly mystics involved in Maghribi religious renewal.

Chapter 3 shows how the French conquest of Algiers in 1830 gave the ruling ᶜAlawī sultan, Mawlay ᶜAbd al-Raḥmān, an opportunity to convert ᶜAlawī religio-cultural influence in west Algeria into political control, using jihad against the infidel and against disruptive forces in society as a justification to occupy the city of Tlemsen. It also looks at how the failure of this attempt led to an ᶜAlawī withdrawal from Tlemsen and rebellion within the sultanate, but provided local leaders in west Algeria with a chance to bid for power using ᶜAlawī ideologies.

Chapter 4 investigates the rise to power of the most successful of these leaders, ᶜAbd al-Qādir b. Muḥyī al-Dīn, and interprets it from the 'Moroccan' rather than 'Algerian' perspective as an attempt to replicate the ᶜAlawī sharifian jihad state. It then explores the relationship between Mawlay ᶜAbd al-Raḥmān and ᶜAbd al-Qādir in the 1830s as that of cautious religio-political allies. This chapter also looks at the formative years of ᶜAbd al-Qādir's state as a significant period in the evolution of the theory of holy war against rebellion due to ᶜAbd al-Qādir's interpretation of it as a facet of jihad against the infidel in the context of impending colonial conquest.

Chapter 5 investigates the broadening of participation in anti-colonial jihad, the political and diplomatic tensions which this engendered and the ensuing breakdown of the alliance between Mawlay ᶜAbd al-Raḥmān and ᶜAbd al-Qādir. This period began by engaging the inhabitants of west Algeria and the northern sultanate in a common jihad against the infidel, headed by ᶜAbd al-Qādir. The French responded by placing intense diplomatic pressure on the sultan to close the border. Although Mawlay ᶜAbd al-Raḥmān did not publicly disavow the jihad, he started to view holy war as a spatially bounded rather than universal obligation and opposition to this view as rebelliousness. His evident reluctance to lead a regional jihad led to a decline in his prestige and finally popular recognition of ᶜAbd al-Qādir, the sharifian holy warrior from the periphery, as a better candidate for power.

Chapter 6 traces the story of ideological and military contest for power which took place between Mawlay ^{c}Abd al-Raḥmān and ^{c}Abd al-Qādir in the late 1840s as religio-political rivals within the sultanate. At this point both men claimed to be rightful definers and leaders of holy war against the corruption/rebellion (*fasād*) of the other. ^{c}Abd al-Qādir harangued the sultan to fulfil his religious commitment to lead a regional jihad, while the sultan denied the former's right to make such judgements. ^{c}Abd al-Qādir's arguments and Mawlay ^{c}Abd al-Raḥmān's responses laid bare the parameters of Islamic statehood in Morocco in the early nineteenth century. Chapter 7 concludes by showing how they formed the basis for state–society discourse during the ensuing decades of state modernisation and European penetration which culminated in the imposition of the French and Spanish protectorates in 1912.

2

THE EVOLUTION OF THE SHARIFIAN JIHAD STATE OF MOROCCO

Historical antecedents

The sharifian jihad state of nineteenth century Morocco was the product of centuries of interplay between the Berber tribes of the western Maghrib, Islam and incoming Arab populations. After the Arabo-Islamic conquest of North Africa in the late seventh to eighth century AD, different political forms emerged as the slow and discrete processes of Islamisation and Arabisation got underway. Situated between the emergent cultural poles of Ifriqiya and al-Andalus, the barely conquered western Berber provinces of the Umayyad and then ᶜAbbāsid empires were an ideal refuge for religious and political dissidents. Many found a ready audience for their religio-political doctrines among the Berber tribes and established city states which became the nuclei of trading networks and centres for the dissemination of Islam among the Berbers. Early states of this type were Rustamid Tahart and Midrārid Sijilmasa founded by Khārijīs, and Idrīsī Fes founded by Idrīs b. ᶜAbd Allah, a descendant of the Prophet and refugee from ᶜAbbāsid persecution. In the formation of each of these states charismatic leadership, a distinct religio-political doctrine, and the backing of a tribe or tribal grouping were essential, prefiguring the large-scale Berber religio-political enterprises of the eleventh and twelfth centuries, the Almoravid and Almohad movements.

The Almoravid movement grew out of the Islamisation of the Saharan Ṣanhāja by Ibn Yāsīn and his dedicated followers, the Murābiṭūn, in the eleventh century. Ibn Yāsīn was supported in his religious undertaking by Ṣanhāja tribal notables who put the unification of the Ṣanhāja under the banner of Mālikī orthodoxy to political ends and launched a jihad against the Zanāta Berbers of Sijilmasa, their heretical Khārijī rivals for the trans-Saharan trade. The Almoravids then expanded south across the Sahara and north across the High Atlas mountains to incorporate the Atlantic plains into their empire. Finally, they crossed the Straits of Gibraltar to wage jihad against the Iberian Christians after the Castilian capture of Toledo in 1085. They ruled al-Andalus and Morocco until ousted by a rival Berber religio-political movement, that of the Almohads.

Like the Almoravid jihad, the Almohad movement was the product of rural Berber Islamisation, this time among the Maṣmūda Berbers of the High Atlas.

It differed from the Almoravid movement, however, in that Almohad religious and political leadership were fused in the charismatic personnages of Ibn Tumārt, the Almohad *mahdī*, and his successor, ^{c}Abd al-Mu'min. Ibn Tumārt united the Maṣmūda as the true and enlightened monotheists in a dark world of imperfect faith. After his death, ^{c}Abd al-Mu'min led the Almohads in the successive conquests of the western Maghrib, al-Andalus and Ifriqiya to return their Muslim populations to the true faith and drive out the infidel Christians. The implementation of Almohadism across this vast area proved impossible as did the defence of the Andalusī frontier against the Christians. Less than a century after the triumphant Almohad capture of the Almoravid capital of Marrakesh in 1148 their empire crumbled and a series of successor dynasties emerged across the Islamic West: the Naṣrids of Granada, the Marīnids of Fes, the Zayyānids of Tlemsen and the Hafsids of Tunis.

All these dynasties were the products of new alliances between state and society which sought legitimation in older religio-political paradigms. The Naṣrids of Granada presented themselves as indigenous heirs to the Andalusī heritage, dedicated to the defence of Mālikī orthodoxy, and indeed Islam, against the Christian offensive. The Hafsid lineage of Almohad governors took power in Tunis as the Almohads true successors. The Zayyānids and Marīnids were Zanāta Berber chieftains from the pasture lands east of the Middle Atlas in what is now western Algeria. Their respective bids for power depended upon their control of the cities of the Maghrib and their acceptance by its tribes, now a mixture of recently arrived Arab tribes who had migrated from the east during the Almohad era and indigenous Berber tribes of differing cultural backgrounds.

The Zayyānids served as Almohad governors of Tlemsen then carved out an independent central Maghribi domain after the Almohad demise. The Marīnids, the most important dynasty for the future geo-political shape of Morocco, pushed through the Taza corridor to the northern Moroccan plains. They captured Fes then Marrakesh and founded a state which encompassed an area roughly coterminous with the later sharifian sultanates and modern Morocco. However, as Zanāta from east of the Middle Atlas, the Marīnids viewed Zayyānid Tlemsen as rightfully theirs, an attitude inherited by the ^{c}Alawī dynasty.

Since the Marīnids could not claim Almohad governorial status and were not champions of a new religious movement they faced a difficult task of legitimation in a milieu where religious and political status tended to go hand in hand. The types of Islamic leadership adopted during previous centuries and their modes of legitimation nonetheless offered them various possibilities. Successive Marīnid sultans moulded these into an ingenious solution to the problem of legitimation. In the process they laid the foundations for the subsequent development of the sharifian jihad state of Morocco.

In the Islamic east the Saljuq sultans had legitimised their usurpation of the temporal political aspect of the caliph's role by posing as defenders of the caliphate and protectors of Sunnī orthodoxy against Shī^{c}ism. The Marīnid sultans came to power in the mid-thirteenth century in a post-caliphal age, but also understood that sultanic power needed to be legitimised by preservation of the faith in some form. One emotive religious ideal in the Far West was that of jihad, holy war to preserve al-Andalus from the Iberian Christian Reconquista. The Almoravids and Almohads had mobilised the Berbers for jihad and transferred that militancy to al-Andalus. Ongoing Christian pressure on the Muslim frontier and attacks across the Straits of Gibraltar ensured that defence of Muslim land remained a crucial part of a western Muslim ruler's task to preserve the faith, and an important aspect of his legitimation.

The task of preserving Islam in the Iberian peninsula largely fell on the Naṣrids of Granada, but the Marīnids also endeavoured to pose as fighters for the faith. Before they achieved power they had distinguished themselves in the Battle of Alarcos (1195), thereby gaining a reputation as holy warriors. On gaining power they consolidated their position by publicly dedicating themselves to holy war. One of the first acts of the early Marīnid sultan, Abū Yūsuf, was to expell a Christian garrison from Salé. In subsequent years he drove the Castilians from Ceuta and directed four campaigns in al-Andalus. Although Abū Yūsuf's attack on Ceuta involved an alliance with Aragón and his campaigns in al-Andalus were as often directed against the Naṣrids as the Castilians, courtly histories portrayed them as *jihād fī sabīl illah*, 'military endeavour in the service of God', and discreetly ignored actions which contravened this image.[1]

Military defence of the faith was not in itself enough to legitimise Marīnid rule. By the thirteenth century Morocco possessed a network of cities whose population included an indigenous scholarly elite and a sophisticated Andalusī element. In the countryside, especially in the water courses south and east of the Atlas mountains, the already complex Berber tribal map had been complicated by the arrival of the Arab tribes of Banū Sulaym and Banū Ma^{c}qīl origin from the east. Many elements in this heterogeneous population were reluctant to accept Zanāta warlords as their rulers. To broaden their appeal the early Marīnid sultans supplemented defence of the faith abroad with the 'restoration' of Islamic orthodoxy at home.[2] This entailed the development of a multi-faceted strategy to counter eclectic religious and political challenges.

The Marīnids political opponents included the ^{c}Azafī amirs of Ceuta whose status was enhanced by their sharifian ancestry and rival tribal warlords who resented their monopoly of power. Religious challenges came from Almohad mahdism which had outlived the Almohad empire in many rural areas, rural Shī^{c}ī movements and popular Sufism, many of whose exponents believed social and political engagement to be an integral part of the Sufi lifestyle.[3] The emphasis on charismatic leadership common to these religious orientations generated the uncomfortable possibility of supra-tribal mobilisation by holy men. Marīnid fears were realised in 1318 when the unexpected 'discovery' of the body of Idrīs I, descendant of the Prophet and eponymous founder of the ninth century Idrīsī dynasty of Fes, caused mass gatherings of tribesmen which they had to disperse by force.

In order to counter these challenges to their authority the Marīnids endeavoured to harness the evident prestige of the *shurafā'* to their own ends. First, they inter-married with sharifian lineages to invest themselves with some of the aura of the *shurafā'*, thereby elevating themselves above their Zanāta rivals and other political contenders. More importantly, they exploited the evident popularity of the Idrīsī lineage by making Fes, the city founded by the Idrīsids, their capital and promoting selected Idrīsī lineages resident in the city as foci for popular respect and veneration.[4] These lineages received state patronage in return for their support for Marīnid efforts to channel the fervour demonstrated by the tribesmen at the discovery of the body of Idrīs I into veneration of his son, Idrīs II, now cast as the patron of Fes.

The Marīnids augmented their 'Idrīsī' policy with efforts to strengthen the hold of text-based urban orthodoxy in their domains thereby enlisting the support of the urban *ᶜulamā'*. This entailed the foundation of residential theological colleges (*madrasa, madāris*), an institution new to the western Islamic world, in Fes and several provincial towns. Marīnid *madāris* provided a standardised education in the Islamic religious sciences to large numbers of students, thereby forming a body of more or less loyal *ᶜulamā'* capable of legitimising sultanic policies as consonant with Islam.

The aim of this cluster of policies was to transform a lineage of tribal warlords into sultans whose temporal power was legitimised by their dedication to the maintenance and protection of the patrimony of the iconic western Islamic rulers, Idrīs I and Idrīs II. In the Marīnid worldview the proto-Shīᶜī Idrīsids were transformed into archetypal Sunnī Muslim rulers dedicated to the spread of Mālikī orthodoxy. As the protectors of, and heirs to, the Idrīsī religio-political tradition, the Marīnids became rulers of an inclusive Islamic state rather than a tribal polity, able to integrate urban, rural, Arab and Berber constituents. The Idrīsī construct also legitimised ultimately unsuccessful Marīnid ambitions to incorporate Zayyānid Tlemsen into the sultanate since Tlemsen was popularly viewed as an Idrīsī foundation.[5]

The domestic religio-political constructs of the Marīnid sultans firmly established an Idrīsī, and by extension, sharifian paradigm of religio-political rule in Morocco which spilled over to Tlemsen where the Zayyānids also cultivated an Idrīsī genealogy.[6] Marīnid policies also transformed sharifian lineages into a religious aristocracy of sorts, a development which gradually disseminated eastwards across the Maghrib encouraging those who had previously claimed Arab ancestry as a mark of their standing (*jāh*) to also claim sharifian ancestry.[7] In addition, Marīnid stress upon their participation in the Andalusī jihad as a facet of sultanic legitimation perpetuated the view that military defence of the faith was incumbent upon a western Muslim ruler.

These ideological developments gained in import during the fifteenth century as Portugal and Spain carried the Reconquista across the Straits of Gibraltar into Africa. Although Iberian raids on the Maghribi coast had been common since the late Almohad period Christian gains were of a temporary nature until the Portuguese capture of Ceuta in 1415. This was followed by constant Portuguese raids on Tanger, Asila and Laraish, their eventual capture in the late fifteenth century and Portuguese construction of fortified trading posts down the Atlantic seaboard as far south as Agadir in the Sus in the early sixteenth century. Spain joined the fray after the fall of Granada in 1492 with the capture of Melilla on the Mediterranean coast in 1497.

The spectre of Christian expansion in the Maghrib sparked a crisis of confidence in the Marīnids, internal political fragmentation, and the rise of political opponents who took Marīnid religio-political theories to their logical conclusions. The Banū Waṭṭās, a Zanāta lineage which had produced generations of Marīnid chief ministers, contested the Marīnid right to rule by contrasting Marīnid inability to defend the coasts from the Portuguese with their own leadership of Muslim counter-attacks. Across the northern part of the sultanate sharifian lineages set themselves up as independent holy warriors, while the Idrīsī lineages of Fes attempted to use their religious prestige to found a new Idrīsī state in alliance with the Banū Waṭṭās. In 1465 they led a revolt, conceptualised as a jihad, against the last Marīnid sultan whom they put to death.[8] The head of the Idrīsī *shurafā'* of Fes, Muḥammad b. ᶜImrān, then seized power in Fes, claiming that sharifian ancestry took precedence over any other criteria for rule.[9] A struggle for power ensued between the Idrīsī *shurafā'* and the Waṭṭāsid *mujāhidūn* in which the latter were eventually victorious.

This episode was critically important on several levels. First, the Idrīsī and Waṭṭāsid claims to legitimacy demonstrated that sharifian ancestry and dedication to the jihad had become crucial to political legitimation. Second, the rebels claim that the rebellion was, in itself, a jihad demonstrated the flexibility of the concept and the possibility of applying it not only to major religio-political movements, as had the Almoravids and Almohads, but also to more varied forms of political action. Of particular importance to later political developments was the implication that, in the context of a serious external threat, military action to unite the Muslim community for defence was a form of jihad whether it was instigated by the state or by its opponents. In effect the Idrīsī–Waṭṭāsid destruction of the Marīnid sultanate generated a new supra-tribal state-building paradigm which was then implemented by two consecutive lineages of *shurafā'* who consolidated their sharifian appeal by assuming direction of the jihad to expell the Portuguese and then the Spanish from their coastal enclaves.

The first sharifian jihad state to come into being was that of the Saᶜdī *shurafā'*, Arab tribal warlords from the Darᶜa valley. Their chance for power came in the early sixteenth century as Portuguese incursions into the Muslim hinterland increased, unchecked and in some cases abetted by the Waṭṭāsids. Defence of the littoral devolved upon local communities led by tribal notables and holy men of sharifian and non-sharifian origin. In many areas holy warriors organised resistance through ribats and regional Sufi networks. One important network of this kind was the Jazūliyya, an amorphous *ṭarīqa* which disseminated the teachings of the charismatic sharifian mystic, al-Jazūlī (d.1465), a firm supporter of both jihad and *ijtihād*.[10] His successors maintained his politically activist stance, opposing the Marīnids and their Waṭṭāsī successors in the name of the sharifian *mujāhidīn*.[11]

The Saᶜdī rise to power began when they assumed the active sharifian profile which Marīnid adoption of the Idrīsī *shurafā'* as religio-political emblems had promoted and Muḥammad b. ᶜImrān's bid for power had politicised. Their recognition by the Arab and Berber tribes of the Darᶜa and Sus as suitable communal representatives by virtue of their ancestry consolidated their local tribal power-base. They broadened their appeal by allying themselves with the Jazūliyya thereby gaining extensive southern support for their bid to be recognised as *shurafā'*, as the rightful representatives of sharifian Sufism and as political challengers to the Waṭṭāsids. They framed their opposition in terms of jihad, claiming that, as *shurafā'*, they possessed a superior right to unify the Muslim community and lead the jihad against the Portuguese. The Saᶜdī jihad was initially a matter of gaining control over the towns and tribes of the south, a task completed with the capture of Marrakesh in 1525. They then turned against the Portuguese and in a spectacular campaign expelled them from the fortress of Santa Cruz at Agadir in 1541. Portugal's subsequent abandonment of several *feitorias* confirmed the Saᶜdī reputation as holy warriors and thus as legitimate rulers of the south.

Despite their prestige, it took the Saᶜdī *shurafā'* four more decades to conquer the north and put an end to external interference in the affairs of the sultanate. They faced internal opposition from other lineages of *shurafā'*, in particular the sharifian holy warriors of Jabal al-ᶜAlam and Shafshawan and the Idrīsī *shurafā'* of Fes who opposed rule by tribesmen from the south who were non-Idrīsī *shurafā'*. Their difficulties were compounded by the fracturing of the dynasty into competing factions backed by the Portuguese and the Ottomans. The Battle of Wad al-Makhazin in 1578, in which both Portuguese and Ottoman-backed contenders for power died, and the accession of Aḥmad al-Manṣūr marked the end of this difficult period. Aḥmad al-Manṣūr's contribution to the evolution of a sharifian jihad state was to weave the ideological threads apparent in the early Saᶜdī movement into a theory of sharifian rule which augmented the religious aura of the Saᶜdī *shurafā'* by an appeal to Muslim eschatology.

The Saᶜdiyyīn came to power during a time of great political upheaval in the Maghrib which stirred up millenarian expectations as the first Muslim millenium in 1576 approached. This enabled early Saᶜdī rulers to combine their claim to sharifian ancestry with hints that the herald of the *mahdī* and perhaps the *mahdī* himself would come from their lineage, thereby underlining their religious status and also legitimising its utilisation for political ends. Aḥmad al-Manṣūr attempted to routinise the charismatic mahdistic appeal of his predecessors by reconstructing the family necropolis in Marrakesh to serve as a shrine for their veneration. The necropolis not only housed the dead *shurafā'* of the lineage but also the charismatic sharifian saint, al-Jazūlī who was reburied within its precincts. Aḥmad al-Manṣūr hoped that it would become a sharifian shrine comparable to that of Idrīs II in Fes, thereby promoting the Saᶜdī *shurafā'* not merely as temporal rulers but as religio-political leaders comparable to the Idrīsids.

Alongside the necropolis Aḥmad al-Manṣūr built a palace to provide a stage for Saᶜdī court ceremonial which was gauged to heighten the distance between the sultan and his subjects and emphasise his sacred status as a descendant of the Prophet. Using this sharifian base, Aḥmad al-Manṣūr transformed the sharifian sultan into a latter-day caliph and imam, the 'Shadow of God' and the 'Sun of the Prophetic Caliphate'.[12] By cultivating the image of a religio-political ruler who was in effect God's representative on earth, Aḥmad al-Manṣūr endowed the Saᶜdī sultanate with a theoretically universal character which could only be realised by means of a jihad. During his reign this expansionist impulse was directed southwards across the Sahara to avoid conflict with the Iberian powers to the north or the Ottomans to the east. It found its ultimate expression in Aḥmad al-Manṣūr's so-called jihad against Songhai in 1591, launched ostensibly to assert Saᶜdī religio-political primacy over the Muslim ruler of Songhai and incorporate the western Sudan more fully into the Islamic oikumene.

Aḥmad al-Manṣūr's religio-political constructs were a vital stage in the evolution of the sharifian jihad state and signalled the transfer of the sharifian cult which had sprung up during the Marīnid and Waṭṭāsid periods from the religious to the political sphere. The Idrīsī *shurafā'* of Fes had tried to make the transition in 1465 and failed, leaving the way open for other sharifian bids for power. The Saᶜdī *shurafā'* succeeded by using mahdism to bridge the gap between religious prestige and political leadership, a move they legitimised by successful jihad against the Portuguese. Aḥmad al-Manṣūr completed the process by formulating the theory of a sharifian divine right to rule and lead the jihad. The religio-political appeal of the Saᶜdī dynasty was tempered, however, by the heavy taxation which they imposed upon the population who interpreted it as oppression. The disgruntled *ᶜulamā'* seized on the famines and epidemics which followed Aḥmad al-Manṣūr's 'jihad' against Songhai as proof that God's wrath had been aroused by the sultan's attack on another Muslim society and disrespect for Islamic norms.[13] Scholarly rejection of Saᶜdī political sharifism triggered a political breakdown after the death of Aḥmad al-Manṣūr in 1603. It was exploited by local power-brokers and the Spanish who occupied several towns on the Atlantic coast, claiming that they were havens for Morisco corsairs bent on attacking Spanish New World shipping.

Renewed Christian Iberian imperialism stimulated the emergence of a new generation of holy warriors along the Atlantic coast. Inland, regional political configurations emerged such as the maraboutic principalities of Dila' in the Middle Atlas and Iligh in the Sus. The ability of each of these small political entities to expand and assume central control of Morocco, however, proved to be limited by their association with specific tribal blocs. The marabouts of Dila' in particular, despite their supra-tribal appeal as religious scholars and holy men, were unable to surmount the antipathy of Fes towards their perceived identification with the Ṣanhāja Berbers of the Middle Atlas, an antipathy compounded by their non-sharifian ancestry.[14] The inability of the marabouts of Dila' and other local leaders to restore Maghribi political unity enabled a second lineage of *shurafā'* from the south, the ᶜAlawī *shurafā'* of Tafilalt, to launch a bid for power.

Sharifism and jihad in the early ᶜAlawī sultanate

The ᶜAlawī *shurafā'* of Tafilalt in the Wad Ziz used their religious prestige to protect caravans travelling south to Tuat or north to Marrakesh and Fes. They became the political representatives of the Filālī tribes when the marabouts of Dila' and Iligh endeavoured to impose their control over the oasis. Between the 1640s and 1660s the ᶜAlawī *shurafā'* built a reputation as sharifian warlords among the tribes of the eastern Middle Atlas, an area which fell between the political spheres of the Ottomans of Algiers and the marabouts of Dila'. Then, like the Marīnids four centuries earlier, they pushed into the Moroccan plains through the Taza corridor, capturing first Fes then Marrakesh, sacking Dila' *en route* in 1668. At this point ᶜAlawī control over Morocco was extremely tenuous and when their chief, Mawlay al-Rashīd, died unexpectedly in 1672, the future of the lineage remained in the balance while his successor, Mawlay Ismāᶜīl, struggled to consolidate his power.

Mawlay Ismāᶜīl's first step was to secure the allegiance of Fes and Marrakesh. His second was to construct a system of central government and formulate a theory to legitimate it.[15] Unlike earlier dynasties which had enjoyed the backing of specific tribal groups, the ᶜAlawī *shurafā'* lacked a distinct tribal power-base. During their rise to power they had made alliances with Arab and Berber tribes from Tafilalt to the Rif but they remained in need of a reliable armed force to consolidate their power. Mawlay Ismāᶜīl responded to this need by founding a black slave army, modelled partly on the Ottoman Janissary army and partly on earlier Maghribi tribal forces. His army fitted the Ottoman paradigm by making a socially and geographically marginal group, black slaves, into a loyal military elite. However, the ᶜAbīd al-Bukhārī, as the army was known, also exhibited tribal characteristics. After recruitment they became a self-perpetuating servile kin-group defined by service to the sultan, described in later centuries as a 'tribe' (*qabīla*) of the army. The army's tribal aspect was heightened by the blood relations which developed between the ᶜAlawī *shurafā'* and the ᶜAbīd through sultanic use of ᶜAbīd concubines. The army also included a subsidiary free black cavalry force known as the Udāyā, similarly endowed with tribal characteristics through intermarriage with the ᶜAlawī *shurafā'*. This gave the ᶜAlawī army something of the character of a black sharifian tribal confederation.

Mawlay Ismāᶜīl housed the ᶜAbīd al-Bukhārī in his vast custom-built royal city at Meknes and deployed them in garrisons throughout his domains to maintain security and extract taxes. At this point the ᶜAlawī sultanate was a tributary state levying what it could from the country by deployment of its coercive power, tangibly represented to tribute payers by sultanic acts of arbitrary violence performed in the palace of Meknes. Mawlay Ismāᶜīl softened the coercive nature of the state by incorporating tribal notables into its structure as provincial ᶜAlawī governors (*qā'id, quwwād*) who enjoyed the prestige of their position in return for assisting the state in gathering taxes. He consolidated such relations by taking women from important tribes as wives thereby giving selected tribal chiefs the same relations with the dynasty as the ᶜAbīd and Udāyā, that of *akhwāl* or maternal kin. The ᶜAbīd al-Bukhārī and co-opted tribal *quwwād* functioned as a rudimentary system of government but the composition of the army also raised issues of legitimacy, especially in Fes where the ᶜAlawī *shurafā'* were regarded as southern warlords who had raised their servile black kin to rule over free Muslims.

To address the pressing problem of Islamic legitimation, Mawlay Ismāᶜīl looked to past paradigms to develop a multi-faceted strategy for legitimacy. Unlike the Saᶜdiyyīn, the ᶜAlawī *shurafā'* did not come to power as religio-political leaders but the failure of non-sharifian contenders for power such as the marabouts of Dila' suggested that political sharifism of the Saᶜdī type was the obvious foundation for ᶜAlawī political legitimation. In a similar way, the success of the Saᶜdī jihad and the continued popularity of jihad leaders along the Atlantic coast where the Spanish enclaves were located indicated that dedication to the jihad could be an equally useful tool in the ᶜAlawī endeavour to accrue prestige and legitimacy. Third, Mawlay Ismāᶜīl looked to Marīnid precedent to improve ᶜAlawī relations with the Idrīsī *shurafā'* and Fes.

Mawlay Ismāᶜīl therefore adopted the nomenclature and attitude of a sharifian sultan, the western equivalent to the caliph–imam of traditional Islamic religio-political discourse. He took the title '*amīr al-mu'minīn*' and then demonstrated his right to hold it by dedicating his army to universal Islamic aims: the maintenance of domestic unity and the continuation of the jihad. In the Maghribi context this meant the expulsion of Christian European powers from their coastal enclaves. During the 1680s ᶜAbīd forces regularly attacked the European enclaves, securing the British evacuation from Tanger in 1684 and expelling the Spanish from al-Ma'mura and Laraish in 1689. These incidents were hailed as jihad victories and signs of Divine favour which proved the legitimate right of the ᶜAlawī *shurafā'* to rule.[16] From the strategic perspective, devotion of state resources to the jihad also possessed the advantage of legitimising the state's collection of taxes as vital for defence of the faith.

In addition to posing as the sharifian leader of the jihad in the Saᶜdī mould, Mawlay Ismāᶜīl attempted to surmount Idrīsī hostility by presenting the ᶜAlawī sultanate as a lineal descendant of the Marīnid and Idrīsī states. First, he assumed the role of patron of sharifian lineages. This involved engaging numerous scholars to investigate the genealogies of the *shurafā'*. He then bestowed pensions on accredited lineages with the most prestigious Idrīsī lineages receiving the most generous pensions.[17] This benefitted the *shurafā'* but also made the ᶜAlawī sultan the *de facto* head of the sharifian religious elite, thereby enhancing his own sharifian status. In addition, Mawlay Ismāᶜīl paid for the repair and reconstruction of the Idrīsī shrines in Fes and the Jabal Zarhun and granted powerful sharifian lineages such as the *shurafā'* of Wazzan the revenues of the areas they controlled.[18]

As well as placing the ᶜAlawī *shurafā'* at the apex of the Maghribi *shurafā'*, Mawlay Ismāᶜīl assumed the responsibility of reconstituting the proto-typical Idrīsī state. To this end he embarked on an ambitious military campaign to incorporate

Ottoman-held Tlemsen into the sultanate as the Marīnids had previously done. Although a logical move in terms of the close commercial relations between Fes and Tlemsen and their geo-political connection as the main towns at either end of the Taza corridor, Mawlay Ismā^{c}īl's campaign provoked an Ottoman counter-offensive from Algiers. The Ottoman forces easily defeated the ^{c}Abīd and the sultan was forced to terms in 1701. The ensuing treaty confirmed Ottoman possession of Tlemsen but accepted ^{c}Alawī assertions that the border should lie along the Tafna river rather than the more westerly Muluwiya river which the Sa^{c}dī sultans had recognised as the border.[19]

Although a failure, Mawlay Ismā^{c}īl's Tlemsen campaign signalled the importance of the commercial and cultural links between Fes and Tlemsen. These links were strengthened by the fact that Tlemsen was no longer a political rival to Fes after the Ottoman takeover of power in the central Maghrib but a border town on the very edge of the Ottoman sphere. Tlemsen's demise as a political and cultural centre meant that from the sixteenth century religious scholars from Tlemsen and its hinterland gravitated towards Fes as the most prestigious centre of learning in the region. This traffic in turn encouraged the dissemination of sharifism and sharifian religio-political constructs eastwards into the deylik of Algiers, whilst the growing cultural affinities between the two cities gave weight to their mythic common Idrīsī origin. As a result, Tlemsen grew in symbolic stature for the ^{c}Alawī sultans and the phenomenon of lineages claiming to be *shurafā'* (*mutasharrifūn*) for prestige or material benefit, already common in the sultanate, spread into rural west Algeria.[20]

Mawlay Ismā^{c}īl was thus the architect of a new sharifian jihad state which relocated the centre of sharifian power from the south to the north and tried to smooth over tensions with the Idrīsī *shurafā'* by adopting Marīnid-style policies of patronage and association with the proto-typical Idrīsī state. His formation of a black slave army, although resented by many, freed the dynasty from dependence on the military support of particular tribes, giving the state a character which blended tribal and Ottoman forms. The existence of this army was legitimised by its deployment to wage the jihad against European coastal enclaves and restore the boundaries of the Idrīsī state. Meanwhile its supra-local identity facilitated the merging of the northern and southern halves of Morocco, represented by Fes and Marrakesh respectively, thereby creating the framework for a more integrated and centralised state. The consolidation of the ^{c}Alawī state and its ideological elaboration was the task of Mawlay Ismā^{c}īl's successors and, in particular, his grandson, Sīdī Muḥammad b. ^{c}Abd Allah.

Mawlay Ismā^{c}īl's death in 1727 initiated a thirty year period of civil unrest during which the heterogeneous elements in Maghribi society jostled to attain maximum political and economic advantage. Despite this political breakdown, the right to rule of the ^{c}Alawī *shurafā'* was not seriously questioned at any time. Although the tribal fringe slipped out of government control, in the heartlands of the sultanate rival factions battled it out by backing different scions of the ^{c}Alawī house rather than by offering their allegiance to rival sharifian lineages or tribal chiefs. This meant that the skeleton of the ᶜAlawī state remained in place, ready to be fleshed out by a sultan of determination and ability. That sultan was Sīdī Muḥammad b. ᶜAbd Allah, an urbane man who had gained an appreciation of Ottoman forms of government during his pilgrimage to Mecca as a young man.

During his thirty year reign from 1757 to 1790, Sīdī Muḥammad steadily extended ᶜAlawī power, centralised the state, and developed a new absolutist theory of sharifian government strongly reminiscent of sixteenth century Ottoman imperial ideology but also distinctively Maghribi. His reign marked a new era in the evolution of the sharifian jihad state in both the political and ideological spheres. On the political side, Sīdī Muḥammad more fully integrated the tribes into the military elite to counter-balance the power of the ᶜAbīd and Udāyā and diversified the state's revenues by promoting trade with Europe. On the religio-political side, he looked to the Ottoman circle of equity to explain the new relationship between state and society and give it an Islamic veneer which complemented his assertion of authority in both the temporal and religious spheres. As the religio-political leader of the Maghribi *umma*, Sīdī Muḥammad also assumed responsibility for leadership of the jihad, a position which he interpreted as including the right to define what was jihad. Sīdī Muḥammad's assistant and ideologue was his chief minister, al-Zayyānī, whose knowledge of Maghribi government was supplemented by experience of the Ottoman world including Istanbul which he visited on diplomatic missions for his master.[21]

Sīdī Muḥammad envisaged a state supported by a disciplined military which performed the function of tax gathering in an equitable way regulated by religious and customary precedent. The revenue collected would then fund the state thus perpetuating the model described in classical Islamic treatises of government and Ottoman sources as the circle of equity. In the ᶜAlawī context, however, the level of taxation viewed as equitable by the tribes rarely coincided with the financial requirements of the state. One solution to the problem was for the state to assume a mercantile role by participating in and taxing foreign trade. To this end Sīdī Muḥammad founded the royal port of Essawira on the barren Atlantic coast west of Marrakesh in 1764 and appointed a cartel of mainly Jewish 'Merchants of the Sultan'.[22] These merchants traded on behalf of the sultan, receiving in return privileges such as state loans and reduced liability for import and export duties.

State sponsorship of trade was not controversial when Muslim trading partners were involved, but since the fifteenth century a proportion of Morocco's trade had been in the hands of merchants from England, the Netherlands, Genoa, Portugal and Spain. When Sīdī Muḥammad decided to impose state control over this trade he put himself in the position of publicly condoning commerce with the infidel, a position which contradicted his role as the sharifian leader of the jihad. His diversion of the trans-Saharan trade to Essawira at the expense of Fes and his privileging of Jewish over Muslim merchants exacerbated the situation by striking at the interests of the Fāsī scholarly and mercantile elites who were in a position to raise the issue of the sultan's legitimacy. To pre-empt potential religious opposition in Fes and the north, Sīdī Muḥammad activated the implicit right of a sharifian sultan to rule in both the religious and politico-military spheres, to become in effect imam as well as *amīr al-mu'minīn*. He then used his self-proclaimed religio-political status to define his jihad and a new relationship between the Makhzan and the *ᶜulamā'*.[23]

With regard to the jihad, Sīdī Muḥammad followed the paradigm put in place by the Saᶜdī sultans and Mawlay Ismāᶜīl and directed state military forces against the remaining Iberian enclaves. When ᶜAlawī contingents besieged Mazagan in 1769 the Portuguese soon evacuated the enclave enabling Sīdī Muḥammad to claim a significant victory, the proof of his right to rule as leader of the jihad. In 1774 he besieged Melilla. The enclave's defences and the resources of Spain were greater than he had anticipated: his offensive provoked a brief war with Spain which forced him to sue for peace, thereby losing considerable face before his subjects.

The continued Spanish presence in Ceuta and Melilla was both a blessing and a curse. On the one hand, it perpetuated the notion that the jihad was not over, especially in the north, enabling subsequent sultans to manipulate the concept to various political ends. On the other hand it was a symbol of ᶜAlawī military failure which could be used by rivals at any time. Sīdī Muḥammad tried to avoid its repercussions by careful representation of sultanic initiatives in the areas of trade and international relations as aspects of jihad. First, he portrayed the formation of a small ᶜAlawī fleet to impose state control over coastal trade and participate in Mediterranean corsairing as part of a sharifian undertaking to wage maritime jihad (*jihād al-baḥr*) against infidel European powers. Makhzan historians presented ᶜAlawī financial assistance to the Ottomans in Istanbul and efforts to create a Mediterranean Muslim alliance in the same light. Another important aspect of Sīdī Muḥammad's jihad was his devotion to ransoming Muslim captives, both Ottoman and ᶜAlawī, who had been captured by Christian Mediterranean corsairs. Makhzan sources specifically describe this as a form of jihad.[24] Meanwhile the Makhzan interpreted treaties signed between the sultanate and European states such as England, France and Spain as acts of submission which placed these powers in a tributary relationship with the sultanate, a relationship considered an acceptable alternative to active military jihad by Islamic jurists.[25]

Sīdī Muḥammad accompanied his tactical extension of the meaning of jihad with a radical reassessment of the relationship between the Makhzan and the *ᶜulamā'*. This entailed Makhzan assertion of the sultan's religio-political right to determine the curriculum offered in *madāris*, to categorise the educational achievements of students coming out of them and to control scholarly appointments and payment of salaries to the *ᶜulamā'*, an approach seemingly inspired by Ottoman precedents. Sīdī Muḥammad's apparent aim was to assert Makhzan control over the *ᶜulamā'*, but he also hoped to break the monopoly on learning held by the Fāsī *ᶜulamā'* and increase the size of the scholarly elite by making education more accessible to poorer students. This aspect of his religious policy is clearly revealed in the changes he made which involved a reduction in time spent on studying the Mālikī *mukhtaṣar* or commentary literature and an increase in time devoted to studying the sources of Islamic law, in particular the Ṣaḥīḥ of al-Bukhārī and the

Muwaṭṭa' of Mālik. The relative accessibility of these sources meant that religio-legal education became simpler and it took students considerably less time to grasp its essentials, thereby creating a niche within the *ᶜulamā'* for students of limited resources who could gain a basic knowledge of Islamic theology and law. Sīdī Muḥammad hoped that these *ᶜulamā'* would then propagate this simpler more inclusive type of urban orthodoxy in their home communities, thereby drawing urban and tribal legal and religious practice closer together and extending the sultan's religio-political role in the tribal countryside.

In many ways the sultan's initiative replicated the Marīnid effort to form a loyal scholarly elite. It also reflected the impact of the central Ottoman paradigm which appeared to the ᶜAlawī Makhzan to have achieved the kind of sultanic autocracy as yet unrealised in the sultanate.[26] However, Sīdī Muḥammad's actions were also rooted in the specifically Maghribi perception that the *shurafā'* possessed unique spiritual powers and that the sharifian sultans were by birthright religio-political leaders rather than simply temporal defenders of a faith defined by the *ᶜulamā'*. Implicit in Sīdī Muḥammad's self-portrayal was a bid for sacred kingship and for the divine right of the ᶜAlawī *shurafā'* to rule, a bid encapsulated in use of the title 'Shadow of God on Earth' (*ẓillu'llahi fī'l-arḍ*), an ᶜAbbāsid caliphal title also used by the Ottomans and the Safavids of Iran to signal the potential universality of their rule.

In the case of Sīdī Muḥammad and his successors, their claim to religio-political universality was aimed not so much at foreign Muslim rivals but towards their domestic audience to give ᶜAlawī sharifian pretensions a firmer underpinning. Such a claim, however, also changed the implications of opposition by charging it with religious significance. This laid the foundations for a widening of the semantic field of jihad from defending the frontier against the infidel to extending sultanic power and authority at home. For this to work ᶜAlawī religio-political legitimacy needed constant reiteration and demonstration before an often sceptical audience of *ᶜulamā'*, rival sharifian lineages and tribesmen. The demonstration of each sultan's legitimacy could best be achieved by successful waging of jihad against the infidel however token such performances might be. This meant that the concept of jihad began to oscillate between the two poles of military actions on land or sea and ᶜAlawī assertions of power within the sultanate. The latter process of state centralisation by means of 'holy war' against 'rebellion' did not go unchallenged and was periodically contested by groups which couched their opposition in the same ideological language as the Makhzan: as righteous jihad against a sultan who failed to fulfil the religio-political obligations he claimed as Shadow of God on Earth. However, at no point before the 1840s when the presence of the French in neighbouring Algiers heightened societal expectations of the sultan did such contestation, verbal or military, seriously challenge the right to rule of the dynasty as opposed to its individual representatives.

Further elaboration of the concept of jihad began in the political crisis which followed Sīdī Muḥammad's death in 1790 and lasted until 1799 when Mawlay Sulaymān finally defeated two other ᶜAlawī claimants to the sultanate. The origins of the crisis lay in Sīdī Muḥammad's religious and commercial policies which had benefitted Marrakesh and the south but undermined the economic standing and religious prestige of the Fāsī elite. Northern alienation expressed itself after Sīdī Muḥammad's death when northern elites offered their allegiance to Mawlay al-Yazīd, a prince of the blood known for his dislike of Sīdī Muḥammad's policies and his desire to prosecute the jihad against the enemies of the faith, the Spanish and the Jews. On his accession, Mawlay al-Yazīd quickly fulfilled his supporters hopes: he incarcerated al-Zayyānī, his father's chief ally, swept away Sīdī Muḥammad's carefully nurtured commercial structures, and turned a blind eye to a wave of violence against Jewish communities in northern towns.[27] He then personally led his armies to besiege Ceuta.[28]

Such reactionary policies, however, had little resonance in the south where the merchants of Marrakesh and Essawira feared that the Ceuta campaign would trigger a war with Spain which would endanger the south's foreign trade.[29] The south therefore transferred its allegiance to Mawlay Hishām, another of Sīdī Muḥammad's sons, initiating a struggle for power between the rival sultans. In February 1792 Mawlay al-Yazīd recaptured Marrakesh from his brother but died of wounds sustained during his Ceuta offensive days afterwards.[30] His sudden death initiated a seven-year civil war during which three ᶜAlawī princes – Mawlay Hishām, Mawlay Salāma and Mawlay Sulaymān – battled to gain the support of key constituents, the cities of Fes and Marrakesh, the Idrīsī *shurafā'* and the main tribal confederations of the plains. The three ᶜAlawī rivals represented distinct sectors of the population. Mawlay Hishām was supported by Marrakesh and the south, Mawlay Salāma inherited Mawlay al-Yazīd's northern constituency,[31] while the Berber tribes of the Meknes region, and subsequently Fes, backed Mawlay Sulaymān due to their reluctance to support either of the other contenders.[32]

Their struggle was both a material one to build up sufficient military resources to defeat rivals and a moral one for legitimacy during which the qualifications for rule were aired and debated in a legal exchange recorded in al-Ḍuᶜayyif's dynastic history.[33] This exchange gives a rare indication of how society perceived the relationship between a sharifian sultan and his subjects and a glimpse of the societal obverse of Makhzan jihad theory, in particular how the spokesmen of society, the *ᶜulamā'* and *shurafā'*, viewed the sharifian sultanate's rights and responsibilities regarding the jihad. The exchange arose when Sīdī ᶜAlī b. Aḥmad al-Ṭayyib of Wazzan, a supporter of the martial Mawlay Salāma, received a missive from the Fāsī *ᶜulamā'* stating that Mawlay Sulaymān held a superior right to allegiance as the most scholarly contender for rule (*khilāfa*). Sīdī ᶜAlī challenged this assertion by airing an anonymous legal question submitted fifty years before to the *shurafā'* of Wazzan during a struggle for power between two of Mawlay Ismāᶜīl's sons, Mawlay ᶜAbd Allah and Mawlay al-Mustaḍī' bi-Nūr Allah.

Al-Ḍuᶜayyif's account shows that from the societal perspective the ultimate qualification for rule was the community's acceptance of a sultan by giving him their oath of allegiance (*bayᶜa*). However, the question is, in case of a conflict what qualities or conditions should dictate which sultan rules: circumstantial conditions such as which contender received the *bayᶜa* first or in the place where the previous sultan died, or personal qualities such as learning, religiosity, or ability to fight the jihad? In addition it asks whether the *bayᶜa* of holy warriors counts for more than that of other groups:

> Do the holy warriors (*mujāhidūn*) serving on the frontier possess a greater right than others to give the *bayᶜa* and is the warrior (*shujāᶜ*) more eligible [to be sultan] than the scholar?[34]

The *shurafā'* of Wazzan had replied that if the community recognised that one *bayᶜa* had plainly been offered first then that contender was the rightful sultan, even if everyone had not offered him their allegiance. After discussing the minimum number of those in authority (*ahl al-ḥall wa'l-ᶜaqd*) needed to validate a *bayᶜa*, the *shurafā'* confirmed that 'those dedicated to the jihad and defence of the frontier' did possess special authority in this respect and that a warrior was most suited to hold religio-political office (*al-imāma*). The ruling was signed by several Wazzani *shurafā'*. Its airing in 1792 and citing by al-Ḍuᶜayyif indicated that ᶜAlawī jihad theory was not simply a Makhzan construct, but that important representatives of society considered devotion to the jihad a source of prestige and authority, and expected those in power to be qualified to lead it. Especially in the north many understood the relationship between the sultan and his subjects as that of a sharifian *mujāhid* elevated by the *mujāhidīn*.

Societal assertion of the contractual nature of power heralded increasing competition between the ᶜAlawī sultan and his subjects to define what constituted jihad, the guarantor of the contract, at any given time. This was obscured in the short term because other factors determined the outcome of the 1792–9 struggle, but its ideological implications emerged in the central years of Mawlay Sulaymān's reign when he devoted his authority as sharifian sultan–imam to the perpetual task of state centralisation. Unlike his father who had used his religio-political status to assert state power over the *ᶜulamā'* and engage in trade with Europe, Mawlay Sulaymān allied with the Fāsī *ᶜulamā'* and reduced state reliance on sources of revenue considered illicit in Islamic law. This necessitated the intensification of Makhzan tax-gathering in the mountainous tribal fringe of the sultanate, an approach sanctioned by the Sharīᶜa and consonant with Fāsī economic interests, but liable to alienate the tribes as inequitable and oppressive. Mawlay Sulaymān focused particular attention on the Middle Atlas and the old Idrīsī nexus from Fes towards Ottoman Algiers and recaptured the border town of Wajda from the Ottomans in 1792. To assist state expansion in what were predominantly Berber-speaking areas the sultan sidelined the northern Berber tribes which had served his father and incorporated a number of Arabic-speaking tribes from the south into the ᶜAlawī armed forces.[35]

Mawlay Sulaymān legitimised his activities by reference to his status as God's representative on earth which made tribal obedience – and tax payment – a religious duty, and implied that tribal dissidence was tantamount to rebellion against God. He accompanied this religio-political offensive against the tribes with a doctrinal offensive against rural religious practices, in particular those associated with the cult of holy men, which he dismissed as contrary to the Sharīᶜa. At the same time he shunned token public displays of his devotion to the jihad such as attacks on the Spanish enclaves, patronage of corsair captains, or expenditure on ransoming Muslims in Christian captivity.

The movement of the state's interpretation of jihad towards the pole of state centralisation and imposition of urban definitions of the faith in the countryside coincided with significant changes in the tribal religious milieu. These were prompted in part by Sīdī Muḥammad's religious policies and in part by the wider phenomenon of religious renewal in the Islamic world in the eighteenth century. In the half century prior to 1830 several Sufi shaykhs from tribal areas north and east of Fes, including the hinterland of Tlemsen, adopted a more activist stance towards religion and the state. They were generally scholars as well as mystics and devoted themselves to invigorating the rural *ṭuruq* by incorporating individual maraboutic lodges into trans-regional networks of lodges affiliated to a single brotherhood. They used these networks to transmit basic religious knowledge and simple mysticism to their tribal memberships, and to combat to a greater or lesser extent the more unorthodox aspects of popular faith. Many of these shaykhs were also *shurafā'*, or claimed to be, thus embuing their mission with additional prestige.

The most important brotherhood of this type to emerge in the ᶜAlawī sultanate was the Darqāwa, a brotherhood headed by al-ᶜArabī al-Darqāwī, which rapidly spread through the Rif, into the Middle Atlas and onwards along the trade and pilgrimage route east into the Algerian province of Oran. The spread of the Darqāwa was matched by the spread of the Wazzāniyya, the brotherhood of the *shurafā'* of Wazzan, roughly throughout the same area. The emergence of the Tijāniyya at ᶜAyn Madi in the Algerian pre-Sahara south of Tlemsen and the renewal of the west Algerian Qādiriyya led to a converse spread of these brotherhoods into the sultanate: the Tijāniyya to the urban centres of Fes and Marrakesh, and the Qādiriyya among the Rif tribes. This created a large northern zone from the Atlantic through the Rif and Middle Atlas into west Algeria culturally and religiously dominated by revived sharifian Sufi brotherhoods.

The relationship between these brotherhoods and the ᶜAlawī sultanate was highly ambiguous. Since many of the shaykhs involved were *shurafā'* their authority within the tribes affiliated to their brotherhoods mirrored in microcosm that of the sultans within the sultanate. On the one hand their common reliance on the prestige associated with sharifian origin made sultan and shaykh natural allies, as did their shared interest in educating the tribes in Islamic orthodoxy. On the other hand, the possibility always existed that sharifian shaykhs might use their religious authority to challenge the sultan's interpretation of his religio-political role, especially in the context of changing relations between the state and tribal society. The ambiguity was deepened by the fact that most brotherhoods bridged the border between the ᶜAlawī sultanate and the deylik of Algiers and tended to promote the ᶜAlawī sharifian religio-political ideal within Algerian territory whatever their domestic relations with the sultan. A case in point was the long-lasting rebellion of the Darqāwa shaykh, Ibn al-Sharīf, against the beys of Oran (1805–13), during which rebel towns and tribes, including Tlemsen, repeatedly offered their oath of allegiance to Mawlay Sulaymān as a result of the pro-ᶜAlawī stance of the Darqāwa, despite his often tense relations with the brotherhood's eponymous head, al-ᶜArabī al-Darqāwī.

Another factor in the relations between Mawlay Sulaymān's Makhzan and the northern tribes was the impact upon the Maghrib of Napoleon's expedition to Egypt (1798–1801) and the Napoleonic Wars (1793–1815). North Africans, conditioned by their past experiences of Iberian imperialism and the prominence of jihad within regional political discourse, responded more immediately and more strongly to French and British expansion into the Mediterranean than Muslim societies further east. The inhabitants of the ᶜAlawī sultanate viewed the French occupation of Egypt as the start of a renewed Christian offensive against the *dār al-islām*.[36] Napoleon's invasion of Spain and the regular passage of French and British naval squadrons through the Straits of Gibraltar fostered local fears of an imminent Christian invasion to which Rif tribes responded with repeated mobilisations to wage the jihad.[37]

In these circumstances, Mawlay Sulaymān's failure to launch any attacks on Ceuta or Melilla or to promote maritime jihad implied a serious failure to fulfil his obligation to provide jihad leadership and defend the country and, by extension, raised the issue of his legitimacy to rule. This in turn undermined his centralisation drive in the Rif and Middle Atlas which had included efforts to control the circulation of firearms and limit their possession to those in Makhzan service. In view of the European naval presence in the Straits of Gibraltar the *ᶜulamā'* of coastal towns demanded that the sultan permit the free sale of weapons because every Muslim had a religious obligation to prepare for jihad.[38] By 1818 his neglect of the jihad against the infidel had become a convenient peg upon which the northern Berber tribes, disaffected by Makhzan efforts to extract revenue, could hang their grievances.

At around the same time Mawlay Sulaymān extended his avowed dislike of the excesses of popular Sufism to public approval of the doctrine of the iconoclastic Wahhābī movement in the Arabian peninsula. The Wahhābīs attempted destruction of the Prophet's tomb in Medina, their disruption of the ḥajj and their denunciation of popular Sufism as polytheism (*shirk*) had given them an extremely bad reputation in the sultanate, as in other parts of the Islamic world. Mawlay Sulaymān's sympathy for their doctrines further soured his relations with the shaykhs of the Darqāwa, whose followers came from the disgruntled Berber tribes of the northern mountains and plains.[39] It also fractured the long-standing alliance between the sultan and the Fāsī *ᶜulamā'*, creating a strong religio-political front ready to challenge his doctrinal position and remind him of his duty to lead the jihad. The stage was thus set for a major ideological confrontation when the sultan marched into the Middle Atlas to force the Berber tribes to pay their taxes in 1819.

When the Makhzan armies met the tribes the Makhzan's Berber allies defected and joined the Middle Atlas Berbers in a rout of Mawlay Sulaymān's remaining, mainly Arab, tribal forces.[40] In order to rally support, Mawlay Sulaymān refined his previous position that tribal opposition to God's Shadow on Earth was equivalent to a rebellion against God, and publicly stated that rebellion against the ᶜAlawī sultan was corruption (*fasād*) of the Islamic body politic which must be resisted by the faithful. Although a Muslim rebel (*bāghī*) is not an apostate in Islamic law, Mawlay Sulaymān asserted that the term 'rebel' (*bāghī, mufsid*) was synonymous with that of dissenter (*khārijī*) and 'infidel' (*kāfir*) thus effacing the juridical possibility of legitimate rebellion and placing all rebels outside the Muslim *umma*. This in turn made Makhan action against rebels a jihad. In a letter demanding aid from the governor of Tetuan Mawlay Sulaymān described the campaign against the Middle Atlas Berbers as a jihad more meritorious than the jihad against the infidel enemy (*al-ᶜadū al-kāfir*) because the Berbers were dissenters (*khawārij*) who, by opposing the sharifian sultan, had left the community of Muslims (*jamāᶜat al-muslimīn*).[41]

The sultan's assertion that his subjects had a religious duty to join him in a holy war against rebellion was strongly contested by his own army, the northern Berber tribes, Fes and the northern coastal *mujāhidūn* who felt, as they had in 1792, that loyalty was conditional upon the military and jihadist credentials of the sultan. Between 1819 and 1820 the situation slipped out of the sultan's control, his military reputation shattered, and he left the anarchic north for Marrakesh. There he took the unusual step of submitting a letter to the Fāsī *ᶜulamā'* implying that having lost the consent of his subjects he had decided to abdicate. This initiated an ambitious northern 'jihad' to replace the failed sultan with a *sharīf* who possessed the qualities to restore the sultanate and defend it from the infidel. Key players in this righteous rebellion were the Idrīsī *shurafā'* of Fes and Wazzan, some of the Fāsī *ᶜulamā'*, the coastal towns, and the northern Berber tribes affiliated to the Darqāwa and Wazzāniyya brotherhoods. Two main choices for a new sharifian sultan emerged: Ibrāhīm, son of the warrior sultan, Mawlay al-Yazīd, or an Idrīsī *sharīf*.

Mawlay Ibrāhīm b. Yazīd was an obvious choice for those who identified legitimacy with jihad leadership. The suggestion of an Idrīsī *sharīf* was more startling, and brought into the open the latent rivalry between the southern ᶜAlawī *shurafā'* and the prestigious northern Idrīsī *shurafā'* of Wazzan and Fes who had never fully accepted prestige and wealth under ᶜAlawī rule as sufficient compensation for putting aside their own political ambitions. The Idrīsī option found support not only among the Idrīsī *shurafā'* themselves but also among the tribes affiliated to the Darqāwa whose founder was an Idrīsī *sharīf*. The strength of the Idrīsī *shurafā'* in northern society was, however, their downfall: different lineages could not agree on which *sharīf* should become sultan, and the non-sharifian elite of Fes resisted the idea of an Idrīsī sultanate as bound to lead to the permanent dominance of Idrīsī social and economic interests.[42] This cleared the way for the elevation of Mawlay Ibrāhīm who received the *bayᶜa* of Fes and then Tetuan during the winter of 1820–1. He was backed by his brother, Mawlay Sa^cīd, who succeeded him after his unexpected death during 1821.

The declaration of an ᶜAlawī counter-sultan split the sultanate in two, rupturing the tenuous political unity of Mawlay Sulaymān's central years and deepening the crisis in central power which had begun in 1819. Between spring 1821 and 1822 two rival sultans in effect waged jihad against each other. Until a clear victor emerged with Mawlay Sulaymān's reduction of Fes and Tetuan's capitulation in April 1822, the legitimacy of each remained suspended. The situation opened the gate to other religio-political challenges to Makhzan authority. This process of fragmentation affected the southern sultanate in addition to the north. In the countryside west of Marrakesh the ambitious shaykh of the Sharāda *zāwiya*, al-Mahdī al-Sharādī, rallied the Sharārda – the descendants of Saᶜdī *jaysh* tribes – against their Makhzan governor.[43] On one level the dispute reflected a struggle for power between two rival Sharāda notables, al-Mahdī and the Makhzan governor of the Sharārda. On another level it expressed a feeling that a sultan's seat should be Marrakesh, the capital of the Saᶜdī sultans, not Fes.

In order to prevent the formation of a rival power base outside Marrakesh, Mawlay Sulaymān marched against the Sharāda *zāwiya* in autumn 1822 only to suffer a humiliating defeat at the hands of al-Mahdī al-Sharādī and the loss of most of his artillery. He returned to Marrakesh where he died shortly afterwards, his life-long effort to extend the reach of the ᶜAlawī state into the tribal fringe ending in disaster. As the sharifian sultan–imam he had located his political initiatives in the wider context of maintenance of the Sharīᶜa, and then, from a position of weakness, interpreted them as a jihad against those 'rebels' who refused to accept the hegemony of the Sharīᶜa. Such religio-political constructs were, however, a double-edged sword. They were turned against the sultan by his opponents who maintained that the sharifian sultan's religio-political status, and therefore right to wage jihad against those who resisted his authority, depended on his fulfilment of his prior duty to wage jihad against the infidel. The multiple meanings of jihad and *fasād* – holy war and rebellion – thus became the shared possession of the sultan and his subjects on the eve of the European colonial era.

The sharifian jihad state on the eve of colonialism

Mawlay Sulaymān was succeeded by his nephew, Mawlay ᶜAbd al-Raḥmān, whom he named as his successor in a testamentary letter which he dictated on his deathbed and immediately sent to Fes.[44] In many ways, Mawlay ᶜAbd al-Raḥmān was an ideal choice. He was the son of Mawlay Hishām, sultan of the south between 1792 and 1799, and Mawlay Sulaymān's protegé and thus theoretically acceptable to both northern and southern constituencies. He had shown considerable military skill during Mawlay Sulaymān's campaign against Mawlay Ibrāhīm and thus fitted the cherished paradigm of the *mujāhid*–sultan. Furthermore, as governor of Essawira and then Fes, he had proved himself a capable administrator. He had also adopted a conciliatory policy towards the rebel faction and the Idrīsī *shurafā'* in Fes. He had limited Makhzan reprisals for the revolt to the detention of its leaders[45] and appointed a young Idrīsī *sharīf*, Muḥammad b. Idrīs, as his chief scribe.[46] His acceptance as sultan by the army and the notables of Fes was therefore likely.

Despite Mawlay ᶜAbd al-Raḥmān's eligibility, Mawlay Sulaymān's death did trigger a struggle for power between different ᶜAlawī *shurafā'* which again possessed a discursive aspect. The main contenders apart from Mawlay ᶜAbd al-Raḥmān were Mawlay Sulaymān's brother, Mawlay Mūsā, in Marrakesh and two of his sons, Mawlay ᶜAbd al-Wāḥid in Tafilalt and Mawlay ᶜAbd al-Raḥmān in Meknes. Mawlay Mūsā, the senior ᶜAlawī *sharīf* present at Mawlay Sulaymān's place of death, was in an advantageous position but the *qāḍī* of Marrakesh, who had been alerted to the testament in favour of Mawlay ᶜAbd al-Raḥmān, contested his claim. The *qāḍī* asserted that the *bayᶜa* of Fes and the Makhzan forces in the north took precedence over the *bayᶜa* of Marrakesh and that he could not therefore offer the city's allegiance to Mawlay Mūsā before receiving news from Fes. This assertion, albeit tactical, echoed the argument of 1792 that the *bayᶜa* of the *mujāhidīn* had greater weight than that of other constituents, and confirmed the growing political weight of Fes within the sultanate. The arrival of an ᶜAlawī envoy from Tafilalt announcing that the oasis had given its *bayᶜa* to Mawlay ᶜAbd al-Wāḥid further complicated the situation. Neither of these southern contenders, however, represented major factions within the sultanate and they dropped their bids when news arrived that Fes and the northern army had offered Mawlay ᶜAbd al-Raḥmān their *bayᶜa*.[47]

The new sultan immediately began to define the character of his government. The recognition of Fes and Marrakesh confirmed his accession but Mawlay ᶜAbd al-Raḥmān b. Sulaymān, the ᶜAbīd under his command and the northern Berber tribes withheld their allegiance. Elsewhere, tribal raiding and brigandage occurred unchecked in the absence of a strong central power. In the circumstances Mawlay ᶜAbd al-Raḥmān's most pressing needs were to secure full allegiance and restore a degree of centralised order to the sultanate. His longer term goal was the same as that of his ᶜAlawī predecessors, the extension of the state's authority and power to their optimum limits, a process lately defined by Mawlay Sulaymān as state jihad against the propagators of *fasād*. The events of previous years suggested that his success would depend upon his skill in employing both the material and ideological resources available to him and his ability to create an equilibrium between the state's two interpretations of jihad: military action against the infidel and military action against domestic dissent.

During the first years of his reign Mawlay ᶜAbd al-Raḥmān evinced willingness for reconciliation and integration but combined it with an evident determination to use force if necessary. His restoration of Makhzan power and authority began in Fes where he adopted a dual policy of punitive action against the leaders of the 1820–1 revolt, whom he temporarily exiled, and patronage of the Idrīsī *shurafā'*. He promoted his Idrīsī scribe, Muḥammad b. Idrīs, to the position of chief minister and commissioned the renovation of the shrine of Idrīs II, Fes's patron and the ancestor of the Idrīsī *shurafā'*.[48] The message was plain: loyal Idrīsī *shurafā'* could play an influential part in ᶜAlawī government and would gain more through alliance than opposition.

Having consolidated his position in Fes, Mawlay ᶜAbd al-Raḥmān tackled the problem of tribal insubordination and the Berber–Darqāwa revolt. The rebels planned to attack and drive him from the north before he had a chance to build up a rural tribal following. The one card in Mawlay ᶜAbd al-Raḥmān's hand was the fact that Mawlay Sulaymān had arrested al-ᶜArabī al-Darqāwī in 1821 to punish him for inciting the revolt. This gave the sultan a bargaining chip which he used to divide the Berber leadership by offering one of its heads, Ibn al-Ghāzī, the release of al-Darqāwī, his spiritual mentor, in return for his oath of allegiance. Ibn al-Ghāzī complied and the other Berber leaders hurried to submit to the new sultan.[49] Mawlay ᶜAbd al-Raḥmān reinforced his diplomatic victory with a series of military progresses among the tribes of the northern plains and the Rif which enabled him to demonstrate his military power in relation to individual tribes, thereby proving his martial skills and his sharifian right to rule as imam and *amīr al-mu'minīn*.[50] By early 1823 the British consul in Tanger could report:

> The affairs of this Empire seem to go with success, many provinces who were in a state of independence under the late sultan have come into the present one and sworn allegiance … among others the whole of the tribes of the Berebers or the mountaineers of the Atlas.[51]

After a year in Fes, Mawlay ᶜAbd al-Raḥmān proceeded to Meknes where he secured the grudging submission of the ᶜAbīd before continuing south to Marrakesh, receiving the *bayᶜa* from each tribe in turn.[52] He took in his entourage several notables, including the Berber chief Ibn al-Ghāzī, as hostages for the good behaviour of their tribes. Despite such precautions his departure was followed by an ᶜAbīd insurrection in Meknes led by Mawlay ᶜAbd al-Raḥmān b. Sulaymān who sent out feelers to the Berber tribes in an effort to reconstitute the Berber opposition under his own leadership.[53] In response, Mawlay ᶜAbd al-Raḥmān incarcerated Ibn al-Ghāzī in the notorious Jazira prison at Essawira where he died a year later.[54] This ended co-ordinated Berber opposition to Mawlay ᶜAbd al-Raḥmān but the countryside remained anarchic throughout 1824 and 1825. In the words of the British consul:

> The Empire is in the greatest possible state of confusion at present, no taxes are received but at the customs houses, and battles take place frequently of tribe against tribe and province against province.[55]

The situation altered over the winter of 1825–6 as a result of a summer drought which ruined the harvest. Famine, heavy winter rains, flooding, and epidemics followed, decimating the already weakened population. This human disaster radically altered the balance of power between the Makhzan and its subjects in favour of the former. Although natural disasters could undermine central power by weakening the sultan's army and triggering desperate internal struggles for scanty resources, in this case famine and epidemic brought the cycle of violence which had started with Mawlay Sulaymān's ill-fated campaign against the Middle Atlas Berbers to an end. In an atypical inversion of the usual association between divine favour and prosperity, Makhzan sources presented the famine as divine intervention on behalf of the sultan. Since Mawlay ᶜAbd al-Raḥmān lacked the military resources to force the tribes 'to enter into obedience', God sent the famine to remove the obstacles to his institution of a new era of Islamic justice and prosperity. It was thus 'a mercy to the country and the servants of God' which ended years of tribal insurrection (*fasād*) and facilitated the reconstitution of an integrative Islamic state.[56]

A detailed presentation of Makhzan religio-political constructs during the 1820s appears in the *ᶜAqd al-jumān fī shamā'il al-sulṭān sayyidnā wa mawlānā ᶜAbd al-Raḥmān*, a chronicle of Mawlay ᶜAbd al-Raḥmān's early years written by Sīdī Muḥammad's former chief minister, al-Zayyānī. Al-Zayyānī recounts in detail the sultan's expeditions to secure the allegiance of the tribes and towns, making plain the ideological aspect of his activities during this period. He describes Mawlay ᶜAbd al-Raḥmān using the caliphal titles 'imam' and '*amīr al-mu'mīnīn*' and presents reform (*iṣlāḥ*) of a corrupt and fragmented society as his foremost religio-political obligation. In al-Zayyānī's view, *iṣlāḥ* entailed the unification of the *umma* under the ᶜAlawī sultan and his restoration of the Sharīᶜa as the overarching law of the land, a construct reminiscent of the Ottoman–sharifian synthesis achieved by Sīdī Muḥammad:

> When God entrusted the affairs of the Muslims to the sultan … Mawlānā ᶜAbd al-Rahmān, he found the world in darkness, her affairs gone awry and the tribes in revolt (*fitan*). He began his reign by exiling the rebels (*mufsidīn*) from the city of Fes and re-imposing the Islamic bounds (*al-ḥudūd*) upon those who had overstepped them.[57]

The sultan achieved his ends in the countryside by means of military progresses (*maḥallāt, ḥarakāt*) which were both practical demonstrations of power and symbolic performances, as al-Zayyānī's highly formulaic accounts show.[58] The historian presents several vignettes in which Mawlay ᶜAbd al-Raḥmān and his 'Muslim' army march against tribal 'rebels' (*mufsidīn, fussād*), whose anarchic behaviour or refusal to give their allegiance is presented as a temporary departure from the *umma*. The sultan then proves his military credentials by decimating the tribe's crops and livestock, 'eating' them in Makhzan and popular parlance. The cycle of violence ceases when the tribesmen sue for pardon. In several cases the symbolic dimension of this exchange is emphasised by reference to delegations of youths from the tribe involved approaching the sultan brandishing copies of the Qur'ān, thereby announcing their tribe's desire to be readmitted to the Muslim community by submitting to its head, the sultan. The final stage in each account is the restoration of the hegemony of the Sharīᶜa by the sultan who imposes Sharīᶜa penalties 'on those rebels (*fussād*) who had tyrannized the land with their disobedience (*fasād*)'.[59]

Prominent in al-Zayyānī's history is the idea that those who obey the sultan–imam are Muslims and that those who resist are not. This finds its fullest expression in panegyrics celebrating Mawlay ᶜAbd al-Raḥmān's early campaigns:

> Good news to all Muslims about the raid carried out by the custodian of God (*amīn allah*) against the depraved Berbers ... tidings of security and felicity to the people of goodness and warnings of shame and despair to the evil doers ... for the pride of kings and the most just among them has come to you, Abu Zayd, [Mawlay ᶜAbd al-Raḥmān] the sword of God.[60]

> Good tidings to all Muslims of the victory of the party of the faithful directed by the just custodian, the lion of all kings, the servant of the Merciful, the imam, son of Hishām and descendant of he who revived existence, Muḥammad, source of perfection, by his destruction of those who spread corruption (*al-mufsidīn*).[61]

The arguments that obedience to the sharifian sultan defined Muslim identity and that *fasād* was equivalent to *ᶜaṣyān* or rebellion against God, were evidently Makhzan constructs, but al-Zayyānī was aware of the contractual aspect of the relationship between sultan and *umma*. In his account, he not only denounces tribal *fasād* but also criticises misgovernment by Makhzan governors (*quwwād*) as an injustice liable to destabilise state–society relations.[62] He implies that obedience to the sharifian sultan is conditional upon probity in government, without which the sultan becomes himself an accessory to Makhzan *fasād*. In this context, al-Zayyānī also refers to the sharifian sultan's obligation to defend the *umma* against infidel encroachment, the necessary counterweight to domestic jihad.

After Mawlay Sulaymān's troubled last years, Mawlay ᶜAbd al-Raḥmān was well aware that reconstruction of ᶜAlawī prestige in general, and his own prestige in particular, required a balancing of jihad against *fasād* with jihad against the infidel. To achieve this balance, he made tentative efforts to restart the maritime jihad. Aggressive jihadist behaviour towards non-Muslims was not feasible in the years immediately following his accession when the unsettled state of the countryside kept rural tax income low and made the Makhzan heavily dependent upon customs revenue. Mawlay ᶜAbd al-Raḥmān therefore followed the precedent set by Sīdī Muḥammad and combined cautious encouragement of existing trade relations with European states with reconstitution of the ᶜAlawī çorsair fleet which had fallen into disrepair during the reign of Mawlay Sulaymān. In 1822 he confirmed existing commercial treaties and during the 1825–6 famine he opened several Atlantic ports to European traders bringing grain from Europe, Tunis and Egypt.[63] Meanwhile, ᶜAlawī commercial agents in Gibraltar sought information about secondhand European vessels up for sale.[64] During 1825 their enquiries bore fruit and they purchased ships in Cadiz and Gibraltar which they transported to ᶜAlawī ports to be refitted.[65] ᶜAlawī agents purchased additional ships in 1827.[66]

As Mawlay ᶜAbd al-Raḥmān consolidated his domestic position he adopted a more aggressive stance towards European traders. After the food crisis of 1825–6 was over he attempted to close ports opened to import grain and restrict European trading to Tanger and Essawira. In March 1826 he rejected European requests to open the southern port of Azzammur.[67] A year later he expelled European traders from Rabat on the grounds that their illicit relations with Muslim women made their presence morally unacceptable.[68] Such policies met with a positive local response from all except the Muslim and Jewish merchants of the littoral since they harmonised with religious sentiment and eased the inflation in basic commodity prices which accompanied commerce with Europeans. The disturbing news that a French fleet had blockaded the port of Algiers as a result of a debt dispute made an active jihad strategy more pressing. In autumn 1827 the sultan ordered Makhzan authorities in coastal towns to repair sea defences and in spring 1828 he toured the defences of Tetuan and Tanger. Whilst in Tanger he informed the European consuls that henceforth maritime jihad would be waged against the shipping of nations unrepresented in the sultanate.[69] This threat was designed to combine maritime jihad for his domestic audience with the preservation of good relations with the sultanate's main European trading partners. He then authorised the corsair captains to go to sea. In the following months ᶜAlawī corsairs detained several vessels, paying scant attention to whether they belong to states in a treaty relationship with the sultanate or not.[70]

Mawlay ᶜAbd al-Raḥmān's resumption of maritime jihad coincided with a serious southern revolt against his authority. Disturbances began with tribal attacks on a ḥajj caravan travelling up from the Sus valley which seriously challenged the legitimacy of a state bound to defend religious rituals such as the ḥajj. These raids were accompanied by a revolt of the Sharārda tribes against the recent restitution of Makhzan power in the south which had manifested itself in higher tax demands on the Sharārda and the appointment of additional Makhzan *quwwād* to administer the confederation. The revolt was led by the marabout al-Mahdī al-Sharādī who had defeated Mawlay Sulaymān six years previously and now used Sharārda discontent to challenge the Makhzan for a second time. His challenge was both military and ideological: while the Sharārda dispossessed their Makhzan-appointed *quwwād* and ambushed traffic to and from nearby Marrakesh, al-Mahdī al-Sharādī proclaimed that he was the awaited *mahdī* (*al-mahdī al-muntaẓar*) who would institute a new era of justice in place of ᶜAlawī oppression. Al-Mahdī thus took on the role of the righteous warrior leading a tribal jihad against a bankrupt central power.

Al-Mahdī's appropriation and reversal of the Makhzan construct of jihad against *fasād*, forced Mawlay ᶜAbd al-Raḥmān to immediate action. A Makhzan victory was crucial to prevent the unravelling of the hard-won consensus which the sultan had built up over the previous years, a fact underlined by the prominence given to the campaign in contemporary sources.[71] He collected reinforcments and proceeded down the Atlantic coast, punishing the Hashtuka and Shiadma for raiding the ḥajj caravan *en route*.[72] He then prepared his offensive against the

Sharārda in concert with Makhzan troops from Marrakesh and besieged the Sharāda *zāwiya* in the hope of securing the surrender of al-Mahdī. After a fruitless wait, Mawlay ᶜAbd al-Raḥmān ordered his artillery to open fire. After several days of sustained bombardment, al-Mahdī fled by night, leaving his relatives and followers to sue for peace. The sultan accepted their surrender but the seriousness of their revolt and their delayed surrender deprived them of the right to an armistice (*aman*). Makhzan troops entered the shrine, plundered it and burnt it to the ground. They stripped and chained male members of the Sharāda maraboutic lineage then completed their humiliation by loading them onto camels to be taken to Fes. Finally, the Makhzan forces left the *zāwiya*, driving several hundred subjugated Sharārda tribesmen to Marrakesh in a triumphal procession accompanied by the sultan himself. They were then dispersed between Makhzan prisons in Rabat, Meknes and Fes where they languished for a year before being resettled on the Azghar plain north of Fes in return for entering Makhzan service as a new military tribe.[73]

The Sharārda episode was significant in many ways. First, while al-Mahdī's revolt threatened the sultan's rule, it also demonstrated the validity of the ideological system constructed by the ᶜAlawī Makhzan. Al-Mahdī and Mawlay ᶜAbd al-Raḥmān shared and manipulated the same symbols – jihad against *fasād* – and competed to prove their right to define each term by military means. The legitimation of al-Mahdī's claim to be the *mahdī* required that he win the fight. His defeat and Mawlay ᶜAbd al-Raḥmān's victory enabled the latter to categorise the revolt as *fasād*, its perpetrators as *mufsidīn* and the Sharāda marabouts as false holy men. Makhzan desecration of the *zāwiya* and humiliation of the Sharāda lineage was a public demonstration that their claim to holiness and the right to define jihad and *fasād* was unfounded. The legitimisation of the system implicit in the terms of al-Mahdī's challenge and the legitimisation of Mawlay ᶜAbd al-Raḥmān implicit in al-Mahdī's subsequent defeat were maximised by means of sultanic rescripts which informed provincial Makhzan authorities of the ᶜAlawī victory.

Second, Mawlay ᶜAbd al-Raḥmān's success gave him a fresh opportunity to convey messages about the nature of the sultanate and its relationship with its subjects. His treatment of the Sharārda tribesmen involved several stages which demonstrated the sharifian sultan's religio-political right to punish rebellion and treat it as apostasy but also his duty to maintain a just balance in society guided by the Sharīᶜa. Although he publicly asserted his right to execute the captive Sharārda tribesmen for rebellion, he then graciously allowed the *ᶜulamā'* to intervene on their behalf.[74] The incorporation of the Sharārda into the ᶜAlawī army a year later completed their reintegration into the state and society. Like Mawlay ᶜAbd al-Raḥmān's treatment of the Idrīsī rebels in Fes, his treatment of the Sharārda was carefully gauged to show that there was a place for all within the sultanate but that rebellion would not be tolerated.

While the Makhzan *jihād* against the Sharārda was successful, Mawlay ᶜAbd al-Raḥmān's maritime jihad had more mixed results. European attitudes towards corsairing had changed significantly during the Napoleonic wars as a result of the growth of European navies and their modernisation. From being a useful means of undermining rivals corsairing had become an outmoded obstacle to British and French commerce and communication in the Mediterranean. The apprehension of European merchant ships by ᶜAlawī corsairs therefore sparked a response which Mawlay ᶜAbd al-Raḥmān had not expected. In retaliation for the seizure of British vessels, a British naval squadron blockaded Tanger harbour during winter 1828–9 and threatened to open fire if the Makhzan failed to release the ships and pay compensation. The Austrians similarly demanded reparations for the detention of an Austrian ship, and when negotiations faltered in May 1829 an Austrian squadron arrived off Tanger with an ultimatum and then attacked Laraish and Tetuan.[75] Neither attack was particularly successful and ᶜAlawī–Austrian differences were only resolved in 1830 when representatives of the two parties brokered a treaty in Gibraltar.[76]

The sultanate held its own in these disputes with Britain and Austria but European naval blockades and bombardments were not the spectacle which Mawlay ᶜAbd al-Raḥmān sought to present by renewing the maritime jihad. A strategy intended to deter European aggression and demonstrate ᶜAlawī power at home and abroad had in fact encouraged British and Austrian attacks. These attacks destabilised the northern coastal regions where the jihad ethic was strongest without gaining the sultan the prestige he had hoped for. Moreover, the Makhzan found itself ill-equipped to deal with the wearisome rounds of negotiations which ensued, and unable to shoulder the combined costs of keeping the corsair fleet at sea and paying compensation to European powers who felt that their shipping had been illegally detained. The era of the corsairs was at an end but the era of jihad was not as events soon demonstrated.

Shortly after the ᶜAlawī–Austrian settlement was reached, news reached the sultanate that the French, frustrated by the ineffectiveness of their naval blockade of Algiers, intended to attack the city to secure satisfaction in their debt dispute. The French let it be known that their sole target was the regime in Algiers but the name of the campaign – *l'éxpedition de l'Afrique* – revived the fear of a general offensive against Muslim lands aroused by Napoleon's expedition to Egypt thirty years before.[77] The sultan ordered the governors of Tetuan and Tanger to prepare for a possible French attack by doubling the coastal guard and drilling the artillerymen.[78] At the same time he attempted to deter possible French aggression against the sultanate by assuring them that they would be able to provision their fleet in ᶜAlawī ports. He also suggested that, given Maghribi attitudes towards Christians, a diplomatic solution would be better for everyone.[79] The popular mood was summed up in comments made by Makhzan officials to the French consul in Tanger:

> Les Maures ne pouvaient voir, sans une espèce de chagrin, le sol des Mahometans foulé par des armées Chrétiennes et des fidèles attaqués par elles, quelque légitimes et justes que soient les motifs.[80]

Such concern over the unfolding situation in Algiers reflected the importance of jihad within ᶜAlawī political and religious culture. By the early nineteenth century the sharifian jihad state founded by the ᶜAlawī *shurafā'* in the seventeenth century had reached maturity. On the domestic front, the jihad against *fasād* construct had gained acceptance throughout society and formed one of the pillars of state–society relations, equally likely to be manipulated by opponents of the Makhzan as by the Makhzan itself. On the international front, jihad against the infidel retained its hold as the primary responsibility of a sharifian sultan and in fact started to loom larger as European imperialism began to send tremors through Maghribi society. The unexpected capture of Algiers by the French in summer 1830 and the subsequent conquest of the deylik during the 1830s and 1840s heralded a new phase in the evolution of the sharifian jihad state. This phase was marked by tremendous religio-political upheaval as the ᶜAlawī Makhzan, the subjects of the sultanate and many in the western Algerian province of Oran attempted to employ ᶜAlawī jihad constructs to establish a new Muslim regime in Algerian territory and combat French imperialism in North Africa.

3

FRENCH COLONIALISM AND SHARIFIAN JIHAD IN ALGERIA, 1830–2

Algiers was the westernmost province of the Ottoman empire. Like the other Maghribi Ottoman provinces, it functioned as an autonomous unit, its ruling elite bound to Istanbul by ties of loyalty, language and political culture. This elite was formed of Janissaries and corsairs of Mediterranean origin united by their use of Turkish and adherence to the Ḥanafī school of Islamic religious law. Although the Algerian ruling elite tried to bar the entry to its ranks of sons of 'Turks' and local women, known as *kulogullari* (Turkish) or Kulughlān (Arabic), these individuals were important as Ḥanafī scholars, merchants and militiamen in provincial towns.

The Turks of Algiers ruled over a society composed of Arab and Berber townsmen and tribesmen as heterogeneous as that of the neighbouring ᶜAlawī sultanate. Their legitimacy lay in the authority delegated to them by the Ottoman sultan to defend Algiers from the infidel and uphold the Sharīᶜa within its confines. They ruled through a strategically placed network of garrisons and a system of alliances with a number of *makhzan* tribes who gained tax exemptions in return for helping them to collect taxes from the remaining *raᶜāyā* tribes. A secular elite of tribal notables (*ajwād*) and a religious elite of marabouts provided local leadership. The degree of integration between the Turks and local society varied across the deylik. Relatively close association characterised relations in Algiers itself and the eastern province of Constantine whilst considerable tensions existed between the Turks and the indigenous population in the western province of Oran which was exposed to ᶜAlawī influence from the west.

The frontier between the sultanate and the deylik had always been a permeable one. As mentioned above, tribal migrations, trade, pilgrimage and educational travel along the Taza corridor created an intimate connection between the northern sultanate and Oran. In particular, the formation of generations of students within the *madāris* and mosques of Fes ensured their exposure to the religio-political theories of the Saᶜdī then ᶜAlawī regimes and their export back to the western deylik. Concrete signs of sharifian religio-political influence in Oran date to the seventeenth century with the formation of a religious elite of maraboutic lineages which supplemented their qualities of learning (*ᶜilm*), saintliness (*walāya*) and nobility (*jāh*) with claims to Idrīsī sharifian ancestry, confirmed in some cases by textual accreditation and in others by miraculous and visionary means.[1] As in the sultanate, the result was a steady increase in the number of marabouts recognised as *shurafāʾ*, a phenomenon which older lineages contested in a plethora of genealogical works.[2]

This broadening of the sharifian base in Oran coincided with the reign of the ᶜAlawī sultan, Sīdī Muḥammad b. ᶜAbd Allah, whose religious policies were instrumental in the advent of Sufi revival in North Africa. Its importance to the sultanate and Oran lay in its invigoration of rural religious culture by means of new and reformed religious brotherhoods – the Darqāwa, the Wazzāniyya–Ṭayyibiyya, the Tijāniyya and the Qādiriyya – who possessed adherents on both sides of the frontier thereby furthering cross-border links. In Oran these brotherhoods tended to be headed by lineages from the old sharifian religious elite who seem to have used Sufi revival as a means to extend their authority among the tribes and counteract the 'democratisation' of sharifian ancestry which threatened their status.

A case in point were the Qādirī marabouts of the Gharis plain outside Mascara, the lineage of ᶜAbd al-Qādir, a distinguished Idrīsī lineage whose ancestor was reputed to have come from Morocco in the thirteenth century and fathered not only the Mascaran lineage but also the inhabitants of the Rif.[3] The lineage had traditionally enjoyed the qualified support of local Arabic-speaking tribes such as the Ḥashem and the Banū ᶜAmir. By participating in Islamic renewal it consolidated its influence over these tribes and extended it westwards into the northern sultanate. The lineage's transformation into shaykhs of the revived Qādiriyya began with ᶜAbd al-Qādir's grandfather, Muṣṭafā al-Mukhtār, who visited Baghdad, home of the Qādiriyya, and received the *khirqa* (robe of investiture) from the head of the Baghdadi *shurafāʾ*, the *naqīb al-ashrāf*.[4] Armed with these validations, he returned to Gharis and began recruiting tribes to the Qādiriyya. ᶜAbd al-Qādir's father, Muḥyī al-Dīn, the next head of the lineage, continued his work and in the decades before 1830 the Qādiriyya became the favoured brotherhood of the Arab tribes of the Mascara region and a scattering of Arab and Berber tribes between Mascara, Tlemsen and the ᶜAlawī Rif.[5]

Another characteristic of the revived religious brotherhoods was their adoption of centralised organisation. In earlier eras, the *zawāyā* of the Sufi *ṭuruq* were generally autonomous entities run by independent holy lineages. The *zawāyā* of these new brotherhoods were more closely bound to the mother *zāwiya* which controlled appointments to subsidiary *zawāyā*, monitored the doctrines taught in them, and often insisted that local dues collected from devotees were forwarded to the centre. Mother lodges also acted as centres for pilgrimage. Such centralisation multiplied the connections between Oran and the ᶜAlawī sultanate. Certainly the Wazzāniyya–Ṭayyibiyya *zāwiya* at Wazzan and the shrine of Aḥmad al-Tijānī in Fes attracted a constant flow of visitors from the deylik who joined those paying their respects at the older shrines of Idrīs I and II.

The centralisation of these brotherhoods endowed them with wide-reaching religious authority which they began to utilise for political ends in the early nineteenth century. Doctrinally Sufi revival was distinguished by its emphasis on the characteristics of a good Islamic society. This gave the brotherhoods an interest in a range of issues as disparate as the acceptability of heterodox rural religious practices and the legitimacy of regional political authorities. Given the ᶜAlawī componant in Sufi revival, the political perspective of the brotherhoods generally took the form of opposition to perceived lapses in governmental integrity which became more frequent in the early nineteenth century as Turkish government became more intrusive.

Previously, the Turks had been able to tax the tribes relatively lightly because of the supplementary income they drew from Algiers thriving commercial and corsairing economy. Changing European attitudes to Mediterranean corsairing signalled by the 1816 Anglo–Dutch bombardment of Algiers for refusing to sign an undertaking to outlaw piracy, forced the Turks to look to the interior for a higher proportion of their revenue. This entailed higher taxation of the tribes from the coast to the Sahara, a development which the latter deeply resented and viewed as oppression. Tribal resentment found its voice in the oppositional discourse of the religious brotherhoods who challenged new Turkish tax-gathering practices as unjust and un-Islamic. Between 1805 and 1830 criticism escalated into brotherhood revolts, conceptualised by their authors as Islamic opposition to the irreligious activities of the Turks, or jihad against *fasād*.

The first of these revolts was the Darqāwa revolt led by Ibn al-Sharīf, a sharifian shaykh admitted to the brotherhood in Fes. ᶜAbd al-Qādir's son, Muḥammad, and the late nineteenth century historian, Muḥammad al-Sulaymānī, report that the Darqāwa revolt was populist, sharifian and mahdistic in nature. Ibn al-Sharīf drummed up tremendous support among the coastal tribes as the awaited *mahdī* (*al-mahdī al-muntaẓar*) who would replace the injustice of the Turks with a just Islamic order.[6] Although Ibn al-Sharīf probably envisaged himself as the head of this new order, he and many of the Darqāwa rebels viewed the ᶜAlawī sultanate as their model of Islamic government and a possible source of religio-political authority. Consequently, Tlemsen and several rebel tribes gave Mawlay Sulaymān their allegiance during the revolt. The second brotherhood revolt was a Tijānī revolt in 1826 triggered by repeated Turkish campaigns to extract taxes from the Tijāniyya *zāwiya* at ᶜAyn Madi on the edge of the Sahara. The head of the brotherhood, Muḥammad al-Tijānī, gathered a large force of Tijānī tribesmen and marched northwards towards Mascara, proclaiming that allegiance to the Turks was contrary to Islam.[7]

These revolts were symptomatic of the changing relationship between the population of Oran and the Turks on the one hand and the ᶜAlawī sultanate on the other in the decades before 1830. With the demise of corsairing governmental structures in place since the sixteenth century had broken down, leading to a delegitimisation of the Turks and growing tribal opposition, directed and given ideological weight by the religious brotherhoods. Meanwhile, the political activism of the religious brotherhoods encouraged the religious and cultural relations between Oran and the ᶜAlawī sultanate to take on a political colour. The ᶜAlawī sultans viewed this development with ambivalence. Whilst expansion into Oran and, in particular, the integration of Tlemsen into the sultanate was a cherished ᶜAlawī ambition, the sultans did not wish to involve themselves in a war with the Turks of Algiers.

The French occupation of Algiers in 1830 transformed the situation by replacing legitimate Islamic authority with infidel rule. The demise of the Turks provided Mawlay ᶜAbd al-Raḥmān, a young and ambitious sultan, with an unprecedented opportunity to transform the historic ties between the sultanate and Oran into political overlordship. If he succeeded, he would greatly increase his prestige and that of his lineage and finally achieve the elusive goal of sultans since the Marīnid era to reconstitute the archetypal Idrīsī state. The sultan's dual obligation to provide integrative Islamic rule by means of jihad against *fasād* and protect Islamic territory by means of jihad against the infidel provided the ideological framework for sharifian expansion. Such constructs had immense popular appeal in the ᶜAlawī sultanate and in Oran where significant sections of the population viewed the sultanate as a natural source of religio-political authority and were keen to sieze the opportunity provided by the French conquest of Algiers to implement a new sharifian Islamic order.

The French conquest of Algiers

The French conquest of Algiers ostensibly marked the culmination of a trade dispute of several years' duration. The conquest was preceded by a naval blockade of Algiers harbour to force the dey to come to terms. When this proved ineffective more aggressive French voices called for an attack on Algiers. While the dispute provided a superficial incentive for the French offensive, its underlying rationale came from Europe's new perception of its global role to 'civilise' which found its practical realisation in imperialism. In the case of Algiers, conquest and civilisation of the country under French auspices was seen as an ideal way to discourage corsairing by busying the population with agriculture.[8] The surplus grain, fruit and olive oil produced could then be exported from Algiers to Marseille to help feed the population of France.

Napoleon had found this vision seductive, based as it was on the idea of making North Africa the bread basket of a European Mediterranean empire as in the days of the Romans, and the first plans for the conquest of Algiers were drawn up during his era. They were revived in 1830 by a French government desperate to distract public attention from domestic problems and gain prestige through an assertive policy abroad. Under pressure from the military and the Marseille commercial lobby, the Bourbon government finally authorised the campaign in June 1830. In the interim, reports of French plans persuaded the dey to summon troops from Constantine and Oran to the capital and call up tribal auxiliaries. He assumed that his armies would easily repel the French.[9]

The French offensive began on 13 June 1830 when an expeditionary force landed west of Algiers. It advanced without difficulty and by July the French had secured the foothills surrounding Algiers and trained their cannon on the city.[10] Algiers inland defences were limited to a single fort which the French quickly reduced when hostilities began on 4 July. Many of the ruling elite wished to fight on but the dey decided to come to terms. By noon of the following day he had signed a convention surrendering the city in return for French guarantees of life, property, freedom to practice Islam, and respect for the city's mores. French forces entered the city soon after, unchallenged and unresisted by its inhabitants.[11]

In order to consolidate their position, French forces rounded up the Janissaries, corsairs and eminent Kulughlān present in the city, sequestered their property and then deported them to Izmir *en masse*. To complete the campaign, they sent additional units to secure key coastal cities such as Oran and ᶜAnnaba. The Turkish authorities in both cities, isolated by the capitulation of the dey, co-operated with the incoming French units in the hope that they would be retained as French client rulers. At this point the French did not attempt to make inroads into the interior. From the perspective of inland authorities it thus appeared that they intended to establish a chain of coastal enclaves in the same manner as the Spanish and Portuguese, leaving the rest of the deylik to govern itself. The provincial beys of Constantine and Titteri, local Turkish garrisons and tribal notables therefore took steps to secure their own positions.

In the eastern province of Constantine this led to the emergence of a new Turco-Arab regime headed by the Kulughlī, al-Ḥājj Aḥmad Bey. In the western province of Oran Turkish authority, contested for decades, faltered as soon as it was no longer backed by the military power of Algiers itself. The result was extensive disorder as isolated Turkish and Kulughlī garrisons, the religious brotherhoods, and rival tribal factions jostled for power. Lacking any significant local support, Ḥasan Bey of Oran solicited French assistance. This was a calculated risk: alliance with the French was morally dangerous but might give him the material power he needed to reassert his authority. The arrival of French troops boded well for Ḥasan Bey but the collapse of the Bourbon government which had organised the *éxpedition de l'Afrique* necessitated their immediate return to France. In fact, the change of metropolitan government not only reduced troop numbers outside Algiers but brought the French occupation of the city itself into question. Throughout the deylik local powers expected a full French withdrawal and turned on those who had collaborated with them. In Oran the French withdrawal signalled the final discrediting of Turkish authority: Ḥasan Bey was beseiged in the city of Oran by hostile tribes while the Turkish and Kulughlī garrisons of Mustaghanim, Mascara and Tlemsen found themselves similarly confined.

This forceful rejection of Turkish rule created a situation verging on anarchy in Oran province as inter-tribal raiding, perpetuation of blood feuds, and faction fighting escalated. Political fracture lines followed the pattern set in previous decades. Tribes such as the Dawā'ir and Zmāla which had served the Turkish authorities banded together against the Arab Qādirī tribes of the Mascara area, their erstwhile rivals for beylical patronage. Similar fissures occurred between the tribes affiliated to the Darqāwa, the Wazzāniyya–Ṭayyibiyya and the Tijāniyya.

The resulting insecurity in the countryside disrupted agriculture and commerce, both local and trans-regional. In the words of Muḥammad b. ᶜAbd al-Qādir:

> The urge to revenge surged in the breasts of the people and everyone who had a murder to avenge by blood endeavored to settle the score. As a result the mantle of security was pulled away, the wheels of trade ceased to turn and agriculture was neglected.[12]

Among those most attentive to the unfolding situation were the ᶜAlawī sultan and his subjects. News of the French conquest of Algiers reached Tanger on 13 July 1830, causing a public furore which gradually subsided into resignation.[13] In a society embued with a strong jihad tradition and recently exposed to European blockades and threats the campaign was seen as the next stage in a major infidel offensive against the *dār al-islām*. Mawlay ᶜAbd al-Raḥmān himself expressed the general mood in a letter to the governor of Tetuan in which he said:

> O God recompense the Muslims for this great disaster and let the return of this port be preordained. Make the enemy unbeliever choke on his own saliva and hasten the destruction of his faction and strengthen Islam by the glory of the Prophet – peace be upon him.[14]

The sultan's words conveyed the sentiments expected of a sharifian *mujāhid* sultan but they also revealed a religio-political perspective which could pave the way for ᶜAlawī expansion eastwards. The fall of Algiers and resultant fluidity of politics in the deylik implied that an opportunity for ᶜAlawī expansion existed but the sultan, like his predecessors, did not wish to risk a clash with Istanbul or the remnants of the Turkish administration in the deylik. By emphasising that Algiers was Muslim territory threatened by non-Muslims, he pointed to the existence of a religious obligation to intervene which surmounted internal Muslim political boundaries.

In the months that followed Mawlay ᶜAbd al-Raḥmān's Makhzan used the services of its mercantile agents in Gibraltar and other Mediterranean ports to monitor the situation in Algiers closely. As it became clearer that Turkish authority had all but collapsed, the ᶜAlawī Makhzan intensified its stress on the Muslim community of interest which existed between the deylik and the sultanate and played up the sultan's universalist role to protect Muslims and Muslim territory from the infidel. ᶜAlawī policy involved active intervention on behalf of Muslims, such as a request to the French to repatriate sharifian lineages from Algiers in the sultanate, and the admittance of shiploads of refugees from Algiers and other French-held coastal cities which arrived in Tetuan and Tanger in late summer.[15]

Makhzan directives from autumn 1830 indicate that the receipt of refugees from Algiers had the air of a public relations exercise. In letters to the governors of Tanger and Tetuan, Mawlay ᶜAbd al-Raḥmān identified the refugees as *muhājirūn* performing a *hijra* from the *dār al-ḥarb*, terminology obviously drawn from the Prophetic period but also resonant with echoes of the troubled centuries of the Reconquista for a Maghribi audience. He then commanded Makhzan governors to receive the refugees as 'brothers in religion' whose willingness to sacrifice their land and property to avoid living under infidel control was moving testimony to the strength of their faith.[16] The Makhzan backed up such rhetoric with generous resettlement packages: refugees were helped to find housing in northern towns, particularly Tetuan and Fes, and given permission to practice their customary occupations without hindrance from the state or the guilds.[17] Poor refugees were added to the list of those entitled to receive sultanic largesse on the occasion of major Muslim festivals. This publicised Makhzan beneficence before the sultan's subjects whilst also extending the patron–client relationship established between the Makhzan and more affluent refugees to poorer, more potentially disruptive, elements within the migrant community.

Mawlay ᶜAbd al-Raḥmān's response to the French conquest highlighted the difference between Maghribi perceptions of the relationship between religion and politics and contemporary European attitudes which viewed states as national and territorial entities. The French in Algiers believed that their conquest of the deylik's capital gave them legal sovereignty over all its territory, even though they held little more than the city of Algiers itself. The Maghribi population had a very different view. Within the Islamic sphere the political division of territory into different states under different rulers by no means conferred upon such states a permanent existence within defined territorial boundaries irrespective of the regime in power. Their existence, as in the case of the deylik of Algiers, was contingent upon their being under Muslim rule and the capture of such territory by a non-Muslim power justified, and in fact necessitated, Muslim intervention to expell that non-Muslim power. Such views were particularly deeply held in the ᶜAlawī sultanate and areas within its sphere of influence, a part of the Islamic world where centuries of warfare with Christian Europe had deeply influenced religio-political theory.

From the Maghribi perspective, the French were the masters of Algiers but their possession of the city rested on *de facto* coercive power rather than on any legal right of sovereignty and did not extend beyond the area they directly controlled. Elsewhere in the deylik the sudden collapse of central Muslim authority meant a devolution of authority to other power-brokers: the provincial beys of Oran, Titteri and Constantine, neighbouring Muslim regimes in Tunis and Morocco and indigenous tribal and religious leaders. It was the responsibility of these competing political players to perpetuate Muslim authority outside Algiers and oppose the city's shameful occupation by a non-Muslim power. For many of the inhabitants of Oran and the ᶜAlawī sultanate the natural source of Muslim authority for the deylik and champion of Islam against the infidel was the ᶜAlawī sultan, Mawlay ᶜAbd al-Raḥmān.

The ᶜAlawī occupation of Tlemsen

In autumn 1830 Mawlay ᶜAbd al-Raḥmān took the weighty step of initiating sharifian expansion into Oran with the aim of enhancing his prestige as a *mujāhid* sultan and realising the long-standing ᶜAlawī goal of incorporating Tlemsen into the sultanate. His decision was informed by two developments, the withdrawal of French troops from Oran and a plea from Tlemsen and nearby tribes for him to accept their allegiance and restore order to the area. The decrease in French troop numbers suggested to the sultan that the French occupation of Algiers would be limited and temporary, while Tlemsen's invitation to him to intervene indicated that sharifian expansion into Oran would have local backing.[18] It also stressed the affective bonds tying Tlemsen to the sultanate in general and to Fes in particular.

Since the seventeenth century the ᶜAlawī sultans had viewed Tlemsen as an Idrīsī and therefore Moroccan city and in 1830 it became clear that its inhabitants held similar views.[19] The group most attached to the sultanate were the civilian elite of merchants and *ᶜulamā'*, many of whom claimed either Idrīsī or Fāsī ancestry. It was the head of this elite, Muḥammad b. Nūna, who contacted the ᶜAlawī Makhzan through Idrīs al-Jirārī, governor of the nearby border town of Wajda, and informed him that the people of Tlemsen wished to submit to the sultan.[20] When the news reached Mawlay ᶜAbd al-Raḥmān he travelled to Meknes where a Tlemsenī *sharīf* resident in Fes offered him the city's allegiance.[21] Tlemsen's choice of a *sharīf* resident in Fes as their representative symbolised the intimate relationship between the two cities and their shared sharifian culture, and suggested that its inhabitants foresaw no Makhzan opposition to their decision. Indeed Mawlay ᶜAbd al-Raḥmān and his military commanders were eager to accept Tlemsen's *bayᶜa* without further ado.

However, the sultan hesitated to act without approval from the religious establishment in Fes. Unexpectedly, many of the *ᶜulamā'* harboured misgivings about the legality of the undertaking and ruled that the sultan could not accept the *bayᶜa* of Tlemsen because the city remained bound by its oath of allegiance to the Ottoman sultan. At this point the French consul in Tanger seized the opportunity presented by the dissenting *fatwa* of the Fāsī *ᶜulamā'* to claim that, in fact, the French had replaced the dey of Algiers on behalf of the Ottoman sultan and thus possessed sovereign rights over all parts of the deylik, including Tlemsen.[22] The unforeseen French assertion of *de jure* sovereignty over Tlemsen was religiously untenable from the Muslim perspective, but their claim to be acting on behalf of the Ottomans and the issue of Ottoman sovereignty could not be lightly dismissed.

The first to contest the opinion of the Fāsī *ᶜulamā'* were the notables of Tlemsen who sent a delegation to present Mawlay ᶜAbd al-Raḥmān with a refutation of the Fāsī ruling. This refutation is one of the clearest statements of western Maghribi political thought in the 1830s and demonstrates that for the inhabitants of Tlemsen as much as for the inhabitants of Fes or Marrakesh religio-political legitimacy was tied to a ruler's ability to preserve his territory from internal disorder and external threat. The refutation, which is preserved in several nineteenth century Maghribi histories, divides into two sections each of which presented a different argument to deny that Tlemsen owed the Ottoman sultan allegiance and demonstrate that Mawlay ᶜAbd al-Raḥmān had an obligation to assume rule over the city.

The first part of the refutation denied that Algiers was part of the Ottoman empire by attributing independent sovereign power to the dey. It then denied that its inhabitants owed the dey and his regime allegiance on the grounds that he had acted in an oppressive and unjust fashion. His removal by the French was an act of God which cleared the way for a true Muslim ruler such as Mawlay ᶜAbd al-Raḥmān to re-establish justice.

> [The Ottoman sultan] was merely a name there. The governor of Algiers seized power for himself and made a mockery of his religion, so God destroyed him for his tyranny.
>
> His lack of concern for the command and consent of the Ottoman [sultan] indicate his usurpation of power and independence, indeed he paid no heed to him and obeyed him in neither word nor deed. [The Ottoman sultan] had ordered him to sign a truce with the Christians but he accepted neither word nor advice from him, but then asked him for resources to help allay the disasters which awaited him at the hands of the Christians. [The Ottoman sultan] completely refused … and the infidel enemy took [Algiers].
>
> All people are the servants of God and the sultan is no exception. God has charged him with their affairs as a trial and tribulation. If he rules them with justice and mercy, equity and fairness as does our Lord [Mawlay ᶜAbd al-Raḥmān] – may God make him victorious – then he is God's deputy upon earth and the shadow of God over his servants and he has high status with God Almighty. But if he rules them with tyranny and violence, oppression and corruption as this tyrant did, then he is showing insolence to God in his kingdom and he has no right to hold sway and swagger about, exposing himself to God's harsh punishment and scorn.

This justification for ᶜAlawī intervention was based on the concept that the legitimacy of a ruler depended upon his fulfilment of the task entrusted him by God, which was to maintain justice within his domains. This notion underlay both the Ottoman circle of equity and the ᶜAlawī theory of sultanic jihad against *fasād*. Both constructs perceived the sultan as the representative and deputy of God on earth, an absolute and divinely appointed ruler, but made his absolute power conditional upon his fulfilment of his responsibility to rule justly in accordance with the Sharīᶜa. The dey ruled by delegation from Istanbul but his independence and oppression had broken that link leaving the inhabitants of Algiers in need of a Muslim ruler to restore the Sharīᶜa. In presenting this argument to Mawlay ᶜAbd al-Raḥmān the notables of Tlemsen implicitly called upon him to continue the 'holy war' to establish just Islamic government which the revolts of the Darqāwa and Tijāniyya had begun.

The second part of the refutation argued that even if Algiers was part of the Ottoman empire the inability of the Ottomans to offer its inhabitants military assistance against the French or any other non-Muslim attacker invalidated their oath of allegiance and transferred the responsibility to rule and defend to a Muslim sovereign capable of fulfilling these obligations. Again Mawlay ᶜAbd al-Raḥmān was cited as the ruler most suited to the task.

> If one were obliged to accept that we were bound by an oath to the Ottoman [sultan] there would still be no argument against us because his land is far from us, and his rule does not benefit us in any way because of the deserts, seas, towns and villages which lie between us. Perhaps his residence is closer to us by sea but the infidel has prevented him from sailing upon it.
>
> In the circumstances, how can he defend our land and home. The news from Egypt and the district of Syria is another indication of how far he is from fulfilling this wish, for the enemies of religion overran these [regions] more than five years ago and he could not find a way to help them or a king to defend them until he sought the help of the infidel enemy. In his explanation of [the Ṣaḥīḥ of] Muslim which analyses a case similar to ours, al-Abī states that when the imam's power does not reach a district and awaiting his assistance will lead to peril, the establishment of another [ruler] in his place and resort to his assistance is permitted.
>
> We approach the threshold of the gate of our Lord – may God make him victorious – seeking to enter under his sway and devote ourselves to his service with the agreement of the tribes, the cities and the people of insight for we know that our Lord is fully qualified for this noble task, and worthy of the honoured imamate by the fact that one great man after another has inherited it and received due praise. We ask our Lord – may God make him victorious – to accept this oath of allegiance from us by his grace as we appeal to him by the glory of his ancestor the Prophet – may God's blessing be upon him, his noble family and his chosen companions.[23]

This second argument drew on other aspects of ᶜAlawī jihad theory: the notion that the prime responsibility of an Islamic ruler was to defend his domains from infidel attack and that those best qualified to perform this religio-political duty were the *shurafā'*. Although the notables of Tlemsen made no overt connection between defence of the realm and sharifian rule, their reference to Mawlay ᶜAbd al-Raḥmān's sharifian ancestry and his worthiness to hold the imamate after listing the reasons why the Ottoman sultan could not defend the regency certainly implied that his suitability to defend Muslim territory was intimately linked to his descent from the Prophet. The Tlemsenī refutation of the Fāsī *fatwa* thus called upon Mawlay ᶜAbd al-Raḥmān to accept the *bayᶜa* of Tlemsen as a sharifian ruler with a dual role: that of establishing Islamic justice within his domains as the shadow of God on earth and defending them from infidel attack as God's holy warrior. The notables of Tlemsen informally added that the sultan might find the wealth of the city and its weapon stores a useful resource in his perpetual struggle against his own rebellious subjects![24]

The arguments marshalled by the notables of Tlemsen provided a set of religio-political justifications for sharifian expansion which received a ready response from the sultan and more militant members of the Makhzan. They appealed to Mawlay ᶜAbd al-Raḥmān's personal ambition to prove himself as a warrior and his desire to divert the ever-restive energies of the army into an undertaking likely to bring prestige and material reward without costing too much given Tlemsen's eagerness for ᶜAlawī rule and the limited scope of the French occupation. More cautious members of the Makhzan remained doubtful of the legality and practicality of the undertaking. From the legal perspective, they contested the notion that the provision of military assistance for jihad required a change in sovereignty. From the pragmatic perspective, they questioned the feasibility of turning the cultural bond between the sultanate and west Algeria into a political reality. Although the demise of the deylical regime decreased the likelihood that another Muslim power would contest the ᶜAlawī claim to Tlemsen, the disruption that the involvement in Algerian affairs had caused during the reigns of Mawlay Ismāᶜīl and Mawlay Sulaymān made senior members of the sultan's entourage and the Fāsī establishment uneasy. They claimed that intervention 'would not contribute anything to this state but the stirring up of insurrection and trouble'.[25]

Despite such dissenting voices, Mawlay ᶜAbd al-Raḥmān accepted the *bayᶜa* and prepared an expeditionary force (*maḥalla*) to assume control of Tlemsen in his name. The ᶜAlawī force consisted of ᶜAbīd and Udāyā units headed by a handful of commanders mostly from the Udāyā, and Makhzan servants to administer the sultanate's new province. The *maḥalla* was led by an ᶜAlawī *sharīf*, Mawlay ᶜAlī b. Sulaymān, a young cousin of the sultan whose lack of military experience or an independent military following meant that he was unlikely to use Tlemsen as a base from which to challenge Mawlay ᶜAbd al-Raḥmān for power. Another important member of the entourage was al-Ḥājj al-ᶜArabī, head of the Wazzāniyya–Ṭayyibiyya brotherhood which had numerous adherents in the deylik as well as the sultanate.[26] His presence in the *maḥalla* underlined the fact that the relationship between the sultanate and Oran was rooted in rural religious networks as much as in urban commercial and cultural exchange, and that the successful incorporation of the tribes of the Tlemsen area into the sultanate would require the assistance of the marabouts.

The *maḥalla* left Fes for Tlemsen in October 1830. As it moved east along the Taza corridor tribal delegations from the Tlemsen and Mascara areas came to offer their allegiance to Mawlay ᶜAlī, the representative of ᶜAlawī authority and power. Among those who offered their allegiance were the Dawā'ir and Zmāla, Turkish Makhzan tribes whose decision to submit to the ᶜAlawī sultan signalled how complete the collapse of Turkish authority was.[27] When the *maḥalla* reached Tlemsen it received an exuberant welcome from the inhabitants who lined the route into the city cheering and waving as Mawlay ᶜAlī passed by.[28] This was, however, only the first step in the process of incorporating the region into the sultanate. Mawlay ᶜAlī and his commanders faced the tasks of establishing control over the Turkish–Kulughlī garrison which held the citadel of Tlemsen, winning over the tribes of the region and countering potential opposition from Ḥasan Bey in Oran and the French. These interrelated tasks required measures which the Makhzan constantly legitimised by reference to the expedition's avowed objectives – the restoration of order in Oran and its defence against the infidel – objectives which were regularly reformulated to parry verbal attacks by Ḥasan Bey and the French who returned to Oran in December 1830.

The most pressing task for the ᶜAlawī commanders was the resolution of tensions between the *maḥalla* and the Turkish garrison which still held the citadel of the city. Although identified with the Turkish regime, the garrison consisted largely of Kulughlān who had maternal ties with the inhabitants of the city and local tribes. When the link between the garrison and the Turks in Oran and Algiers was severed these local affiliations persuaded the Kulughlān to join the civilian elite in offering Mawlay ᶜAbd al-Raḥmān their allegiance.[29] They had assumed, however, that the sultan would rule Tlemsen indirectly and expected to retain their role as the politico-military wing of the urban elite. They had not expected to be supplanted by an ᶜAlawī garrison or sidelined by the mercantile sharifian elite which had originally solicited ᶜAlawī intervention.

The arrival of the *maḥalla* to institute direct ᶜAlawī rule therefore created a conflict of interests which centred on control of Tlemsen's citadel. In order to preserve their position, the Kulughlān refused the *maḥalla* access to the citadel. In retaliation the ᶜAlawī commanders arrested several members of the Kulughlān and their allies, the Dawā'ir and Zmāla tribes, and dispatched them to Fes in chains. The remainder of the garrison barricaded themselves in the citadel with their artillery trained on the ᶜAlawī positions outside and informed Mawlay ᶜAbd al-Raḥmān that they had decided to withdraw their *bayᶜa* to him.[30] To avoid bombardment the *maḥalla* retreated to the market gardens outside Tlemsen. Mawlay ᶜAbd al-Raḥmān attempted to resolve the conflict by receiving the Kulughlī prisoners with apologies, but the fragile consensus formulated before the arrival of the *maḥalla* was broken and the tentative alliance between the Makhzan and the ex-Turkish elite severely damaged.[31] Henceforth, the Kulughlān considered the ᶜAlawī *maḥalla* an occupying force with whom they were at war. The conflict diverted the latter's energies and necessitated its regular re-inforcement with men and munitions from Fes.[32] This unexpected drain on resources was compounded by the loss of prestige involved in the expedition's failure to reduce the citadel of Tlemsen and force the Kulughlān into submission.

The second task faced by the *maḥalla* was to pacify the countryside and gain the submission of the tribes of the region who had not offered their allegiance. Their limited resources and the importance of local consent to the legitimation of ᶜAlawī intervention required that the commanders of the *maḥalla* secure the allegiance of the tribes and persuade them to supply the *maḥalla* with food by peaceable means. To achieve this they activated the maraboutic networks and tribal alliances which operated across the frontier. The *sharīf* and head of the Wazzāniyya–Ṭayyibiyya, al-Ḥājj al-ᶜArabī, deployed his considerable spiritual authority to persuade Ṭayyibiyya tribes to supply the *maḥalla* and give the ᶜAlawī sultan their allegiance. At the same time, Bū Zayyān, a Makhzan *qā'id* and tribal notable of the Wajda area, acted as a bridge between the ᶜAlawī lineage to which he was affiliated by marriage and the tribes of the area lying between Wajda and Tlemsen.[33]

The activation of cross-border social and religious connections could not, however, surmount the divisions which existed between different confederations of tribes, between tribes which had served the beys of Oran and tribes forced to pay taxes to them, and between tribal blocs affiliated to different religious brotherhoods. Past ᶜAlawī experience had shown that one way to surmount such divisions was to proclaim a jihad. Mawlay ᶜAbd al-Raḥmān therefore sent instructions to the tribes to bury their differences and unite behind the new ᶜAlawī administration to wage jihad against the infidel French.[34]

The ᶜAlawī's call for a jihad struck a chord, particularly among the leadership and clientele of the sharifian religious brotherhoods. It was given added weight by the return of French troops to the towns of Oran, Médea and Blida after the resolution of the political crisis in France. Tribal delegations began to arrive in Tlemsen from all over the province to submit to the ᶜAlawī sultan as sharifian leader of the jihad. One of the most important new submissions came from the Qādirī tribes of the Mascara region east of Tlemsen. The tribal delegation which arrived in Tlemsen was led by the head of the Qādiriyya, Muḥyī al-Dīn, who informed Mawlay ᶜAlī that all the Qādirī tribes from Mascara to Blida in the east would join the sultan if he led a jihad against the French. This exchange marked the beginning of the relationship between the ᶜAlawī Makhzan and the Qādirī marabouts of Gharis, Muḥyī al-Dīn and his son, ᶜAbd al-Qādir, which would make them the staunchest allies of the sultan in Oran and eventually the greatest danger to him.

The widespread response to the ᶜAlawī summons to jihad created a loose web of affiliation over a vast area in which Mawlay ᶜAbd al-Raḥmān was perceived first and foremost as a leader of jihad rather than as a sultan. For many his acceptance as ruler required that he first prove himself as a *mujāhid* in the time-honoured fashion of sharifian sultans. Emphasis on the military and religious aspects of intervention also glossed over the tendentious issue of sovereignty which was now contested by the ᶜAlawī sultan, Ḥasan Bey in Oran and the French. At this point Mawlay ᶜAbd al-Raḥmān hoped to secure the submission of the population of Oran by means of a jihad and deflect Turkish and French criticism while he consolidated his position. His policy was therefore two-fold: military action on the ground to organise the tribes for an attack on Oran combined with diplomatic initiatives to counter the claims of Ḥasan Bey and the French.

Ḥasan Bey, although beseiged in Oran, responded immediately to the ᶜAlawī occupation of Tlemsen with a message that ᶜAlawī actions were illegal as Tlemsen was an Ottoman possession. Mawlay ᶜAbd al-Raḥmān replied with a statement which reworked the arguments of the notables of Tlemsen and asserted that ᶜAlawī intervention was primarily a religious undertaking to quell communal unrest, unite the Muslims of the deylik and lead them in a jihad against the infidel. Mawlay ᶜAbd al-Raḥmān agreed that Ḥasan Bey had been the representative of deylical authority and that the dey in his turn had been the representative of the Ottoman sultan. He claimed, however, that the departure of the dey had severed the link between Algiers and Istanbul and terminated the authority of the provincial beys, including Ḥasan Bey. He further asserted that Ḥasan Bey's failure to maintain control confirmed his loss of legitimate authority because the inhabitants of Tlemsen had been forced to beg for ᶜAlawī aid to 'extinguish the flames of strife' and restore law and order.[35] He ended by implying that the imposition of ᶜAlawī rule in Oran was simply a by-product of his religious responsibility to defend Muslim territory against the French on behalf of all Muslims, including the Ottoman sultan. In the words of a French report on the situation:

> [Le sultan] a donné à ses projets la couleur d'une croisade religieuse; il répand le bruit, sans doute mensonger, que son entreprise est concerté avec la Porte dans l'interêt generale de l'Islamisme.[36]

Ḥasan Bey's protest was soon drowned out by the more strident complaints of the French authorities in Algiers, conveyed to Mawlay ᶜAbd al-Raḥmān by the French consul in Tanger. The French government was ambivalent about holding Algiers and debates in Paris weighed up the advantages and disadvantages of withdrawal, limited occupation, or full conquest of the deylik. The ambivalence of the centre was not fully replicated in Algiers, however, where the military leadership tended to uphold more actively 'colonial' views than the politicians in Paris. After the resolution of the crisis caused by the fall of the Bourbon government General Clauzel, a firm supporter of the French presence in Africa, became commander in charge of the *armée de l'Afrique* in Algiers. He started by consolidating French control in Algiers by offering French nationals plots of land to buy or rent on a four-year lease. He then sent units to re-establish garrisons in Oran, Médea and Blida between October and December 1830, a development which coincided with the ᶜAlawī arrival in Tlemsen and subsequent call to jihad.[37] The arrival of both the French and the ᶜAlawī army in Oran province provoked a serious diplomatic row.

During the debates over the viability of the *bayᶜa* of Tlemsen the French consul in Tanger had warned Mawlay ᶜAbd al-Raḥmān that the French considered Tlemsen theirs by right of conquest and law. The sultan had countered that Algiers was French by right of conquest but that their occupation of the capital did not give them sovereign rights over the rest of the deylik.[38] The French were not prepared to accept such an argument and sent a warship to Tanger in December 1830 to demand that Mawlay ᶜAbd al-Raḥmān withdraw the *maḥalla* from Tlemsen. The officer-in-charge delivered a letter to the French consul which stated that by their conquest of the city of Algiers the French had inherited all deylical territories and expected the *maḥalla* to leave Tlemsen immediately.[39] The substance of this letter was conveyed to the governor of Tanger, who duly informed Mawlay ᶜAbd al-Raḥmān of the French position. The sultan had underestimated French interest in the territories of the deylik and now realised that sharifian expansion might entail conflict with France. To maintain his domestic prestige, however, he had to stand firm. The arrival of the warship in ᶜAlawī waters had generated a surge of hostile feeling against the French in the Tanger area where tribesmen intimidated the European community with their 'bloodthirsty eyes'. It had also spread panic among coastal populations who became agitated by the movement of all European ships through the Straits of Gibraltar, whatever flag they flew.[40]

This turbulent combination of popular hostility and hysteria obliged Mawlay ᶜAbd al-Raḥmān to publicly prepare to defend the Mediterranean coast and Tlemsen from French attack.[41] Simultaneously, the Qādirī tribes of the Mascara area began their jihad against Oran under the ᶜAlawī flag. Such measures not only increased French ire but also stretched ᶜAlawī resources to their limit. In order to maintain the supply line to Tlemsen and support the jihad the sultan suspended all commercial licences allowing the export of grain and requisitioned large numbers of pack animals. The result was a wave of inflation within the sultanate which rapidly aroused popular anger and made Makhzan collection of taxes increasingly difficult. By January 1831 Mawlay ᶜAbd al-Raḥmān had to instruct the *maḥalla* to draw its own provisions from the hinterland of Tlemsen.[42] This was no easy task since the failure of repeated offensives to dislodge the French from the city of Oran had brought the viability, and hence legitimacy, of the ᶜAlawī jihad into question. In the absence of any notable victories, tribal support for the ᶜAlawī presence began to decrease and it became impossible for the *maḥalla* to levy provisions. ᶜAlawī problems were compounded by the fact that the emergence of a French claim to the province encouraged those disillusioned with the ᶜAlawī regime to solicit French assistance. One such group was the Kulughlān of Tlemsen who informed the French that they would surrender the citadel to them if they sent aid to the city. The British consul in Tanger, Drummond Hay, noted:

> There is reported to be a party of hill country Arabs, who are holding out some castle in Tlemsan (wherein it is reported there is a large treasure) for the French, and the Sultan of Marocco has resolved, or is urged on blindly by the ignorant and uninstructed bigots around him, to make the best efforts he can to take that place.[43]

At this juncture events took an unexpected turn. The French government, reluctant to devote the resources necessary for a full conquest of the territories they claimed, but equally reluctant to abandon their claim, decided to establish a Muslim client regime in the deylik. The independent ambitions of the ᶜAlawī sultan in the west and al-Ḥājj Aḥmad Bey of Constantine in the east precluded their appointment as French clients. Instead, the French approached their only ally in the Maghrib, the Ḥusaynid Bey of Tunis, who agreed that his sons should become client beys of Constantine and Oran respectively. The first troops from Tunis arrived in Oran in January 1831.[44] Soon afterwards the French stripped the unlucky Ḥasan Bey of his wealth and position and exiled him to Egypt. Aḥmad, son of the bey of Tunis, was named bey of Oran in his stead.[45]

In response to the arrival of troops from Tunis, Mawlay ʿAbd al-Raḥmān reiterated and intensified his claim to Tlemsen by stating not only that the city's *bayʿa* to him was legal but that it was historically part of the sultanate and had belonged to the deylik of Algiers only temporarily.[46] To back up his assertion the sultan made one last effort to secure the citadel of Tlemsen and firmly establish ʿAlawī rule. Further troops were despatched to the region under the command of Mawlay ʿAbd al-Malik, another scion of the ʿAlawī lineage, with instructions to take the citadel, lead a tax-gathering expedition among the tribes of the Tlemsen hinterland and prosecute the jihad against Oran.[47] To forestall the defection of the Kulughlān and former Turkish Makhzan tribes to the French or the new Tunisian bey of Oran, Mawlay ʿAbd al-Raḥmān offered their representatives in Fes posts as ʿAlawī governors in Oran.[48]

Despite the sultan's efforts, the sudden appearance of an alternative source of Muslim authority in the region, albeit as a French client, exacerbated the divisions which already existed among the tribes of the deylik and further weakened the ʿAlawī position.[49] Unable to dislodge the Kulughlān from the citadel of Tlemsen, unable to secure a victory against the French or their Tunisian clients and unable to extract provisions from the tribes, the ʿAbīd and Udāyā corps in the *maḥalla* mutinied in March 1831.[50] Their hopes of prestige and material reward dashed, they ran amok through Tlemsen breaking into houses and looting as they went.[51] Mawlay ʿAbd al-Raḥmān had little option but to acquiese in the return of the *maḥalla* to Fes.[52] The retreat was an ignominious affair which contrasted dramatically with its triumphant entry to Tlemsen six months earlier: in their hurry to leave the troops of the *maḥalla* abandoned all vestige of order and were jeered at by the now hostile local population. To give some semblance of forethought to the ʿAlawī withdrawal Mawlay ʿAlī entrusted the continued direction of the ʿAlawī jihad to Muḥyī al-Dīn, head of the Qādiriyya, as he departed.

Mawlay ʿAbd al-Raḥmān's policy of intervention in Tlemsen in the name of Muslim unity and resistance to infidel encroachment on Muslim territory was in tatters, and with it his reputation. Direct ʿAlawī rule over Tlemsen was no longer feasible and, although Mawlay ʿAbd al-Raḥmān was not prepared to relinquish his claim to the city or admit failure in the jihad, it was clear that the only possible way to maintain his position was through local clients. The situation in the sultanate was more desperate. Mawlay ʿAbd al-Raḥmān had decided to accept the allegiance of Tlemsen and impose direct ʿAlawī rule over the city primarily for reasons of prestige. He had hoped to be the sharifian sultan who succeeded in incorporating Tlemsen into the sultanate where his predecessors had failed. He had also aspired to prove himself to be a true holy warrior against the infidel without actually having to engage in hostilities.

Popular feeling, as recorded in Makhzan letters and consular reports of the time, was strongly pro-jihad in the wake of the French conquest of Algiers. The occupation of a nearby Muslim city by a non-Muslim power stoked the prejudice towards Christian Europe which had been rooted in the collective memory since the traumatic loss of al-Andalus. This prejudice, and the fear that accompanied it, had been reawakened during the Napoleonic wars and the French *éxpedition de l'Egypte*. It had been further intensified by the conflicts with Britain and Austria over ᶜAlawī corsairing and peaked with the French offensive against Algiers. The sultan had a moral obligation to react but the failure of the *maḥalla* to secure Tlemsen or expell the French from Oran, and the Makhzan's timid response to French claims, conveyed the impression that Mawlay ᶜAbd al-Raḥmān lacked the strength of character to actively fulfil the obligation he bore to direct Muslim resistance to the French. Popular discontent was exacerbated by the socio-economic impact of the Tlemsen campaign: inflation in grain prices, food shortages, and a degree of social dislocation in northern towns which had received large numbers of immigrants from French-held towns. The situation reached a head in April 1831 with the return to Fes of the *maḥalla*.

The revolt of the Udāyā

Mawlay ᶜAbd al-Raḥmān was fully aware of his subjects' hostility to the French presence in Algiers, and the domestic implications of his apparent suspension of the jihad and abandonment of west Algeria's population to infidel rule. To divert their dissatisfaction, he decided to make the commanders of the *maḥalla* scapegoats for the Tlemsen debacle. In response, the Udāyā launched a major revolt against him. Other northern elements disgruntled by Makhzan policies, both political and economic, aligned themselves behind the Udāyā rebels, transforming the revolt from a military mutiny into a widespread rebellion of the magnitude of the revolt of Fes and the Berbers a decade before.

The Udāyā revolt lasted throughout the summer of 1831 and almost toppled Mawlay ᶜAbd al-Raḥmān from power. Its significance lay in the extent to which the sultan's perceived failure to provide jihad leadership in Oran undermined his credibility at home and enabled the Udāyā, whose mutiny was primarily about their status within the ᶜAlawī army and access to Makhzan resources, to manipulate the concept of jihad against *fasād* to their own advantage. Once the revolt had gained wider ideological significance in the north it escalated into a crisis of ᶜAlawī authority during which the rebels not only questioned Mawlay ᶜAbd al-Raḥmān's personal qualifications to rule but also contested the legitimacy of the ᶜAlawī lineage itself. Like Mawlay Sulaymān a decade earlier, Mawlay ᶜAbd al-Raḥmān thus found himself obliged to engage in an ideological as well as military contest to preserve his position and the control of the ᶜAlawī *shurafā'* over the sharifian sultanate.

The drama began as the *maḥalla* travelled westwards along the Taza Corridor towards Fes. Acting on instructions from Fes, the Makhzan garrison in Wajda arrested Idrīs al-Jirārī, the most prominent Udāyā commander, for his part in the

Tlemsen mutiny and incarcerated him in Taza prison.[53] When the *maḥalla* reached the outskirts of Fes instead of being greeted by the usual guard of honour it was met by an ᶜAbīd cohort led by a man distasteful to the Udāyā, the sultan's chief minister, Muḥammad b. Idrīs. Udāyā hostility towards Bin Idrīs dated to the revolt of Fes against Mawlay Sulaymān when he had publicly criticised Udāyā behaviour as unjust and unacceptable.[54] The ᶜAbīd cohort was in itself an irritant since the Udāyā and ᶜAbīd were rivals for the sultan's favour in the charged political atmosphere of the central Makhzan and the Udāyā considered the ᶜAbīd as their inferiors due to their servile status. To add insult to injury Muḥammad b. Idrīs carried an order from the sultan commanding the Udāyā to relinquish their baggage and thus surrender the booty they had collected in the pillage of Tlemsen.[55]

The manner in which the *maḥalla* was met inverted the usual rituals of return – a triumphal procession back into the city and the distribution of largesse among the troops – and was calculated to dishonour the Udāyā and make evident the sultan's displeasure. Its implications were not lost on the Udāyā and feelings ran high as Muḥammad b. Idrīs approached the commanders of the column, Muḥammad b. al-Ṭāhir al-ᶜAqīlī and al-Ṭāhir b. Masᶜūd, to convey the sultan's order. As he drew close:

> A sub-officer of the devoted Kaids rushed at Ben Drees with a sword or dagger: the minister retired as quickly, and by help of his attendants was rescued from a violent and certain death.[56]

This scuffle was followed by an exchange of fire between the column and the ᶜAbīd as the latter retreated to Fes to inform Mawlay ᶜAbd al-Raḥmān what had transpired. Meanwhile, the rebellious troops of the *maḥalla* marched to their quarters in Fes al-Jadid where they discussed their options. All was quiet until Mawlay ᶜAbd al-Raḥmān summoned Muḥammad al-ᶜAqīlī and Aḥmad b. al-Maḥjūb, commanders of the Udāyā and ᶜAbīd units which had served in Tlemsen respectively, and castigated them for the expedition's failure and the mutiny of their troops. He then had them arrested.[57]

The commanders of the Udāyā had expected that one or more of their number would be arrested and had arranged a contingency plan.[58] As the two men were led out of the *dār al-sulṭān*, a group of Udāyā led by al-Ṭāhir b. Masᶜūd forcibly released al-ᶜAqīlī from Makhzan custody, an action which marked their crossing of the line from obedience to revolt. Aware of the significance of the moment, the ᶜAbīd commander, Ibn al-Maḥjub, decided to remain a prisoner.[59] Al-ᶜAqīlī and al-Ṭāhir b. Masᶜūd rode straight to the centre of the Udāyā quarter and called their kinsmen to revolt. Members of the Maghāfira section of the Udāyā immediately rode to the *dār al-sulṭān* and attacked the Makhzan guard outside. The latter retreated and fastened the outer gates against the insurgents. The revolt of the Udāyā had begun.

When Mawlay ᶜAbd al-Raḥmān was informed that the Udāyā had risen in revolt, he turned to his entourage for advice. They suggested that he leave immediately for Meknes to avoid becoming a prisoner of the rebels and rally the ᶜAbīd against them. As the light faded, the sultan slipped out of Fes al-Jadid with a small coterie of followers, but someone alerted the Udāyā who hurried out to prevent his departure. They overtook him at the ᶜAyyad bridge over the Wad Sebu a short distance from Fes and protested their loyalty but asserted that they could not allow him to leave for Meknes and gather the ᶜAbīd against them. In a last-ditch attempt to evade them Mawlay ᶜAbd al-Raḥmān offered to abdicate and retire to Tafilalt.[60] The Udāyā, seeing this offer as a ploy, refused to accept it and began to kiss his horse's hooves as a symbol of their devotion to him while insisting that he remain in his rightful place, the city of Fes.[61]

The sultan had no choice but to comply and the Udāyā escorted him to the residence of the *qā'id* Muḥammad b. Farḥūn in the Sharāga citadel. His situation was perilous. He was at the mercy of the Udāyā protected only by his *baraka* as an ᶜAlawī *sharīf* and the sanctity of his office as Shadow of God on Earth. Accounts of the revolt demonstrate that these qualities proved sufficient to prevent the Udāyā from physically harming him. Although they mocked him and expressed their grievances to him with vehemence, they dared not strike him and indeed felt obliged to escort him back to the *dār al-sulṭān* at some point during the night, their anger tempered by their reverence for his sharifian blood and the inviolability of the office of imam.[62]

Instead, the Udāyā directed their ire at Muḥammad b. Idrīs and al-Wadīnī al-Bukhārī, the ᶜAbīd governor of Fes, whom they claimed were responsible both for the trouble in Tlemsen and the rupture between themselves and the sultan. They asserted that Muḥammad b. Idrīs had made a grave error of judgement in advocating ᶜAlawī acceptance of the *bayᶜa* of Tlemsen, an error which illustrated how inappropriate it was for a 'man of the pen' to interfere in military affairs and mediate the relationship between a warrior sultan and his 'men of the sword'. Their anger towards Muḥammad b. Idrīs was compounded by their belief that he and al-Wadīnī al-Bukhārī had worked together to promote the ᶜAbīd at the expense of the Udāyā. Specifically, they accused him of reducing Udāyā salaries and only paying them to members of the corps who presented themselves to collect them, whilst pocketing the wages of those who were entitled to them but absent for some reason.[63] In recompense they demanded Muḥammad b. Idrīs's dismissal and prompt payment of the wages owed to them. The complaints of the Udāyā pointed to the root cause of their revolt: resentment at their perceived loss of precedence within the ᶜAlawī military elite and the material rewards which went with it.

During the following days Mawlay ᶜAbd al-Raḥmān remained under house arrest while the Udāyā debated their next move in the great mosque of Fes al-Jadid: if the sultan were to refuse their demands, should they accept his offer to retire to the ᶜAlawī ancestral home in Tafilalt or should they murder him, an act which would protect them from retribution in this life but possibly incur the greatest penalties in the afterlife? Meanwhile rumours of the crisis in Fes al-Jadid had spread to the surrounding countryside, triggering outbreaks of disorder with tribes attacking markets and seizing goods to compensate for the shortages they had suffered as a result of sharifian expansion into Oran. The growing disruption persuaded the inhabitants of Fes al-Bali to send a delegation to beg Mawlay ᶜAbd al-Raḥmān to accede to the demands of the Udāyā and end the impasse.[64] It was headed by the merchant al-Ḥājj al-Ṭālib b. Jallūn, an advisor and associate of the sultan since 1820. Mawlay ᶜAbd al-Raḥmān complied and sacrificed Muḥammad b. Idrīs to the rebels: his minister was dismissed, stripped of his wealth and confined to his house in Fes al-Bali. He also reluctantly dipped into the treasury and distributed a large sum among the Udāyā in order to satisfy their wages complaints.[65]

Mawlay ᶜAbd al-Raḥmān's capitulation to the demands of the Udāyā ended the first stage of the revolt but he remained at their mercy, unable to leave Fes and make his presence felt in other parts of the sultanate where rumours of his humiliation were spreading. Mawlay ᶜAbd al-Raḥmān was, however, a consummate tactician and began to plot his escape. During the summer months he commonly relaxed in the Bu Jallud gardens located between Fes al-Jadid and Fes al-Bali. Under the pretext of wiling away a couple of hours in the gardens, Mawlay ᶜAbd al-Raḥmān gathered his immediate family and servants together and left the *dār al-sulṭān*. Once in the Bu Jallud complex he ordered his servants to bolt the gates and position the ten or so pieces of artillery stored in the complex to defend it from Udāyā attack.[66] Using the Bu Jallud gate into Fes al-Bali he then sent a messenger to Meknes to summon ᶜAbīd reinforcements. He calculated the time it would take for the message to reach Meknes and the ᶜAbīd to make their way to Fes. He then asked the Udāyā for permission to take a ride in the countryside at the same time. The Udāyā insisted on accompanying him and did not realise they had been lured into a trap until they saw the ᶜAbīd corps approaching. A bloody battle ensued with horrifically high losses on both sides, but the sultan and the ᶜAbīd gradually forced the Udāyā back into Fes al-Jadid and beseiged them.[67]

Mawlay ᶜAbd al-Raḥmān took the opportunity of his release to send requests for aid to provincial governors throughout the north. The letters he sent out were also intended to downplay the seriousness of the situation in Fes and deny the legitimacy of Udāyā complaints about the injustice of their treatment by Makhzan officials. In an extant letter to the governor of Tetuan, the sultan adopted the rhetoric of holy war against rebellion which had become a standard part of the state's ideological armoury in preceding decades. He stated that he had offered the 'rebellious faction' a settlement which they had rejected. The ᶜAbīd had then served as the instrument of God by chastising the Udāyā for their obduracy towards the sultan and the Divine order which he represented.[68] Mawlay ᶜAbd al-Raḥmān thus countered the Udāyā claim that they had risen against Makhzan injustice by transferring the accusation of *fasād* to the Udāyā themselves for refusing to accept the settlement he had offered them.

Mawlay ᶜAbd al-Raḥmān's proclamations were not simply a show of bravado but also a plea to the inhabitants of the sultanate to rally behind their sultan in his jihad against *fasād*. A reconciliation between himself and the Udāyā was now unlikely but, in order to defeat this important military corps, he needed active assistance not only from the ᶜAbīd of Meknes but also from other power-brokers in the north: the inhabitants of Fes al-Bali, the Awlād Jāmi^{c} and Sharāga *jaysh* tribes settled to the north of Fes, and Makhzan forces from the northern provinces of Taza, Tetuan, Tanger and Rabat. After the events of the previous year, however, Mawlay ^{c}Abd al-Raḥmān's appeal to the paradigm of jihad against *fasād* was not sufficient to align his subjects behind him. Although to a large extent material, the complaints of the Udāyā touched on the legitimacy of Mawlay ^{c}Abd al-Raḥmān's religio-political, military and financial policies which appeared to have been tested and proved flawed by his abortive attempt to incorporate Tlemsen into the sultanate. Whilst the prerogatives of the Udāyā were of little concern to northern urban elites and tribes, they too had grievances about 'corruption' (*fasād*) at the centre. A key theme was that of the sultan's avarice, an accusation which did not imply a personal lack of generosity but a failure to appropriately circulate resources by means of patronage and inclusion in government. Such a failure suggested that the sultan lacked *baraka* in the sense of an ability to bestow material wellbeing upon his subjects.

The elite of Fes, in particular, harboured a range of barely submerged grievances against the Makhzan which dated from the revolt of Fes against Mawlay Sulaymān over a decade before. Although Mawlay ^{c}Abd al-Raḥmān had endeavoured to improve Makhzan relations with Fes, his neglect of the advice of the Fāsī *^{c}ulamā'* against intervention in Tlemsen had re-awakening Fāsī resentment about their exclusion from government. Fāsī feelings that they were not being treated with due respect had been exacerbated by the sultan's appointment of the ^{c}Abīd commander, al-Wadīnī al-Bukhārī, as governor in place of a member of the ^{c}Alawī lineage. Market gossip in Tanger said that the sultan had raised the servile black ^{c}Abīd from the south over the free white inhabitants of the north who traced their ancestry to the aristocratic Arab conquerors of the region, to the *sharīf* Idrīs I and to the elite of al-Andalus.

Such gossip encapsulated the Fāsī elite's self-perception that they were guardians of a high Arabo-Islamic tradition associated with the Idrīsids and al-Andalus. It also expressed their concomitant expectation of a relationship with the ^{c}Alawī Makhzan which acknowledged their religious and cultural pre-eminence in return for their loyalty. Mawlay ^{c}Abd al-Raḥmān appeared not to have respected this unwritten contract. The Fāsīs also had economic complaints. Many merchants had suffered as a result of the Makhzan's temporary withdrawal of commercial licences for export and requisitioning of basic commodities during the Tlemsen campaign. Fes, therefore, held aloof from the sultan and refused to declare its support for him or allow him to utilise Fāsī resources.[69]

The situation among the tribes of the north was a complex mixture of local competition for resources and rivalries generated by ^{c}Alawī policies towards the tribes. On the one hand, the humiliation of the ^{c}Alawī forces in Tlemsen and the breakdown of relations between Mawlay ^{c}Abd al-Raḥmān and the Udāyā undermined the coercive power which underwrote ^{c}Alawī authority among the tribes. As a result, rural order began to break down and several tribes attacked their rivals or unprotected market towns, aware that punishment from the centre was unlikely to be forthcoming. On the other hand, such disorder was intimately related to the economic strain put on the north by the Tlemsen campaign and longstanding grievances between the ᶜAlawī Makhzan and the Berber Darqāwa tribes ousted from service by Mawlay Sulaymān. These tribes were not only resentful of their exclusion from power but also hostile to their Arab counterparts whom they felt had usurped their position – the Awlād Jāmiᶜ, the Sharāga and the Sharārda newcomers from the south. As a result the Berber tribes of the Meknes area declared for the Udāyā.

The perceptions of sultanic *fasād* implicit in the complaints lodged against Mawlay ᶜAbd al-Raḥmān fed speculation about possible replacements for him. The most commonly cited contenders were the sons of Mawlay Sulaymān who had been passed over by their father's choice of Mawlay ᶜAbd al-Raḥmān as his successor. It is likely that the restive and warlike Mawlay ᶜAbd al-Raḥmān b. Sulaymān who had never fully accepted his cousin's accession was a strong challenger. The rumour mill also named a more startling candidate for power, al-Ṭālib Idrīs, an Idrīsī *sharīf* and the keeper of the shrine of Idrīs I at Zarhun, who had no personal desire to enter the political arena but whose name was bandied around as a symbolic reference to the northern archetype of Idrīsī sharifian rule.[70]

Speculation about an Idrīsī contender for the sultanate challenged the legitimacy of the southern ᶜAlawī lineage in its entirety and evoked northern loyalties to the Idrīsī *shurafā'* as an alternative source of sharifian leadership more likely to respect northern interests. It also inverted the Makhzan paradigm of jihad against *fasād* and replaced it with the reverse model of a holy man taking the role of *mujāhid* to challenge the corruption of a sultan.[71] The fact that the issue of Idrīsī sharifian rule and the right of society to rise behind a holy man in a *jihād* against a corrupt sultan arose in the aftermath of the French conquest of Algiers and the failed campaign to institute direct ᶜAlawī rule over Tlemsen was not coincidental. Success in Tlemsen would have brought Mawlay ᶜAbd al-Raḥmān prestige and resources, failure in the jihad brought everything into question. A general revolt of the north seemed imminent.

Aware of the possibility of a major northern insurrection Mawlay ᶜAbd al-Raḥmān made a bid to align Fes behind him using the mediation of al-Ṭayyib al-Bayyāz, a Fāsī *sharīf* who had been involved in the 1820 revolt of Fes but subsequently pardoned and appointed Makhzan overseer (*amīn*) of the customs house in Tanger. The sultan summoned al-Bayyāz to Fes with the dual purpose of bringing him much-needed funds from the treasury in Tanger and acting as his go-between in negotiations with the Fāsī elite. At the same time he prepared to transfer his base of operations from Fes to Meknes in order to create a centre loyal to himself as a counter-balance to the oppositional centre created by the Udāyā and their Fāsī sympathisers.

In mid-June 1831, Mawlay ᶜAbd al-Raḥmān left Fes accompanied by his family, a large baggage train and the ᶜAbīd. The convoy moved north in order to loop around the rebellious Berber tribes of the Sais plain but was soon intercepted by the Udāyā who again wished to prevent the sultan from evading their control.[72]

A second vicious battle between the ᶜAbīd and Udāyā developed. During the fighting Mawlay ᶜAbd al-Raḥmān escaped and headed for Meknes as a fugitive, harassed and threatened by rebellious tribes along the way. He reached the city on 21 June and battled his way in through the hostile Berber tribes of the hinterland which included the powerful Garwān.[73] His family and possessions fell into the hands of the Udāyā who put his relatives under house arrest and took his possessions to the markets of Fes where they coerced the reluctant population into purchasing them to generate much needed funds for their revolt.[74] They also appropriated the artillery which the sultan had left in the Bu Jallud munitions store, aware that if he remained in power he would return and beseige them in Fes al-Jadid. The immediate outlook for the sultan was not good:

> All the discontents against the present monarch … continue so great, and the moral influence of the monarch, as well as the number of troops on which he can depend, is so small, that I am persuaded that he would ere this have been deposed, could the people have found in the Imperial family … one individual against whom greater objections are not presented.[75]

In the months that followed, however, Mawlay ᶜAbd al-Raḥmān slowly built up his resource base and reasserted his authority in the north. He began by gathering military supplies from the Makhzan governors of Tetuan, Tanger and Rabat.[76] He also approached the British and Portuguese representatives in Tanger to request that their governments supply him with artillery to beseige the Udāyā.[77] Both governments hesitated to become involved: the British stalled through the summer and finally stated that Mawlay ᶜAbd al-Raḥmān was free to purchase artillery privately from the Gibraltar military store but that the British government could not be involved in the transaction.[78] Opinions in Tanger differed as to whether the Portuguese finally provided the sultan with the artillery he had requested or not.[79] In addition to stockpiling weapons, ammunition and artillery, Mawlay ᶜAbd al-Raḥmān cast around for allies to join him. Although tribal loyalty to the sultan was tenuous, he was able to exploit local rivalries and recruit auxiliaries from tribes opposed to those who had joined the revolt. Soon his army included auxiliaries from the Arab Banū Ḥasan, the Berber Mjāt and Zammūr of the Meknes area, and the Rifi Ait Idrāsen. Across the Sais plain, the Awlād Jāmiᶜ and Sharāga waited outside Fes for his return to assist in the seige of the Udāyā.

The sultan found another unexpected ally in the person of Idrīs al-Jirārī, the Udāyā commander of the *maḥalla* to Tlemsen whom he had imprisoned several months before. He escaped from Taza prison by a ruse: during the occupation of Tlemsen the sultan had sent several blank papers bearing his personal seal so that Mawlay ᶜAlī could issue sultanic decrees without having to send them back to Fes first. Idrīs al-Jirārī wrote an order for his own release on one of these papers and smuggled it to the Makhzan governor of Taza who thereby released him. When Mawlay ᶜAbd al-Raḥmān was informed of his escape he ordered an immediate search of the countryside, feared that if Idrīs reached Fes, his leadership would give the revolt new impetus.[80] His fears were unfounded: for reasons best known to himself, Idrīs al-Jirārī threw in his lot with the sultan and offered to use his influence with the Udāyā to negotiate with them and protect the sultan's family detained in the *dār al-sulṭān*.[81]

When he had built up sufficient military reserves, Mawlay ᶜAbd al-Raḥmān began a counter-offensive to defeat his enemies and restore his military prestige. His first target was the Garwān tribe which stood at the centre of the tribal bloc which had declared for the Udāyā. The majority of the tribal auxiliaries whom he had gathered in Meknes were inimical to the Garwān and eagerly took the opportunity to advance out of Meknes with the ᶜAbīd and plunder their territory. The sultan used the apparently successful raid as an occasion to publicly reclaim jihad against *fasād* as a sultanic prerogative. In letters to provincial governors, he described the Makhzan forces as a united Muslim front which had scored a just victory over the 'enemies of God', the Garwān. Makhzan treatment of the dead Garwān underlined the message that rebellion against the sharifian sultan was equivalent to apostasy: the corpses were decapitated, a form of mutilation reserved for infidels and rebels who had placed themselves outside the Muslim community.[82] The success of the raid gave weight to Mawlay ᶜAbd al-Raḥmān's rhetoric but he knew that his power and authority would be contested across the north until he reasserted Makhzan control over Fes and the Udāyā. He therefore followed up his victory against the Garwān with a general call to arms circulated through Tanger–Laraish and Tetuan provinces.[83] The tribes of the north slowly came forward to renew their oaths of allegiance and a shift began to occur from widespread support for the Udāyā to renewed loyalty to Mawlay ᶜAbd al-Raḥmān. The British consul noted:

> Appearances are considerably in favour of the ultimate success of the Sultan, who is declared to have vowed to exterminate the Oodaiah, the popularity of whom seems also to decline in full proportion to the diminuation of their strength.[84]

A significant factor in the declining popularity of the Udāyā was their lack of a coherent policy beyond opposition to Mawlay ᶜAbd al-Raḥmān. They also made several serious tactical errors after the sultan's escape from Fes. Their first error was to attack the Awlād Jāmiᶜ and Sharāga *jaysh* tribes loyal to the sultan. They hoped to weaken these tribes and seize what weapons and horses they could to augment their own limited supplies, but the Awlād Jāmiᶜ and Sharāga defeated them and chased them back into Fes al-Jadid with heavy losses. The inhabitants of Fes al-Bali gathered to watch the debacle which entailed a considerable loss of prestige for the Udāyā and a concomitant decrease in Fāsī support for them.[85] It seemed increasingly likely that Mawlay ᶜAbd al-Raḥmān would defeat the Udāyā and the Fāsī population knew that its interests lay in being on the side of the victor rather than the vanquished.

To bolster their waning support, the Udāyā committed a second grave error: they proclaimed an alternative ᶜAlawī sultan as a new figurehead for the revolt. Their appointee was Muḥammad b. al-Ṭayyib, a collateral member of the ᶜAlawī lineage who had previously served as governor of Fes and was currently governor of Taza. Muḥammad b. al-Ṭayyib was a military man, infamous for his violent administration in an age when violence was the norm. Although the reasons why the Udāyā selected him are opaque, it seems likely that they perceived him as a man ideally suited to fulfil the military obligations of a sharifian sultan and someone who would be indebted to them for his position and, therefore, respectful of their wishes. The Udāyā were joined in their support of Muḥammad b. al-Ṭayyib by disgruntled sections of the Fāsī population and proclaimed him sultan in the great mosque of the al-Andalus quarter. Shortly afterwards he arrived from Taza and took up residence in Fes al-Jadid.[86]

The selection of Muḥammad b. al-Ṭayyib as sultan was a fatal mistake on the part of the Udāyā. He was unpopular with the majority of Fāsīs who had suffered under his administration at the beginning of the reign of Mawlay ᶜAbd al-Raḥmān, and equally unpopular in other parts of the sultanate where the sultan had deployed him as an 'iron fist' to quell insurgencies and collect taxes.[87] In addition, the Udāyā proclamation of a counter-sultan brought their confrontation with Mawlay ᶜAbd al-Raḥmān to a head. In the wake of their *bayᶜa* to Muḥammad b. al-Ṭayyib, Mawlay ᶜAbd al-Raḥmān approached Fes at the head of a *maḥalla* consisting of the ᶜAbīd, the Sharāga, tribal auxiliaries and the Makhzan's artillery. As he drew near, the Udāyā and their Fāsī allies closed the gates of Fes al-Bali and Fes al-Jadid. In order to finally break the alliance between Fes al-Bali and the Udāyā, the sultan trained his guns on the main gates of the civilian city rather than the royal complex of Fes al-Jadid where the Udāyā resided.[88] The inhabitants of Fes al-Bali who had expected him to beseige Fes al-Jadid suddenly found themselves threatened by artillery bombardment and seige, a development which enabled those already inclined to support Mawlay ᶜAbd al-Raḥmān to secure a consensus in favour of submission to him. Within days al-Ḥājj al-Ṭālib b. Jallūn emerged from the city to offer the sultan Fes al-Bali's surrender in return for a guarantee that those involved in the revolt would not be punished. He agreed to the terms and Fes al-Bali opened its gates, enabling him to procure provisions from the city and concentrate his military might on beseiging the Udāyā.

According to al-Nāṣirī, Mawlay ᶜAbd al-Raḥmān's seige of the Udāyā in Fes al-Jadid lasted for forty bitter days.[89] The humiliation he had suffered at the hands of the Udāyā and the implicit challenge to his legitimacy in their proclamation of a counter-sultan had strengthened the sultan's resolve to make a salutary example of them. He was in no mood to compromise with a military corps which had betrayed the sacred bonds of obedience and blood tying it to his lineage. Muḥammad b. al-Ṭayyib and the Udāyā were similarly aware that they had reached the point of no return. As summer turned to autumn Mawlay ᶜAbd al-Raḥmān ordered the *maḥalla* to construct a fortress from which to continue the seige through the winter.

At this point mediating forces intervened in the persons of loyal Makhzan commanders and al-Ḥājj al-Ṭālib b. Jallūn who pointed out to the sultan that the Udāyā would probably prefer to capitulate than endure a winter seige. Aware of the cost of a seige and the still tenuous state of public order and obedience, Mawlay ᶜAbd al-Raḥmān reluctantly agreed to offer the Udāyā terms. His conditions for their surrender were, however, harsh – permanent expulsion from their traditional barracks in Fes al-Jadid and their dispersal throughout the sultanate.[90] This meant, in effect, the disgrace of the corps, the severing of their link with the ᶜAlawī dynasty in place since the seventeenth century and their permanent exclusion from the centre of power and patronage. The sultan's terms were conveyed to the Udāyā who had the choice of risking starvation over the winter in Fes al-Jadid, fighting the superior forces of the sultan or accepting his terms for their surrender. They decided to surrender and the rebel commanders and their counter-sultan rode out of Fes al-Jadid and threw themselves at the sultan's feet in a symbolic plea for mercy. The revolt of the Udāyā was over.

The surrender of the Udāyā, however, did not end the crisis of authority of which the revolt was only the most dramatic manifestation. Mawlay ᶜAbd al-Raḥmān's prestige, and hence his authority over his army, the population of Fes and the tribes, remained fragile. In order to consolidate his own position and revalidate central ᶜAlawī authority he needed to tackle the tensions between the ᶜAbīd, Udāyā and Makhzan officials at the centre, reinstate ᶜAlawī authority among the tribes and address the issue of his responsibilities towards the Muslims of Algiers.

The sultan's first task was to forestall further military insubordination. Although he wished to disband the Udāyā he was loathe to push them into a new revolt. On the other hand he could not treat them too leniently without risking a mutiny of the ᶜAbīd who expected to see their Udāyā rivals punished and themselves well rewarded for their loyalty. He therefore decided to split the Udāyā between Fes and Marrakesh. He made Idrīs al-Jirārī commander of the Fes section as a reward for his loyalty during the crisis and put the rebel leader Muḥammad b. Farḥūn under his jurisdiction. Al-Ṭāhir b. Masᶜūd and Muḥammad b. Ṭāhir al-ᶜAqīlī were forced to leave Fes with several hundred Udāyā and settle on the lands of the Sharārda near Marrakesh which had been empty since the Sharārda revolt of 1828.[91] This relocation left the Udāyā isolated and shorn of the complex web of relationships they had built up in the Fes area over generations and thus less able to stir up widespread insurrection.

The Udāyā sultan, Muḥammad b. al-Ṭayyib, paid a heavy price for his involvement in the revolt. Mawlay ᶜAbd al-Raḥmān spared his life since he was an ᶜAlawī *sharīf* whose execution would undermine the impression of the lineage's inviolability but he stripped him of his offices, wealth and pension and exiled him to the ancestral home of Tafilalt in 'ignominy and shame'.[92] Muḥammad b. al-Ṭayyib's political career and participation in the fruits of government were over. Mawlay ᶜAbd al-Raḥmān then travelled to Meknes where he was obliged to quell rumblings of discontent among the ᶜAbīd. They had almost certainly expected to be allowed to pillage the Udāyā quarters of Fes al-Jadid after their capitulation to gain the material reward which they felt they were owed for their loyalty during the crisis. Mawlay ᶜAbd al-Raḥmān's restraint towards the Udāyā was a source of considerable ᶜAbīd dissatisfaction likely to escalate into a mutiny unless they got immediate recompense for the services they had rendered. He therefore dipped into the treasury and gave the corps a generous sum of money and new uniforms, a benefice usually reserved for annual feast days.[93]

The dispatch of a section of the Udāyā to Marrakesh and the distribution of monies among the ᶜAbīd solved Mawlay ᶜAbd al-Raḥmān's immediate problems. The larger task facing him was the restoration of his domestic prestige and power, a task heavily dependent on his performance in Oran. The fate of the deylik of Algiers remained at the forefront of popular consciousness as a result of the steady trickle of refugees from French-held cities and the arrival of ᶜAlawī merchants with tales of abuses against Muslims committed by the French. In addition, the Tunisian beys appointed by the French as Muslim client rulers had not secured local support, obliging the French to reimpose direct rule over their coastal possessions.[94] Direct infidel rule and abuse of Muslims in Oran made it impossible for Mawlay ᶜAbd al-Raḥmān to relinquish his claim to the region since that would imply its abandonment to French sovereignty and a total abnegation of his responsibilities as a sharifian sultan and leader of the jihad.

In fact, Mawlay ᶜAbd al-Raḥmān maintained his interest in Oran province throughout the Udāyā crisis and took steps to substitute direct ᶜAlawī rule for indirect control using local notables. The notables he selected represented the most important power-brokers in the northwestern deylik: Bū Rasālī of the Kulughlān; Muṣṭafā b. Ismāᶜīl of the Dawā'ir who also represented the other ex-Turkish *makhzan* tribe, the Zmāla; and Muḥyī al-Dīn, shaykh of the Qādiriyya and representative of the Qādirī tribes of the Mascara area. These notables agreed to act under the direction of a newly appointed ᶜAlawī governor, Muḥammad b. al-ᶜAmirī, whose name suggests that he may have been a descendant of the Mascaran Banū ᶜAmir who had fled to the sultanate during the Darqāwa revolt of 1805–13.

The sultan gave Ibn al-ᶜAmirī no military assistance beyond a small cohort of Udāyā troops, and his instructions were considerably more cautious than those given to Mawlay ᶜAlī: he was to co-ordinate a jihad against Oran in association with ᶜAlawī allies and secure the allegiance of the tribes of the western deylik. He was to withdraw if he could not achieve these aims.[95] Mawlay ᶜAbd al-Raḥmān hoped that without the divisive presence of a large ᶜAlawī army, Ibn al-ᶜAmirī would be able to pull together the disparate elements in the western deylik for a jihad against Oran. If the campaign was successful it would restore his reputation as a *mujāhid* and enable the pro-ᶜAlawī 'holy warriors' to assert their authority over the tribes in the name of Muslim unity against the infidel, a process of religio-political consolidation tried and proven in the sultanate many times over.

When Ibn al-ᶜAmirī reached Tlemsen, he found the situation little changed from March when the *maḥalla* had departed. Many towns and tribes accepted the notion of ᶜAlawī sovereignty but expected to see some proof of ᶜAlawī might before paying taxes or offering regular military assistance. Many of Ibn al-ᶜAmirī's local allies held themselves similarly aloof. For instance, in Tlemsen the Kulughlān expressed their acceptance of Ibn al-ᶜAmirī's appointment but refused to allow him access to the citadel, pending the outcome of his planned offensive against Oran. Nonetheless, the Kulughlān, the Dawā'ir, the Zmāla and the Qādirī tribes led by Muḥyī al-Dīn and his son ᶜAbd al-Qādir assisted Ibn al-ᶜAmirī's ᶜAlawī troops when he beseiged Oran in October 1831. Despite numerous examples of bravery, the Muslim fighters lacked any overall command or co-ordination and were unable to break into the city as a result. After twelve days they withdrew.[96] The ᶜAlawī jihad had failed.

As Mawlay ᶜAbd al-Raḥmān had feared, the failure of the offensive sparked the collapse of the fragile unity the seige had fostered among the tribes of Oran and a general falling away of support for ᶜAlawī overlordship. Henceforth, the divisions between groups previously affiliated with the Turks – the Kulughlān, Dawā'ir and Zmāla – and the tribes who had opposed the Turks – the affiliates of the Qādiriyya, the Tijāniyya, the Darqāwa and the Wazzāniyya–Ṭayyibiyya – became insurmountable and unification of the region under ᶜAlawī rule virtually impossible. The former group, no longer convinced that an alliance with the sultan offered them any advantage, began to consider allying with the French in return for a continued role in government. The latter group increasingly resorted to maraboutic authority in place of sultanic authority, including that of Muḥyī al-Dīn and his son, ᶜAbd al-Qādir.[97] Despite reservations about the value of ᶜAlawī rule, however, the concept of an ᶜAlawī jihad steadily gained ground across the deylik and several towns in the central deylik, namely Blida, Miliana and Médea offered their allegiance and support to Mawlay ᶜAbd al-Raḥmān if he would lead an offensive against the French.[98]

In the sultanate itself, renewed ᶜAlawī involvement in the affairs of Oran and, in particular, the stirring up of jihadist sentiment triggered a second round of French protests backed by the arrival of a French naval squadron off Tanger in December 1831.[99] The French government then sent a formal diplomatic mission to the sultanate to insist that Mawlay ᶜAbd al-Raḥmān abandon all claims to sovereignty over territory in the deylik and immediately withdraw all ᶜAlawī personnel or risk war with France. The military in Oran believed that 'if the Emperor manifested the least opposition to France, the fate of his Empire would quickly follow that of Algiers'.[100] The French mission, headed by the Comte De Mornay, arrived off Tanger on 24 January 1832. At around the same time the sultan received news of the approach of delegations from Tlemsen and the towns of the central deylik.

The simultaneous arrival of Muslim delegations, begging him to fulfil his religious responsibility to defend Muslim land from infidel appropriation, and a French delegation, demanding that he abandon all claims to that same land, put Mawlay ᶜAbd al-Raḥmān in an extremely awkward situation. The problem was compounded by De Mornay's insistence that he personally convey the French government's demands to the sultan in Meknes rather than handing them over to

Makhzan officials in Tanger, increasing the visibility of the French mission and the likelihood of the rival delegations meeting. Mawlay ᶜAbd al-Raḥmān's reconstruction of sultanic authority in the wake of the revolt of the Udāyā was not complete and would be again brought into question if he appeared to yield in any way to French pressure. On the other hand, although he was eager to appear to challenge the French, he wished to discourage further confrontation with them either in the diplomatic arena of Tanger or the politico-military arena of Oran. In the event, he used the procession of De Mornay's mission from Tanger to Meknes and the reception of the Muslim delegations from the regency as a theatrical enterprise during which multiple messages were conveyed to a multi-faceted audience made up of the delegations themselves, the European consuls in Tanger and the inhabitants of the sultanate. Although the sultan privately gave the French verbal assurances that ᶜAlawī interference in the deylik was a thing of the past, his primary objective was to publicly perform the role of an all-powerful monarch approached by petitioners from the *dār al-islām* and *dār al-ḥarb* but resolute in his devotion to his faith. The French thus became tools in Mawlay ᶜAbd al-Raḥmān's endeavour to reconstruct his place at the pinnacle of the sharifian political system.

The sultan's first action on receiving news of the French mission's arrival was to assure De Mornay that he had ordered ᶜAlawī troops to withdraw from the regency.[101] At the same time he instructed the governor of Tanger and Laraish, ᶜAbd al-Salām al-Slāwī, to keep De Mornay in Tanger during the fast month of Ramaḍān which was just beginning and use the month to prepare for his journey to Meknes. The sultan envisaged the journey as a chance to demonstrate the strength of the ᶜAlawī military to De Mornay as a sign of the 'power and glory of Islam which so angers [the infidel]'.[102] In the meantime he entrusted a cluster of Makhzan officials and advisors experienced in European mores with the task of mollifying De Mornay and explaining why he could not publicly disavow his responsibilities towards the Muslims of the deylik. For this task he chose al-Ṭayyib al-Bayyāz, the Fāsī customs administrator of Tanger whose mediation he had used during the revolt of the Udāyā, Muḥammad b. ᶜAbd al-Malik, known as Bin Abū, a native of the Rif and the deputy governor of Tanger, and the Fāsī merchant, al-Ḥājj al-Ṭālib b. Jallūn. All three were northerners who bridged the gap between the Makhzan and its northern subjects and also comprehended the conceptual gap between the politics of the sultanate and Europe as a result of their service in Tanger, the 'City of the Consuls', and their involvement in foreign trade.

In discussions with De Mornay, the French consul Delaporte and the British consul Drummond Hay, al-Ṭayyib al-Bayyāz and Bin Abū presented the sultan's dilemma over Tlemsen and other territories in the deylik. They pointed out that as a Muslim ruler he could not publicly renounce his claim to Muslim territory in favour of a non-Muslim power, especially when he had only laid claim to that land under the pressure of a communal consensus that he should do so in the form of the *bayᶜa* of Tlemsen and other tribes and towns.[103] The French assertion that the lands of the regency belonged to themselves as the successors of the dey of

Algiers was inadmissible from the perspective of Islamic law and the perspective of the inhabitants of the territories concerned. They could only claim *de facto* possession of occupied territory, and even then the sultan was religiously bound to contest them by word and action. If Mawlay ᶜAbd al-Raḥmān were to order an ᶜAlawī withdrawal from the deylik, he would not only be reneging on his religious obligations towards Muslims who had given him their allegiance but also abandoning the jihad which he had himself urged the Muslims of the region to undertake. Such an act would not only affect his reputation in Oran but, more importantly, could undermine the fragile domestic political balance which he had achieved since the revolt of the Udāyā.

Whilst al-Ṭayyib al-Bayyāz and Bin Abū justified the Makhzan's public stance towards the deylik, Mawlay ᶜAbd al-Raḥmān received the delegations from Tlemsen, Blida, Médea and Miliana. Each of them offered him allegiance if he would lead them in a jihad against the French. The point was most concisely made by the Tlemsen delegation which assured the sultan that all the Muslims of the central Maghrib, including those resident in French-occupied areas, would join the jihad if only he would personally lead it rather than delegating authority to someone else.[104] The delegates' remonstrances indicated that ᶜAlawī efforts to legitimise sovereignty as a means to re-establish order and unite the community for jihad had confirmed the gradual drift towards a situation in which the issue of Muslim sovereignty was submerged within the larger issue of defence of Muslim territory: successful and personal performance as a *mujāhid* had become a pre-condition of sovereignty rather than its confirmation. It was this change in religio-political emphasis which enabled maraboutic holy warriors to step into the political arena and structure a new relationship between the ᶜAlawī sultanate and the western deylik in the course of 1832.

In March 1832 after the celebrations of *ᶜīd al-fiṭr* marked the conclusion of Ramaḍān, De Mornay left Tanger for Meknes accompanied by al-Ṭayyib al-Bayyāz, Bin Abū and a sizeable Makhzan cavalry escort. As the cavalcade travelled through the Gharb district it was mobbed by hostile crowds of armed tribesmen, mobilised by the Makhzan for the occasion, who made the strength of popular feeling against the French occupation of Algiers abundantly clear.[105] The sultan had orchestrated these gatherings of tribesmen along the mission's route to impress upon De Mornay how great the military resources of the sultanate were but they also provided a controlled outlet for popular hostility towards the French and a tableau in which the French actors were disempowered by their need for sultanic protection and approached him as supplicants.

Once in Meknes, the mission was quartered discreetly within the city in order to prevent De Mornay accidentally coming across the petitioners from the regency, although he was well aware of their presence and made his own enquiries as to their identity. Finally, on 22 March 1832 Mawlay ᶜAbd al-Raḥmān received De Mornay in a private audience. The latter listed the French government's demands from the most important that the sultan renounce all claims to territory within the regency and withdraw all ᶜAlawī agents, to minor demands concerning diplomatic and commercial interactions between the sultanate and French-held territories. Lastly he requested that the sultan ignore the petitioners from the deylik as a token of goodwill towards the French.[106] Mawlay ᶜAbd al-Raḥmān responded vaguely that he had authorised al-Ṭayyib al-Bayyāz to deal with the matters raised by De Mornay.

On paper the Makhzan did indeed acquiese to the demands made by De Mornay but political realities in the sultanate and the deylik were much more complex. The Muslim delegations' request that Mawlay ᶜAbd al-Raḥmān personally lead the jihad underlined the fact that Mawlay ᶜAlī and Ibn al-ᶜAmirī lacked the authority to rally the community behind them. In fact, wherever Ibn al-ᶜAmirī went urban communities and tribes made their submission to ᶜAlawī authority conditional on the personal appearance of the sultan, the personification of the sharifian ideal. Just as the Kulughlān in Tlemsen had refused to surrender their position in 1830–1 without some guarantee that the sultan had the power and authority to implement ᶜAlawī rule, the Kulughlān of Mascara now refused to submit to Ibn al-ᶜAmirī for the same reason. The tribes meanwhile, imbued with the concept of sharifian *baraka*, wished to see it proved in the ᶜAlawī case by a successful attack on the infidel. In a sense the sultan was caught by the success of the sharifian jihad model which made him God's representative on earth and the repository of the values the position encapsulated.

Understanding this, Ibn al-ᶜAmirī had organised the delegations to Mawlay ᶜAbd al-Raḥmān in the hope of persuading him to come east in person. Instead the sultan summoned him back, thereby removing his main representative in the deylik and appearing to ignore the appeal of the Muslim delegations. In May 1832 Ibn al-ᶜAmirī arrived in Fes. Before his departure he delegated responsibility for the ᶜAlawī project in Oran to the most faithful of the sultan's allies, Muḥyī al-Dīn, shaykh of the Qādiriyya. Mawlay ᶜAbd al-Rahmān's decision to further limit ᶜAlawī involvement in Oran was partly a product of French pressure but also a response to ongoing political instability in the sultanate: the sultan dared not leave for the deylik with the issues raised by the Udāyā revolt largely unresolved.

During the winter of 1831–2 the Udāyā had remained quiescent but they resented their loss of status. The great commanders of the corps were restive under the surveillance of Idrīs al-Jirārī and the sultan's son, Sīdī Muḥammad, and in May 1832 rumours that they planned a new revolt began to circulate.[107] Mawlay ᶜAbd al-Raḥmān reacted swiftly and ordered their arrest. Muḥammad b. Farḥūn was transferred to the Jazira prison at Essawira whilst al-Ṭāhir b. Masᶜūd and al-ᶜAqīlī were transferred to Fes and incarcerated.[108] The sultan took the opportunity to also strike against those who had supported the Udāyā during the revolt. A Makhzan *maḥalla* assisted by tribal auxiliaries from the Gharb pillaged the territories of the Zaᶜīr and Zammūr tribes which had participated in the rebellion alongside the Garwān. They trampled the green crops and pastured their horses on them, attacked villages and seized livestock to replenish Makhzan stocks.[109] In the meantime more than thirty members of the Fāsī élite were arrested and imprisoned in Marrakesh. They were to remain in prison for three years, after which time they were released on the condition that they and their families left Fes for good.[110] During this wave of reprisals the Udāyā resident in Fes al-Jadid, deprived of leadership, hesitated to react. Their hesitancy enabled the sultan to carry through his project of disbanding the corps, exiling it from Fes and executing the rebel commanders. Drummond Hay reported in September 1832:

> There are said to have occurred of late numerous incidents of faithless revenge on the part of the Sultan or his advisors, and among the victims are some of high rank who were implicated in the revolt of the Oodaiah soldiery last year … some of whom have been tortured and maimed and others put to death although their safety had been guaranteed by the royal word.[111]

The executions of al-ᶜAqīlī and al-Ṭāhir b. Masᶜūd took place outside the *dār al-sulṭān* in Fes al-Jadid where al-Ṭāhir had released al-ᶜAqīlī from Makhzan custody so starting the Udāyā revolt, a symbolic reminder that rebellion against the sharifian sultan merited death.[112] In the same month rumours reached Tanger that Mawlay ᶜAbd al-Raḥmān intended to disperse the Udāyā throughout the sultanate and form a new corps in their place.[113] The disbanding of the Udāyā took several months: the Ahl Sūs contingents of the corps were sent to the citadel of Rabat while the remainder were transferred to the small port of Laraish where each soldier was given a plot of land and a quarter of his previous salary.[114] The Udāyā quarters in Fes al-Jadid and their duties were taken over by the ᶜAbīd, the Sharāga, and the Awlād Jāmiᶜ. The Udāyā were, thus, physically and metaphorically banished from the centre of power. Their physical resettlement in the vicinity of Marrakesh, Rabat and Laraish away from the northern centres of power, Meknes and Fes, symbolised their decreased status in the ᶜAlawī army: they were, in Drummond Hay's words, 'degraded in the line of march from their former post of honour near the monarch'.[115] Although they were not actually expelled from the army and remained on the Makhzan payroll on reduced salaries, they played no major part in military engagements until their recall in August 1847.

After a two-year struggle to reassert his authority, Mawlay ᶜAbd al-Raḥmān seemed victorious. However, the rebellion of such an important corps underlined the serious domestic political consequences of his policy of expansion into the western deylik. He assumed sovereignty over Tlemsen as a *sharīf* and a *mujāhid*. His decision to accept political responsibility for Tlemsen in the absence of any alternative Muslim authority thus entailed a religious as well as political obligation which could neither be easily fulfilled nor disavowed. The undertaking proved more hazardous than the sultan had imagined. Voices within the sultanate had warned him not to embark upon a course which would raise domestic expectations of a spectacular sultanic victory against the infidel but also leave him vulnerable to domestic accusations of failure and French reprisals.

Mawlay ᶜAbd al-Raḥmān had not heeded these warnings and his inability to impose ᶜAlawī control over Oran did result in a domestic political breakdown which was spearheaded by the revolt of the Udāyā commanders who had led the *maḥalla* to Tlemsen and found themselves involved in conflict with their new subjects rather than in the vanguard of a glorious campaign against the French. The connection between the revolt of the Udāyā and the Tlemsen campaign was implied not simply by the leadership of the revolt but by the Udāyā search for a warrior sultan who would better serve the needs of the time. Other disgruntled elements joined the revolt because the failure of such an evidently meritorious undertaking as the rescue of Tlemsen from anarchy and non-Muslim attack implied that Mawlay ʿAbd al-Raḥmān had forfeited God's favour and that opposition to him was legitimate. The failure appeared so dramatic that it momentarily brought not just the sultan but the dynasty into disrepute, expressed by the search for an Idrīsī *sharīf* and holy man to restore righteousness at the heart of the state.

Mawlay ʿAbd al-Raḥmān countered the rebellion by exploiting societal divisions to reconstruct a network of allies to resist the Udāyā and promote the ʿAlawī religio-political model in Oran. Between 1831 and 1832 he slowly rebuilt his power base and skilfully manipulated the arrival of Muslim delegations begging him to lead a jihad and De Mornay's mission to restore his reputation. By the second half of 1832 he felt strong enough to finally strike against his enemies and disband the Udāyā, but this significantly reduced the military power of the sultanate at a time when the inhabitants of the western Maghrib were becoming increasingly aware of the real dangers posed to Muslim autonomy by the presence of the French in Algiers and their unexpectedly intense opposition to ʿAlawī intervention in Tlemsen. The danger of employing a religio-political construct which was predicated on the existence of an infidel threat, but not its materialisation, was becoming clear. After two years of propagating the idea that the deylik needed a Muslim government and that its prime responsibility was to unite the community and lead a jihad against the French, Mawlay ʿAbd al-Raḥmān could not disengage, but nor could he actively re-engage without risking further domestic unrest. His solution was to patronise autonomous religio-political leaders in Oran who were prepared to acknowledge ʿAlawī overlordship in return for the prestige which their association with the sharifian sultan brought them in relation to their own communities. The most successful of these local religio-political leaders were the Qādirī marabouts of Gharis, Muḥyī al-Dīn and his son ʿAbd al-Qādir, who had been allies of the sultan since 1830, avid participants in the ʿAlawī jihad against Oran in 1831 and trustees of the ʿAlawī cause after the departure of Ibn al-ʿAmirī in 1832. ʿAbd al-Qādir himself would go on to appropriate the sharifian jihad model and challenge Mawlay ʿAbd al-Raḥmān for power not only in Oran but in the northern half of the sultanate itself.

4

AN AMBIVALENT ALLIANCE

Morocco and cAbd al-Qādir's jihad, 1832–9

The recall of Ibn al-cAmirī terminated cAlawī efforts to rule the western deylik either directly or indirectly. It did not, however, end cAlawī involvement in the region's affairs which henceforth took the form of patronage of one or more of those jostling for power in the ex-Turkish territories: the Kulughlān, tribal notables and the heads of the religious brotherhoods. These local power-brokers did not look exclusively to the sultanate for legitimation and support but also flirted with the new power in the area, the French military. Sharifian marabouts tended to prefer the religio-political backing which the cAlawī sultan offered, but the Kulughlān and ex-Makhzan tribes increasingly turned to the French as a surer source of material, if not moral, support. The absence of strong leadership from either of the competing foreign claimants for the territory created a power vacuum. At grassroots level this perpetuated the breakdown of law and order which had begun in 1830 and precluded coordinated jihad offensives against French-held towns, despite a growing will for such attacks to take place. The beneficiaries of popular dissatisfaction with the situation were the marabouts whom the French quickly identified as a much more serious threat than the sultan's delegates:

> Les autres plus dangereux encore parcequ'ils se presentent sur plusieurs points à la foi, qui excitent le fanatisme des populations crédules et musulmanes, ce sont des marabouts espèce de religieux joissant des toutes les prérogatives des missionaires, vénéres dans tout l'empire ottoman et plus particulièrement dans le territoire de la Regence.[1]

The term 'marabout' as used by the French at this point included all those who possessed religious prestige among the tribes: local holy men, the *shurafā'* and the shaykhs of the revived religious brotherhoods. The prestige and potential power of these individuals varied extensively but even the most influential rarely possessed the ideological means to gain the support of competing tribal groups or their own rivals. Both the Darqāwa and Tijāniyya revolts had demonstrated that the limits of religious solidarity tended to coincide with the limits of tribal solidarity. Prestigious marabouts and *shurafā'* now looked to the cAlawī sultan to legitimise their respective bids to lead the jihad and surmount previous divisions with the hope of assuming the mantle of rule in the ex-deylik. For his part, Mawlay ᶜAbd al-Raḥmān accepted the role of patron as a useful way to demonstrate his continued concern for the Muslims of the deylik. The mutual benefits of this patron–client relationship enabled the Qādirī shaykhs of Gharis, Muḥyī al-Dīn and his son, ᶜAbd al-Qādir, to launch a bid for religio-political power which they legitimised not only as a delegation of ᶜAlawī sharifian authority, but also as its independent replica.

Muḥyī al-Dīn, ᶜAbd al-Qādir and the Qādirī bid for power

Muḥyī al-Dīn's lineage had constructed a sphere of influence in the Mascaran hinterland long before 1830. As mentioned in Chapter 3, they actively promoted Idrīsī sharifism and subsequently Sufi revival in the province of Oran and thus inhabited the ᶜAlawī-influenced religious and cultural milieu which had developed since the seventeenth century. Their connections with the northern sultanate found expression in foundation myths stating that their ancestor was an Idrīsī *sharīf* who had also fathered the inhabitants of the Rif. Their revival of the Qādiriyya in the eighteenth century elevated them from the growing ranks of rural *shurafā'* to the level of regional religious figures comparable to the heads of the Tijāniyya, Wazzāniyya–Ṭayyibiyya and Darqāwa brotherhoods.

Like other sharifian shaykhs, Muḥyī al-Dīn was a critic of Turkish rule and, although he did not lead a revolt against them, Ḥasan Bey of Oran had considered a Qādirī revolt not only possible but likely in the late 1820s. The complicated web of affiliation and opposition which bound local society, however, meant that the sharifian marabouts of Gharis could not fully unite the community under their leadership. The other religious brotherhoods opposed them and considerable hostility existed between their closest supporters, the Ḥashem and Banū ᶜAmir, and the ex-Makhzan Dawā'ir and Zmāla tribes. These fissures had prevented Muḥyī al-Dīn launching a Qādirī bid for power prior to 1830.

The substitution of infidel French rule for Turkish rule along the coast and ᶜAlawī interest in expanding east presented the Qādirī shaykhs with a unique opportunity to try their hand at the political game. One reason for the failure of the Darqāwa and Tijāniyya revolts was the absence of a consensus that their action constituted a righteous struggle against impious rulers. Such a consensus did emerge after 1830. On the one hand the fall of Algiers was popularly interpreted as Divine punishment of the Turks for oppression. On the other, unity for jihad against infidel rulers was a clear moral imperative in the way that revolt against the Turks had never been.

In 1830 Mawlay ᶜAbd al-Raḥmān had appeared most suited to take power and Muḥyī al-Dīn had quickly allied himself with the rising ᶜAlawī star, acting both as a propagandist for the ᶜAlawī jihad and informal deputy for Ibn al-ᶜAmirī when he was absent from Tlemsen. During this period, Muḥyī al-Dīn's tribal following had repeatedly offered him their political allegiance but he consistently supported the ᶜAlawī administration rather than setting himself up as a political rival to it.

The advantages of this were twofold. First, Muḥyī al-Dīn's association with the ^{c}Alawī hierarchy and promotion of jihad against the infidel augmented his religious prestige in relation to that of other marabouts. Second, it enabled him to manoeuvere his lineage closer to the source of ^{c}Alawī power and prestige without sacrificing his religious integrity as head of the Qādiriyya.

Muḥyī al-Dīn's appointment as ^{c}Alawī deputy (*khalīfa*) when Ibn al-^{c}Amirī departed in 1832 marked his transition into the realm of politics.[2] He confirmed his crossing from the religious to religio-political sphere by renewing the jihad against Oran during the summer of 1832.[3] As in the sultanate, a jihad was an opportunity for the marabouts of Gharis to prove their religio-political legitimacy by means of military victory and a way to unite the population under their leadership. Muḥyī al-Dīn directed the Qādirī jihad but actual leadership in the field devolved in part upon his son, ^{c}Abd al-Qādir, who demonstrated considerable fighting flair. The Qādirī jihad enjoyed no greater overall success than the earlier ^{c}Alawī campaign, but scattered victories against French foraging columns and a successful economic blockade of Oran gained the marabouts of Gharis the extra prestige which they sought and paved the way for the next stage in their bid for power.

When the Mascaran tribes again asked Muḥyī al-Dīn to accept their allegiance in autumn 1832 he did not reject their advance. Nonetheless, he was aware of the perils involved in using religious authority for political ends and in order to avoid risking the religious prestige of the lineage he refused to accept the *bay^{c}a* himself, but suggested that the tribes offer it to ^{c}Abd al-Qādir instead. Since ^{c}Abd al-Qādir's older brother, Muḥammad al-Sa^{c}īd, was to be Muḥyī al-Dīn's successor as shaykh of the Qādiriyya, the shifting of the *bay^{c}a* to ^{c}Abd al-Qādir prepared the way for a division of labour in the next generation which would insulate the lineage and its *zāwiya* from the effects of a possible defeat in the political sphere.

^{c}Abd al-Qādir's youth caused the tribes to hesitate but Muḥyī al-Dīn's prestige and authority gave weight to his wish and the Banū ^{c}Amir and Ḥashem finally agreed to give their allegiance to his son in November 1832.[4] Shortly afterwards, Muḥyī al-Dīn and ^{c}Abd al-Qādir proceeded to Mascara where the latter addressed the crowds before entering the city and taking possession of the old beylical residence. When he had installed himself in the palace he received the *bay^{c}a* of Mascara. His inauguration culminated in a sermon to his new subjects and the circulation of written exhortations to the region's tribes to submit and join the jihad.

^{c}Abd al-Qādir's appropriation of Mascara with the support of the Qādirī tribes recalled the Khaldunian pattern and like similar tribal bids for power, gained strength from a legitimating religious ideology. The account of ^{c}Abd al-Qādir's rise to power in Muḥammad b. ^{c}Abd al-Qādir's *Tuḥfat al-zā'ir* indicates that Muḥyī al-Dīn and ^{c}Abd al-Qādir consciously drew on Islamic political archetypes and that ^{c}Alawī-derived notions of sharifism and jihad, mediated in part through Sufi revivalism, were central legitimating constructs. Muḥammad b. ^{c}Abd al-Qādir explicitly describes his father's receipt of the *bay^{c}a* as a replay of the Prophet's receipt of the *bay^c^a* at Hudaybiyya, thereby setting up a comparison between the establishment of the first Islamic state and ᶜAbd al-Qādir's state-building activities.[5] In the same vein, both Muḥammad b. ᶜAbd al-Qādir and Churchill recount that ᶜAbd al-Qādir's mission was to command the good and prohibit the evil in the tradition of the Prophet and the early Muslim caliphs.[6]

His legitimate right to take on such a mission, however, lay in his qualifications as a *sharīf* and *mujāhid* in the ᶜAlawī mould. Muḥyī al-Dīn and ᶜAbd al-Qādir's interpretation of what commanding the good and prohibiting the evil entailed was also a product of the ᶜAlawī-inspired religio-political milieu and bore similarities to the stated objectives of the earlier Darqāwa and Tijāniyya rebels. At the heart of their undertaking lay the belief that the French occupation of Algiers signified divine displeasure at the tyranny of the Turks and the moral transgressions of their subjects.[7] From this perspective only the restoration of Islamic values in government and society could secure the departure of the infidel from Muslim territory. To achieve such a restoration, a new Sharīᶜa-based system of central government had to be formed. The evident righteousness of this new order would lead to its acceptance by the population who could then direct their martial energies against the infidel. The creation of a new Sharīᶜa-based regime and resistance to infidel encroachment were thus two sides of the same coin, a view clearly expressed by one of ᶜAbd al-Qādir's close associates in later years:

> He came to the assistance of the religion of his prophet, our Lord Muhammad – peace be upon him – and he gathered what forces he could against the unbelievers and he used his judgement (*ijtahada*) to restore the Muhammadan community (*al-milla al-muḥammadiyya*). He spent the most precious years of his life on this, fighting in the path of God … God made him ruler of His lands from Wajda to Tunis and he propagated the rulings of the Sharīᶜa after they had been swept away.[8]

In its call for the implementation of a just, Sharīᶜa-based government headed by a scholar and *mujtahid*, Qādirī ideology resembled that of other religious brotherhoods and Sufi-inspired jihad movements in West Africa and further afield. The Qādirī mission, however, intended to substitute *ṭarīqa* organisation for an Islamic state structure. ᶜAbd al-Qādir's titles indicate this shift. In the classical Islamic period, the caliphal titles – '*amīr al-mu'minīn*' and 'imam' or '*khalīfa*' – were exclusive and universal but in early nineteenth century northwest Africa their utilisation indicated an established Islamic regime.[9] A feeling existed that only the ᶜAlawī and Ottoman sultans could legitimately assume them because of their dynastic longevity, the recognised scope of their political and religious authority and their ability to unite the community under their leadership for the purposes of jihad.[10] In the words of Aḥmad al-Bakkay, the shaykh of the Kunta branch of the Qādiriyya in Timbuctu:

> The imam of the Muslims today is his excellency Abdurrahman, or the sultan Abdul Mejid, because his excellency Abdurrahman is the

> religiously sanctioned leader and the sultan Abdul Mejid is the greatest and has the most extensive domain.[11]

He added that only the imam could be called *amīr al-mu'minīn* and lead a jihad. In other words, jihad leadership was the prerogative of established sultanic regimes, a view which Mawlay ^{c}Abd al-Raḥmān and his predecessors would have upheld. A counter-view existed, however, among the shaykhs of activist religious brotherhoods who reversed the equation and claimed that successful jihad to institute a just and hegemonic Islamic order entitled the victor to assume the titles 'imam' and '*amīr al-mu'minīn*'. Usuman dan Fodio had first taken this path when he established the Sokoto caliphate and the shaykhs of Masina claimed a similar privilege. Such views corresponded to the notion of societal jihad to replace a corrupt ruler current in the ^{c}Alawī sultanate and the Qādirī project.

In the Qādirī case, ^{c}Abd al-Qādir came to power first as an '*amīr*', a generic politico-military title meaning 'commander', 'prince' or 'leader'. His regnal title, Nāṣir al-Dīn (Champion of Religion), given to him by Muḥyī al-Dīn, underlined, however, that his responsibilities as *amīr* were not merely political but religio-political, to exert his efforts to restore the faith internally and protect it from infidel encroachment.[12] There are also hints that he assumed the more overtly religious title, 'imam', thereby indicating that he saw himself not only as a defender of the faith in a military sense but also as a spiritual leader in the caliphal tradition.[13] This conformed with his avowed aim to reform Islamic practice and reinstate the limits defined by the Sharī^{c}a. In the following years he sometimes substituted the title '*amīr*' for the more highly charged title of '*amīr al-mu'minīn*' which implied a bid for equality with the ^{c}Alawī and Ottoman sultans. However, he appears to have used the title primarily in communication with French colonial authorities and non-Muslim governments to imply much wider sovereignty than he actually held.[14]

The terms which Muḥammad b. ^{c}Abd al-Qādir employed to describe his father's political opponents – *khawārij, murtaddūn, ahl al-fasād* – all confirm the religious dimension of the Qādirī project. The term '*murtadd*' (apostate), used for those who gave their allegiance and then broke with ^{c}Abd al-Qādir, maintained the comparison between ^{c}Abd al-Qādir's undertaking and the early Islamic era when political dissidence after the Prophet's death was categorised as apostasy from the new faith. The terms '*khārijī*' (seceder) and '*ahl al-fasād*' (people of rebellion) came from the ^{c}Alawī repertoire where they denoted not merely opposition to the sultan but opposition to Islam itself. In sum, Muḥyī al-Dīn and ^{c}Abd al-Qādir envisaged the establishment of a centralising sharifian jihad state of the ^{c}Alawī type with its capital at Mascara. Although the titles ^{c}Abd al-Qādir accepted were not necessarily universalist, references to the Prophetic paradigm and the absence of any territorial definition of his state allowed for unlimited expansion and a possible challenge to ^{c}Alawī hegemony in the western Maghrib.

Similarities between the Qādirī state and the sultanate were not limited to ideology but extended to governmental institutions. ^{c}Abd al-Qādir relied heavily on Turkish and ᶜAlawī precedents, modified by elements from the *niẓām-i cedīd* regimes of Egypt and the central Ottoman lands which he had witnessed when he performed the ḥajj with Muḥyī al-Dīn in 1827. ᶜAbd al-Qādir stood at the apex of the governmental pyramid assisted by a *makhzan* composed of his father, other members of his kin group and close associates. These men held the main offices of state: chief minister (*wazīr*), scribes (*kuttāb*), chancellor (*ḥājib*), keeper of the state treasury (*nāẓir khazīnat al-mamlaka*), keeper of the household treasury (*nāẓir khazīnat al-khaṣṣa*), keeper of pious endowments (*nāẓir al-awqāf*), head of taxes (*ma'mūr al-ḍarā'ib*), and overseer of foreign affairs (*nāẓir al-umūr al-khārijiyya*).[15]

A distinguishing feature of ᶜAbd al-Qādir's new order was his formation of a consultative assembly (*majlis*) composed of tribal notables, marabouts and *ᶜulamā'* who gathered irregularly in Mascara to advise on important matters. Whilst evoking the consultative practice (*shūrā*) of the early Islamic state, this institution was also an enlarged version of a tribal council which counter-balanced the new state's autocratic character and an early example of a Muslim political assembly recruited from the *raᶜāyā*. On the military side, the Qādirī tribes closest to Muḥyī al-Dīn and ᶜAbd al-Qādir became the regime's military tribes and enjoyed tax exemptions in return for permanent military service. In addition, ᶜAbd al-Qādir soon created a professional *niẓām-i cedīd* army trained in modern European tactics, comparable in style, although not in size, to the armies of Aḥmad Bey of Tunis, Muḥammad ᶜAlī of Egypt and the Ottoman sultan, Maḥmūd II.[16] He entrusted provincial government to regional deputies (*khulafā'*) and governors (*ᶜummāl*) either chosen from local elites or sent out from Mascara. Finally, he took a special interest in the appointment of judges and teachers to participate in the restoration of Islamic faith and law, or more properly, its homogenisation under the new state's auspices.

The Qādirī–ᶜAlawī alliance

In accepting the *bayᶜa* and creating a sharifian jihad state modelled upon the sultanate in a region nominally subject to it, ᶜAbd al-Qādir both acknowledged and challenged the ᶜAlawī sultan. Although dangerous, his rise to power and authority also presented Mawlay ᶜAbd al-Raḥmān with a new opportunity. In deciding to intervene in Tlemsen Mawlay ᶜAbd al-Raḥmān had chosen between two learned opinions on his responsibilities towards the ex-Turkish deylik and its predicament. The alternatives recommended by the jurists now presented themselves afresh as a choice between support for ᶜAbd al-Qādir as a surrogate holy warrior waging jihad on his behalf or distance from a rival to his power and authority. The choice governed the relationship between the two leaders throughout the formative period of the 1830s and was made all the more difficult by ᶜAbd al-Qādir's own dilemma, to lead his subjects in a war they could not win or compromise with the infidel.

In November 1832 when ᶜAbd al-Qādir received the *bayᶜa* his support base was limited to the Mascara area. To extend his authority he immediately sent out letters to the tribes and towns of the region, including Tlemsen, calling upon them to submit to him as their legitimate ruler and leader of the jihad.[17] In doing this he adopted the 'statist' line that jihad leadership was the prerogative of the centre and that Muslims had a religious obligation to submit to a *mujāhid* ruler. Like the ᶜAlawī sultans he further asserted that failure to submit was an act of rebellion (*fasād*) which undermined Muslim unity and ability to wage an effective jihad against the French infidel.

Since the region he purported to rule was theoretically under ᶜAlawī sovereignty his efforts to impose his authority in this manner raised the issue of his relations with ᶜAlawī clients such as the Kulughlān, the *ḥaḍar* of Tlemsen, the Dawā'ir and Zmāla, and, more importantly, with Mawlay ᶜAbd al-Raḥmān himself. ᶜAlawī clients initially rejected ᶜAbd al-Qādir's call to submit on the grounds that ᶜAbd al-Qādir had no right to assume religio-political precedence over them and therefore no right to lead the jihad which was, in any case, an individual rather than a communal obligation. Many clients insisted that the right to lead the jihad belonged to Mawlay ᶜAbd al-Raḥmān and that ᶜAbd al-Qādir could only demand allegiance if he were his agent. The *ḥaḍar* of Tlemsen, for instance, made their submission to ᶜAbd al-Qādir conditional upon his submission to Mawlay ᶜAbd al-Raḥmān. It was clear that for Muḥyī al-Dīn and ᶜAbd al-Qādir's bid for power to succeed they would have to retain the client relationship with the ᶜAlawī sultanate which they had hoped to throw off. They thus set in train the creation of an alliance with Mawlay ᶜAbd al-Raḥmān which would last until 1840.

This alliance began when ᶜAbd al-Qādir wrote to Mawlay ᶜAbd al-Raḥmān to offer him his *bayᶜa* and his services as leader of the jihad in return for the position of ᶜAlawī deputy in Oran. Mawlay ᶜAbd al-Raḥmān's response was cautious. French reports state that he was in communication with Muḥyī al-Dīn and ᶜAbd al-Qādir in January 1833 and that ᶜAbd al-Qādir was publicly claiming to be the sultan's deputy by March.[18] However, Danziger suggests that an appointment letter circulated by ᶜAbd al-Qādir in early 1833 was a forgery and French reports say that Mawlay ᶜAbd al-Raḥmān had broken off the correspondence by April.[19] What is certain is that for about nine months after ᶜAbd al-Qādir received the *bayᶜa* of Mascara Mawlay ᶜAbd al-Raḥmān remained aloof. He viewed him as a petty chief trying to carve a niche for himself whom it was not worth supporting given his bad relations with ᶜAlawī clients and French warnings against further ᶜAlawī involvement in the region.[20]

During summer 1833 ᶜAbd al-Qādir emerged as a major political player in Oran. He forcibly imposed his authority over the recalcitrant Dawā'ir and Zmāla who complained to Mawlay ᶜAbd al-Raḥmān;[21] he captured Tlemsen bar the citadel and forced the pro-ᶜAlawī governor, Muḥammad b. Nūna, to flee to the sultanate; and he began to negotiate with the French military governor of Oran, Desmichels, as the representative of the Muslims of the region. His attitude towards ᶜAlawī clients and capture of Tlemsen struck at Mawlay ᶜAbd al-Raḥmān's claim to sovereignty in Oran while his negotiations with Desmichels appeared to contravene the ethics of jihad and create the possibility of a French client state on the sultanate's doorstep. These factors forced Mawlay ᶜAbd al-Raḥmān to engage with the situation. He therefore encouraged Muṣṭafā b. Ismāᶜīl, chief of the Dawā'ir, to set himself up as an alternative source of power and authority to ᶜAbd al-Qādir.[22] In a letter to the chief, the sultan warned him that the French would undoubtedly exploit the rifts caused by ᶜAbd al-Qādir and urged him to promote Muslim unity, to 'command the good and prohibit the evil', exhort the tribes to hold fast to the Qur'ān and Sunna and wage the jihad. He added that he would send an envoy to monitor ᶜAbd al-Qādir's negotiations with the French to prevent any agreement detrimental to the Muslims. To underline his disapproval of ᶜAbd al-Qādir's behaviour he suspended the export of munitions from the sultanate to Oran and ordered Makhzan authorities at Wajda to check all caravans for contraband.[23]

Mawlay ᶜAbd al-Raḥmān's stance was almost immediately undermined by the place ᶜAbd al-Qādir secured in the imagination of his subjects. Although those whom ᶜAbd al-Qādir claimed to rule had mixed feelings towards him, the inhabitants of the sultanate considered him 'l'élu de Dieu soutenant à lui seul tout les poids de la guerre contre les infidels qui evahissent les pays musulmans', in other words an emblematic *sharīf* and *mujāhid*.[24] From this perspective, Mawlay ᶜAbd al-Raḥmān's suspension of the arms trade was not punishment of a collaborator but opposition to a holy warrior and it was rumoured that it was the French themselves who had demanded that he suspend the export of arms. Public recognition of ᶜAbd al-Qādir as a legitimate holy warrior obliged Mawlay ᶜAbd al-Raḥmān to reconsider his position and accept the former's allegiance. The British consul in Tanger, Drummond Hay, summed up the situation:

> Nothing would assuredly render Mulai Abd Errachman, who is the acknowledged vice-gerant of Heaven … in this part of the world, than that the priests could console their flocks from the minbar with an assurance that their monarch was helping the holy war.[25]

An exchange of gifts sealed the new relationship between the two men: ᶜAbd al-Qādir sent the sultan thirty horses and the equivalent of 35,000 francs in gold, in lieu of taxes, whilst Mawlay ᶜAbd al-Raḥmān sent decorated rifles and daggers as tokens of investiture and supplies of swords, rifles and ammunition to signal his support for the jihad.[26] This gift of munitions indicated to the merchants of Fes that the sultan had lifted the Makhzan ban on arms trading with Oran and by January 1834 munitions from Europe were arriving in Tanger for transportation to ᶜAbd al-Qādir.[27]

A month later, ᶜAbd al-Qādir secured the recognition of the French in the Desmichel's treaty, a bipartite treaty in two separate versions, one French and one Arabic. This treaty defined a French coastal zone and acknowledged ᶜAbd al-Qādir as the sovereign of the interior. In return ᶜAbd al-Qādir agreed to provision French outposts. In an Arabic clause absent from the French version of the treaty sent to Paris, Desmichels also promised ᶜAbd al-Qādir weapons, ammunition and training for his *niẓāmī* corps.[28] This treaty meant all things to all men. For Desmichels, recognising and assisting ᶜAbd al-Qādir enabled him to deal with a single friendly Muslim representative rather than multiple competing chiefs. He believed that in the process he had created a channel for French influence into the interior and secured the provisioning of French garrisons. Although he acted beyond his powers, his reasoning was similar to that applied in many cases where an imperial European power considered strengthening a native ally the cheapest and most effective means to consolidate their influence.

On the Muslim side the treaty secured ᶜAbd al-Qādir precedence over other local leaders as the Muslims' representative before the French. Although an agreement with the infidel, the treaty could be seen as a religiously acceptable truce which had bought the Muslims time to prepare for war and munitions with which to eventually fight it. The treaty also mollified Mawlay ᶜAbd al-Raḥmān who viewed it as a tactical truce sanctioned by the Sharīᶜa which had not created the French client state he had feared but an allied buffer zone between ᶜAlawī and infidel territory, headed by a *mujāhid* who would fight on his behalf.

ᶜAbd al-Qādir's definition of relationships with the French and Mawlay ᶜAbd al-Raḥmān inaugurated a new stage in his political career. During the 1830s he ruled his state with the qualified acceptance of both the French and the ᶜAlawī sultan and reconciled local and regional imperatives by operating on two levels. On one level he operated as an independent sultan of the ᶜAlawī type, determined to establish himself and coerce local tribes into accepting his religio-political authority. On another level he operated as the deputy (*khalīfa*) of the ᶜAlawī sultan–imam and the disciple of his ᶜAlawī master. Despite the tensions inherent in it, both men saw the establishment of this fictional hierarchy of power as an effective way to prevent French expansion into the interior and secure the prestige which they needed. ᶜAbd al-Qādir gained persuasive proof of his legitimate right to implement the sharifian model in Oran, religious backing against his tribal opponents and access to ᶜAlawī military resources. Mawlay ᶜAbd al-Raḥmān, meanwhile, assuaged the impression that he had abandoned the Muslims of Oran to the infidel and perpetuated the fiction that he was the sovereign of the region.

The most significant variable in their relationship was whether a jihad was actually in progress. ᶜAbd al-Qādir needed peace to consolidate his rule but the tribes of Oran tended to secede when the imperative for state formation – waging jihad – was absent. Mawlay ᶜAbd al-Raḥmān's support was also lukewarm during peacetime. Conversely, ᶜAbd al-Qādir's reputation among his subjects and the inhabitants of the sultanate soared during periods of warfare with the French, bringing him massive amounts of aid from the sultanate and Mawlay ᶜAbd al-Raḥmān's acclaim. Despite the growing risks of fighting the French, this remained generally true throughout the 1830s as a result of pressures on both ᶜAbd al-Qādir and Mawlay ᶜAbd al-Raḥmān to prove themselves in the theatre of war. Their relationship nonetheless constantly shifted as the domestic and international pressures on each altered.

During the first year of the alliance peace with the French held and ᶜAbd al-Qādir concentrated upon internal consolidation. His signing of the Desmichels treaty had constrained the French to the coast and secured military aid from them, but it nevertheless ruptured his tribal support base and gave rivals to power their chance. The situation was compounded by the death of Muḥyī al-Dīn which deprived ^{c}Abd al-Qādir of the religious prestige which his father's backing had bestowed upon him. Tribal opposition took several forms. First, many tribes, including the Banū ^{c}Amir, resisted ^{c}Abd al-Qādir's efforts to continue collection of the *ma^{c}ūna*, an extraordinary war tax, during peacetime. They refused to pay on the grounds that ^{c}Abd al-Qādir had promised to respect Sharī^{c}a rules on taxation which meant that the *ma^{c}ūna* could not be levied unless the state was at war. Only the use of force convinced the Banū ^{c}Amir to pay the tax.[29]

In addition to resistance to taxation, ^{c}Abd al-Qādir also faced opposition from tribal notables and marabouts who still questioned his right to rule despite his recognition by the French and Mawlay ^{c}Abd al-Raḥmān. In particular, the Dawā'ir and Zmāla in alliance with the Kulughlān of Tlemsen gradually distanced themselves from him and sought a rapprochement with the French which would give them greater authority than he was prepared to offer. Maraboutic opposition took the shape of rival attempts to lead the jihad which rejected ^{c}Abd al-Qādir's right to sign a truce on behalf of the entire population. The most serious challenge of this kind was a Darqāwa bid to lead the jihad in central Algeria headed by a shaykh called al-Ḥājj al-Darqāwī and one of ^{c}Abd al-Qādir's own brothers.

^{c}Abd al-Qādir met these challenges by building a professional *niẓām-i cedīd* corps using technological and military instructors, weapons and ammunition from Desmichels and the ^{c}Alawī sultanate. This marked the westward movement of the military New Order already employed by Muslim rulers further east to consolidate state power using techniques borrowed from industrial Europe. In order to secure approval for its formation ^{c}Abd al-Qādir summoned a meeting of the *majlis*. Armed with the concurrence of the tribal notables and *^{c}ulamā'*, he then sent criers to urban and rural markets to request volunteers for the new corps which was legitimised as an instrument for the jihad:

> Let it be known that the undertaking of Mawlānā Nāṣir al-Dīn (^{c}Abd al-Qādir) starts with the formation of an army and the training of soldiers from throughout the country. He who wishes to enter under the Muḥammadī banner and be imbued by the glory of the [new] order (*niẓām*) should hurry to the capital of the emirate, Mascara, to have his name entered in the rolls.[30]

After its establishment ^{c}Abd al-Qādir used the corps to extend state power over tribes still resisting centralisation and fight the rival Darqāwa *mujāhidīn* into submission.[31] He legitimised deployment of state forces against fellow Muslims by appealing to his religio-political status and the necessity of unifying the Muslims before initiating the jihad. In the same vein as the ^{c}Alawī sultans he attempted to define political allegiance in religious terms by designating his followers Muslims and his opponents *khawārij* and *murtaddīn* who had seceded from the Muslim *umma* by rejecting his leadership.[32] He applied these terms most liberally in relation to the Dawā'ir and Zmāla when their chiefs started to court the French during the course of 1835 as a result of their inability to secure a satisfactory position within the political hierarchy of ᶜAbd al-Qādir's sharifian state. The Dawā'ir and Zmāla formalised their secession in June 1835 when they placed themselves under the protection of the new governor of Oran, General Trezel.[33]

Unlike Desmichels, Trezel was no admirer of ᶜAbd al-Qādir and the dispute which ensued over his granting of the Dawā'ir and Zmāla protection triggered the first serious round of hostilities in the west Algerian interior. A more or less active state of war continued until ᶜAbd al-Qādir signed the Tafna treaty with the French in 1837. Although eventually detrimental to ᶜAbd al-Qādir in territorial and material terms, the resumption of the jihad dramatically improved his standing among his own subjects, generated a huge surge of support for him in the ᶜAlawī sultanate and transformed his alliance with Mawlay ᶜAbd al-Raḥmān into a reality. War began in late June 1835 when Trezel's column left the French coastal zone to attack ᶜAbd al-Qādir. The latter's tribal forces ambushed the French column in the narrow Maqtaᶜ defile along the course of the Wadi Habra. Both sides sustained heavy losses but the victory went to ᶜAbd al-Qādir while the remnants of Trezel's column staggered back to Oran. Rumours of Trezel's defeat reached Tanger in July when Drummond Hay noted:

> There has been for about a fortnight past, a strange rumour of one or more battles upon the coast, near to the eastern frontier of this country, between the natives and a considerable body of French troops, in which, as some Moors who have lately come hither pretend, there were many slain on both sides, and that, after three days of fighting the natives captured some twelve field guns.[34]

ᶜAbd al-Qādir himself confirmed the victory by sending a deputation to the Makhzan with various military trophies: five French prisoners, captured munitions and several severed French heads.[35] The nature of the deputation suggested ᶜAbd al-Qādir's political agenda. The Battle of the Maqtaᶜ was the victory which the inhabitants of the sultanate and Oran had been waiting for since the French arrived in Algiers in 1830. Both ᶜAbd al-Qādir and Mawlay ᶜAbd al-Raḥmān desperately needed it to maintain their religio-political credibility in societies where military victory and legitimacy were closely entwined. As a result the deputation was a public relations exercise which ensured that ᶜAbd al-Qādir's victory received extensive exposure thereby encouraging the sultan and his subjects to more fully support his project. In order to reach Mawlay ᶜAbd al-Raḥmān in Marrakesh, the French prisoners and captured guns had to be paraded through the sultanate in a highly visible statement of the triumph of Islam over the infidel.

Although it's impact is difficult to gauge, Drummond Hay's note on the response of the people of Fes was probably widely applicable:

> The people did not hesitate ... to display the usual signs of a public rejoicing – such as the hanging out of their doors and decking the shops in particular with silks and damasks suspended.[36]

The arrival of ^{c}Abd al-Qādir's deputation coincided fortuitiously with a sea change in the Makhzan attitude towards the situation in Algeria. Although Mawlay ^{c}Abd al-Raḥmān had accepted ^{c}Abd al-Qādir's allegiance a year previously the dominant voice in the Makhzan had been one of caution, represented by the person of al-Mukhtār al-Jāmi^{c}ī, the sultan's chief minister. When Mukhtār al-Jāmi^{c}ī died in June 1835 he was replaced by a supporter of ^{c}Alawī involvement in Algeria, Muḥammad b. Idrīs, disgraced in 1831 to pacify the Udāyā.[37] Muḥammad b. Idrīs's return to favour signalled the rise of a distinct pro-jihad party within Makhzan circles. Another supporter of the jihad was Sīdī Muḥammad, the sultan's son and deputy in Fes.

The presence of jihad supporters in key positions fostered a rise in military aid to ^{c}Abd al-Qādir accompanied by public Makhzan support for him. Sīdī Muḥammad actively assisted in the organisation of several caravans from Fes to Mascara between August and October 1835 and Mawlay ^{c}Abd al-Raḥmān made his first extant statement confirming his patronage of ^{c}Abd al-Qādir.[38] This statement took the form of a letter to ^{c}Abd al-Qādir preserved in the *Ibtisām*, a contemporary chronicle written by the unidentified Abū'l-^{c}Alā Idrīs.[39] The letter's superficial objective was to congratulate ^{c}Abd al-Qādir upon his success in the jihad but it was carefully formulated to associate Mawlay ^{c}Abd al-Raḥmān with that success and make plain the hierarchy of power between them. To achieve these ends it adopted the paradigm of Sufi master and disciple. Mawlay ^{c}Abd al-Raḥmān addressed ^{c}Abd al-Qādir as 'our most revered son' (*waladnā al-abarr*), a formula common in Sufi as well as Makhzan correspondence, and then proceeded to pray for his continued success and preach the merits of jihad:

> For, as you know, we envy the benefits gained by the participants in the jihad, because they are the armour of happiness and the key to mercy in the unknown and the known, and you have earned what God has prepared for the fighters of jihad in this world and the next and the high rank and elevated status he distinguishes them with.[40]

Mawlay ^{c}Abd al-Raḥmān conveyed a series of messages by adopting the didactic tone of a Sufi shaykh. The interaction between master and disciple was characterised by the total obedience of the latter to the former, and reference to it reminded ^{c}Abd al-Qādir of the sultan's authority. At the same time, it also identified the source of that authority as religious, thereby tacitly asserting Mawlay ^{c}Abd al-Raḥmān's sharifian seniority and his right to define the jihad and bestow its prosecution upon ᶜAbd al-Qādir as a gift. The relationship between a Sufi master and disciple, however, was an interaction of ambivalence in the Maghribi context. In his analysis of contemporary Moroccan politics and society, Abdellah Hammoudi identifies the dominant interaction between male superiors and inferiors as one of total submission which eventually enables the inferior to challenge the superior for power or rise above him at a later time. He suggests that this interaction originates in the relationship between a Sufi master and disciple in which the master demanded exemplary obedience and self-abnegation from the disciple before the latter could receive his *baraka* and take on the role of master himself. The ambivalence in the relationship lay in the humiliation of submission for the inferior and the potential challenge contained in such submission for the superior.[41] Mawlay ᶜAbd al-Raḥmān certainly felt ambivalent towards ᶜAbd al-Qādir and perceived the potential threat which lay in the rise to power of an Idrīsī *sharīf* and *mujāhid* on the edge of his domains, however submissive he was in the short term.

Active prosecution of the jihad gained ᶜAbd al-Qādir enormous prestige among the inhabitants of the western Maghrib, but it also unleashed a wave of outrage in France which enabled those committed to expansion in Algeria to proceed.[42] The war against ᶜAbd al-Qādir was prosecuted by Trezel's successor in Oran, General Clauzel, a man who had already demonstrated his commitment to French expansion in the early 1830s in Algiers. Clauzel's objectives between 1835 and 1837 were twofold: to undermine ᶜAbd al-Qādir politically by strengthening French ties with his enemies, the Dawā'ir, the Zmāla and the Kulughlān of Tlemsen, and to undermine him economically by extending French control of coastal trade and the interior caravan route from the ᶜAlawī sultanate through Tlemsen to Mascara. Clauzel estimated that the sultanate's commercial relations with Tlemsen were worth about 25,000,000 francs a year, and he had high hopes that the establishment of a French garrison in Tlemsen would not only damage ᶜAbd al-Qādir but facilitate the development of French commerce along the routes from Algiers and Oran to Tlemsen and Fes.[43]

Clauzel therefore planned a two-pronged campaign from Oran: a land offensive against Mascara and Tlemsen and the simultaneous establishment of a French garrison on the island of Rashgun, located at the mouth of the Tafna river north of Tlemsen.[44] Once the French forces reached Tlemsen they would be able to receive assistance from the Rashgun garrison. For ᶜAbd al-Qādir the planned attack on Mascara would damage his prestige, but the prospect of an alliance between the French and the Kulughlān and the establishment of a French post at Tlemsen was a much more serious threat to his autonomy. Therefore, when Clauzel's campaign started in November 1835, ᶜAbd al-Qādir abandoned Mascara to French sack and pillage and concentrated his energies on a final attempt to expel the Kulughlān from the citadel of Tlemsen and secure the city, along with his vital supply line to Fes. Despite rumours that he had successfully stormed the citadel, ᶜAbd al-Qādir's inability to prevent French penetration into the interior seriously reduced his tribal following and he was unable to even defend Tlemsen.

As Clauzel's forces approached, he and the *ḥaḍar* retreated to the nearby mountains. The Kulughlān pillaged the deserted city and on 13 January 1836 Clauzel entered its gates. From Tlemsen he sent out a contingent which destroyed ᶜAbd al-Qādir's mountain camp.[45] ᶜAbd al-Qādir escaped but his defeat seemed complete: he had lost his indigenous support and the two cities most important to his state, Mascara and Tlemsen.

Clauzel's campaign had, however, brought infidel troops within a stone's throw of the sultanate. Their presence, in combination with the fall of Tlemsen, Fes's sister city, provoked considerable agitation among the tribes of the northeastern Rif and in Fes itself. Commercially, the merchants of the Fes viewed the fall of Tlemsen as a disaster. Despite Clauzel's sanguine hopes of establishing a profitable trade with the sultanate, a large proportion of Tlemsen's trade with Fes in the 1830s was in munitions to ᶜAbd al-Qādir, a trade which the French were unlikely to permit. The city's fall also had strategic and political implications. Strategically, French control of Tlemsen made Fes vulnerable to French attack by way of the Taza corridor, a fact reflected in a sudden rise in wheat prices when news of the French occupation reached the city.[46] Politically, it reflected extremely badly on the sultan whose policy towards Oran should have kept the infidel away from the sultanate rather than bringing him to its door. In addition, the sultan had a particular responsibility for Tlemsen as the city which had first solicited his protection and offered him the *bayᶜa* in 1830. As refugees from Tlemsen straggled into Fes popular pressure for Makhzan intervention increased, and for the first time since the ᶜAlawī occupation of Tlemsen the Makhzan was forced to directly proclaim a jihad.[47]

Over the next months the sultanate was heavily involved in resistance to Clauzel's efforts to establish control over the area between Tlemsen and Rashgun. Massive donations enabled the Fāsī merchant, al-Ḥājj Ṭālib b. Jallūn, to purchase munitions in Gibraltar for ᶜAbd al-Qādir and the Tlemsen evacuees, whilst Rif tribesmen and Makhzan troops stationed at Wajda mobilised to assist him against the French.[48] The two sides came to blows in late January 1836 when Clauzel's tribal auxiliaries recruited from ᶜAbd al-Qādir's old rivals, the Dawā'ir, attacked him. Rif tribesmen rushed to his defence and the next day a heterogeneous force of tribesmen and Makhzan cavalry attacked Clauzel's column. The French dispersed the attackers with their artillery and retreated to Tlemsen. In the engagement's aftermath the extent of ᶜAlawī participation became clear: Clauzel estimated that 5,000 of the 8,000 attackers were inhabitants of the sultanate.[49] The discovery of letters on the body of a dead marabout exhorting the tribes to jihad in the name of the sultan implicated the Banū Yznāsen, the Aḥlāf and several sections of the Angād in the fighting, along with the erstwhile governor of Tlemsen, Muḥammad b. Nūna, and the governor of Wajda, al-ᶜArabī al-Qabībī.[50] ᶜAlawī aid continued to stiffen local resistance to the French garrisons in Tlemsen and Rashgun after Clauzel's departure for Algiers in February and by April both posts were in trouble. ᶜAlawī assistance also enabled ᶜAbd al-Qādir to slowly rebuild his following and reassert his authority, convincing French commanders that ᶜAlawī involvement had prejudiced their position in west Algeria more than anything else.[51]

ᶜAlawī complicity resulted in fresh French complaints to Mawlay ᶜAbd al-Raḥmān transmitted through the French consul in Tanger. Their protests included reference to the Wajda garrison's part in the attack on Clauzel's column and Makhzan involvement in the arms trade to ᶜAbd al-Qādir.[52] The sultan responded with a letter which completely denied Makhzan involvement in the fighting and attributed the trouble to the endemic dissidence of the border tribes and their clumsy handling by the French, a reference to French employment of the Dawā'ir and other auxiliaries who had a record of feuds with local tribes.[53] The sultan's statement was accompanied by a similar statement from his representative in Tanger, al-Ṭayyib Bayyāz, who presented the Makhzan case even more strongly by asserting that since the sultan desired good relations with the French it was inconceivable that his officers had openly assisted France's enemies.[54] Al-Bayyāz further dissociated the Makhzan from the situation by reviving the argument of those opposed to ᶜAlawī involvement in Tlemsen in 1830 that the area's rebelliousness was the reason that Mawlay Sulaymān had refused the Darqāwa *bayᶜa* and Mawlay ᶜAbd al-Raḥmān had now dropped his claim to Tlemsen.

These two Makhzan statements to the French consul attempted to portray the border situation as an example of localised tribal feuding rather than a regional jihad. The sultan's domestic correspondence, however, revealed a strong Makhzan impulse to condone popular participation in the jihad at this point. In a letter to the governor of Tanger intercepted and translated by the British consul, he asserted that:

> He would not interfere to prevent any of his people assisting their brethren of Islam and as to the complaint of the French government that a body of troops had been collected by him, the Sultan, at Ooschda (Wajda), no person had a right to dictate what he should do within his own territories.[55]

In addition to condoning tribal participation in ᶜAbd al-Qādir's war, the Makhzan further increased the level of military aid sent to Algeria. This aid represented a 'virtual military alliance' between ᶜAbd al-Qādir and Mawlay ᶜAbd al-Raḥmān which served both men's interests.[56] It enabled ᶜAbd al-Qādir to continue the jihad against the French and reconstruct his state which served Mawlay ᶜAbd al-Raḥmān's purposes by transferring the theatre of war from the borders of the sultanate to areas further east. If fully occupied by ᶜAbd al-Qādir, the sultan assumed, the French would not invade the sultanate. The French military, however, considered this alliance unacceptable and stepped up pressure on Paris to use military and diplomatic channels to force Mawlay ᶜAbd al-Raḥmān to desist from aiding ᶜAbd al-Qādir.

The result was another French diplomatic mission to the sultanate headed by Baron de la Rue who held instructions to demand an explanation for ᶜAlawī involvement in the attack on Clauzel's column and firm assurances that it would not happen again. The arrival of the French mission escorted by warships in Tanger in early July 1836 provoked popular fears that an infidel invasion was imminent, fears exacerbated by the simultaneous arrival of French reinforcements commanded by General Bugeaud at Rashgun. Concomitant popular agitation for military mobilisation against the French put the sultan in an awkward situation which he tried to handle in the same way as he had handled De Mornay's mission in 1832. This entailed adopting strategies to assure France of his amity and simultaneously reassure his subjects that he would resist infidel pressure and continue to assist ᶜAbd al-Qādir, in sum, a policy of dissimilation.

First he dispatched a force of 4,000 Makhzan troops to Wajda which, he assured De La Rue, would prevent Rif tribesmen joining ᶜAbd al-Qādir, but also gave the impression to his subjects that he was fortifying the northeast against a possible French invasion.[57] When De la Rue made his visit to Meknes to meet the sultan he was treated to the same Makhzan parades and armed tribal gatherings as De Mornay had been in 1832. These displays of ᶜAlawī military power were intended to convince the envoy that the sultanate was a power to be reckoned with and present the infidel to the population as a suppliant.[58] De la Rue remained in Meknes for a week under close guard. During that time he had a single short audience with Mawlay ᶜAbd al-Raḥmān and several meetings with his representative, al-Ṭayyib al-Bayyāz, at which he demanded written explanations of border incidents and assurances of future neutrality. The Makhzan maintained substantially the same position as in its exchanges with the French consul, denying Makhzan involvement in the arms trade and describing the attack on Clauzel as a non-governmental initiative instigated by 'freebooters of the border' historically beyond the control of central government.[59] Al-Bayyāz defended ᶜAlawī contacts with ᶜAbd al-Qādir and other figures in his administration as normal diplomatic practice and defended the sultan's right to offer refuge to Muslims from the French zone as a religious duty he could not shirk. Under intense pressure from De la Rue, al-Bayyāz reluctantly promised that the Makhzan would prohibit trade with ᶜAbd al-Qādir in munitions, horses and foodstuffs but retained some room for manoevere by warning De la Rue that it would be impossible for the Makhzan to police the entire march area from the Mediterranean to the Sahara.[60]

De la Rue's correspondence recognised the serious political problems faced by Mawlay ᶜAbd al-Raḥmān at home and the potential dangers for him in his association with ᶜAbd al-Qādir. Whatever undertakings the Makhzan made, the sultan's ability to implement them depended on the extent of his authority. However, the fact that he had neither led his army to Tlemsen nor personally taken charge of resistance to the French had undermined that authority.[61] Although ᶜAbd al-Qādir's nominal status as an ᶜAlawī deputy had eased the pressure on him to participate in the jihad, the former's prosecution of the jihad made him a popular hero who seemed more able to defend the sultanate from French attack than the sultan. ᶜAbd al-Qādir's popularity had reached the point where the implicit challenge to Mawlay ᶜAbd al-Raḥmān which he represented had entered the public consciousness.

In Tanger De la Rue received word of rumours that ᶜAbd al-Qādir had entered into an alliance with a nephew of the sultan and crossed into the sultanate 'en revolte vrai ou simulée contre lui'.[62]

The problems he had in imposing his authority were compounded by the popularity of ᶜAbd al-Qādir and the poor state of Makhzan military discipline. De la Rue commented that the ᶜAlawī troops were courageous but badly armed, undisciplined and ignorant of the simplest manouveres.[63] Although Mawlay ᶜAbd al-Raḥmān and his subjects thought that they would be equal to repulsing a French force if it entered the sultanate, in training, tactics and equipment they lagged behind not only the modern French military machine but also ᶜAbd al-Qādir's *niẓām-i cedīd* corps. In the circumstances Mawlay ᶜAbd al-Raḥmān could not deter the tribes from joining ᶜAbd al-Qādir's jihad and in fact needed to associate himself as closely as possible with him to improve his domestic standing. Despite the threat contained in De la Rue's mission, the sultan believed that he could avert a French attack by paying lip-service to their demands while simultaneously pursuing the much more important task of satisfying his subjects that he was not a vassal of the infidel but a defender of the faith.

Mawlay ᶜAbd al-Raḥmān maintained this policy through 1836 hoping that if he kept the French occupied in Algeria they would not turn their attention to the subjugation of other Muslim territories. In fact, he stepped up Makhzan aid to ᶜAbd al-Qādir to strengthen him after his defeat by General Bugeaud in the Battle of the Sikkak near Tlemsen in July 1836. During late summer, the Makhzan issued summons to jihad throughout the sultanate. The British explorer, Davidson, reported in August that tribes in the Sus and Wad Nun in the deep south were mobilising because the sultan had exhorted them to arms claiming that Islam itself was under threat.[64] A month later a large caravan carrying uniforms, provisions and money enabled ᶜAbd al-Qādir to re-equip, pay and feed his *niẓām-i cedīd* corps which he would otherwise have had to disband.[65] Makhzan policy appeared to have paid off when Bugeaud returned to France and the *armée de l'Afrique* turned to the pacification of the eastern region of Constantine rather than Oran. The main French military effort of winter 1836 was Clauzel's unsuccessful campaign to capture the city of Constantine, the seat of Aḥmad Bey, leader of resistance in the east.

ᶜAbd al-Qādir maintained the alliance for different reasons. Although his subjects had demanded that he prove himself in the jihad, steady French encroachment into the interior during the war significantly reduced his support and his resource base. ᶜAlawī material aid was essential and Mawlay ᶜAbd al-Raḥmān's moral backing an important source of legitimation. The value of the sultan's support emerged when ᶜAbd al-Qādir returned to the perpetual task of consolidating his authority in west and central Algeria in the second half of 1836. His major problems were the secession of tribes to the French to protect their lands and goods and the refusal of the shaykhs of the religious brotherhoods to accept his authority. In order to justify military action against such tribes, he sent an embassy to the sultan with a series of legal questions in which he appealed to the Fāsī *ᶜulamā'* to confirm his legitimate right to demand communal participation in the jihad; to collect extraordinary war taxes; to attack those who supplied the French or gave them information; and to consider those who opposed him as rebels, (*bughāt*) whose wealth was forfeit.[66] In effect ᶜAbd al-Qādir was asking for a *fatwa* confirming that, as the sultan's representative, he was the only legitimate source of political authority in west Algeria and that his opponents could be treated as rebels against Islamic order in the ᶜAlawī mode.

The embassy, headed by Muḥammad b. ᶜAbd Allah al-Saqāt, set off in late 1836. Mawlay ᶜAbd al-Raḥmān received it warmly and passed ᶜAbd al-Qādir's questions to one of the foremost *ᶜulamā'* in Fes, ᶜAlī al-Tasūlī. Al-Tasūlī's lengthy reply is preserved in the *Tuḥfat al-zā'ir* and an important nineteenth century *fatwa* collection, the *Miᶜyār*. Like Mawlay ᶜAbd al-Raḥmān's earlier letter, al-Tasūlī's *fatwa* gave ᶜAbd al-Qādir the encouragement he sought, but qualified it by stressing that he derived his authority from his submission to the ᶜAlawī sultan. He achieved this by addressing him not as '*amīr*' or '*mujāhid*' but as '*nā'ib al-imām*', the deputy of the imam, Mawlay ᶜAbd al-Raḥmān, who was himself God's deputy. He then answered ᶜAbd al-Qādir's questions on the status of his opponents in two parts: a first part which expressed the sharifian state's ideological response to internal dissidence, and a second part which defined the rights and responsibilities of the state and its subjects with respect to leadership of the jihad and participation in it.

In the first part of the *fatwa* al-Tasūlī stated that both the imam and those who held power from him had the same right to punish those who threatened the well-being of the Muslim *umma*. Crimes (*fasād*) against the *umma* included harbouring spies for the infidel, trading with the infidel in prohibited commodities such as metals, weapons and foodstuffs, banditry and unspecified violations of 'the rights of God servants'. Alliance with those who were guilty of such dissidence was also a punishable offence. Al-Tasūlī's comments on the state response to *fasād* formed a prelude to the second part of the *fatwa* which emphasised the religio-political nature of government in the western Maghrib.

He began by stating that the imam had a divinely imposed responsibility to maintain the Sharīᶜa since communal failure to adhere to it would lead to the destruction of the faith. An aspect of this task was leadership of holy war and the executive right to decide when the *umma* was spiritually and militarily competent to fight. In contrast to the widely held view that Muslims had an individual responsibility to wage a defensive jihad, al-Tasūlī argued that their responsibility was dependent on authorisation from the imam. Conversely, failure to fight when God's representative on earth commanded it was a form of rebellion (*maᶜṣiya*) against God. Refusal to pay extraordinary taxes to raise and provision a Muslim army similarly transformed a Muslim into a rebel (*bāghī qaṭᶜan*) and entitled the state to fight him and seize his wealth. Although reserving the state's right to decide when a jihad was appropriate and thus allowing the possibility of state truces, al-Tasūlī denied the legitimacy of pacts between Muslims and infidels when Muslims were under attack. He also insisted that Muslims living under infidel rule should migrate to Muslim controlled territory.[67]

Al-Tasūlī's *fatwa* gave ᶜAbd al-Qādir the religious backing he sought for his perennial struggle against dissidents and publicly confirmed his association with Mawlay ᶜAbd al-Raḥmān, albeit as a servant within the ᶜAlawī hierarchy. The nature of their relationship was underscored by the gifts which the sultan sent with the *fatwa*: seven cloaks of investiture and richly caparisoned horses for ᶜAbd al-Qādir's regional governors, other horses and artillery. He also deposited 10,000 mithqals with ᶜAbd al-Qādir's commercial agent in Fes, al-Ḥājj al-Ṭālib b. Jallūn, for the purchase of munitions.[68] These gifts located ᶜAbd al-Qādir and his officers within the ᶜAlawī governmental structure but stressed that ᶜAlawī support was primarily for prosecution of the jihad.

Late 1836 was a point of concurrence between Mawlay ᶜAbd al-Raḥmān and ᶜAbd al-Qādir but tensions existed below the surface. Although ᶜAbd al-Qādir was deferential in his correspondence with Mawlay ᶜAbd al-Raḥmān, his use of symbols of sharifian sovereignty such as the imperial parasol and his adoption of the title '*amīr al-mu'minīn*' in correspondence with non-Muslim powers suggested ambitions beyond the bounds of his alliance with the sultan. The European consuls in Tanger suspected that the sultan believed that if ᶜAbd al-Qādir was successful in Algeria he would launch a bid for power further west:

> However the Moors of this country might appear to rejoice in the successes of their Algerine neighbours against the French, the Sultan Mulai Abd Errachman was very jealous of the great marabout Abd-el-Kader – inasmuch as it was well known that the marabout's purpose was to make his way if possible, through feat of arms in Tlemsan to the throne of Fes.[69]

It was thus of great importance to Mawlay ᶜAbd al-Raḥmān that ᶜAbd al-Qādir should remain at war with France. By 1837, however, ᶜAbd al-Qādir and his subjects were war weary and eager to come to terms with the French. Their first overtures to the authorities in Oran were rejected but in March General Bugeaud returned to Algeria with instructions to either destroy ᶜAbd al-Qādir or force him to accept French sovereignty in order to release French forces for a new campaign against Constantine in the east. Bugeaud decided to negotiate with ᶜAbd al-Qādir rather than continue the war. In late May the two sides agreed the terms of the Tafna treaty which came into force a month later. Like the Desmichels treaty the Tafna treaty existed in two distinct versions, one Arabic and one French, intended to satisfy two different audiences. In the French version, ᶜAbd al-Qādir accepted French sovereignty and agreed to suspend hostilities whilst the French made their second assault on Constantine. In the Arabic version, Bugeaud recognised ᶜAbd al-Qādir as the ruler of the old Turkish provinces of Oran and Titteri and agreed to withdraw the French garrison from Tlemsen and terminate French relations with the Dawā'ir and Zmāla. In a clause kept secret from the French government he also promised to sell ᶜAbd al-Qādir 3,000 rifles and bayonets and 100,000 pounds of gunpowder.[70]

The ᶜAlawī sultan's initial reaction to the Tafna treaty was similar to his reaction to the Desmichels negotiations. He immediately suspended the transfer and trade in munitions and other supplies to ᶜAbd al-Qādir and made their resumption conditional upon the renewal of hostilities within Algeria. At this point Mawlay ᶜAbd al-Raḥmān probably not only feared ᶜAbd al-Qādir's transformation into a French client but his possible use of French backing to attack the sultanate. He was mollified, however, by the positive effect of the Tafna treaty upon public opinion within his domains. The French withdrawal from Tlemsen and Rashgun in July 1837 led to public celebrations across the sultanate and the continued involvement of the French in eastern Algeria relieved popular fears of a French attack.[71] In addition, ᶜAbd al-Qādir made no move to exploit the peace by invading the sultanate. Instead both he and Mawlay ᶜAbd al-Raḥmān used the breathing space created by the Tafna treaty to stabilise their respective domestic positions.

For ᶜAbd al-Qādir this meant a new round of hostilities against domestic rivals including the Tijāniyya religious brotherhood based at ᶜAyn Madi on the edge of the Sahara. By the late 1830s the viability of ᶜAbd al-Qādir's state depended upon his ability to reach an accommodation with the French and surmount the political divisions within the area he pertained to rule. The refusal of the shaykhs of the Tijāniyya and other religious brotherhoods to put their religious authority behind ᶜAbd al-Qādir, however, made political unification of the region virtually impossible. The aloofness of the Tijāniyya was especially problematic since the shaykh of the brotherhood was extremely prestigious and Tijānī tribes controlled much of the western Algerian pre-Sahara, an area of strategic importance for ᶜAbd al-Qādir as the French pushed southwards from the coast. He therefore took the gamble of forcing the Tijāniyya into submission in 1838 during the post-Tafna peace. The gamble failed: ᶜAyn Madi closed its gates to ᶜAbd al-Qādir and the ensuing seige dragged on for eight months at the end of which Muḥammad al-Tijānī chose exile over recognition of ᶜAbd al-Qādir's authority. The refusal of the Tijāniyya to recognise him, coupled with his failure to defeat them, severely tarnished his reputation.

For Mawlay ᶜAbd al-Raḥmān domestic consolidation entailed initiatives to improve his own jihad credentials and strengthen the ᶜAlawī military machine in the context of possible war with either ᶜAbd al-Qādir or the French. During summer 1837 he began to prepare an offensive against the Spanish-held enclave of Ceuta. Although the French consul feared that the Ceuta campaign would be a trial run for fresh ᶜAlawī involvement in Algeria, it is likely that Mawlay ᶜAbd al-Raḥmān simply hoped for a personal military victory to show that he was as much of a *mujāhid* as ᶜAbd al-Qādir.[72] In the event he was dissuaded from attacking Ceuta by the possibility that the British or French might intervene on behalf of Spain. News of the French capture of Constantine was another disincentive to engaging with a European power: Constantine was well-known for its unassailable location and strong fortifications and its fall increased ᶜAlawī respect for French, and by extension European, military might.[73]

Makhzan concern about the military capabilities of European powers translated into a programme of military reorganisation to fill the gap created by the demotion of the Udāyā five years before. In a letter to the governor of Tanger and Laraish, the sultan stated that a strong army was essential to defend the faith but that the ᶜAbīd corps had degenerated and ᶜAlawī contingents from the southern heartlands of the dynasty were reluctant to serve in the north. The letter's unstated implication was that the jihad in Algeria had generated a need for a strong force in the north which could not be met by the southern army. Mawlay ᶜAbd al-Raḥmān's solution was to rationalise the internal command structure of his most important corps, the ᶜAbīd al-Bukhārī, and reinvigorate it by admitting new recruits. First, he ordered the governor of Tanger and Laraish to make sure that all ᶜAbīd units had a commander (*qā'id*) and their full complement of one hundred men divided into four sub-units of twenty five men, each headed by a captain.[74] A month later he ordered the governor to search the Gharb and Jbala regions for members of the ᶜAbīd and their descendants who were living 'hidden' among the tribesmen, conscript them and resettle them in the countryside outside Laraish alongside the exiled Udāyā.[75]

These rather cryptic orders suggest a Makhzan initiative to requisition black agricultural labourers in the north reminiscent of Mawlay Ismāᶜīl's attempt to recruit ᶜAbīd in a similar way in the 1690s. Although Mawlay ᶜAbd al-Raḥmān ordered a search for renegade ᶜAbīd it is unlikely that sufficient numbers of deserters existed to boost the corps, despite the fact that some garrisons had certainly melted into the local population during the eighteenth century. The likely target of Mawlay ᶜAbd al-Raḥmān's recruitment drive were thus black servitors and slave labourers working on the estates of religious brotherhoods such as the Wazzāniyya on the tenuous assumption that their ancestors must have been sharifian slaves. Local communities and Makhzan officials, however, proved equally reluctant to co-operate and Makhzan efforts to increase the size of the ᶜAbīd corps without significant financial outlay failed. The project nonetheless marked the moment when the Makhzan started to become aware of its military weakness and need to address the problem in view of the smouldering conflict in Algeria.

Mawlay ᶜAbd al-Raḥmān's recognition of European military strength coupled with ᶜAbd al-Qādir's substitution of warfare for the Tafna peace led to a new shift in their attitudes towards each other. Although the Makhzan allowed the resumption of convoys of munitions from the sultanate to ᶜAbd al-Qādir in 1838, their correspondence showed a growing caution on the part of the sultan contrasted with greater eagerness for the alliance on the part of the *amīr*. ᶜAbd al-Qādir's keenness to associate himself with the sultan reflected his desire to compensate for the blow to his religious prestige struck by the stubborn resistance of the Tijāniyya at ᶜAyn Madi. He also wished to get the sultan's backing to negotiate an undertaking with the French government that the provisions of the Tafna treaty would be honoured by the military command in Algiers. He therefore sent his brother, Muḥammad al-Saᶜīd, head of the Qādiriyya, to Mawlay ᶜAbd al-Raḥmān with a new communication. In this letter, ᶜAbd al-Qādir fell back on the relationship formed between Muḥyī al-Dīn and the Makhzan in the early 1830s, a relationship in which the marabout had put his religious prestige at the service of the ᶜAlawī dynasty without assuming a formal political role. He claimed that he had subdued western Algeria – and also by implication attacked the Tijāniyya – on behalf of the ᶜAlawī sultan and now wished to hand over political control of the region to a member of the ᶜAlawī family so that he could retire to a life of religious contemplation.[76] He simultaneously tried to make Mawlay ᶜAbd al-Raḥmān responsible for his relations with the French by asking his permission to send a representative to Paris.[77]

Mawlay ᶜAbd al-Raḥmān handled the situation adroitly in a reply to ᶜAbd al-Qādir which praised his efforts but denied any ᶜAlawī responsibility for Algerian affairs.[78] He achieved this by picking up ᶜAbd al-Qādir's reference to his religious aspirations and again framing his response as that of a Sufi master to his disciple, a ploy which enabled him to ignore the political aspect of their alliance. The sultan began by addressing ᶜAbd al-Qādir as:

> Our son who has unified the *umma* and illuminated our dark troubles by the light of his sincerity, protector of Islam and the Muslims, the commander and *mujāhid*.

He then insisted that ᶜAbd al-Qādir had a religious obligation in his self-appointed role as *mujāhid* to continue fighting the French. Furthermore, he reminded him that he did not need to seek religious retreat to gain spiritual rewards since in man's relationship with God intention (*niyya*) is all and if he acted for the greater glory of God, even in the politico-military sphere, he would reap the rewards. He also gave guarded approval to ᶜAbd al-Qādir's wish to send a representative to France. Mawlay ᶜAbd al-Raḥmān had clearly grown wary of the Algerian morass and was seeking the best of both worlds, disengagement coupled with prestige. The mission nevertheless partially achieved ᶜAbd al-Qādir's aims by securing the maintenance of his supply line through the sultanate and complimenting his integrity and actions, despite his campaign against the Tijāniyya.[79]

In the wake of this mission to Mawlay ᶜAbd al-Raḥmān, ᶜAbd al-Qādir sent his trusted lieutenant, Milūd b. ᶜArrāsh, to Paris to inform the government of violations of the Tafna treaty by Governor-General Vallée and discuss the real possibilities of indigenous–French accommodation in Algeria. Milūd b. ᶜArrāsh was well received but it was obvious that Paris did not intend to support ᶜAbd al-Qādir against the military authorities in Algeria.[80] Governor-General Vallée had virtual *carte blanche* and on Milūd b. ᶜArrāsh's return to Algiers he refused to let him pass back into ᶜAbd al-Qādir's zone without signing a revision of the Tafna treaty.[81] ᶜAbd al-Qādir rejected the revision but realised that the co-existence of indigenous and French authority in Algeria would not last and that French power would only increase. He also realised that despite the danger of renewed conflict with the French, his best chance to prevent their encroachment into territory he regarded as his lay in an immediate offensive.

In preparation for a resumption of the jihad, ᶜAbd al-Qādir sent a new set of questions to the Fāsī *ᶜulamā'* with the aim of drawing a clear line between his supporters and indigenous allies of the French by defining the former as Muslims and the latter as apostates. His questions were conveyed to the sultan in spring 1839 by two experienced emissaries, his brother Muḥammad al-Saᶜīd and Muḥammad al-Saqāt. They also asked for renewed confirmation of ᶜAbd al-Qādir's role as ᶜAlawī *khalīfa* and military aid so that he could resume the jihad.[82] Mawlay ᶜAbd al-Raḥmān forwarded his questions to the *qāḍī* of Fes, Mawlay ᶜAbd al-Hādī. His ensuing *fatwa* sounded a much more cautious note than al-Tasūlī's earlier ruling. He substituted ᶜAlawī ideology that rebellion was equivalent to apostasy with a more conventional statement that Muslims should be wary of accusing other Muslims of apostasy and even more wary of attacking or killing them. In fact, he argued that in the case of alliance with the infidel it was preferable to shun those culpable than kill them since it was a lesser sin to allow an apostate to live than to kill a Muslim.[83]

Despite Mawlay ᶜAbd al-Hādī's reluctance to authorise ᶜAbd al-Qādir to wage jihad against *fasād*, the news that he was about to restart the jihad was enthusiatically received by the population of the northern sultanate who began to call him by his father's title, Muḥyī al-Dīn, 'Reviver of Religion'.[84] He also enjoyed considerable support in high Makhzan circles, counting among his devotees marabouts, ᶜAlawī ministers, one of the sultan's wives and members of the ᶜAlawī lineage.[85] Mawlay ᶜAbd al-Raḥmān himself, distrustful as ever of ᶜAbd al-Qādir's ultimate objectives, probably preferred to see him involved in an unequal struggle with the French than at peace with them and in a position to become a political threat. In any case, he had little choice but to support ᶜAbd al-Qādir's jihad initiative. He sent him a set of ceremonial robes of the kind bestowed upon Makhzan officers at their appointment to confirm that he was indeed his servant and authorised the sale of weapons from Makhzan stores to his commercial agents. At the same time the most important of these agents, al-Ḥājj al-Ṭālib b. Jallūn, started to purchase British weapons from the Gibraltar garrison, a sale condoned by the British who viewed ᶜAbd al-Qādir as a useful thorn in the side of the French.[86]

War between the French and ᶜAbd al-Qādir resumed in October 1839. It was precipitated by the passage of a French column led by Governor-General Vallée and the Duc d'Orléans from Algiers to Constantine through territory which ᶜAbd al-Qādir considered his by the terms of the Tafna treaty. ᶜAbd al-Qādir reacted to this deliberately provocative act by informing the French military authorities that he viewed it as an act of war and would respond accordingly. He followed this declaration, which the French failed to take seriously, with a spectacular raid on the Mitija Plain outside Algiers, the heart of the nascent colony of *l'Algérie française*. His *niẓām-i cedīd* corps and tribal cavalry swept across the plain killing European colonists, burning their farms and stealing their cattle. The raid was as successful as it was unexpected and shocked the French out of their complacency. Their response was to finally launch an all-out war to conquer Algeria after nearly a decade of indecision.

Whether ᶜAbd al-Qādir realised the seriousness of the impending war or not, he was aware of the unequal nature of conflict with the French unless he could bring the ᶜAlawī sultanate into the fray. Immediately after the Mitija raid, he wrote to Sīdī Muḥammad in Fes to inform the Makhzan of his victory, plead for further military supplies and reiterate his argument of the previous year that the lands he had subdued had capitulated not to him but to the ᶜAlawī sultan who thus had an obligation to expell the French from them.[87] His object was to use the impetus created by the raid to draw the sultanate into a jihad which was now no longer an issue of negotiating boundaries between French and indigenous spheres of authority but a war for control of Algeria.

He was partly successful: the resumption of war initiated a burst of activity in the northern sultanate in support of the jihad and the participation of Rif tribesmen in western Algeria. However, the sultan was keenly aware of the danger of French reprisals and increasingly tried to reorient popular desire to fight the infidel towards garrisoning the ᶜAlawī heartlands rather than ᶜAbd al-Qādir's zone. This change in emphasis naturally affected their alliance and brought Mawlay ᶜAbd al-Raḥmān slowly to a position, ironically similar to that of the French, that Algeria was a separate territory to the sultanate and that ᶜAlawī subjects had no business intervening in the war to the east. This eventually put him at odds not only with ᶜAbd al-Qādir who insisted that Muslims had a common obligation to defend the *dār al-islām*, but also with many of his own subjects who upheld the same view. The gulf between the sultan and his subjects was not fully evident until 1844 but it opened during the early 1840s as the conflict between ᶜAbd al-Qādir and the French escalated to encompass the northern sultanate.

5

THE ᶜALAWĪ JIHAD DURING THE FRENCH WAR TO CONQUER ALGERIA, 1839–45

The resumption of the war in Algeria in 1839 initiated a period in which the sultanate as a whole perceived itself to be at war with France and the north actively participated in ᶜAbd al-Qādir's jihad. When hostilities restarted donations poured into the coffers of ᶜAbd al-Qādir's commercial agents in Fes and many Rif tribesmen joined him. This placed considerable pressure on Mawlay ᶜAbd al-Raḥmān to fulfil his obligations to lead the community against the infidel. He initially discharged these obligations by the usual means: support for the arms and supply trade through the northern sultanate to ᶜAbd al-Qādir. However, the resulting French demands for ᶜAlawī neutrality and their relentless advance towards the sultanate brought the war to the sultan's door. As popular fears of a French attack intensified, Mawlay ᶜAbd al-Raḥmān was forced to respond more fully to the expectations which his role as a *mujāhid*–sultan aroused. He deregulated the arms trade to allow coastal tribes to prepare themselves adequately and commanded annual mobilisations to prevent the expected French landing. Such mobilisations reflected a common will to defend the *dār al-islām* from the infidel, but for the sultan the real issue was no longer assistance to ᶜAbd al-Qādir but defence of the ᶜAlawī patrimony.

This change in emphasis gradually destroyed the unity of state and society. Despite the collapse of ᶜAbd al-Qādir's state in Algeria, his careful propaganda ensured that Mawlay ᶜAbd al-Raḥmān's subjects continued to see him as a dedicated and successful *mujāhid* and to view the sultan's insistence on domestic defence as tantamount to a failure to sufficiently assist him. Popular dissatisfaction was compounded by the expense and disruption to daily life incurred by the annual military mobilisations and the frustrations aroused in the absence of actual engagement with the infidel. As the consensus between the sultan and his subjects unravelled, he and his son, Sīdī Muḥammad, fell back on the theocratic constructs developed by his predecessor, Mawlay Sulaymān, and used by ᶜAbd al-Qādir during the 1830s: the right of the sultan to decide when jihad was appropriate and lead it and the obligation for subjects to obey their sultan as the Shadow of God on Earth or expose themselves to a sultanic jihad against their *fasād*. The moment for the Makhzan to prove the righteousness of its cause came in 1844 when the French finally attacked the sultanate. The spectacular defeat of the ᶜAlawī army provoked a political collapse and the rise of ᶜAbd al-Qādir's star as a serious challenger for the position of sharifian sultan.

The first mobilisations

When news of ᶜAbd al-Qādir's successful attack on the Mitija plain reached the sultanate it was received with jubilation and immediate activity to assist, characterised by the French consul as a resurgence of fanaticism.[1] Gifts of horses, pack animals, grain and other provisions poured into Fes where Sīdī Muḥammad organised their conveyance to ᶜAbd al-Qādir. The flood of pious donations was matched by an intensification of the arms trade as local merchants, eager to exploit the war's commercial potential, started to import European rifles and gunpowder which joined the other commodities carried from Fes to ᶜAbd al-Qādir.[2] Although the weapons trade was not new it gained international import at this point due to the participation of foreigners. Most of those involved were British merchants and adventurers, whose activities were tacitly condoned by a British government keen to undermine France's imperial ambitions and Jewish merchants from Tunis with contacts throughout the Mediterranean. All liaised with ᶜAbd al-Qādir's agents in Fes and many also received Makhzan support for their operations.

The first conclusive reference to direct European involvement in the arms trade dates to February 1840 when a group of unidentified Europeans arrived in Tetuan with cases of rifles for ᶜAbd al-Qādir. Mawlay ᶜAbd al-Raḥmān authorised their passage to the war zone but insisted that the Makhzan deliver the rifles.[3] Such incidents became commonplace over the next few years. Foremost among the Jewish merchants involved in the arms trade were Natale Manucci and Isaac Cardozo from Tunis. Natale Manucci worked for ᶜAbd al-Qādir throughout the early 1840s as a commercial agent and roving diplomat, enlisting support where he could. During 1840 he not only arranged the purchase of British rifles in Gibraltar for ᶜAbd al-Qādir using funds processed by the Makhzan, but also approached European officers in Spain left without commissions after the conclusion of the civil war and offered them generous wages to serve with ᶜAbd al-Qādir.[4] His activities were instrumental in recruiting an English officer, Captain James Scott, who subsequently published his memoirs which helped romanticise ᶜAbd al-Qādir's cause in Britain.

The liveliness of the arms trade did not escape the attention of the French consul, De Nion, who protested to the Makhzan that ᶜAbd al-Qādir's ability to restart the war was largely due to the aid he had received from the sultanate over the previous years.[5] Mawlay ᶜAbd al-Raḥmān countered by reminding De Nion that the French had themselves given ᶜAbd al-Qādir weapons and ammunition after both the Desmichels and Tafna treaties.[6] Interestingly, in his reply to the French consul, the sultan described ᶜAbd al-Qādir as a danger to stability in the sultanate as well as in Algeria, the first extant statement of this kind. The sultan's domestic policy, however, remained dictated by ᶜAbd al-Qādir's popularity and his subjects' expectations that a French attack on the north was imminent.

During spring of 1840, he ordered the first of several annual tribal mobilisations for war in the northern provinces. The first phase primarily affected the hinterland of Tanger, the 'City of the Consuls', and appeared to be a performance directed against the European consular community. The governor warned Europeans to remain indoors for the *ᶜīd al-aḍḥā* celebrations in late February during which tribesmen from the Rif and Jbala poured into Tanger and shot at several consular residences.[7] Simultaneously, Mawlay ᶜAbd al-Raḥmān informed the French consul that he would try to prevent his subjects joining ᶜAbd al-Qādir but that their wish to assist a man fighting for his faith and country was natural.[8] Further domestic preparations for war followed as rumours of an impending conflict with France circulated.[9] Preparations included the repair of Tanger and Tetuan's sea defences, the distribution of extra money to their garrisons, regular drills by the artillery corps of Tanger and a rise in northern rifle production.[10] The sultan also prohibited the export of livestock to French Algeria.[11] In June he dispatched extra troops to Wajda to guard the frontier zone,[12] authorised tribal chiefs in the northwest to prepare their men for jihad and raised controls on the importation of arms and ammunition to enable the tribesmen to arm themselves.[13] The lifting of the usually tight Makhzan controls on weapon imports indicated that the sultan thought that the dangers of a French attack, or failure to adequately prepare for it, outweighed the risks of public disorder which accompanied tribal armament.

While Mawlay ᶜAbd al-Raḥmān's domestic policy focused on aiding ᶜAbd al-Qādir and preparing for a French offensive against the sultanate, he also became receptive to the prospect of alliance with other Muslim powers fearful of European expansionism. In early 1840 a colourful character called Nādir Bey arrived in Tanger, claiming to be a relative of the Ottoman sultan. He was rapidly discredited as a Polish imposter but not before Mawlay ᶜAbd al-Raḥmān had publicised his visit as an Ottoman initiative to create closer links between the two regimes.[14] Although the consuls speculated that the Ottomans wanted ᶜAlawī help against ᶜAbd al-Qādir as a usurper of their authority, it was more important for Mawlay ᶜAbd al-Raḥmān to use the visit to suggest the existence of an Ottoman–ᶜAlawī alliance against the French.[15] Soon after the Nādir Bey incident an envoy from Tunis visited the sultan, generating speculation that the Ḥusaynid beys wished to ally with him to discourage French encroachment on their respective territories.[16]

Despite Mawlay ᶜAbd al-Raḥmān's extensive preparations, the French did not attack. ᶜAbd al-Qādir's Fāsī contact, al-Ḥājj al-Ṭālib b. Jallūn, asserted that an offensive had not transpired because the French were fully engaged with ᶜAbd al-Qādir but if they captured Tlemsen they would advance on Fes via the Taza corridor. To avoid this, Makhzan policy shifted from garrisoning the coast to supplying ᶜAbd al-Qādir and mobilising the northeastern tribes to assist him. The Makhzan put al-Ḥājj al-Ṭālib b. Jallūn in charge of the supply operation and issued orders to border commanders that tribesmen from the Angād, Aḥlāf and Banū Saᶜīd should be allowed to join ᶜAbd al-Qādir if they wished and provided with weapons from the Makhzan store in Wajda.[17] This partially obviated the discontent of mobilised tribesmen who had paid their own expenses and resented being obliged to guard the sultanate rather than join ᶜAbd al-Qādir. During summer 1840, the *qā'id* of the Aḥlāf, Bu Zayyān b. al-Shāwī, established closer links with ᶜAbd al-Qādir's governor of Tlemsen, Bū Ḥamīdī, and together they mobilised the tribesmen of the Muluwiya basin for service with ᶜAbd al-Qādir.[18]

The Makhzan maintained its policy of backing the Muslim resistance to keep France occupied in Algeria until unrelated diplomatic incidents involving France persuaded Mawlay ᶜAbd al-Raḥmān that the war in Algeria did not completely preclude French expansion into the sultanate and that he must devote at least a proportion of his resources to guarding his own domains. Both incidents occurred in the south. First, reports reached the sultan of French initiatives to build a fortified trading post on the coast at Wad Nun without Makhzan permission.[19] This breach of ᶜAlawī sovereignty was compounded by a dispute between the French consul in Essawira and the port's Makhzan governor over the status of an Algerian refugee. The dispute escalated into a scuffle during which Makhzan troops manhandled two French residents. The consul temporarily closed the consulate and enlisted the aid of the senior French consul in Tanger.[20] De Nion wrote a complaint to Mawlay ᶜAbd al-Raḥmān which not only criticised the behaviour of the governor of Essawira but also warned that if ᶜAlawī aid to ᶜAbd al-Qādir continued France would consider Morocco an enemy power.[21] This sparked rumours that the French government intended to send a diplomatic mission or even a war fleet to further protest about ᶜAlawī involvement in Algeria. The British press in London and Gibraltar was certain that a war was imminent and published reports to that effect.[22]

These rumours compounded Makhzan feelings of an irreparable rupture with France and the need to prepare for war as well as support ᶜAbd al-Qādir. Spring 1841 thus witnessed a replay of the 1840 mobilisations. During the *ᶜīd al-aḍḥā* celebrations in February, tribesmen from the Rif, Jbala and Gharb again poured into Tanger and opened fire on consular residences to express their hostility towards the 'Nazarenes'.[23] In the north the Makhzan called upon the tribes to mobilise for the jihad, distributed gunpowder to them and allowed ᶜAbd al-Qādir's emissaries to circulate freely calling for jihad volunteers.[24] These mobilisations were accompanied by considerable internal disorder as a result of the uncontrollable hostility towards Christians which they unleashed among the tribes. In addition, the Makhzan faced ᶜAbīd insubordination because the economic strain of supporting ᶜAbd al-Qādir and mobilising the country had left the state barely able to pay their salaries.[25]

Within the Makhzan itself the different groupings of the 1830s crystallised into three main factions: a Tanger-based faction which advocated accommodation with European powers; the pro-jihad administration in Fes headed by the sultan's son, Sīdī Muḥammad; and a Marrakesh party which considered neutrality and minimal contact with Europe the best policy. The disunity within the Makhzan became evident during the 1841 mobilisations when the governor of Tanger, Bu Silhām, admitted to the British consul that, although the sultan and Sīdī Muḥammad supposed that the tribesmen's presence would 'impress the Christians with wholesome awe', he was worried about their disruptive behaviour.[26] Furthermore he asked Drummond Hay how he should suggest the sultan respond to France's protests about aid to ᶜAbd al-Qādir.[27] The consul warned him that the sultanate's continued independence depended on Mawlay ᶜAbd al-Raḥmān reassessing his relations with European powers and adopting a 'generous and conciliatory' tone in his dealings with them.[28]

Although logical, popular anti-Christian feeling was too strong for the generous and conciliatory tone Drummond Hay suggested to be a viable option. The sultan was in no position to allow himself to be seen as a friend of France. An insight into the atmosphere comes from the memoirs of Captain Scott, the English officer enlisted to assist ᶜAbd al-Qādir by Natale Manucci in 1840. Scott first attempted to join ᶜAbd al-Qādir in September 1840 when he arrived in Tanger intending to travel across the sultanate to ᶜAbd al-Qādir's base at Tagdempt on the edge of the Sahara. He was deterred by Drummond Hay but returned in February 1841 determined to carry through his plan. Before proceeding east he met up with Natale Manucci and a small party of Europeans who had already arrived in Tetuan.[29] The entire group waited for Makhzan permission and then set off along the trade route east wearing local dress to make them less conspicuous.[30]

Scott's account reveals the depth of popular antipathy to Europeans aroused by France's struggle with ᶜAbd al-Qādir, the degree of ᶜAlawī help he enjoyed, and the conflicting demands which jihad obligations and French calls for neutrality placed upon Mawlay ᶜAbd al-Raḥmān. Scott was struck by the overt hostility of the Rif tribes to 'Christian dogs', including his own party, and the inability of the Makhzan to control it. He also commented on the operation of the Fez–Taza–Tlemsen trade route and the close liaison between the Makhzan and ᶜAbd al-Qādir's men in the frontier zone. As a result of this liaison, he reported, Mawlay ᶜAbd al-Raḥmān had actually ceded the land between the Muluwiya and Tafna rivers to ᶜAbd al-Qādir.[31] He analysed the relationship between Mawlay ᶜAbd al-Raḥmān and ᶜAbd al-Qādir in much the same terms as the Makhzan, stating that the sultan viewed the *amīr* as the commander-in-chief of his jihad forces.[32] Although ᶜAbd al-Qādir claimed greater autonomy that such a title suggested, styling himself 'sultan' according to Scott, he too recognised the hierarchy of power which existed between himself and Mawlay ᶜAbd al-Raḥmān, whom Scott described as 'emperor'. At the least, ᶜAbd al-Qādir found it expedient to treat him with respect and gratitude in order to maintain his supply line.[33] For the sultan's part, Scott believed that ᶜAbd al-Qādir's popularity in the sultanate actually made it impossible for him to do as the French demanded:

> Are they [the French] aware that the Emperor is bound by the ties of his religion to protect the Emir? And that whatever excuses the Emperor (not being possessed of a martial spirit) may be induced to offer in order to avoid an open rupture with them, yet he would rather chose the latter alternative than attempt any violence or attach any blame whatever to the

> Emir, who is considered the champion of his religion; for under these circumstances he would be joined by the whole of Morocco against the Emperor, and the result would in all probability be a transfer of that sceptre to more martial hands.[34]

The passage of Europeans from Tanger and Tetuan to ᶜAbd al-Qādir bought the simmering crisis between France and the sultanate to a head. Shortly before Scott's arrival, the French informed Mawlay ᶜAbd al-Raḥmān that if he allowed ᶜAbd al-Qādir's European supporters to travel through the sultanate they would declare war on him. The conviction of the Europeans in Gibraltar and Tanger that the French would at last attack conveyed the gravity of the situation to the Makhzan. As Scott pointed out, however, it was not feasible for Mawlay ᶜAbd al-Raḥmān to simply abandon his alliance with ᶜAbd al-Qādir. In fact, the intensification of French threats against the sultanate only strengthened popular support for a jihad unbounded by the territorial divisions which the French insisted existed.

In order to reconcile these conflicting demands, Mawlay ᶜAbd al-Raḥmān attempted to revert to more clandestine support of ᶜAbd al-Qādir and bring the supply route under closer Makhzan control. For him the problem was not assistance to ᶜAbd al-Qādir, which was still a political imperative, but the obvious involvement of Europeans and foreign agents.[35] He, therefore, cancelled permission previously given to Manucci to reside in the sultanate and ordered the governor of Tetuan, Muḥammad Ashᶜāsh, to apprehend Europeans arriving in the port and send them back to Gibraltar. Five officers who arrived in Tetuan in March with supplies of gunpowder for ᶜAbd al-Qādir were duly deported.[36] The sultan suspected that the French gained their information from renegades, or spies posing as renegades, and therefore sent orders to the governors of the northern provinces to apprehend any such persons found in their areas and send them to him in chains.[37] By May 1841 fifteen were in custody.[38] At the same time the Makhzan opened negotiations with the French and agreed to sell them livestock to provision the army in Algeria in return for peace.[39]

The collapse of consensus and the rise of '*fasād*'

The spring 1841 crisis was a turning point for Mawlay ᶜAbd al-Raḥmān and ᶜAbd al-Qādir. Although both remained committed to the jihad, they henceforth interpreted its meaning differently and the inherent tension in their relationship emerged. As ᶜAbd al-Qādir started to retreat westwards and France's military capabilities became more obvious, Mawlay ᶜAbd al-Raḥmān ceased to believe that assisting him was the best way to prevent a French offensive against the sultanate. Conversely, as his resource base diminished, ᶜAbd al-Qādir's requests for Makhzan aid became more strident. They were well publicised and widely supported in the sultanate. This concordance between ᶜAbd al-Qādir's demands and northern public opinion posed a grave political danger to Mawlay ᶜAbd al-Raḥmān and forced him to sway back and forth between capitulating to the French and satisfying his subjects' wishes that he support the jihad. The result was an inconsistent policy which pleased no-one and a growing gulf between the sultan on the one hand and his subjects and ᶜAbd al-Qādir on the other.

Within weeks of granting the French livestock export licences popular pressure forced the Makhzan to revoke them. Drummond Hay reported that ᶜAbd al-Qādir had rebuked the sultan for selling provisions to 'the common enemies of their faith', and that he had revoked the licences, fearing 'greater unpopularity among his own people' if he failed to heed the rebuke.[40] Although the trade would have helped ease the strain put on the Makhzan treasury by two seasons of military mobilisations, the demands of ideology outweighed those of economy. Nonetheless, the Makhzan's priority over summer 1841 was to improve relations with France rather than assist ᶜAbd al-Qādir. The Makhzan ceased supplying him with munitions and the volume of trade between Fes and Tlemsen slowed.[41] When the French consul paid a visit to Essawira in July, scene of the winter clash between Makhzan and consular authorities, Sīdī Muḥammad paid special attention to him.[42]

This stance had to be adjusted as French successes in Algeria drove refugees into the sultanate. In particular, the arrival of refugees from Mascara, which had fallen to the French in late May, heightened popular awareness of ᶜAbd al-Qādir's dire need for reinforcements and created a gulf between the position of the sultan and his subjects. There were popular demonstrations of support for ᶜAbd al-Qādir and concomitant criticism of the sultan's failure to adequately help him, as well as collections of money and provisions for the refugees in mosques and marketplaces.[43] As a result, Mawlay ᶜAbd al-Raḥmān felt obliged to renew his commitment to supplying ᶜAbd al-Qādir and by August fresh convoys were on their way to Tlemsen.[44]

In a vain attempt to distract attention from the Algerian theatre of war, the sultan launched an initiative against illegal Rif trading in provisions to Spain. He ordered the governor of Tetuan to patrol the Rif coast with the Makhzan's few seaworthy ships and act against tribes known to be involved in smuggling.[45] This initiative did more harm than good: instead of stopping Rīfī boats the ᶜAlawī patrol impounded a Spanish felucca in October 1841, triggering Spanish recriminations. The prospect of a Spanish attack prompted the sultan to order the imams of the mosques in Tetuan province to preach that a Muslim's foremost religious obligation was to wage jihad.[46] These sermons exacerbated the popular clamour for war in the north which the sultan needed to quell.

Over the winter of 1841–2, domestic calls for more active ᶜAlawī participation in ᶜAbd al-Qādir's jihad turned into rebellion and the Franco–Algerian war spilled into the northeastern sultanate. Internal discontent manifested itself in Tafilalt, the ᶜAlawī dynasty's ancestral home, where the sons of Mawlay Sulaymān launched a revolt against their cousin. The trigger to revolt was Mawlay ᶜAbd al-Raḥmān's reduction of his relatives' allowances by three-quarters to improve his finances. The sultan's penuriousness provoked an angry reaction from Mawlay al-Ṭayyib b. Sulaymān who seized control of Tafilalt's citadel. In alliance with his siblings and many southern tribes, he then transformed the complaint about pensions into a wider movement against Mawlay ᶜAbd al-Raḥmān's policies in general and his reluctance to lead the jihad, in particular. Rumours reached the consuls in Tanger that he was in league with ᶜAbd al-Qādir.[47] Mawlay ᶜAbd al-Raḥmān managed to confine the revolt to Tafilalt but he could not recapture the citadel and he was eventually forced to come to terms with his cousins and make one of them, Mawlay al-Ḥasan, governor.[48]

Whilst this small drama was enacted in Tafilalt, the conflict between the French and ᶜAbd al-Qādir moved into the territory that the ᶜAlawī sultan claimed as his own. By early 1842 ᶜAbd al-Qādir had lost his towns and created a mobile centre of operations known as the Zmāla, a vast tent city able to move within hours to avoid French columns. The Zmāla travelled widely and in early 1842 arrived near Tlemsen to defend it from advancing French forces. The presence of both ᶜAbd al-Qādir and the French in the area provoked the same reaction as Clauzel's 1835 campaign – immediate tribal mobilisation to join the jihad. This time the sultan begged ᶜAbd al-Qādir to leave the region, but instead he exploited popular antipathy to the 'infidel' to recruit among the Rif and Angad tribes. He also sent jihad propagandists to solicit support in the eastern and southern sultanate.[49] In January he forcibly dissuaded tribes around Nedroma from capitulating to the French with the assistance of Rif auxiliaries. Soon after he retreated to Wajda with several Algerian tribes to prepare a new offensive against the French.[50] Reports of his retreat across the Tafna river, which the French considered the border, led to demands from the French consul that Mawlay ᶜAbd al-Raḥmān close the border or, if ᶜAbd al-Qādir was in ᶜAlawī territory, force him to abandon the jihad and retire to another part of the sultanate.[51]

ᶜAbd al-Qādir's use of ᶜAlawī territory as a refuge and recruiting ground marked the definitive transfer of the conflict to the sultanate and the transformation of the conceptual state of war which had existed since 1840 into a real, albeit limited, war in the northeast. Growing numbers of Rif tribesmen gathered to observe French movements between Tlemsen and Wajda and when a French column advanced to the small shrine of Lalla Maghnia near Wajda, a joint force of Rif tribesmen, Makhzan troops and Algerians repelled it.[52] Meanwhile auxiliaries from border tribes joined ᶜAbd al-Qādir in several engagements around Tlemsen, harrying French columns involved in constructing border forts.[53] The intensification of border hostilities and the ensuing French protests impelled Mawlay ᶜAbd al-Raḥmān to initiate a third season of coastal mobilisations which as usual involved sermons on the merits of participating in the jihad, distribution of gunpowder and arms and repair of seaward defences.[54]

Whether ᶜAbd al-Qādir was in Algeria or the sultanate, ᶜAlawī involvement in the conflict was now a *fait accompli* for which Mawlay ᶜAbd al-Raḥmān was blamed by both supporters and opponents of the jihad. On the one hand, ᶜAbd al-Qādir's supporters saw the movement of the jihad west as a reflection of the sultan's lukewarm commitment over the previous years. On the other hand, proponants of peace blamed the situation upon the sultan's failure to maintain strict neutrality.[55]

Meanwhile the French asserted that they did not intend to invade the sultanate but insisted that the sultan reduce the troop presence on the border and punish the governor of Wajda, Bū Zayyān, for assisting ʿAbd al-Qādir.[56] In a letter to the sultan, De Nion attempted to ally the French and the Makhzan as two sovereign powers both troubled by the activities of ʿAbd al-Qādir whom he characterised as an instigator of civil strife (*fitna*) rather than a holy warrior. Although Mawlay ʿAbd al-Raḥmān was not ready to recast ʿAbd al-Qādir as a rebel at this time, the French consul's argument prefigured the ideological line which the Makhzan would later take to delegitimise him.

Mawlay ʿAbd al-Raḥmān responded to the French protest with the same tactics of dissimulation and limited compliance as in earlier years. In his reply to the consul he denied Makhzan involvement in border skirmishing and shirked responsibility for Rīfī participation in it on the grounds that the Rif tribes had customarily been beyond the political reach of both the Makhzan and the Turks of Algiers.[57] On the contrary, he insisted, the Makhzan garrison at Wajda was endeavouring to hold the tribes in check but French trespass upon their land, a reference to the French advance on Lalla Maghnia, naturally provoked them.
Nonetheless, he took steps to reduce th... ...rison to a few hundred men
and move tribal auxili... ...though the French were not
... the military commanders
... ...ation in the jihad and thus

... ...ol the border *mujāhidīn*
... ...uthorise punitive actions
... ...rily eased in April when
... ...his return to the Rif in
... ...rench immediately sent
... ...tan to prove that he was
... ...es and forcing ʿAbd al-
... in the jihad was not
... ...r the authority of the
... ...an oppose them. The
... ...te of alert in coastal
... the establishment of
... In the ports of the
... ...had which generated
... ...ropean warships.[64]
... ...y at a time when
... ...for the jihad were
... ...ials.[65] Their anxi-
... ...s the sultan made
... ...tic political risk,
... ...Britain in the process.
... ...rummond Hay approached the sultan's chief

THE WAY OF SALVATION

What must I do to be saved? *Saved from what?* What is it you wish to be saved from? Hell? That proves nothing. Nobody wants to go there. The issue between God and man is SIN. Do you wish to be saved from it? WHAT IS SIN? Sin is a species of rebellion against God. It is self-pleasing; it is the utter ignoring of God's claims,—being completely indifferent whether my conduct pleases or displeases Him.

Before God saves a man, He convicts him of his sinnership. By this I do not mean that he says with everybody else, "Oh yes, we are all sinners, I know that." Rather do I mean that the Holy Spirit makes me feel in my heart that I have been a life-long rebel against God, and that my sins are so many, so great, so black, that I have transgressed beyond the reach of divine mercy.

Have *you* ever had that experience? Have *you* seen yourself to be totally unfit for heaven, and for the presence of a Holy God? Do *you* now perceive that there is no good thing in you, nothing good credited to your account, that all the way through you have loved the things God hates and hated the things God loves?

Has the realization of this *broken your heart* before God? Has it made you *mourn* that you have so despised His mercies, misused His blessings, broken His sabbaths, neglected His Word, and given Him no real place at all in your thoughts, affections and life? If you have not yet seen and felt this minister, Muḥammad b. Idrīs to offer the Makhzan advice on how to weather the crisis. After some hesitation, Mawlay ᶜAbd al-Raḥmān permitted Drummond Hay to visit Meknes and meet Muḥammad b. Idrīs.[66] The mission took place in June 1842. The discussions between the consul and Muḥammad b. Idrīs revolved around the problem which lay at the heart of the continuous disputes between France and the sultanate over ᶜAbd al-Qādir: how the sultan could reconcile his traditional religio-political obligations with alien European concepts of territorial sovereignty and neutrality.

Drummond Hay repeated Britain's earlier advice that Mawlay ᶜAbd al-Raḥmān should be conciliatory in his dealings with France. In reply, Muḥammad b. Idrīs reiterated that the sultan, as imam of the community, was under tremendous pressure to resist French demands. Not only could he not personally renounce the jihad, but he had to encourage his subjects to fulfil 'so essential a point of their religion'. Although Islamic law made the maintenance of truces, even with infidel powers, a religious obligation, the public considered the French to have themselves violated the truce by trespassing upon the land of the Lalla Maghnia shrine. This had created a consensus for war not only among the general public but also the *ᶜulamā'*. Mawlay ᶜAbd al-Raḥmān's attempts to go against this surge of popular feeling and prevent acts of aggression against the French had led to:

> Complaints, outcries, resistance and applications [from his subjects] displaying an asperity of hostile disposition, following one other in multitudes, uttering threats and menaces, bringing forward arguments from the Oolamma … in support of their representations, urging that it is the duty of the chiefs to go to the Holy War.[67]

Mawlay ᶜAbd al-Raḥmān nonetheless tried to respond to British advice. Muḥammad b. Idrīs assured Drummond Hay that the Makhzan was not personally involved in supplying ᶜAbd al-Qādir, and it subsequently took steps to further limit trade in arms and supplies from Fes. The sultan issued orders that no merchants, muleteers or soldiers should approach the border zone beyond Wajda. If they did they would incur penalties including corporal punishment, life imprisonment and confiscation of their property.[68] These measures were badly received by the population but insufficient to satisfy the French who now called on the Makhzan to agree to a firm demarcation of the ᶜAlawī–Algerian border as a prelude to its closure.[69]

As Mawlay ᶜAbd al-Raḥmān considered his response to this new demand, he was offered an Ottoman straw which he grasped eagerly. The straw took the form of the arrival of Yūsuf Badr al-Dīn al-Madanī, an official Ottoman envoy bearing a letter from Sultan Abdülmecid in August 1842.[70] The Ottomans faced their own problems as they tried to modernise the empire by implementing the Tanzimat reforms and stave off European encroachment. They had lost significant territories in the north to Russia and Egypt had gained *de facto* autonomy under

Muḥammad ᶜAlī. The combination of territorial losses to the infidel and a distinctly secular modernisation programme had raised issues of Ottoman legitimacy which Abdülmecid, like Mawlay ᶜAbd al-Raḥmān, tried to address through a demonstration of Muslim solidarity against the infidel. His letter emphasised the brotherhood of all Muslims and their responsibility to aid each other and offered Mawlay ᶜAbd al-Raḥmān whatever artillery, provisions or instructors he required to prepare his subjects for jihad.

Abdülmecid's letter provided Mawlay ᶜAbd al-Raḥmān with an opportunity to divert attention from ᶜAbd al-Qādir and gain the prestige of an alliance with a major Muslim power. He widely publicised the contents of the letter and ordered the Makhzan artillery corps in Tanger and other towns to fire cannon salutes to celebrate the formation of an ᶜAlawī–Ottoman alliance against the infidel.[71] Since Ottoman aid for a Mediterranean jihad was not actually forthcoming, however, his efforts fell on stony ground and his subjects continued to view support for ᶜAbd al-Qādir rather than domestic mobilisation as his foremost religious obligation. He therefore met the French demand for demarcation of the border with a refusal.[72] The French had not expected a positive response and did not pursue the matter at this time.

As the likelihood of a French offensive receded, popular dissatisfaction with Makhzan policy again manifested itself in rebellion. Like the Tafilalt rebellion of the previous winter, insurgency in autumn 1842 involved the sons of Mawlay Sulaymān. This time the instigator was Mawlay ᶜAbd al-Raḥmān b. Sulaymān who was extremely popular among the ᶜAbīd and had a history of opposition to his cousin and support for ᶜAbd al-Qādir. Although based in Meknes, Mawlay ᶜAbd al-Raḥmān b. Sulaymān was in close contact with his ᶜAlawī relatives in Tafilalt and represented the war party within the ᶜAlawī lineage. His fellow conspirators, the commander of the ᶜAbīd, Ibn al-ᶜAwwād, and al-Ṭayyib al-Bayyāz, also sympathised with ᶜAbd al-Qādir and had grievances against the sultan. Al-Ṭayyib al-Bayyāz was a member of the Fāsī *shurafā'* and, although a respected Makhzan servant, his first loyalty was to Fes. He had been involved in the revolt of Fes in 1821 and now opposed the sultan on the grounds that he should not only support ᶜAbd al-Qādir but also reside in Fes.[73] This indicated that the Fāsī elite felt snubbed by the sultan's preference for living in Marrakesh. Ibn al-ᶜAwwād meanwhile shared the grievances of the rest of the ᶜAbīd corps over their irregularly paid salaries.

The separate complaints of the conspirators contributed to a common feeling that the sultan had betrayed the trust put in him by his subjects, a betrayal most glaringly demonstrated in his failure to fully support ᶜAbd al-Qādir. To rectify the situation they formented a plot to assassinate him.[74] The sultan, forewarned of the conspiracy, had both Mawlay ᶜAbd al-Raḥmān b. Sulaymān and Ibn al-ᶜAwwād imprisoned. In response the ᶜAbīd staged daily protests outside the prison.[75] To calm the situation, Mawlay ᶜAbd al-Raḥmān distributed a generous sum to them for *ᶜīd al-fiṭr* in November and transferred Ibn al-ᶜAwwād to the Makhzan prison in Tanger.[76] The commander's transfer provoked further ᶜAbīd demonstrations which forced Mawlay ᶜAbd al-Raḥmān to flee from Meknes to Fes. In Fes he was greeted by remonstrances from merchants and partisans about his cutting of the supply line to ᶜAbd al-Qādir.[77] These complaints were accompanied by pleas from ᶜAbd al-Qādir himself that the sultan release arms and ammunition stockpiled for him in Fes and permit the supply trade to resume. The connection between support for ᶜAbd al-Qādir and what the sultan considered *fasād* against himself, however, rendered him unsympathetic. Instead of releasing the goods, Mawlay ᶜAbd al-Raḥmān impounded them.

The nature of opposition in 1841 and 1842 indicated the steady development of a faction with an ideological stance similar to that of Mawlay Sulaymān's opponents between 1818 and 1822. Despite its connections with the ᶜAlawī house and Tafilalt, the opposition was primarily northern and Fes-based and considered the sultan to have failed in his military obligations. The solution, from the opposition's perspective, was to replace Mawlay ᶜAbd al-Raḥmān with a more martial member of the ᶜAlawī lineage who would renew aid to ᶜAbd al-Qādir and actively lead a jihad against the French. The opposition saw their cause as a righteous struggle against a corrupt sultan, in other words, societal jihad against sultanic *fasād*, an ideological interpretation aided by their association with ᶜAbd al-Qādir and the jihad against the French. Although the opposition did not put ᶜAbd al-Qādir forward as a candidate for rule, his Idrīsī ancestry combined with the high degree of Idrīsī support for the movement suggested that such a development was only one small step away. From late 1842 onwards, Mawlay ᶜAbd al-Raḥmān therefore started to view support for ᶜAbd al-Qādir as *de facto* opposition to himself and, in effect, as *fasād* against the ᶜAlawī state.

This unravelling of the consensus between the sultan and his subjects began to affect Makhzan policy in 1843 when the struggle in Algeria reached a new level of intensity and ᶜAbd al-Qādir needed ᶜAlawī aid more urgently than ever. By the start of the spring 1843 campaigning season the French logistical advantage over him was considerable. The *armée de l'Afrique* was continually replenished by new recruits from France, all the towns were in French hands and General Bugeaud had copied the Algerian method of provisioning. His troops now travelled as lightly as the tribesmen and fed themselves by stealing grain from the underground hoards of the tribes. French destruction of villages and trees, slaughter of livestock and murder of women and children had undermined the will of many tribes to resist and ᶜAbd al-Qādir could no longer count on his support across the Algerian countryside. The offensive launched by Bugeaud in April 1843 proved to be decisive. In May the Zmāla was tracked down and destroyed and by the end of the year the campaign had turned into what Bugeaud described as a *chouannerie*, a manhunt, in which ᶜAbd al-Qādir was almost captured and the nucleus of his army all but destroyed.

During the same period the French also endeavoured to consolidate their position in the border area. Tlemsen and nearby Nedroma now served as French bases and columns from both towns regularly marched into the border area opposed by Rif tribesmen and displaced Algerians, often commanded by ᶜAbd al-Qādir's former governor of Tlemsen, Bū Ḥamīdī.[78] A major incident occurred in March 1843 when Bū Ḥamīdī and Makhzan troops from Wajda attacked a column commanded by General Bedeau who pursued his assailants deep into the sultanate.[79] Mawlay ᶜAbd al-Raḥmān's subjects saw it as the prelude to a French invasion and began to purchase extra rifles in preparation. Officially, the Makhzan denounced Bedeau's actions as a violation of ᶜAlawī sovereignty. Unofficially, both the Makhzan and European consular authorities believed that Bū Ḥamīdī had orchestrated the clash to stir up popular hostility towards the French and force Mawlay ᶜAbd al-Raḥmān to war. It was thus a further indication of *fasād*.

When the French military in Algeria chose to view the incident as an ᶜAlawī declaration of war and made the usual protests accompanied by the dispatch of warships to Tanger, Mawlay ᶜAbd al-Raḥmān countered by criticising French violations of the border but also took active steps to reassert control in the area.[80] He ordered the dispatch of fresh reinforcements to Wajda, the preparation of a task force which Makhzan authorities in Tanger assumed was to take action against the border tribes and repair of the Makhzan citadel in Taza.[81] Although such preparations were perhaps designed to deter a French advance along the Taza corridor, they coincided with rumours that ᶜAbd al-Qādir was in the southeast assembling volunteers for an offensive against Tlemsen assisted by Mawlay al-Ḥasan, the ᶜAlawī governor of Tafilalt.[82] To keep support for ᶜAbd al-Qādir alive, his partisans circulated reports of largely fictional victories to conceal his almost total defeat. The destruction of the Zmāla and the French capture of many of ᶜAbd al-Qādir's relatives, for instance, was reported as a minor setback.[83] This made it impossible for the sultan to regain control.

The generals in Algeria repeated that they would advance into the sultanate unless the issue of tribal assistance to ᶜAbd al-Qādir was resolved. Drummond Hay counselled caution, warning the governor of Tanger, Bu Silhām, that incitement of the tribes by exaggerated rumours of ᶜAbd al-Qādir's 'victories' was self-defeating since the French had pledged to conquer Algeria and his minor successes would be of little avail against 'a large and highly disciplined army, sustained by the wealth of a powerful nation'.[84] ᶜAlawī assistance to ᶜAbd al-Qādir simply made a French attack on the sultanate more likely. Drummond Hay, however, offered no solution to the actual dilemma faced by Mawlay ᶜAbd al-Raḥmān, the fact that domestic political discourse did not admit a Makhzan policy which publicly put pragmatic considerations before jihad. As Drummond Hay himself recognised, Makhzan control over the population was minimal and if the sultan openly opposed the Algerian jihad he would risk a more serious rebellion than the small revolts he had already weathered. He had little option but to tolerate the activities of ᶜAbd al-Qādir's Fāsī suppliers, the border tribes and Algerian refugees as his support base narrowed.

Despite his tolerance, Mawlay ᶜAbd al-Raḥmān soon faced another deposition attempt. This time the plot was hatched in the highest Makhzan circles. The main conspirator was the sultan's chief minister, Muḥammad b. Idrīs, who appears to have concocted a plan to do away with the sultan during a summer campaign against the Zammūr Berbers. Before hostilities commenced, the sultan offered the tribe a settlement using the mediation of the head of the Wazzāniyya brotherhood, al-Ḥājj al-ᶜArabī. When the Zammūr rejected the settlement it seems that Muḥammad b. Idrīs approached them suggesting that he would order the Makhzan forces not to engage if the Zammūr would capture the sultan when they charged the Makhzan camp.[85] Muḥammad b. Idrīs duly issued orders under sultanic seal commanding the Makhzan troops to remain at ease whilst the Zammūr advanced.[86] The plot was thwarted when the commander of the Zayyān auxiliaries challenged the orders. The perplexed sultan summoned the other commanders and found that they had received similar orders. He ordered an immediate charge against the surprised Zammūr contingents who beat a hasty retreat.[87] Muḥammad b. Idrīs subsequently pleaded that he had misunderstood the sultan's own instructions and Mawlay ᶜAbd al-Raḥmān allowed him to return to his duties.[88] It was rumoured, however, that Muḥammad b. Idrīs had hoped to overthrow the sultan and make himself or someone else sultan in his place. The reason was again said to be the sultan's lukewarm devotion to ᶜAbd al-Qādir and the jihad, represented by his failure to reside in Fes.

Throughout summer 1843, ᶜAbd al-Qādir and his supporters maintained pressure on Mawlay ᶜAbd al-Raḥmān for money, arms and ammunition, and his brothers promoted his cause in the Rif, probably using Qādirī networks. In September the shattered remnants of the Zmāla, now known as the Dā'ira, crossed into the sultanate. Bū Ḥamīdī and other leaders organised the refugees and local tribesmen into raiding parties which struck at French positions across the frontier.[89] As a result the French consul demanded that Mawlay ᶜAbd al-Raḥmān forcibly remove the Algerians from the frontier zone and accept a firm demarcation of the border.[90] The sultan's reply to the French was as usual evasive but the heightened activity of ᶜAbd al-Qādir's partisans elicited an unusually swift and blunt response from him. He informed ᶜAbd al-Qādir's Makhzan supporters that his priority was to restore domestic unity against those bent on rebellion (*fasād*) and that he lacked the resources to help ᶜAbd al-Qādir fight the French as well.[91] He then had twenty of ᶜAbd al-Qādir's Fāsī supporters arrested on suspicion of plotting against him.[92] His actions were tantamount to an admission that jihad against *fasād* was more important than an offensive against the French and ᶜAbd al-Qādir himself remonstrated with a letter containing 'une mélange bizarre de supplications, de reproches et de menaces'.[93]

To have his ideological stance accepted, Mawlay ᶜAbd al-Raḥmān had to improve his popular standing. To this end he combined his interpretation of support for ᶜAbd al-Qādir as *fasād* with measures to move Algerian refugees away from the border and resettle them elsewhere in the sultanate. Refugee communities consisted of tribal groups which had moved into the sultanate to avoid French reprisals, individuals from Algerian towns and the Dā'ira. Most had a much truer sense of what jihad against the infidel meant than the inhabitants of the sultanate and were exhausted by years of war. Some also considered ᶜAbd al-Qādir's obsession with resistance as pointless. In general, they responded positively to

Makhzan resettlement initiatives which entailed offers of land, houses and tax relief to those who left the border. For instance, a party including ᶜAbd al-Qādir's nephew went to Marrakesh in autumn 1843 to ask the sultan for asylum. He welcomed them and gave them letters to the Makhzan authorities in Fes instructing the latter to take care of them.[94] In the following years resettlement became a major component of Makhzan strategy against the jihad party, serving both to decrease the number of fighters in the northeast and gain the sultan religious credit for aiding Muslims who had left their land to escape infidel domination.

Mawlay ᶜAbd al-Raḥmān's attitude to ᶜAbd al-Qādir himself remained opaque. In December 1843 ᶜAbd al-Qādir's brother, Muḥammad al-Saᶜīd, and Milūd b. ᶜArrāsh visited the sultan in Marrakesh and Sīdī Muḥammad in Fes to ask for weapons.[95] The Makhzan refused the request but shortly afterwards Bū Zayyān, the governor of Wajda, was sent to the Jazira prison in Essawira.[96] It was rumoured that his arrest was a concession to ᶜAbd al-Qādir's envoys and the *parti fanatique*.[97] The fact that Bū Zayyān had been illegally exporting grain to French Algeria contributed to speculation that the jihad party had sought his dismissal. His replacement, al-ᶜArabī al-Qabībī, was certainly a firm supporter of the jihad and had assisted ᶜAbd al-Qādir against General Clauzel in 1835–6. On the other hand Bū Zayyān had a record of co-operation with Algerian refugees. Makhzan policy is perhaps best interpreted as an effort to decrease aid to ᶜAbd al-Qādir for operations within Algeria, but maintain a strong military presence in the northeast from where a French offensive now seemed most likely to come.

The lax discipline of the Makhzan armies, however, and the keenness of the border tribes to participate in Algerian raiding parties meant that the maintenance of a strong military presence near the border involved continual raiding into French territory at a time when France was no longer prepared to tolerate such activity.[98] By winter 1843–4 the French military in Algeria considered the war of conquest over and believed that closure of the border with the sultanate was necessary for internal stability.[99] The French consul therefore informed the governor of Tanger that his government would no longer accept ᶜAlawī hospitality to ᶜAbd al-Qādir and his followers and considered a border demarcation essential.[100] The time for Makhzan prevarication was almost past but Bū Silhām, the governor of Tanger, shrugged off the French demands stating that it was religiously unacceptable for the Makhzan to arrest Muslim asylum-seekers or take action against ᶜAbd al-Qādir because they were neither ᶜAlawī subjects nor resident in the sultanate.[101] At the same time the sultanate's fragile relations with Spain took a turn for the worse. The Spanish had a number of grievances against the sultanate including tribal violations of the *cordon sanitaire* around Ceuta and maritime disputes. Then Makhzan authorities ordered the execution of a Jew under Spanish protection who had unwisely provoked a Muslim crowd in al-Jadida and shot at a Makhzan soldier. Strong Spanish protests joined the perennial French complaints, triggering a fourth season of tribal mobilisations. This time they led inexorably to war.

The Franco–ᶜAlawī war of 1844

The reasons why hostilities eventually broke out in 1844 are not entirely clear but both the French and the Makhzan adopted a more aggressive and resolute tone than previously. ᶜAbd al-Qādir's virtual defeat had brought the French to the ᶜAlawī frontier and beyond to Lalla Maghnia, only twenty odd miles from Wajda, and they were determined to put a stop to Algerian resistance. ᶜAbd al-Qādir was himself in the area with the conflicting aim of ensuring the survival of the resistance by bringing the sultanate fully into the war. This created a dilemma for Mawlay ᶜAbd al-Raḥmān which was intensified by the French presence on ᶜAlawī land. It is possible that he initially hoped to deter the French by a show of strength but that his own rhetoric and the activities of the border commanders and his son, Sīdī Muḥammad, took the matter out of his hands and precipitated the war. On the other hand, there are indications that the Makhzan now considered a successful jihad to restore sultanic prestige the only way to break the opposition and regain popular allegiance. For the first time since 1830 Mawlay ᶜAbd al-Raḥmān himself overtly talked of an ᶜAlawī offensive to put an end towards French insolence (*jasāra*).[102] The heir-apparent, Sīdī Muḥammad, certainly felt a need to prove himself militarily and replace ᶜAbd al-Qādir in popular affections as representative of the *mujāhid* ideal. The governor of Essawira explained the Makhzan's position to the British vice-consul:

> As it was the will of God that the French should become masters of Blad Islam (the land of Islam) meaning Algiers and its territories, it was not for the Sultan to go against the Divine Will, but that His Majesty would at all risks, to the utmost of the power which the Almighty had given him, protect the inviolability of his own dominions and that His Majesty had decided to resist by force of arms, the least encroachment of the French on his frontiers.[103]

In any case the mobilisations of spring 1844 witnessed an unprecedented military build-up. Sīdī Muḥammad in Fes sent 3,000 extra troops, commanded by ᶜAlī b. al-Ṭayyib al-Gnawī of the ᶜAbīd and Mawlay al-Ma'mūn of the ᶜAlawī lineage, to the northeastern border zone and ordered provincial Makhzan garrisons to send reinforcements of men and artillery to Fes for a border campaign.[104] ᶜAbd al-Qādir was also in the area recruiting tribesmen for raids into French territory. High casualties in many of these raids intensified tribal hostility to the French and the cycle of mobilisations and raids now routine in the Wajda area started to affect tribes further west previously less involved.[105] The ᶜAlawī military build-up in the northeast was matched by a French project to fortify the frontier by constructing forts at Jamiᶜat al-Ghazwat (Nemours) on the coast and at Lalla Maghnia.[106] General Bedeau was entrusted with the project, arousing fears that either he or another ambitious French general might, as Drummond Hay put it:

> Dash at Fas, the heart of wealth and capital of the northern kingdom of this country, which place is utterly defenceless and is not capable of being defended by any number of Moors.[107]

Extensive coastal mobilisations also occurred during spring 1844 to resist a possible Spanish attack in the north and discourage a French naval offensive along the Atlantic seaboard. Fears of an allied Christian European naval offensive were intensified by demands from Scandinavian countries who paid tribute in return for trading rights for a cessation of such payments.[108] In the Rif, mobilisation was directed from Tetuan and primarily involved tribes in the vicinity of Ceuta where tribal incursions into territory claimed by the Spanish led to their reinforcement of the Ceuta garrison. In response, the forts opposite Ceuta were repaired and the sultan ordered Muḥammad Ashᶜāsh, governor of Tetuan, to double the Ceuta patrol, hand out gunpowder to the tribes and distribute money among Makhzan artillerymen and sea captains to ensure their loyalty.[109]

In the neighbouring province of Tanger, all men eligible for military service were called up to patrol the Atlantic coast between Asila and Laraish on a daily basis, beating drums and playing ghaytas.[110] Bū Silhām was also ordered to spread the word among the European consuls in Tanger that auxiliaries from the tribes of the Atlantic plains had been reviewed and each tribe could put 20,000 men into the field.[111] In addition, summons to jihad were announced during the Friday prayer in the great mosques of coastal towns, fanning popular expectations of war to new heights.[112] When a French ship sailed past Laraish in May the guns were immediately manned and local tribes rushed to the shore. Behind al-Jadida, further to the south, 'one line of horsemen stretched along the hills to the distance of at least one mile' occasionally discharging blank rounds.[113]

As in previous years the mobilisation of coastal tribes had a detrimental effort on law and order and raised popular antipathy towards the infidel to levels which the Makhzan could not control. Drummond Hay reported in May 1844 that 'the whole population of Morocco is in a state of great ferment' and that a Spanish or French attack would, 'fan the hot embers into a flame which the Moorish government would be unable to quench'.[114] The French consul also recognised the strength of the popular passions, *haineuses et fanatiques*, released by the possibility of French and Spanish offensives and, although sure that the ᶜAlawī troops were no match for the French, he thought that the Rif tribes would defeat the Spanish if they advanced beyond the perimeters of Ceuta and Melilla.[115] However, popular anger was as likely to be turned against the sultan as against the infidel. For instance, Frederick Redman, a British merchant and representative based in al-Jadida, suspected that the tribes were as likely to murder their governors and pillage the coastal towns as resist a European offensive.[116]

The unprecedented scale of these mobilisations strengthened Makhzan resolve to define internal opposition as a religio-political offence meriting punitive action. The aim was to de-legitimise ᶜAbd al-Qādir's supporters by arguing that they were rending the unity of the *umma* and therefore aiding the French. As the sultanate moved closer to war, Sīdī Muḥammad had several of ᶜAbd al-Qādir's partisans in Fes arrested and transferred to Marrakesh in chains.[117] Mawlay ᶜAbd al-Raḥmān explained his actions in an address to assembled Makhzan officers on the occasion of the *mawlid al-nabī* celebrations. He stated that French trespass on ᶜAlawī territory made it essential for him to deal with traitors who conspired against him and spread unrest, asserting that such men were 'more Christian than the Christians' in their desire to undermine Muslim, in other words Makhzan, authority.[118]

Within the Makhzan a gap started to develop between the stance of the sultan in Marrakesh and Sīdī Muḥammad in Fes. Mawlay ᶜAbd al-Raḥmān, older and wiser than he had been when he decided to intervene in Tlemsen in 1830, began to retract his bold words about teaching the French a lesson. Although sure that the Makhzan armies could defeat the French, he hoped that the extensive mobilisations would deter them from invading and that hostilities could be avoided. Sīdī Muḥammad was likewise convinced of ᶜAlawī military capabilities, believing that the defeat of the Algerian resistance indicated not French military superiority but the inferiority of the Algerian *mujāhidīn* to their ᶜAlawī counterparts. Unlike his father, however, he envisaged an ᶜAlawī offensive to regain Tlemsen unaided by ᶜAbd al-Qādir, hoping that such a campaign would enable him to prove himself as a warrior and improve the prestige of the Makhzan which he hoped to inherit. Conversely, ᶜAbd al-Qādir wanted to draw the sultanate into a joint offensive against the French under his direction.

Among the sultan's subjects' support for a jihad and disparagement of the Makhzan subsisted as two sides of the same coin. The distinction which the Makhzan wished to make between an ᶜAlawī jihad, either defensive or offensive, and ᶜAbd al-Qādir's jihad had little popular resonance. For much of the 1830s the Makhzan had claimed sovereignty over western Algeria and claimed that ᶜAbd al-Qādir was acting as an ᶜAlawī deputy in his struggle against the French. For the majority jihad was still an obligation which transcended political boundaries, especially those imposed by an infidel power within the *dār al-islām*. Although French incursions deeper into ᶜAlawī territory heightened popular anger and expectations of a military initiative from the Makhzan, they did not lead to a distinction between domestic defence and fighting with ᶜAbd al-Qādir.

The descent into full-scale war started in May 1844 and revolved around the French project to build a fort at Lalla Maghnia begun by General Bedeau in April. In the view of the Makhzan and local tribes, Lalla Maghnia was undeniably ᶜAlawī land and its violation by the French was intolerable to all for both secular and religious reasons. On the secular side, construction of the fort trespassed upon ᶜAlawī sovereignty and the land rights of the Banū Yznāsen who had sown crops around the shrine. On the religious side, construction of an infidel fort on land dedicated to Lalla Maghnia, a Muslim saint, was viewed as a profanation of the shrine and its *ḥurm* or sacred territory. The actual *casus belli* was this profanation of a shrine which in effect symbolised France's incursion into the Maghrib.

On 22 May 1844 ᶜAlī al-Gnāwī, ᶜAbīd commander of the Makhzan border re-inforcements, demanded that the French withdraw from the fort. He received no response and the following week a French column made camp on land where Banū Yznāsen crops were growing. The irate tribesmen complained to al-Gnāwī that the French had come to destroy or steal their crops. Al-Gnāwī and Mawlay al-Ma'mūn immediately mobilised the ᶜAbīd in Wajda and, in conjunction with Banū Yznāsen auxiliaries, marched to evacuate the French from their camping ground. Although the Makhzan troops had orders to hold their fire, they and the Banū Yznāsen shot at the French troops who drove them back to Wajda.[119]

The die was effectively cast. Rumours quickly circulated through the sultanate that the French had not only violated the shrine of Lalla Maghnia but also entered Wajda and hanged the Makhzan governor. Although untrue, the attention of the Makhzan and its northern subjects now became trained exclusively on their holy war against the French and ᶜAbd al-Qādir's raids into Algeria became a sideshow.[120] After the clash Mawlay al-Ma'mūn returned to Fes for re-inforcements and extra artillery.[121] Mawlay ᶜAbd al-Raḥmān, meanwhile, informed the governor of Tanger that jihad was no longer a communal responsibility (*farḍ kifāya*) which could be fulfilled by Makhzan forces, but had become the personal responsibility (*farḍ ᶜayn*) of all Muslims, including women and youths. He furthermore compared the plight in which the sultanate found itself to the early Islamic era when the Prophet and his small Muslim army had battled against more numerous pagan forces.[122] The Makhzan's moment to prove the righteousness of its cause had come. The French remained unaware of the eschatological significance with which the Makhzan had invested the impending conflict. General Bugeaud, on his way to the border with reinforcements, laconically stated that the disputed land was not ᶜAlawī territory and that any settlement would have to include a definitive demarcation of the border and the cessation of aid to ᶜAbd al-Qādir.[123]

French–Makhzan correspondence on the incident exhibited the same inconclusive and circular nature as earlier exchanges. When the French protested, Muḥammad b. Idrīs denied that the Makhzan was responsible.[124] Consul De Nion reported to Paris that the problem was that Mawlay ᶜAbd al-Raḥmān was in Marrakesh and therefore too far from Fes and the northeastern border to adequately monitor events. He had thus been persuaded by northern jihadists that a French invasion was imminent and had responded predictably by ordering nationwide preparations for a jihad.[125] De Nion's comments recognised that the sultan and his subjects were primarily concerned with French trespass on their land, but the French military remained preoccupied with ᶜAbd al-Qādir and border demarcation. Shortly before his arrival in the area, General Bugeaud instructed Bedeau to meet with the ᶜAlawī commander, al-Gnāwī, and ascertain the Makhzan's stance towards ᶜAbd al-Qādir. He ordered him to demand the forced resettlement of the Dā'ira away from the border, the repatriation of Algerian tribes, the transfer of ᶜAbd al-Qādir westwards if he was to be found in the sultanate, and finally the demarcation of the border along the Muluwiya river, a more westerly line than the Tafna river which the Makhzan considered the frontier.[126]

Bedeau and al-Gnāwī duly met near the French camp on 15 June but negotiations faltered when al-Gnāwī refused to accept a border demarcation west of the Tafna.[127] Shortly afterwards hostilities broke out between restive tribal auxiliaries and the French cavalry, leaving around two hundred tribesmen dead on the field.[128] The Makhzan forces retreated and the French pursued them to Wajda which Bugeaud entered three days later and then abandoned.[129] After the clash the French submitted an ultimatum to the sultan, backed by threats of naval bombardment.[130] Makhzan authorities in Tanger assured De Nion that the Makhzan desired peace with France and blamed the skirmishes on 'disruptive ill wishers'.[131] Drummond Hay, meanwhile, offered to act as a neutral arbiter between the Makhzan and her enemies, France and Spain, in order to avert a war which Britain feared would not be in her interests. He duly set off for Marrakesh in mid-June to persuade Mawlay ᶜAbd al-Raḥmān to capitulate to French and Spanish demands.[132]

The sultan and Sīdī Muḥammad, however, were in no mood to placate European powers. This engagement was the most serious clash between French and ᶜAlawī forces so far and, despite ᶜAlawī expectations that Makhzan forces would be equal to the challenge, Bedeau's forces had routed them and Bugeaud had entered Wajda unresisted. Both events were sources of deep shame to the Makhzan and rendered any disengagement from the conflict politically suicidal. When news of al-Gnāwī's defeat reached Fes the city went into public mourning and the families of the dead clamoured for vengeance. News of Bugeaud's entry into Wajda stirred up further outcry.[133] Mawlay ᶜAbd al-Raḥmān tried to cloak the humiliation of the Makhzan by implying that the responsibility for the double defeat lay with the entire community not just the Makhzan. He lamented that his subjects used to be a 'splinter in the eye of the enemy' but were now shamed by their failure to obey the imam and their resultant defeats at the hands of the infidel.[134] Unusually harsh punishment was meted out to the Makhzan commanders involved and the border command was handed over to Ḥamīda b. ᶜAlī, supported by reinforcements from the ᶜAbīd and the *jaysh* tribes.[135]

In communication with Bū Silhām in Tanger who was responsible for presenting the Makhzan position to the European consuls, the sultan adopted an uncharacteristically firm tone. He stated that fighting had occurred because the French had transgressed the border, constructed a fort on territory never claimed by the Turks and then ignored Sīdī Muḥammad's demands to desist. He added that his subjects had every right to attack infidels who trespassed upon their land and denied that ᶜAbd al-Qādir was in the area. Furthermore, he accused the French of bribing local tribes to usurp Makhzan sovereignty. At the same time he rejected suggestions that he send an ambassador to Paris to discuss Franco–Moroccan differences and asserted that he would not discuss the demarcation of the border unless the French remained within their territory.[136] Muḥammad b. Idrīs, speaking for Sīdī Muḥammad, adopted a similar stance.[137]

From the perspective of the sultan and Sīdī Muḥammad the most worrying issue was the poor performance of the Makhzan army which augured ill for future engagements with the French. Mawlay ᶜAbd al-Raḥmān demanded an explanation from Sīdī Muḥammad for the poor discipline which had led to the clash and the easy defeat of the troops. In communication with the governor of Tanger he suggested that responsibility lay with the rabble (*awbāsh*) of auxiliaries who had joined the Makhzan troops and troublemakers (*mufsidīn*), possibly a reference to the Algerians.[138] Sīdī Muḥammad, however, blamed the army's archaic organisation and poor command structure. He informed his father that al-Gnāwī underpaid the troops and their commanders neglected to organise and drill them properly, thus increasing the likelihood of their disobedience. He suggested that if the *maḥalla* had been disciplined properly and fought in formation (*ṣaff*), the skirmish would have been of little consequence. His comments represented one of the first calls for military modernisation in the sultanate.

It was not the time, however, for modernisation but for continued mobilisation which now started to affect the interior as well as the northeast and coastal regions. Mawlay ᶜAbd al-Raḥmān in Marrakesh took charge of gathering troops in the south as a prelude to coming north, and ordered Sīdī Muḥammad to gather a *maḥalla* of 30,000 men from the ᶜAbīd and 'all the Moroccan tribes' and then advance from Fes to Taza.[139] Although Jules Mayer, a French *médecin renégat* attached to one of the tribal contingents in the *maḥalla* suggested a more conservative number of troops – 4,000 cavalry, 2,000 infantry, and a seventy-man artillery corps of Spanish renegades – the *maḥalla* was nonetheless of a considerable size.[140] The preparations of the Makhzan were complemented by a huge public effort to supply the border *mujāhidīn*. Drummond Hay reported that the citizens of Fes and surrounding areas were said 'to be spontaneously carrying forage and provisions to the Moorish camp' and 'arming against the Infidels'.[141]

Mawlay ᶜAbd al-Raḥmān accompanied the war preparations with a concerted effort to address the rifts within society. The apparently inevitable conflict with the French enabled him to call for unity under his leadership and take action against dissenters, a jihad against *fasād* as a prelude to jihad against the infidel. He again compared the situation faced by the sultanate to that faced by the Prophet and his followers and insisted that feuding tribes and his opponents should recognise that the French were the real enemy.[142] He also ordered the arrest of partisans of ᶜAbd al-Qādir in Fes whose loyalty to the Makhzan he suspected.[143] By July the Makhzan was committed to using the impending war as a means to resolve the ambiguity in Makhzan–society relations which had surfaced in the previous years but, in fact, ran through the history of the dynasty. Resolution, however, required a Makhzan victory.

During July 1844 British hopes of preventing the war by forcing a settlement on the Makhzan faded. Drummond Hay's mission was unsuccessful and the Prince de Joinville, commander of the waiting naval squadron, sent the sultan an ultimatum. His subsequent evacuation of French citizens from Tanger indicated that the French were no longer bluffing.[144] In the next few days the other Europeans resident in Tanger hastily left for Gibraltar and Algeçiras. The town's customs administrator, Aḥmad al-Razīnī, sent a desperate plea to De Joinville to have mercy and hold his fire.[145] Meanwhile public order broke down as the city's inhabitants panicked and Rīfī tribal contingents ran through the streets looting. When news of the city's plight reached Mawlay ᶜAbd al-Raḥmān he furiously accused the Rif tribes of being possessed by the devil and ordered the city's governor, Bū Silhām, to proceed immediately to Tanger from his residence in Laraish with the Gharb and Jbala tribal contingents.[146] To secure their loyalty, he ordered Bū Silhām to distribute money and gunpowder among them.[147] He also sent Makhzan reinforcements commanded by one of his sons, Mawlay Sulaymān, bringing the number of fighters in the Tanger area to several thousand.

On 6 August 1844 the French opened fire on Tanger. Their intention was not to invade but to destroy the city by means of a naval bombardment. This rendered the Makhzan troop presence useless. The only corps involved was Tanger's small artillery unit but the Makhzan cannon did not have sufficient range to actually strike the French ships![148] The French bombardment lasted for six hours and left much of the port area in flames. The following day Aḥmad al-Razīnī returned to the city to assess the damage. He reported to Mawlay cAbd al-Raḥmān that one of the bastions, the lower harbour and the Makhzan stores had been destroyed, while many buildings had been severely damaged, including the great mosque and neighbouring residences.[149] A week later on 15 August De Joinville bombarded Essawira, the sultanate's main Atlantic port. The bombardment lasted from noon until sunset during which the port's artillery unsuccessfully tried to repel the attack. The French also occupied the Jazira, the offshore island holding the sultanate's highest security prison whose inmates they took into custody.[150] As in Tanger, several sections of the port were destroyed or severely damaged.

The day before the bombardment of Essawira, 14 August 1844, French and cAlawī forces in the northeast finally met on the battlefield. Mawlay cAbd al-Raḥmān had given Sīdī Muḥammad orders to advance to Taza and no further, but the heir-apparent advanced to Wad Isly, a tributary of the Tafna river which passed close to Wajda and Lalla Maghnia.[151] He was accompanied by:

> A very large and volunteer assembly of the Kabeal (tribes) clamorous for a conclusion of their troubles [having] left their crops to spoil on the ground … abandoned their houses and their families [for the jihad].[152]

The arrival of Sīdī Muḥammad and tribal auxiliaries from the interior spoiling for a fight with the infidel destroyed the last shreds of hope for a settlement. Sīdī Muḥammad was young, ambitious and keen to prove himself whilst also teaching the French a lesson, and stirred up the passions of his troops by promising that he would not only lead them victorious to Tlemsen but march all the way to Algiers and drive the French into the sea.[153] In the French camp it was rumoured that he intended to launch 'une veritable croisade pour retablir les affaires de l'Islamisme'.[154] cAbd al-Qādir was also present, calling the tribes of the Angad plain between the Tafna and Muluwiya rivers to jihad. On Sīdī Muḥammad's arrival, cAbd al-Qādir came to offer his advice on how to fight the French, suggesting that he avoid pitched battle and adopt the guerilla tactics which had gained the Algerians most of their victories.

Sīdī Muḥammad and his senior commanders rejected cAbd al-Qādir's advice. The late nineteenth century historian, al-Nāṣirī, says that Sīdī Muḥammad did not accept cAbd al-Qādir's advice because he distrusted his motives, a veiled reference to the suspicions harboured by the Makhzan that ᶜAbd al-Qādir's ultimate aim was not jihad against the infidel but a bid for power in the sultanate.[155] Muḥammad Akansūs, a historian who lived through the events, states that Sīdī Muḥammad accepted ᶜAbd al-Qādir's advice because he was aware of the superiority of French discipline and tactics but that his commanders insisted that anything less than a pitched battle was shameful since their numerical superiority would ensure a victory over the French.[156] However al-Mashrafī, a late nineteenth century Makhzan historian whose grandfather was an ardent supporter of ᶜAbd al-Qādir, asserts that both Sīdī Muḥammad and his commanders feared that if they bowed to ᶜAbd al-Qādir's superior experience of engagement with the French they would have to submit to his command in battle.[157] Clearly the Makhzan assumed that the ᶜAlawī army was equal to French infantry and heavy artillery and was jealous to win an exclusively ᶜAlawī victory without ᶜAbd al-Qādir's interference. The confidence of Sīdī Muḥammad and his forces was augmented by the French forces' apparent reluctance to attack which they attributed to fear and weakness.[158] Their assumptions proved deadly.

On the night before the battle of Isly the ᶜAlawī watch was virtually non-existent and the *maḥalla* remained unaware that the French were preparing for battle until local tribesmen raised the alarm. Sīdī Muḥammad's aide did not consider the information important enough to merit waking him and no preparations for battle were undertaken until dawn when the French were already advancing in battle formation. The two armies were significantly different in character: the French army was relatively small but highly disciplined and trained to fight in formation. It also had a unified chain of command. The much larger ᶜAlawī army was of a traditional type and consisted of discrete Makhzan corps and tribal contingents which responded only to their own chiefs and had no knowledge of tactics other than the traditional charge and retreat. Sīdī Muḥammad presided over his fighters in full sultanic regalia with a small bodyguard.

When the two sides met the French infantry advanced in close formation protected by artillery fire and was able to drive a wedge between the two flanks of the ᶜAlawī cavalry.[159] Initially the ᶜAlawī forces fought well, albeit chaotically, but after a couple of hours Sīdī Muḥammad realised that his conspicuous attire was making him a target for French shots and he withdrew to change. His sudden disappearance led many to assume that he was dead. The Sharārda *jaysh* contingent immediately stopped fighting and went to pillage his treasure chests. Others followed their lead and the ᶜAlawī front rapidly collapsed. The only corps to stand firm were the renegade artillery corps and Sīdī Muḥammad's bodyguard.[160] By midday the battle of Isly was over and 800 ᶜAlawī fighters lay dead on the field.[161] The French army occupied the ᶜAlawī camp and Wajda while Sīdī Muḥammad retreated to Taza where he waited for the remnants of his *maḥalla* which had melted into the countryside after the battle.[162]

During the week of hostilities, Mawlay ᶜAbd al-Raḥmān proceeded from Marrakesh to Rabat. When news of Sīdī Muḥammad's defeat at Isly reached him he hurried to Fes.[163] Shortly afterwards he was informed of the French bombardment of Essawira. His worst fears had been realised: the Makhzan had finally been tested in the jihad and failed. Although better leadership, either at the centre or on the field, might have resulted in a satisfactory defence of the sultanate against the infidel, the army had blundered into a debacle made considerably worse by the bombardments of Tanger and Essawira which the Makhzan had been powerless to resist. The defeats destroyed the reputation of the Makhzan army upon which sultanic authority depended and brought down upon Mawlay ᶜAbd al-Raḥmān's head his gamble of using jihad against the infidel to consolidate the position of the Makhzan in relation to society. He and Sīdī Muḥammad appeared incapable of either waging successful war or defending their subjects. The result was a complete political breakdown as endemic skirmishing among tribes escalated into rebellion across the sultanate. After the bombardment of Tanger, tribesmen poured into the city, pillaging the Jewish Mellah and the empty houses of the consuls and wealthy townsmen who had evacuated the town.[164] A similar breakdown in order occurred in Essawira where the Shiadma tribes devastated the Jewish section and looted other quarters. In the northeast the tribes of the Angad and the Rif attacked retreating Makhzan troops and stole what they could from them.

In the circumstances Mawlay ᶜAbd al-Raḥmān saw no option but to make peace with France. The French too wished to conclude hostilities as they felt that their objective – chastisement of the sultanate for assisting ᶜAbd al-Qādir – had been achieved and that further hostilities could lead to a war with Britain.[165] The government therefore appointed the Duc de Glucksberg to negotiate a truce.[166] The sultan viewed French suggestions of a truce with distrust, suspecting some stratagem which would further damage his position, but he duly appointed Bū Silhām, governor of Tanger, as his negotiator. He, however, informed Bū Silhām that he would dispatch envoys to 'London, Vienna, St. Petersburg and the Ottoman Porte to request the support and mediation of those four great powers' if the French rejected his conditions for peace in a rather belated effort to enrol international support.[167]

The French conditions, submitted to Bū Silhām on 10 September 1844 by De Joinville, the Duc de Glucksberg and De Nion, reiterated the demands made before the war. To secure peace Mawlay ᶜAbd al-Raḥmān had to arrest ᶜAbd al-Qādir, remove him from the border and declare him an outlaw. The French also stipulated that the Wajda garrison should be reduced to 2,000 men, that ᶜAlawī tribes should respect the old Turco–ᶜAlawī frontier and that a joint commission should investigate the exact line of that frontier and fix it by a treaty within six months. In return they would halt hostilities and withdraw from Wajda and the Jazira off Essawira. Finally both sides would effect an exchange of prisoners. Bū Silhām accepted the French conditions and the French and ᶜAlawī negotiators signed the treaty.[168] One copy was forwarded to Paris for ratification and the other to the sultan. The French evacuated Wajda and the Jazira in mid-September, but they retained their prisoners of war until Mawlay ᶜAbd al-Raḥmān signed the treaty and the ratified copies had been exchanged in late October 1844.[169]

At the same time the Makhzan resolved its disputes with Spain and addressed the issue of Scandinavian tribute payments. Intense negotiations between Bū Silhām, the Spanish consul, Antonio Beramendi, Drummond Hay, his son, John Hay and Henry Bulwer, the British ambassador in Madrid, produced a preliminary settlement in September 1844 which averted hostilities with Spain. The Queen of Spain accepted it and a final agreement was reached in 1845.[170] On the tribute issue, the sultan promised Denmark and Sweden that he would make new treaties with them within six months.[171]

Peace with the infidel and jihad against '*fasād*'

In the aftermath of the war, Mawlay ᶜAbd al-Raḥmān represented the defeat of the sultanate by France as a tribulation sent by God which did not signify an infidel victory but rather the necessity of patience, faith and better military preparation on the Muslim side. In correspondence to the people of Essawira, the sultan stated, 'we are afflicted as a result of our sins'.[172] The fact that the Muslims had not been ready, either religiously or militarily, was the responsibility not just of the Makhzan but the entire community which had allowed itself to be divided into true Muslims and rebels (*mufsidīn*). Although he and Sīdī Muḥammad had been ready to defend Islam, they had been thwarted by internal opposition, the tribes quick loss of interest in the jihad and the Makhzan troops disobedience.[173] To underline his point, he ordered the imprisonment of the Makhzan commanders who fought at Isly and the shaving of their beards to symbolise their cowardice.[174]

Mawlay ᶜAbd al-Raḥmān attributed his acceptance of the Treaty of Tanger to the parlous state of Islam in his domains and claimed that those who were true Muslims recognised its necessity to allow the Makhzan to restore central authority by 'closing the door on civil strife (*fitna*) and rebellion (*fasād*)'.[175] He later said that he had signed the treaty because Islam's champions were few and his subjects reluctant to defend their faith.[176] The Qur'anic verse stating that if the enemy inclines towards peace, then the Muslims should agree, especially if a truce will prevent their defeat and allow them to prepare properly for war, gave him some religious justification.[177] The author of the *Ibtisām* explained the Makhzan position:

> The scale of the catastrophe impressed itself upon him [Mawlay ᶜAbd al-Raḥmān] and when he saw the enemy rushing at him from every side and the impotence of all he possessed, when he saw the terror which had seized the Muslims in every part of his domain, both in the countryside and in the towns, and the absence of calls to battle as a result of the weakness of Islam and the insurrections among the tribes and their revolts against their governors in every province, then he inclined towards making a treaty with the enemy of God.[178]

By all accounts Makhzan attempts to blame the defeats of 1844 on communal *fasād* and to religiously justify the Treaty of Tanger were not generally accepted.

Victory of the infidel against the Muslims did indeed suggest to the population the corruption of the body politic but they blamed the ᶜAlawī Makhzan not the community. The prestige of both Mawlay ᶜAbd al-Raḥmān and Sīdī Muḥammad had been almost destroyed. Historic ᶜAlawī use of jihad for political legitimation, Mawlay ᶜAbd al-Raḥmān's early justification of intervention in Tlemsen as a jihad and four years of jihad mobilisation within the sultanate had culminated in a war which the sultan himself depicted as a struggle between good and evil. The defeat of the Makhzan therefore seemed to indicate that God had withdrawn his favour not only from Mawlay ᶜAbd al-Raḥmān but perhaps from the entire ᶜAlawī lineage. The political response of the Makhzan's subjects fell into three categories: first, spontaneous rebellions; second, suggestions that another scion of the ᶜAlawī lineage should replace Mawlay ᶜAbd al-Raḥmān as sultan, the martial Mawlay ᶜAbd al-Raḥmān b. Sulaymān being a prime contender; and third, calls for the replacement of the ᶜAlawī *shurafā'* with an Idrīsī *sharīf* of whom the most popular was the Idrīsī holy warrior, ᶜAbd al-Qādir.

Spontaneous rebellions took the form of rural revolt against Makhzan authority which started with the tribal looting in Tanger and Essawira and went on to affect the entire coastal region between Rabat and Essawira. The conclusion of the Treaty of Tanger in mid-September released Makhzan forces for the task of reasserting sultanic authority. Mawlay ᶜAbd al-Raḥmān chose Sīdī Muḥammad and his brother Mawlay Sulaymān for the task. Sīdī Muḥammad left Fes shortly after it was announced in the mosques that peace with France had been concluded. The first leg of his journey to Rabat indicated the close connection between Makhzan defeat and popular insurrection. As he travelled west, Sīdī Muḥammad found that to avoid attack by local tribes 'for being so shamefully defeated by the Christians', he required the protection of the respected marabout and head of the Wazzāniyya brotherhood, Sīdī al-Ḥājj al-ᶜArabī.[179]

He met Mawlay Sulaymān outside Rabat.[180] Together the brothers commanded several thousand men whom they led south to pacify the countryside, a task for which they were barely fit.[181] Frederick Redman witnessed their arrival in al-Jadida and described them as 'a miserable specimen of Moorish troops, fatigued and reluctant for combat' in contrast to the tribes of the neighbouring Dukkala who swore that they would not submit to Makhzan authority unless forced to do so in battle.[182] In the event Sīdī Muḥammad and Mawlay Sulaymān simply struggled to Marrakesh through hostile country without re-imposing any degree of Makhzan authority. Drummond Hay summed up the causes of the widespread disaffection as maladministration and more importantly:

> Wounded national pride – or as it may rather be deemed here religious pride – at the flower of Islam being overcome of late in several conflicts … with the Christians … these disasters the people attribute to pusillanimity in their sultan, rendering him unworthy to receive that religious homage which this people have been for ages accustomed to pay to their shereefian sovereigns.[183]

Evident popular disparagement of himself and Sīdī Muḥammad led the sultan to fear a coup at the centre. He initially imagined that such a coup would come from among disaffected Idrīsī *shurafā'* or the sons of Mawlay Sulaymān, and was deeply concerned by the presence in the south of two Idrīsī *shurafā'* who had escaped from the Jazira prison in Essawira during its occupation by the French. French sources suggested that Mawlay ᶜAbd al-Raḥmān's fear of an Idrīsī coup reflected the latent resentment of northerners to rule by a southern dynasty, a resentment brought out into the open by Mawlay ᶜAbd al-Raḥmān's prolonged absences from Fes and apparent disinclination to support ᶜAbd al-Qādir who was perceived as a product of the northern Idrīsī milieu. They added that the north–south divide in the sultanate included a racial dimension which juxtaposed the 'whiteness' of the Idrīsī *shurafā'* with the generally dark skin of the ᶜAlawī sultans.[184]

Idrīsī aspirations, however, did not focus on local Idrīsī *shurafā'*, who rarely exhibited sultanic qualities, but on ᶜAbd al-Qādir, who had very clearly demonstrated both martial skill and devotion to religious ideals in the previous years. In Algeria ᶜAbd al-Qādir had supporters and detractors and had faced similar problems of legitimacy to Mawlay ᶜAbd al-Raḥmān, but in the sultanate he was perceived as a selfless holy warrior and man of God dedicated to driving the infidel from Islamic shores. Although he had also signed treaties with the infidel, it was his jihad exploits which filled the imagination of the sultan's subjects and Mawlay ᶜAbd al-Raḥmān and Sīdī Muḥammad were compared unflatteringly to him. The French won a military victory at Isly but the moral victory went to ᶜAbd al-Qādir, who underlined his commitment to the jihad by attacking a French column near Tlemsen while the Makhzan negotiated the Treaty of Tanger.[185]

After the raid he moved into the Rif with the Dā'ira and settled at ᶜAyn Zura west of the Muluwiya river for the winter. His residence in the sultanate made him more politically threatening to Mawlay ᶜAbd al-Raḥmān than ever before. Opposition to the sultan had already become conflated with theoretical adherence to ᶜAbd al-Qādir but now there was the possibility that such a conflation would turn into an actual political challenge. ᶜAbd al-Qādir rapidly built up a following. His immediate entourage included his *niẓāmī* corps of 200–300 men and the Algerian tribes closest to him, the Banū ᶜAmir, Ḥashem and Jaᶜāfra. In addition, his brother, Muḥammad al-Saᶜīd, head of the Qādiriyya, had widespread influence among Qādirī tribes in the Rif which he used for ᶜAbd al-Qādir's benefit. This influence was strongest among the Banū Yznāsen tribe with whom Muḥammad al-Saᶜīd had lived since 1843 but also stretched westwards into the Rif along Qādirī networks. It included sections of the Awlād Settūt, Banū Bū Yaḥyā, Aḥlāf, and Qalᶜaya (Iqāriyen), all of whom were willing to continue the jihad under ᶜAbd al-Qādir's leadership.[186]

The crisis came when the news that Mawlay ᶜAbd al-Raḥmān had signed the Treaty of Tanger became public. On receiving news of the treaty the Rīfī *mujāhidīn* decided to offer ᶜAbd al-Qādir not only military assistance but their political allegiance in recognition of his 'courage, bravery and dedication to the jihad in accordance with the obligations of great rulers'.[187] The danger of secession in the northeast coincided with the reassertion of the Idrīsī jihad faction in Fes who also looked to ᶜAbd al-Qādir to solve the political ills plaguing the sultanate. Several members of the Fāsī elite, including Makhzan officials, sent pleas to ᶜAbd al-Qādir to depose Mawlay ᶜAbd al-Raḥmān and 'ascend the throne of his ancestors', a reference to the iconic Idrīsī dynasty of Fes.[188]

The conjunction between Rīfī and Fāsī aspirations marked a political path for ᶜAbd al-Qādir from ᶜAyn Zura to Fes. He, however, chose not to take it, claiming that it would contravene the Sharīᶜa to depose a fellow sovereign appointed by God. Many years later in Damascus he admitted to his biographer, Charles Henry Churchill, that he refused the allegiance of the Rif and Fes because he doubted that he could ever fully impose his authority over the turbulent tribes of the sultanate.[189] He used his popularity, however, to circulate among the tribes of the eastern marches pleading with them to join the jihad while he begged his brothers, Muḥammad al-Saᶜīd and Muṣṭafā, to do the same in the Rif.

Such activities contravened the sultan's undertaking to the French to keep the peace and they maintained pressure upon him to demarcate the border and fulfil his obligation to declare ᶜAbd al-Qādir an outlaw and detain him. They had fought the war to prevent further ᶜAlawī assistance to ᶜAbd al-Qādir and secure Algeria and refused to find their aims thwarted by the deteriorating political situation in the sultanate. The border demarcation and ᶜAbd al-Qādir's detention, they believed, were crucial to prevent him renewing his raids into Algeria in spring 1845.[190] The sultan responded by appealing to ᶜAbd al-Qādir to retire to Fes or leave the sultanate, viewing him, so Drummond Hay suspected, as 'a secret enemy of his throne and a dangerously designing rival for power', as well as a liability in ᶜAlawī–French relations.[191]

Drummond Hay's estimation of Mawlay ᶜAbd al-Raḥmān's feelings towards ᶜAbd al-Qādir probably came through Bū Silhām who received a letter from the sultan, the contents of which he perhaps intended to be circulated among the European consuls. In the letter, the sultan described ᶜAbd al-Qādir bluntly as an 'enemy of religion' (*ᶜadū'l-dīn*'), a phrase applied to infidels and rebels in Makhzan discourse, and strongly criticised his attack on the French near Tlemsen during the peace negotiations as an irreligious act contravening the word of the imam. While he could not denounce the jihad *per se* nor forcibly eject the Dā'ira from the sultanate for moral reasons, he ordered Bū Silhām to send the deputy-governor of Tanger, Muḥammad b. ᶜAbd al-Ṣādiq, through the Rif with 100 cavalrymen reading out a sharifian statement that ᶜAbd al-Qādir was not a true *mujāhid* if his intention was to stir up dissidence (*fasād*) within the sultanate.[192] In addition to questioning ᶜAbd al-Qādir's motives, Mawlay ᶜAbd al-Raḥmān ordered the Makhzan governors of Taza and Wajda, Qā'id Ḥamdūn and Ḥamīda b. ᶜAlī, to stop him crossing into Algeria if he passed through their provinces.[193]

In January 1845 the Bū Maᶜza revolt broke out in Algeria. General Bugeaud had glibly assumed that the war of conquest was over after the defeat of the Makhzan army at Isly, but the French were not welcome masters and when a Darqāwa shaykh, Muḥammad b. ᶜAbd Allah, alias Bū Maᶜza, began to preach jihad, claiming that he was the awaited *mahdī*, he found a ready audience. The revolt he started soon spread across Algeria, and the French unexpectedly found the land they had assumed was pacified up in arms against them. It would take them over a year to reconquer Algeria. News of the revolt encouraged ᶜAbd al-Qādir and his brothers to intensify their efforts to recruit fighters in the sultanate to return to Algeria and the jihad. By early March ᶜAbd al-Qādir was said to have 700 well-equipped cavalrymen, 500 infantrymen and the allegiance of several ᶜAlawī tribes ready to join the struggle in Algeria.[194]

The outbreak of the revolt and ᶜAbd al-Qādir's obvious intention to get involved put the French on the defensive and persuaded them to press for a speedy demarcation of the border as a preliminary to fortifying and closing it to ᶜAbd al-Qādir. Shortly after the Bū Maᶜza revolt began the French government appointed De la Rue, head of the 1836 mission to Meknes, and Leon Roches, a young French renegade with a good command of Arabic, to negotiate a border demarcation with the sultan's men.[195] For his part, the sultan appointed the governor of Wajda, Ḥamīda b. ᶜAlī, and an official called Aḥmad al-Khaḍir as his negotiators.[196] De la Rue had instructions not only to ascertain and demarcate the frontier line but also to protest to the sultan that he had breached the Treaty of Tanger by allowing ᶜAbd al-Qādir to gather fresh *mujāhidīn* in the Rif.[197]

In a communique from his base in Oran, De la Rue pointed out that Mawlay ᶜAbd al-Raḥmān's constant failure to act against ᶜAbd al-Qādir had damaged his own position as well as that of France. He reminded the sultan that he had warned him in 1836 that if ᶜAbd al-Qādir received ᶜAlawī aid he would at some point use it against him. Now that time had come: ᶜAbd al-Qādir had usurped the role of defender of the faith from the sultan and set himself up in opposition to him claiming that 'he alone cares for religion and the jihad'. The underlying message in De la Rue's letter was that it was in the sultan's interest to arrest ᶜAbd al-Qādir. He backed up this 'advice' with a veiled threat of French military intervention, stating that Algerian border tribes loyal to the French were eager to invade the sultanate and attack ᶜAbd al-Qādir's following.[198]

While De la Rue and Leon Roches began to gather Turkish documentation about the border, Mawlay ᶜAbd al-Raḥmān reacted to the French protest by ordering one of his sons to lead an expedition (*ḥarka*) into the Rif with the stated aim of either interning ᶜAbd al-Qādir or forcing him to leave the sultanate.[199] The sultan was well aware that this was unrealistic since ᶜAbd al-Qādir was camped in an inaccessible mountain region supported by tribes whose loyalty to the Makhzan was formal to say the least. The *ḥarka* served, however, as a useful propaganda exercise which could be interpreted in opposing ways. For the Makhzan, it offered an opportunity to investigate the extent of ᶜAbd al-Qādir's support in the Rif, which the sultan hoped the French would read as commitment to the Treaty of Tanger and his subjects would read as commitment to preventing French encroachment on ᶜAlawī territory. In the meantime his border negotiators, Ḥamīda b. ᶜAlī and Aḥmad al-Khaḍir, made their enquiries as to where the border lay.

Actual negotiations began in February 1845 in Tlemsen while cAbd al-Qādir rallied nearby border tribes for jihad.[200] De la Rue reported that the negotiations were difficult because neither Ḥamīda b. cAlī nor Aḥmad al-Khaḍir knew where the old Turco–cAlawī border had been. This was probably dissimilation on the part of the Makhzan team: Ḥamīda b. cAlī was an experienced border commander and it is highly unlikely that he was unaware where the Makhzan believed the border lay. However, the idea of a firm border line was unfamiliar and the border situation tense because of cAbd al-Qādir's presence which put the cAlawī negotiators under pressure not to cede land to the infidel French. The Makhzan had, in fact, maintained that the Tafna was the frontier since 1701 and had been gradually pushing eastwards since Mawlay Sulaymān's recapture of Wajda from the Turks in 1795. Mawlay cAbd al-Raḥmān's occupation of Tlemsen and appointment of cAlawī deputies in central Algeria between 1830 and 1832 had marked the culmination of cAlawī aspirations to extend their sovereignty eastwards. Although forced to retreat, the Tafna remained the westernmost point which the Makhzan would admit as the border and French movements beyond the Tafna since 1835 had consistently provoked a reaction from the Makhzan and border tribes.[201] Turkish documentation, however, cited the more westerly Muluwiya as the border. It seems likely that the cAlawī sultans and Turkish deys had each regarded the border as the delimitation most advantageous to themselves regardless of the situation 'on the ground', a tribal and often nomadic social structure with fluid political allegiances which rendered the concept of a border-line anomalous.

Such flexibility was possible before 1830 because both regimes were Muslim. In contrast, the non-Muslim status of the French made the border issue much more highly charged. Until 1845 the French maintained the Turkish definition that the Muluwiya was the border, dismissing cAlawī claims that it lay on the Tafna as attempts at territorial aggrandizement.[202] De la Rue, however, opted for a more pragmatic border which coincided with the existing line of French fortifications along the Wad Kis, including the forts of Jamicat al-Ghazwat and Lalla Maghnia.[203] This placed the border between the Muluwiya and Tafna rivers presenting the Makhzan negotiators with an insurmountable problem, an apparent compromise which, nonetheless, confirmed cAlawī loss to the infidel of the land over which the battle of Isly was fought. They quibbled with the French team over the attribution of various fortified villages (*qṣūr*) in the pre-Sahara to Algeria but eventually found no option but to sign the French demarcation treaty.[204] They signed it at Lalla Maghnia on 18 March 1845 protected by French soldiers to avoid an attack by cAbd al-Qādir's *mujāhidīn*.[205] Aḥmad al-Khaḍir then took one copy to Tanger for the sultan's imprimatur and Roches took another to Paris.

The Treaty of Lalla Maghnia represented the demise of cAlawī hopes to rule western Algeria, nurtured for centuries, and another political challenge for the sultan to overcome. The situation was worsened by the fact that the border was agreed not between two Muslim powers but between a Muslim and a non-Muslim power which was tantamount to Muslim surrender of a portion of the *dār al-islām*. It was religiously dubious for Mawlay ᶜAbd al-Raḥmān to accept French sovereignty over Algeria but it was totally unacceptable for him to surrender land inhabited by Muslims who believed themselves to be his subjects.[206] The loss of Lalla Maghnia and its environs was therefore something he could not be seen to accept and he rejected the treaty on the grounds that it defined ᶜAlawī tribes and territory as French.[207]

French observers surmised that the sultan's rejection indicated the heavy criticism of a border demarcation *per se* in the circles around him.[208] It also indicated its rejection by ᶜAbd al-Qādir and his following which included tribes adversely affected by the specific line chosen for the border. Throughout the demarcation talks, ᶜAbd al-Qādir had continued to call up tribal fighters to join the Bū Maᶜza revolt and had denounced accommodations with the French. To limit the reach of his propaganda, Mawlay ᶜAbd al-Raḥmān had ordered the governors of Wajda and Taza to forbid his partisans' entry to Rif markets but he feared that ratification of the Treaty of Lalla Maghnia as it stood would impell disgruntled tribes to join him *en masse*.[209] The sultan chose to play for time. First, he shifted responsibility for the definition of the border onto his negotiators whom he accused of succumbing to French bribery.[210] He then insisted that he could not ratify the treaty without consulting the border tribes and legal authorities as to the validity of the new border, an attempt to create an impression of a Muslim consensus.[211] Finally he refused to accept the treaty's commercial articles in deference to the wishes of ᶜAlawī merchants who saw them as part of a French plot to monopolise the sultanate's trade.[212]

The French authorities did not feel that they had time for prevarication, given the revolt in Algeria and their pressing need to prevent ᶜAbd al-Qādir from joining it with reinforcements from the sultanate. De la Rue arrived in Tanger in early May to exchange ratified copies of the treaty and ordered his colleagues, the new French consul, De Chasteau, and Leon Roches, to persuade the sultan that the border demarcation was correct. When informed that the Makhzan would not accept the commercial articles, De la Rue agreed to drop them since his own government had not been convinced of their value.[213] On the issue of the border line, however, the French were adamant.[214] Meanwhile, the sultan's investigations into the veracity of the border line proved inconclusive. Semi-nomadic pre-Saharan tribes subject to the sultan protested against definition of their *qṣūr* as Algerian in a clash between territorial and tribal concepts of space, while the Banū Yznāsen affected by the northern delimitation of the border reported that Ḥamīda b. ᶜAlī had not been duped by the French but added that they had prevented the French moving into their territory.[215]

The vagueness of the Turco–ᶜAlawī frontier and French insistence forced Mawlay ᶜAbd al-Raḥmān to accept the Treaty of Lalla Maghnia shortly afterwards. He managed to save face within the sultanate, however, by insisting that the French release prisoners of war whom they had been holding since the war in the summer as a condition for the treaty's ratification.[216] The French acquiesed and the signing of the Treaty of Lalla Maghnia was thus followed by the return of 136 captives from Essawira and Isly to the sultanate.[217] Their disembarkation at Essawira in July 1845 was accompanied by public rejoicing which partially obscured the surrender of cAlawī land formalised by the treaty.[218]

On the domestic front, Mawlay cAbd al-Raḥmān's reluctant acceptance of the Treaty of Lalla Maghnia marked a definitive break between himself and cAbd al-Qādir and the start of a period of domestic reform to improve the strength of the cAlawī Makhzan. cAbd al-Qādir remained active in the sultanate and Algeria for another three years during which he became steadily more critical of Mawlay cAbd al-Raḥmān's attitude to the plight of Algeria. The sultan responded to cAbd al-Qādir's jihad rhetoric with a counter-rhetoric in which he argued that cAbd al-Qādir no longer had his support and was, therefore, an instrument not of the jihad but of *fasād*. Makhzan villification of cAbd al-Qādir gradually transformed him from a holy warrior (*mujāhid*) to a rebel (*mufsid*). The process began in 1844 with *siyāsa* or political persuasion when Mawlay cAbd al-Raḥmān began to publicly question cAbd al-Qādir's motives. Between the Treaty of Tanger and Lalla Maghnia the sultan's *siyāsa* failed to have much effect due to popular anger at the Makhzan's defeat and the territorial losses which followed. When cAbd al-Qādir finally left the sultanate to join the Bū Macza revolt in September 1845, however, sultanic propaganda against him gained ground among the north-eastern tribes. While criticising the disruption cAbd al-Qādir had caused by waging jihad against the explicit orders of his master, the sultan also increased the Makhzan military presence in the Rif and pursued his policy of resettling displaced Algerians away from the border. This policy was relatively successful until cAbd al-Qādir's return from Algeria in July 1846 after which the real struggle for power between the two men began. The struggle culminated in 1847 in a full-scale Makhzan offensive, presented as a holy war against the rebellion of cAbd al-Qādir.

6

THE [c]ALAWĪ JIHAD AGAINST [c]ABD AL-QĀDIR, 1845–7

In the period between the Treaty of Tanger and the Treaty of Lalla Maghnia six months later, Mawlay [c]Abd al-Raḥmān found himself obliged to also draft new treaties with Spain, Denmark and Sweden. These treaties signalled the sultanate's steady incorporation into a Mediterranean economic and political system dominated by Europe and its imperial networks. The arrival of the French in Algeria, the growing number of European merchants arriving in Tanger, Essawira and other ports, and the increasing influence of the European consuls on Makhzan policy forced the sultan and Sīdī Muḥammad to reassess their relationship with the 'infidel'. As in other Muslim areas, they perceived modern Europe, and in particular its armies, as a model to be emulated and a threat to be averted. The issue was especially pressing after the battle of Isly had dramatically proven [c]Alawī military inferiority to the French. Reform to tackle the related challenges of quelling domestic unrest and defending the realm was clearly essential. As in earlier eras, the sultan believed that if he had a strong army he would be able to protect the sultanate from infidel incursions and thus also keep domestic rivals, including [c]Abd al-Qādir, at bay.

His model for reform was the modern European army developed during the Napoleonic Wars then adopted by the Ottoman empire, Egypt, Tunis and [c]Abd al-Qādir as the *niẓām-i cedīd*, the New Order. Its implementation required economic and political measures which proved unpopular both with the European consuls and the Makhzan's subjects and the project remained smallscale. However, the attempt introduced the concept of military and governmental modernisation into the sultanate and provided Mawlay [c]Abd al-Raḥmān with a new instrument to restore the authority of the Makhzan against the endemic dissidence which followed the defeat at Isly. This first wave of military reform was legitimised as necessary for the jihad and accompanied by an ideological campaign to improve the prestige of the Makhzan and tarnish [c]Abd al-Qādir's reputation.

The [c]Alawī '*niẓām-i cedīd*'

French ambassadors to the sultanate had commented on the poor discipline and impoverishment of the [c]Alawī army throughout the 1830s, but the Makhzan did not recognise the problem until 1844 when Sīdī Muḥammad attributed the poor performance of Makhzan troops before Isly to inadequate training, leadership and payment. The defeat at Isly and the inability of the army to subsequently restore Makhzan authority in the countryside confirmed the seriousness of the problem: a jihad state could not survive without a reputable army. Sīdī Muḥammad believed that the solution was the introduction of modern military organisation. The term he employed was '*niẓām*', used across the Muslim Mediterranean to denote military organisation of a European type. In the ᶜAlawī case this meant the replacement of the traditional army composed of corps born or sold into service with a uniformed and salaried army recruited or conscripted from the subject population.

Shortly after the war with France, ᶜAlawī merchants in London approached the British government to discuss the possibility of British officers training an ᶜAlawī *niẓāmī* corps. In October 1844 an officer arrived in Tanger for that purpose.[1] This tentative start was followed by the arrival of an envoy from Sultan Abdülmecid offering the Makhzan Ottoman assistance in forming the new corps.[2] European powers were supportive of the Makhzan initiative viewing it as the means by which Mawlay ᶜAbd al-Raḥmān could restore control over his domains and finally intern ᶜAbd al-Qādir.[3] The Makhzan certainly intended to use its new corps for such ends, but also envisaged its purpose as defence of the realm against the infidel. As Mawlay ᶜAbd al-Raḥmān's chief minister, Muḥammad b. Idrīs, enthused to a rather dubious Bū Silhām in Tanger:

> My brother, if you had only seen [the *niẓāmī* army's] resolve and courage, you would realise that it is the very thing to tear down the defences of the infidel.[4]

A detailed plan for the formation of the ᶜAlawī *niẓāmī* army was drafted by Muṣṭafā al-Dukkālī, an eminent merchant from the cartel known as the *tujjār al-sulṭān* who traded for the Makhzan and often acted as advisors on foreign affairs. Al-Dukkālī's plan included a detailed set of regulations for the formation and functioning of the corps and an analysis of the economic measures necessary to fund it. Al-Dukkālī stated that members of the corps should be unmarried men without dependents who resided in urban barracks and drilled for several hours each day. They should have no other occupation than being soldiers and should be paid a reasonable and steady wage, al-Dukkālī suggested between one and four dirhams per day, depending on rank. To finance the project, he envisaged an increase in foreign trade and the Makhzan's share of it. He reassured the Makhzan that an increase in imports from Europe would not damage the economy as long as export duties were decreased at the same time, thereby encouraging merchants to pay for imports with local exports rather than specie. To ensure that the Makhzan benefitted from an increase in trade, he advised the sultan to impose monopolies on the export of staple goods. He also suggested that the Makhzan promote indigenous manufactures and improve communications in the sultanate by repairing roads and constructing bridges which could be financed by tolls levied for their use.[5]

Al-Dukkālī's plan appears to have been the basis for Makhzan military modernisation and economic policy during the second half of the 1840s. From the Makhzan's point of view, its virtue was that it suggested sources of revenue other than non-canonical market taxes (*mukūs*) or taxation of the tribes which was nearly impossible in 1845 as rural revolts continued to rage.[6] As Sīdī Muḥammad had found sixty years before, Makhzan involvement in foreign trade with infidel states entailed risks, but al-Dukkālī's plan had the advantage of being protectionist in tendency, enabling the sultan to argue that his aim was not to profit from European trade but to control it and prevent illegal trade, such as blackmarketeering between the Rif and Oran, damaging ᶜAlawī commerce. The first imports to become Makhzan monopolies were iron, steel and sugar.[7] Food exports also became monopolies and customs duties were raised eliciting complaints from the British consul, Drummond Hay, that provisioning the garrison at Gibraltar had become more expensive as a result.[8]

European consuls and merchants attributed the new commercial practices to sultanic avarice but in fact they indicated the sultan's need for revenue to fund the *niẓāmī* army at a time when his domestic tax-gathering power was minimal. The Makhzan established the first *niẓāmī* units of 1–2,000 men in Fes and Meknes in May 1845 with the intention of creating similar units in every major town. The recruits took an oath before the town judge to serve the sultan for seven years and in return they received a daily wage which Drummond Hay estimated was equivalent to thrupence sterling.[9] These units required not only salaries but also uniforms, modern muskets, and other items which were mainly imported from Gibraltar by Makhzan agents.[10]

The Makhzan also needed to find commanders with an adequate knowledge of the *niẓām-i cedīd* to train the recruits. Although the British had offered assistance, the sultan was wary of European instructors and instead selected Maghribi Muslim commanders with some knowledge of *niẓāmī* technique. The first commander of the corps was Ismāᶜīl Bū Darba whom Drummond Hay described as a young, intelligent veteran from the French army in Algeria.[11] Bū Darba was actually the son of one of ᶜAbd al-Qādir's commercial agents and had grown up in Marseilles. He had no military experience and had come to the sultanate to evade creditors in France.[12] Possibly, Mawlay ᶜAbd al-Raḥmān selected him because of his indirect connection with ᶜAbd al-Qādir which associated the new ᶜAlawī units with the latter's *niẓāmī* corps. His lack of actual military knowledge, however, led to his speedy replacement by military instructors from Ḥusaynid Tunis and Tripoli.[13] The Makhzan garnered further information on the *niẓām-i cedīd* by importing military manuals from Muḥammad ᶜAlī's Egypt.[14] The formation of a corps modelled indirectly on modern European armies required religious justification. Association with ᶜAbd al-Qādir's *niẓāmī* corps and its jihad credentials was insufficient to legitimise new units which threatened the position of traditional corps, imposed new military obligations on the population and possessed 'infidel' characteristics. The establishment of the corps was thus accompanied by the emergence of a new genre of literature which promoted military modernisation as religiously acceptable and indeed obligatory to defend the sultanate against colonialism. This genre flourished during the reign of Sīdī Muḥammad after the Tetuan War with Spain (1859–60) had confirmed the lessons of Isly, but it began in the 1840s. Ideologically these works not only justified military modernisation as necessary for jihad, but also reiterated the centrist view that deciding what was necessary for the jihad and when it should be waged was the right and responsibility of the sultan, not his subjects. Modernisation literature thus became a vehicle for the promotion of ᶜAlawī theocracy as well as the *niẓām-i cedīd* and, as such, a weapon against those who tried to appropriate leadership of the jihad as ᶜAbd al-Qādir had done.

The first extant example of this literature is Muḥammad al-Kardūdī's *Kashf al-ghumma bi-bayān inna ḥarb al-niẓām ḥaqq ᶜala al-umma*, a lengthy work which introduced the *niẓām-i cedīd* as the means to victory in the jihad. Its success, however, depended upon the community's fulfilment of certain social, political and religious conditions which al-Kardūdī clearly saw as a three-way contract between God, an Islamic ruler and his subjects.

> Know that God most high is the origin of victory and the origin of defeat. Victory indicates the victory of the religion of God … and God most high says, 'We give power on earth to those who perform the prayers, pay alms, command the good and prohibit the evil'. He guarantees victory to those rulers on four conditions and when their laws are challenged and disruption threatens the borders of their kingdom, or an enemy, rebel or challenger appears, then they must seek refuge with God and restore their relations with him by restoring the balance (*mīzān*) which He has ordained for His servants, by following the path of justice and righteousness by which the earth and sky are held up, and by bringing forth the precepts of religion, succoring the oppressed and staying the hand of the oppressor.[15]

A ruler such as the ᶜAlawī sultan had a contract with God which guaranteed him military victory if he maintained justice within his domains. If he failed to do this, he was liable to face internal political challenges and the threat of attack from outside, a situation which Mawlay ᶜAbd al-Raḥmān certainly faced in the 1840s. The only way to restore central authority was by redressing domestic injustices which would be followed by victory against rebels and invaders. This placed responsibility for the moral and political health of the *umma* squarely upon the sultan but al-Kardūdī added that subjects were obliged to obey the imam, to only wage jihad when he ordered and to fight until he suspended hostilities. Desertion, he asserted, was a sin equivalent to rebellion against God.

In 1845 Mawlay ᶜAbd al-Raḥmān was far from able to assert his right to obedience from his subjects or to lead the jihad. The contraction in state power which had come to a head in 1844 remained severe: large parts of the countryside were still in revolt against the sultan and in many areas power had devolved from the Makhzan to local leaders. The situation was most critical in the northeast where ᶜAbd al-Qādir, the only recognised leader of the jihad, virtually controlled Wajda province. ᶜAbd al-Qādir's authority was strengthened by the French presence across the border which had turned the region into a frontier society where a sense of mission, the jihad, thrived alongside the economic opportunities provided by raiding and blackmarketeering.[16]

The reassertion of local particularism and independent jihad initiatives recalled the moments in the fifteenth and seventeenth centuries when Portuguese and Spanish imperialism respectively had contributed to a severe contraction in the power of a discredited dynasty and its replacement by a new one. In 1845 the ᶜAlawī dynasty, discredited by their failure to resist French colonialism, appeared to have reached the stage in the Khaldunian cycle when they would be challenged and replaced by a new power from the periphery. The European consuls believed that if Mawlay ᶜAbd al-Raḥmān took any steps against ᶜAbd al-Qādir, as he was obliged to do by the terms of the Treaties of Tanger and Lalla Maghnia, the entire disaffected population would rally to 'the saint and warrior of the Mohammedan religion'.[17] ᶜAbd al-Qādir, however, was still intent upon regaining the political power he had lost in Algeria and in September 1845 he left the sultanate to join the Bū Maᶜza revolt, thereby depriving the opposition of its leader. The sultan took the opportunity presented by his absence to tackle the challenge he represented by political means (*siyāsa*) designed to complement the improvement in Makhzan material power which he hoped the *niẓāmī* corps would bring about.

The sultan's '*siyāsa*'

ᶜAbd al-Qādir's return to Algeria took place in late September after a summer of cross-border raiding which had provided him with the resources to provision and arm his following of Algerian tribesmen and Rīfī contingents.[18] He marked his return to the jihad with a spectacular attack on an unsuspecting French column in which most of the French soldiers were killed.[19] The remainder were sent across the border and forced to parade on the field of Isly in symbolic vengeance for that defeat.[20] As the French had feared, ᶜAbd al-Qādir's return inaugurated a new stage in the Bū Maᶜza revolt as large parts of western Algeria rose to join the jihad. The furious French military authorities demanded that Mawlay ᶜAbd al-Raḥmān make good the damage by destroying the Dā'ira, which remained camped in the Muluwiya basin, or they would do it for him.[21] The sultan replied that the only feasible way to undermine ᶜAbd al-Qādir was to counter his jihad rhetoric with Makhzan propaganda. He was helped by the fact that the French consular establishment in Tanger, De Chasteau and Leon Roches, agreed that a French offensive into the Rif to destroy the Dā'ira would do more harm than good.[22] Their attitude bought Mawlay ᶜAbd al-Raḥmān the time to apply his policy of peaceful persuasion. On a mission to Rabat in November 1845, however, Leon Roches warned him that the French army in Algeria would not wait indefinitely for Makhzan action and would pursue ᶜAbd al-Qādir if he crossed back into the sultanate.[23]

Under the looming threat of French incursions into the Rif, Mawlay ᶜAbd al-Raḥmān began the process of reconstructing Makhzan authority across the sultanate. In addition to general disparagement of the Makhzan in the Rif, the south was said to be 'far from peaceful' while tribes in the Gharb were in revolt against the governor of Tanger.[24] Urban troublespots included Meknes, where the ᶜAbīd were threatening to mutiny in protest over the formation of a *niẓāmī* unit, and Rabat, where a revolt against the governor had broken out.[25] The phenomenon of urban revolt indicated the depth of the political breakdown which faced the Makhzan. The immediate cause of the Rabat revolt was the overbearing behaviour of its governor but reports of the social situation in the city at the time suggest that it was driven by the widespread feeling that the sultan had failed in his obligation to defend his subjects from infidel encroachment. In the case of Rabat this had taken the form of increased contact with European merchants who had come to reside in the city and whose behaviour contravened the Sharīᶜa. Complaints directed to the Makhzan included reference to presumptuous behaviour on the part of local Jews working with the Europeans, wine drinking and sexual immorality.[26]

The sultan could only regain control of these cities by making a personal appearance. He therefore left Fes for Meknes after which he continued to Rabat to spend the winter addressing the city's problems. While he was in Rabat, Leon Roches arrived to discuss ᶜAlawī relations with France and the related issue of ᶜAlawī policy towards ᶜAbd al-Qādir and the Dā'ira. The discussions held between Roches and the sultan's chief minister, Muḥammad b. Idrīs, indicate that Makhzan *siyāsa* against ᶜAbd al-Qādir began by questioning the religious legitimacy of his actions. Bin Idrīs characterised ᶜAbd al-Qādir's activities as dissidence (*fasād*) rather than jihad because he was acting without Makhzan authorisation and had created dissension between the sultan and his subjects and between the sultan and France. He added that jihad was a form of selfless service in the way of God but that ᶜAbd al-Qādir's actions were for his own advancement and thus inspired by the devil.[27]

Mawlay ᶜAbd al-Raḥmān expressed the same opinion in letters to Makhzan commanders in the Rif which ordered them to inform the tribes that ᶜAbd al-Qādir was a *mufsid* not a *mujāhid* because he had 'cast the noose of religion from his neck' and thus did not have Makhzan support, making their oaths of allegiance to him invalid.[28] He further countered the jihadists' argument that ᶜAbd al-Qādir was fighting for Islam by stating that, regardless of a man's intention, fighting the infidel was not jihad unless it contributed to the material and moral well-being of Islam and the Muslims. ᶜAbd al-Qādir's participation in the Bū Maᶜza revolt was not jihad because it was a struggle which the Muslims could not win which only increased the likelihood of French reprisals and Muslim suffering.[29]

The sultan and Muḥammad b. Idrīs were not alone in characterising futile resistance as religiously unjustifiable. Al-Ḥājj al-ᶜArabī, head of the Wazzāniyya–Ṭayyibiyya brotherhood, told shaykhs of the brotherhood in Algeria that they should support those to whom God had given the victory, in other words the French. Those who did not were:

> Devils who set themselves up as fighters of the holy war, under the pretext of religion, and mislead those unhappy believers who listen to their lying words, and then draw them into danger and abandon them.[30]

Such arguments against further resistance indicated a conceptual accommodation to the French presence in Algeria based on Muslim belief in the impenetrable will of God. The French occupation of Algeria and attacks on the sultanate could not be other than God's will and to resist indefinitely suggested opposition to that will.

Although the population as a whole remained hostile to the 'infidel' and supportive of ᶜAbd al-Qādir, the sultan's new position found resonance with those who had most experience of Europe, namely the Makhzan authorities of Tanger and Tetuan and merchants from the coastal towns. De Chasteau and Leon Roches hoped to use this small clique to consolidate ᶜAlawī relations with France. To this end, Roches secured the appointment of the deputy governor of Tanger, Muḥammad b. ᶜAbd al-Malik, as governor of the Rif.[31] Muḥammad b. ᶜAbd al-Malik knew the consular community and the French believed that he understood their position and would take the action against ᶜAbd al-Qādir necessary to improve ᶜAlawī–French relations. Roches also persuaded the sultan to send an envoy to Paris.[32] He and De Chasteau hoped that through the embassy they would be able to transform the Makhzan's reluctant co-operation into a more wholehearted alliance.

The sultan chose ᶜAbd al-Qādir Ashᶜāsh, the governor of Tetuan, as his envoy. He hoped that Ashᶜāsh would be able to persuade the French government to revise the border line agreed in the Treaty of Lalla Maghnia and make them comprehend his policy towards ᶜAbd al-Qādir. Ashᶜāsh went to Paris in December 1845 accompanied by De Chasteau, Roches and several Makhzan officers, including Muḥammad al-Ṣaffār who wrote an account of the embassy.[33] On his arrival, Ashᶜāsh presented Mawlay ᶜAbd al-Raḥmān's points to several French ministers. He defended the Makhzan's use of propaganda rather than force against ᶜAbd al-Qādir as a strategy to prevent the entire north rising to join the jihad which the French should support not undermine by constantly threatening invasion. He also raised the issue of the pre-Saharan *qṣūr* designated Algerian in the Treaty of Lalla Maghnia and illicit French attempts to establish a trading post at Wad Nun.[34] The French government paid little heed and devoted their efforts to persuading the delegates of the desirability of closer contacts with France. The ᶜAlawī envoys were treated to tours, royal receptions and gala performances designed to impress upon them the superiority of French culture, society and military power.

The mission was the first of its kind and the comments of its members indicate the responses to France in particular, and Europe in general, which co-existed in the sultanate in the mid-1840s. ᶜAbd al-Qādir Ashᶜāsh's correspondence to his brother shows that he wished to make a good impression and was himself impressed by the French and by Paris which he described as 'among the greatest and most splendid cities in the world'.[35] ᶜAbd al-Qādir Ashᶜāsh was not, however, representative. He enjoyed unusually warm relations with the British and French consuls in Tanger and, after the mission, kept up a personal correspondence with the French minister of war, Guizot.[36] A more mainstream response was that of Muḥammad al-Ṣaffār whose travel account (*riḥla*) of the embassy suggests that he was intimidated by the impersonal industrial order he encountered in France and the workings of a society whose values clearly did not coincide with those of his own.[37] Subsequently, those who participated in the mission seem to have been perceived as tainted by their close interaction with the infidel. Ashᶜāsh paid the price for fraternisation eighteen months later when he came before Mawlay ᶜAbd al-Raḥmān on charges of apostasy levelled against him for his contacts with the infidel.[38]

Ashᶜāsh's mission coincided with the final phase of the Bū Maᶜza revolt in Algeria during which resistance lost all semblance of coherence and became increasingly apocalyptic as the violent French counter-attack destroyed the land and decimated the population. ᶜAbd al-Qādir travelled ceaselessly, retreating and then returning to the offensive, but it had become evident that the Algerians could not expell the French from Algeria.[39] He therefore began to appeal to the population to abandon the jihad and migrate to Muslim territory to render French possession of their land worthless by depriving them of taxable subjects and labour. As a result growing numbers of tribesmen and townsmen crossed into the sultanate.[40] For some the aim was resettlement, for others preparation for the raiding which ᶜAbd al-Qādir envisaged as the next stage in the jihad. For the latter group, which included ᶜAbd al-Qādir's brothers and Bū Ḥamīdī, ᶜAlawī participation in the jihad remained a crucial component in their plans.[41]

Large-scale immigration confirmed the existence of a virtual Algerian protectorate in the northeastern sultanate. The Dā'ira, camped near the Muluwiya river, formed the Algerian headquarters. Its head, Bū Ḥamīdī, controlled the territory between the Muluwiya and the border, including the town of Wajda.[42] He was supported by migrant tribes and sections of the Banū Yznāsen, Angād and Aḥlāf loyal to ᶜAbd al-Qādir.[43] His authority was sufficient for him to levy taxes from migrants and take steps against local raiding.[44] Further afield, ᶜAbd al-Qādir's brothers circulated among the Rif tribes, begging for provisions for the Dā'ira from those gathered at local markets and calling them to jihad.[45] Their tactics included donations to tribal chiefs in return for their support and use of the *ᶜār* ceremony. In the *ᶜār* or 'shame' ceremony a supplicant trespassed on a man's private domain and then made a sacrifice or offering to him to secure his pardon and assistance, in this case supply of the Dā'ira or support for the jihad.[46] The use of the *ᶜār* compulsion by ᶜAbd al-Qādir's brothers hinted that the Rif tribes were becoming less supportive of the Algerian presence than they had previously been, probably as a result of the strain put on limited Rif resources by the presence of large numbers of immigrants.

Their ambivalence may also have derived from Mawlay ᶜAbd al-Raḥmān's *siyāsa* which gained impetus in the eastern and central Rif in early 1846. In

January the sultan commanded Bū Zayyān to inform the border tribes that ᶜAbd al-Qādir was no longer his deputy and that support for him was incompatible with allegiance to the Makhzan. He was to add that the tribes should abandon the Dā'ira and prevent ᶜAbd al-Qādir re-entering the sultanate as proof of their loyalty. Mawlay ᶜAbd al-Raḥmān ordered Muḥammad b. ᶜAbd al-Malik to perform a similar duty in the central Rif.[47] Although the latter had been appointed governor of the Rif at the instigation of Roches, the sultan valued him as a notable of the Rīfī Temsamān tribe with the necessary knowledge and authority to promote a pro-Makhzan alignment against the jihadists among the tribes.[48] His true loyalties are a matter for surmise. During his stint as governor of the Rif he received a French salary in return for keeping De Chasteau informed.[49] On the other hand this gave him access to information on ᶜAbd al-Qādir's movements from French military and espionage sources which would prove essential to the Makhzan counter-offensive in the Rif. Knowledge of French reports also revealed the extent of their information and could be used against them. Indeed De Chasteau was later warned that Muḥammad b. ᶜAbd al-Malik used his French contacts on behalf of ᶜAbd al-Qādir. This accusation was mischievous but underlined the ambiguity in the relations between men like Muḥammad b. ᶜAbd al-Malik and the European consuls.

The Rif tribes, courted by both the Makhzan and ᶜAbd al-Qādir, manoeuvered to their own advantage. The Banū Yznāsen and Angād protested their loyalty to the Makhzan, but requested governors of their own choice in return for closing their territory to ᶜAbd al-Qādir and refused to participate in any action against him.[50] They were also reluctant to cease selling provisions to the Dā'ira, causing Bū Zayyān to appeal to the Makhzan for a renewal of earlier prohibitions against sale of Rif produce to the Algerians.[51] Further west in the central Rif, Muḥammad b. ᶜAbd al-Malik made greater headway. He left Tanger for Tetuan in February 1846 and then travelled to ᶜAyn Badis with a small cavalry corps.[52] Although initially faced with the same dilatory response from the tribes as Bū Zayyān, Muḥammad b. ᶜAbd al-Malik was able to use his tribal allies and Makhzan troops from the central Rif garrison at Tafarsit to attack and defeat pro-jihad sections of the Qalᶜaya and Banū Tūzīn.[53] As a result of this engagement several Rif tribes obeyed his orders to cease provisioning the Dā'ira.

The sultan combined Makhzan infiltration of the Rif with an intensification of his Algerian resettlement policy. Resettlement involved both individuals and entire tribal groups and was targeted at the Dā'ira and the tribal sections camped between the Muluwiya and the border. The provisioning problems experienced by the Dā'ira encouraged several important families to accept resettlement. In March 1846 Milūd b. ᶜArrāsh presented himself to Muḥammad b. ᶜAbd al-Malik seeking asylum.[54] He was escorted to Fes where Sīdī Muḥammad provided him and his family with a rent-free Makhzan property on the orders of the sultan.[55] Many scholars and *shurafā'* from the Dā'ira were similarly welcomed in Fes, provided with lodgings and allowed to teach in the city's mosques, including the prestigious Qarawiyyin. As a result the number of west Algerian *shurafā'* in Fes rose so rapidly that a special communal representative (*naqīb*) was appointed to oversee their affairs.[56]

Makhzan *siyāsa* thus revolved around the characterisation of ᶜAbd al-Qādir's holy war as rebellion a point reinforced by the apparent hopelessness of continued resistance in Algeria, economic pressure on the Dā'ira and generous patronage of Algerian Muslims who left the border zone. It also entailed more general efforts on the part of the sultan to reappropriate the attributes of a sharifian *mujāhid* ruler. In Makhzan campaigns against Berber rebels around Meknes and the tribes of the Dukkala in spring 1846, commanders repeatedly addressed the sultan using the titles adopted by ᶜAbd al-Qādir during the 1830s: 'Commander of the Faithful and Warrior (*mujāhid*) in the way of the Lord of the Worlds';[57] 'Champion of the Community (*milla*) and Religion';[58] and 'Reviver of Religion, Commander of the Faithful and Champion of Religion'.[59] Extensive use of such titles at this juncture suggested a bid by Mawlay ᶜAbd al-Raḥmān to restore the religio-political status he had lost over the preceding years and with it his exclusive right to decide what was jihad and what was *fasād*. He wished to assert that whatever the flaws of his Makhzan tribal revolt at a time when the Muslim community was under threat from an infidel power was irreligious and its perpetrators were as much enemies of God as the infidel.[60]

The sultan's policies began to bear fruit from March 1846, assisted by events involving the French prisoners in the Dā'ira. As the Makhzan's economic blockade on the Dā'ira tightened, the presence of 300 French mouths to feed generated unbearable tension.[61] French demands for the release of the prisoners and threats of a military expedition to free them exacerbated the situation.[62] Although De Chasteau in Tanger advocated caution, Bugeaud, now Governor-General of Algeria, was determined to secure the prisoners' release and punish the border tribes for raiding into Algeria.[63] The aggressive attitude of the French military in Algeria put greater pressure on the Dā'ira while also forcing Mawlay ᶜAbd al-Raḥmān to send more troops to Taza in preparation for a French invasion. The inhabitants of the Dā'ira interpreted the arrival of the Makhzan reinforcements as an indication that the sultan planned to forcibly release the French captives.

Tensions were compounded by ᶜAbd al-Qādir's replacement of Bū Ḥamīdī as the Dā'ira's custodian with Muṣṭafā al-Tuhāmī, his brother-in-law. The change was a mistake. Muṣṭafā lacked the authority of Bū Ḥamīdī and the latter regarded the change as an indication that ᶜAbd al-Qādir no longer trusted him. As a result, those tribes most closely associated with Bū Ḥamīdī decided to leave and by May 1846 the trickle of emigrants from the Dā'ira was a flood. The most important departees were Banū ᶜAmir sections who had supported ᶜAbd al-Qādir since 1832.[64] They travelled to Taza and were finally resettled on the Gharb plain between Fes and Rabat with the blessing of Sīdī Muḥammad and Mawlay ᶜAbd al-Raḥmān.[65] One of ᶜAbd al-Qādir's former governors, Muḥammad b. ᶜIssa al-Barkānī, also departed for Fes at this time in a group of forty individuals.[66]

These departures, economic pressure and fear of attack either by the Makhzan or the French brought the situation in the Dā'ira to crisis point and impelled al-Tuhāmī to take the extraordinary step of slaughtering the French captives with the exception of a handful of officers. The massacre prompted the departure of ᶜAbd al-Qādir's remaining tribal allies, the Ḥashem and the Jaᶜāfra, who arrived in Fes on 22 June.[67] An anonymous letter to Rif shaykhs stated that the Dā'ira had been reduced to the personal households of ᶜAbd al-Qādir, Bū Ḥamīdī and Muṣṭafā al-Tuhāmī plus 500 retainers.[68] The first rumours of the massacre reached Tanger on 1 June and were confirmed by mid-June.[69] The incident elicited French threats of revenge but they took no action and by late June it seemed as if the sultan's *siyāsa*, aided by the internal problems of the Dā'ira, had achieved its aim.[70] Algerian influence in the Rif had been significantly reduced and the sultan felt able to boast that resettlement of migrants, economic embargo of the Dā'ira and propaganda had together succeeded in destroying ᶜAbd al-Qādir's following and restoring Makhzan control over the Rif.

He over-estimated the Makhzan achievement: the decline in support for ᶜAbd al-Qādir was partly a function of his absence and tribal protestations of loyalty to the Makhzan were meaningless unless he had the military power to make them operational. The weakness of Makhzan power was particularly evident with respect to the frontier where Makhzan authorities were totally incapable of preventing cross-border raids.[71] For the sultan's *siyāsa* to really bear fruit he had to close the border to prevent raiding and the return of ᶜAbd al-Qādir, a possibility which the French were equally keen to avert. At French request, Mawlay ᶜAbd al-Raḥmān therefore ordered Sīdī Muḥammad to send more troops to Taza to seal the border. Before his precautions could be implemented rumours arrived that ᶜAbd al-Qādir had crossed the border and was moving westwards towards the Dā'ira at ᶜAyn Zura.[72]

ᶜAbd al-Qādir's return signalled the start of his real struggle with Mawlay ᶜAbd al-Raḥmān. During his 1844–5 sojourn in the northeast he had constructed a power base on the strength of his reputation as a fighter for the faith and his claim that he was acting as the sultan's deputy. Although many ᶜAlawī subjects had cited him as a better candidate for rule than Mawlay ᶜAbd al-Raḥmān, his priority had remained jihad within Algeria. The divergence between his position and that of the sultan with regard to the jihad had nonetheless led the latter to view him as a rebel and opponent, an interpretation he had publicised throughout the Rif. That the sultan should have launched his propaganda campaign and tried to destroy the Dā'ira while he was fighting desperately against the French made ᶜAbd al-Qādir extremely hostile to his former 'master'. On his return he openly accused the sultan of betraying his own people for the sake of a treaty with the French and transformed the Rif into a centre for opposition to him. Not only did he form an army of Rif auxiliaries but he nurtured contacts with the jihadists in Fes and ᶜAlawī opponents of the sultan. Mawlay ᶜAbd al-Raḥmān countered ᶜAbd al-Qādir's accusations of betrayal with renewed denunciations of him as a rebel and insurgent. Between 1846 and early 1847 the struggle between the two men remained a war of words, a jihad of the tongue, but during 1847 it escalated into a civil war for control of the Rif, if not the sultanate as a whole.

The sultan's 'jihad of the tongue' against ᶜAbd al-Qādir

On his return to the Dā'ira, ᶜAbd al-Qādir quickly summoned the remnants of the Banū ᶜAmir, Ḥashem and other Algerian tribes in the Rif to rejoin him.[73] At the same time he exploited the fears of the Rif tribes by asserting that he had returned to mobilise them against an impending French invasion.[74] He then sent his brothers to request camping permission and support among tribes from the border to Taza, a day's journey from Fes.[75] These requests amounted to calls for allegiance and were interpreted as such by the Makhzan.[76] ᶜAbd al-Qādir also openly criticised the sultan's treatment of the Dā'ira, publicly stating that he would rather trust the French than a Muslim who had betrayed his co-religionists, a statement which came close to accusing the sultan of apostasy.[77] His words fueled extravagant rumours that he planned to march on Fes in the vanguard of a French army![78]

While ᶜAbd al-Qādir openly questioned the sultan's faith, the French authorities in Algeria insisted that he prove his commitment to his alliance with them by preventing ᶜAbd al-Qādir from re-establishing a base in the Rif.[79] Mawlay ᶜAbd al-Raḥmān tried to manouevere out of the ideological corner he found himself in by convoking a gathering of ᶜAlawī *ᶜulamā'* at which he asked them to define the respective positions of a ruler and a subject who challenged his definition of jihad. The *ᶜulamā'* predictably ruled that 'true' Muslims could attack those who rejected arguments against jihad when the sultan–imam deemed that it was inappropriate.[80] However, it remained to be seen whether the sultan could retain his position as ruler or whether ᶜAbd al-Qādir would overthrow him, rendering in the process the latter's definition of jihad the correct one.

After ᶜAbd al-Qādir's return Makhzan authorities struggled unsuccessfully to counter his requests for camping rights and allegiance. By the beginning of August, sections of the Tsūl and Brānis of the Taza region had defected to ᶜAbd al-Qādir, along with the Karārma fraction of the border Aḥlāf.[81] Their defection led to skirmishing between themselves and fractions loyal to the Makhzan which culminated in the retreat of the Aḥlāf notable and Makhzan commander, Bū Zayyān, to Taza.[82] Drummond Hay reported that ᶜAbd al-Qādir had been involved in the clashes which had arisen because tribesmen loyal to the Makhzan had refused to supply the Dā'ira with provisions.[83] The Makhzan's position was further undermined by the fact that ᶜAbd al-Qādir's claim that a French invasion was imminent seemed corroborated by the arrival of additional French troops at the border fort of Jamiᶜat al-Ghazwat.

ᶜAbd al-Qādir now had a greater following than ever before in the Rif and French intelligence reports suggested that several tribes had not only given him their allegiance but asked him to replace Mawlay ᶜAbd al-Raḥmān as sultan.[84] An informer told De Chasteau that although ᶜAbd al-Qādir had hesitated to challenge Mawlay ᶜAbd al-Raḥmān in 1844 now that his incapacity to rule and betrayal of Islam was proven, he was ready to wage war against him. Due to his religious scruples he would not attack first but if 'that degenerate Muslim sovereign who has allied with the Christians' attacked him he would accept the title of sultan and religion would triumph.[85] Other reports stated that ᶜAbd al-Qādir did not wish to rule the sultanate, but intended to challenge Mawlay ᶜAbd al-Raḥmān for leadership of the jihad by coming to Fes to preach its merits in the Qarawiyyin mosque and mobilise the population for a new Algerian campaign in defiance of the sultan and Sīdī Muḥammad.[86] Given the close association between jihad leadership and political rule this was hardly less than a direct bid for power.

De Chasteau suspected that there was some exaggeration in these reports but they did reflect the popular mood. Drummond Hay recounted that the people of Tanger were reluctant to rebel against Mawlay ᶜAbd al-Raḥmān but felt that ᶜAbd al-Qādir alone could solve the sultanate's domestic problems and repel a French invasion.[87] He added that the entire population showed a 'manifest desire' for ᶜAbd al-Qādir to overthrow the sultan and place himself or 'another person whom he may elect on the throne of Morocco'.[88] Part of ᶜAbd al-Qādir's enormous popularity lay in the fact that he represented an ideal – altruistic commitment to the jihad devoid of personal ambition – an illusion he fostered by suggesting that he wished to remain a fighter for the faith and make another ᶜAlawī or Idrīsī *sharīf* sultan.

Such rumours, combined with the Makhzan's inability to prevent the tribes between Wajda and Taza from going over to ᶜAbd al-Qādir, convinced Sīdī Muḥammad that he was about to advance on Fes.[89] He begged Mawlay ᶜAbd al-Raḥmān to come north and endeavoured to reinforce the Makhzan position in Taza and the central Rif.[90] The movement of ᶜAbd al-Qādir towards Taza, however, panicked the Makhzan garrison into abandoning the town. In Fes both ᶜAbd al-Qādir's supporters and his opponents began to prepare for his arrival.[91] His partisans, who included natives of the city and Algerian migrants, gathered provisions and money in preparation for the Makhzan seige they knew would follow its occupation by ᶜAbd al-Qādir. Meanwhile, the Makhzan tried to rally its forces to defend Fes and, on discovery of the jihadists' preparations, confiscated their supplies and dispatched their leaders to Marrakesh in chains.[92]

At this point ᶜAbd al-Qādir and Sīdī Muḥammad both decided it was preferable to avert hostilities. It seems that ᶜAbd al-Qādir had expected the French force at Jamiᶜat al-Ghazwat to invade the sultanate, justifying his calls to jihad and creating a broad northern consensus for his replacement of the sultan. The French troops, however, showed no sign of entering the sultanate and ᶜAbd al-Qādir was reluctant to attack the Makhzan without the ideological umbrella provided by the jihad. For his part, Sīdī Muḥammad was unsure of the loyalty of the tribes between Taza and Fes and did not wish to test it by fighting ᶜAbd al-Qādir. He therefore responded positively with gifts of grain when ᶜAbd al-Qādir sent his brother, Muḥammad al-Saᶜīd, to apologise for the clashes which had occurred between his Rīfī supporters and pro-Makhzan tribes.[93] Muḥammad al-Saᶜīd continued to Marrakesh to convey a similar apology to Mawlay ᶜAbd al-Raḥmān and, although southern tribes appealed to ᶜAbd al-Qādir to advance, he remained in the Rif assuring the *ᶜulamā'* and tribesmen who came to pay him their respects that he was a loyal Makhzan servant.[94]

Whether the Rif tribes believed ᶜAbd al-Qādir's protestations of loyalty or not, Mawlay ᶜAbd al-Raḥmān had no doubt that they were false. In the aftermath of the Fes crisis he sent military reinforcements north and warned Sīdī Muḥammad not to be taken in by ᶜAbd al-Qādir whose strength had always lain in his skillful rhetoric.[95] He ordered Muḥammad b. ᶜAbd al-Malik in the central Rif to threaten ᶜAbd al-Qādir with attack if he failed to leave the sultanate and insisted that Makhzan commanders in the Rif stress to the tribes that support for him was contrary to Makhzan wishes. Finally, he instructed Sīdī Muḥammad to ensure that the resettled Banū ᶜAmir and Ḥashem tribes did not rejoin ᶜAbd al-Qādir.[96] The resettled tribes themselves, aware of the tensions and keen to avoid persecution, protested their loyalty to the Makhzan.[97] Their efforts to remain outside the conflict were undermined, however, by later reports that Bū Ḥamīdī had sent envoys asking them to rejoin the Dā'ira.[98]

Towards the end of October 1846 ᶜAbd al-Qādir temporarily left the sultanate for Algeria, having moved the Dā'ira from ᶜAyn Zura to a more defensible position in the nearby Banū Warayn mountains.[99] As previously his departure marked an upswing in Makhzan fortunes in the Rif. The tribes started to respect Makhzan decrees and border commanders regained some control over the tribes under their jurisdiction.[100] As a result raids against the Dā'ira intensified.[101] Ongoing food shortages in the Rif assisted the Makhzan. Although the tribes were as resentful of sharing scant resources with Makhzan troops as with the Dā'ira, the pressure on the Dā'ira was greater.[102] During the autumn its inhabitants pressed ᶜAbd al-Qādir to come to terms with either the French or the sultan to relieve them from their straitened circumstances. He therefore decided to release the French officers still in the Dā'ira's custody and send them to Melilla with a message informing the French authorities that he would consider coming to terms.[103]

The Spanish forwarded ᶜAbd al-Qādir's message to Algiers but the French paid no more heed to it than the Makhzan had to his apology after the Fes crisis. The French military authorities mistrusted him and the consular authorities in Tanger maintained that the best way to secure Algeria was by strengthening the ᶜAlawī Makhzan. To this end De Chasteau and Roches visited the sultan in Marrakesh in November 1846 with a gift of eight field guns plus officers and artillery experts to help train the still embryonic *niẓāmī* corps.[104] They also spread largesse within Makhzan circles, offering Muḥammad b. Idrīs a salary and increasing that already paid to Muḥammad b. ᶜAbd al-Malik in the Rif.[105] French intentions to support Mawlay ᶜAbd al-Raḥmān were confirmed early in 1847 when they rejected a request from the Banū ᶜAmir and Ḥashem for repatriation to Algeria.[106]

An impasse had been reached: the Dā'ira's situation in the Rif was untenable in the long term and France's refusal to countenance an agreement with ᶜAbd al-Qādir left him little option but to fight it out with the sultan. Although he would sporadically claim allegiance to the Makhzan during 1847 as a matter of stategy, both ᶜAbd al-Qādir and Mawlay ᶜAbd al-Raḥmān knew that no accommodation was possible. They were each waging a righteous war against corruption of the body politic and only the outcome would prove who was justified. At about this time Mawlay ᶜAbd al-Raḥmān substituted his rather naïve characterisations of ᶜAbd al-Qādir as a *mufsid* or rebel with a far more intense denunciation of him as evil incarnate. The language of jihad against *fasād* remained in place but the sultan now began to describe ᶜAbd al-Qādir as a demon (*shayṭān*) and a false *mahdī* (*al-dajjāl*).[107] Demonisation of ᶜAbd al-Qādir removed the last traces of ambiguity in their relationship by presenting their rivalry as a dualistic struggle between good and evil.[108] It also allowed the sultan to use ᶜAbd al-Qādir's seeming virtue as proof of his inherent depravity. In letters to Sīdī Muḥammad, Mawlay ᶜAbd al-Raḥmān claimed that ambition had seduced ᶜAbd al-Qādir who had then seduced the Rif tribes with his honeyed tongue and his duplicitous ability to make black seem white which meant that his 'jihad' was actually an unholy war and his 'loyalty' to the Makhzan was in fact opposition to it.[109]

The sultan's ability to employ such constructs resulted in part from the apocalyptic atmosphere generated by the Bū Maᶜza revolt. During the revolt Bū Maᶜza and several other local leaders had claimed to be the *mahdī*. Mawlay ᶜAbd al-Raḥmān was now suggesting that ᶜAbd al-Qādir, whom his subjects had cast in the mahdistic role of Idrīsī champion, was actually the *dajjāl* scheduled to appear before the *mahdī* in Muslim eschatology. ᶜAbd al-Qādir countered the sultan's vehement denunciation by asserting that his jihad was a true mission and that he remained a loyal Makhzan servant who only found himself in opposition to his master because the latter had betrayed his obligation to wage jihad. His criticism of the sultan did not imply a political challenge but was religious admonition (*naṣīḥa*) which he was obliged to give as a pious Muslim. ᶜAbd al-Qādir also insisted that he would not fight Mawlay ᶜAbd al-Raḥmān unless he attacked first. He thus attempted to perpetuate his idealisation as a selfless holy warrior for the greater glory of Islam.

Neither man's ideological position was universally accepted. The sultan faced the same problems of credibility as he had throughout the long crisis and the difficulty that he could not simply denounce jihad, but had to denounce *fasād* disguised as jihad, a particularly subjective category given the French presence across the border. On the other hand, ᶜAbd al-Qādir's presence within the sultanate had produced more realistic estimates of his achievements. He had never been as popular in the south as in the north and as he became more closely associated with the Rif his idealisation in the south lessened. In a report on the marabouts and brotherhood lodges of the Saharan provinces filed in February 1847, Auguste Beaumier wrote that an informant had stated that although the ᶜAlawī *shurafā'* had been discredited by their defeat at Isly and ᶜAbd al-Qādir coveted the sultanate, the south would fight for the ᶜAlawī sultan against 'Riffi dogs' who only supported ᶜAbd al-Qādir because they had no reputable *shurafā'* of their own![110]

The loyalty of the Rif tribes was itself conditional and as ᶜAbd al-Qādir became embroiled in local politics his reputation as a *mujāhid* became besmirched. The main problem he faced was provisioning the Dā'ira which illustrated the difficulties in mixing religious and political authority. The Dā'ira, as the base of the *mujāhidīn*, had been welcomed and provisioned by tribesmen who saw its support as a religious duty or benefitted from economic exchange with it. ᶜAbd al-Qādir's personal presence in the Rif, the reduction in jihad activity in Algeria and the plunder it brought and food shortages in 1846 and 1847 made the tribesmen less keen to supply the Dā'ira. In order to secure food and protect it from raiders, ᶜAbd al-Qādir and his men became involved in raiding themselves. As a consequence the Dā'ira began to assume the character of a migrant tribe competing for scant resources and ᶜAbd al-Qādir began to seem like a tribal chief rather than a religious figure. This alteration in Rif perceptions gave weight to Mawlay ᶜAbd al-Raḥmān's assertion that ᶜAbd al-Qādir was a *mufsid* rather than a *mujāhid* and facilitated the formation of a pro-Makhzan party prepared to support the idea of a Makhzan jihad against ᶜAbd al-Qādir's *fasād*.[111]

Algerian participation in raiding brought civil war nearer in other ways. For instance, in February 1847 a Dā'ira raiding party attacked a pro-Makhzan section of the Aḥlāf for stealing livestock. Several men from both sides were killed and women and children injured.[112] Although Bū Ḥamīdī took steps not to involve other tribes, the raid created a blood feud between the Aḥlāf and the Dā'ira and heightened the possibility of Makhzan intervention in the Rif on behalf of the Aḥlāf.[113] Sīdī Muḥammad interpreted the clash as preliminary to an advance on Fes by ᶜAbd al-Qādir and reacted swiftly. Members of the Dā'ira discovered in Taza were arrested, the route from Taza to Fes put under surveillance and Algerian tribes resettled in the Fes area ordered to migrate to Marrakesh.[114] When they refused several of their chiefs were temporarily imprisoned. Sīdī Muḥammad's fears were compounded when the French consular authorities alerted the Makhzan to the imminent arrival of a party of English adventurers with a consignment of arms for ᶜAbd al-Qādir.[115] The party was refused permission to land at Tetuan and then forced to return to Gibraltar by the Spanish in Ceuta.[116] A single raid thus triggered preparations for war in Taza and Fes, renewed pressure on resettled tribes in the Gharb, and European involvement.

The Makhzan's jihad of the sword against ᶜAbd al-Qādir

War was temporarily averted because ᶜAbd al-Qādir did not advance on Fes and Mawlay ᶜAbd al-Raḥmān vetoed a Makhzan offensive fearing it would play into ᶜAbd al-Qādir's hands.[117] During spring 1847, however, war crept closer as a result of another clash in the Rif. In April 1847, Muḥammad b. ᶜAbd al-Malik abandoned his post, frustrated because the Makhzan had not provided him with adequate resources to take effective action against ᶜAbd al-Qādir, or so he told the consuls.[118] He also complained to Drummond Hay that the French had not paid him for acting as an informant.[119] His replacement was Qā'id al-Aḥmar, a stranger to the Rif who did not speak Rīfī Berber and had no experience of its tribes. Al-Aḥmar had only his status as a Makhzan officer to rely upon and was thus extremely vulnerable. In fact his only supports were the small Makhzan garrison at Tafarsit and tribes in the immediate vicinity such as the Banū Tūzīn.

ᶜAbd al-Qādir in contrast benefitted from the departure of Muḥammad b. ᶜAbd al-Malik to consolidate his position from the central Rif to the border.[120] His strength relative to that of the Makhzan emboldened him to threaten al-Aḥmar and the pro-Makhzan sections of the Banū Tūzīn if they did not allow him safe asylum in the Rif.[121] His threat to attack a Makhzan governor was unprecedented and al-Aḥmar immediately requested reinforcements from Sīdī Muḥammad and begged Mawlay ᶜAbd al-Raḥmān to come north.[122] The situation was worsened by reports that Mawlay ᶜAbd al-Raḥmān b. Sulaymān, long-time ᶜAlawī rival of the sultan, had joined ᶜAbd al-Qādir's camp.[123] During May the two sides prepared for hostilities, both militarily and diplomatically, while the French joined the fray by trying to back every horse in the impending struggle.

Makhzan military preparations involved the mobilisation of around one thousand men from the core corps of the army, the ᶜAbīd, the artillery and the new *niẓāmī* units, and around one thousand five-hundred fighters from the Sharāga, Awlād Jāmiᶜ and Sharārda *jaysh* tribes.[124] The *maḥalla* gathered on the banks of the Wad Sebu east of Fes but could not proceed into the Rif due to a rebellion by the Ghiyāta tribe which blocked the route from Fes to Taza, the first stage on the journey to Tafarsit where al-Aḥmar was based.[125] To compensate the sultan ordered al-Aḥmar to recruit tribal auxiliaries from the Qalᶜaya. Their sympathy for ᶜAbd al-Qādir, however, undermined their reliability. For his part, ᶜAbd al-Qādir mobilised the Dā'ira, which included his *niẓāmī* corps, and moved northwest to Wad Kart around thirteen miles from Tafarsit. A French informant estimated the size of the Dā'ira as 120 tents of infantrymen and 400 tents of Algerian tribesmen all of whom needed food and other supplies and had been reduced to using weapons and gunpowder of local rather than European manufacture.[126]

Aware that the Makhzan possessed greater resources than he did, ᶜAbd al-Qādir sought Spanish intercession to re-open negotiations with France. A remarkable exchange resulted in which the French offered ᶜAbd al-Qādir the arms and material assistance necessary to replace Mawlay ᶜAbd al-Raḥmān as sultan on condition that he abandon all claims to French Algeria and ban British influence from the sultanate.[127] They hoped that the sultanate would be a glittering enough prize to make ᶜAbd al-Qādir renounce his claim to his native land but he refused. The French did not limit their approaches to ᶜAbd al-Qādir. When shaykhs of the Wazzāniyya brotherhood expressed concern about French discussions with him, the French consular mission suggested that al-Ḥājj al-ᶜArabī, head of the brotherhood, use his influence to persuade Mawlay ᶜAbd al-Raḥmān to attack ᶜAbd al-Qādir.[128] Finally, they suggested a secret alliance to the Makhzan itself according to which the sultan would lead a campaign into the Rif against ᶜAbd al-Qādir and a French column from Algeria would attack from the other side, apparently by coincidence, and then retreat to Algeria.[129] They also offered al-Aḥmar a salary and money to bribe the Rif tribes into abandoning ᶜAbd al-Qādir.[130] Mawlay ᶜAbd al-Raḥmān rejected these suggestions and ordered Sīdī Muḥammad to forbid al-Aḥmar to communicate with the French.[131]

In June the two sides came to blows. Makhzan troops and their Qalᶜaya allies stumbled upon the Dā'ira whose inhabitants opened fire killing several men. Al-Aḥmar then mobilised the Tafarsit garrison and his tribal auxiliaries to attack the Dā'ira the next day. The Dā'ira made its own preparations and managed to enlist the assistance of the nearby Mtalsa tribe. As a result ᶜAbd al-Qādir's forces were superior to those of al-Aḥmar who backed down from a confrontation. ᶜAbd al-Qādir was then warned by his informants that al-Aḥmar was planning a guerilla attack on the Dā'ira. Although the veracity of the report was questionable, ᶜAbd al-Qādir decided to pre-empt a Makhzan strike and attack al-Aḥmar first. He and his forces charged into the Makhzan camp at dawn, assuring the bemused troops that he would not harm them if they did not attack him. They immediately complied by casting down their weapons, an indication of ᶜAbd al-Qādir's mystique among rank and file soldiers. Bū Ḥamīdī then rode to the Tafarsit fort where the Makhzan commanders were quartered. A short battle ensued in which Bū Ḥamīdī captured the fort, the military supplies in it and all the Makhzan commanders with the exception of al-Aḥmar, who was killed during the fighting.[132]

ᶜAbd al-Qādir's victory was both logistic and ideological. Not only did he appropriate much needed supplies of arms, clothing and horses, but the reported details of the engagement reinforced his religious reputation across the north. The victory in itself suggested that ᶜAbd al-Qādir was favoured by God while his magnanimous treatment of ordinary Makhzan troops confirmed his religious prestige. A Fāsī courier informed Drummond Hay that al-Aḥmar's fighters had laid down their weapons because whenever ᶜAbd al-Qādir charged:

> The arms of his enemies were by some supernatural force wrested from their hands whilst bullets and stones showered down miraculously from Heaven.

The victory and its miraculous attributes encouraged a swell in public support for ᶜAbd al-Qādir which gave new hope to his northern partisans that he would indeed overthrow the sultan, hope augmented by the presence of Mawlay ᶜAbd al-Raḥmān b. Sulaymān in his camp.[133] Conversely, the Makhzan fared very badly. The troops were angered that Mawlay ᶜAbd al-Raḥmān had ordered them to fight a 'defender of the Faith' and reluctant to engage him again. The general population took the defeat as a sign of continued Makhzan weakness and new insurrections broke out across the country. The breakdown was most evident in the Meknes region where caravans were attacked 'within musket shot of the walls of the town' and a *niẓāmī* unit was attacked by tribesmen.

ᶜAbd al-Qādir insisted that his clash with al-Aḥmar was a localised incident rather than part of a general offensive against the Makhzan but the surge in his popularity convinced Sīdī Muḥammad to order a full mobilisation. He appointed Muḥammad b. ᶜAbd al-Ṣādiq, a native of the Rif, as its new governor and then sent him to clear the route to Taza using Makhzan cannon.[134] He also issued a general call for 'every Muslim… to act in defence of his faith and country' against the rebel ᶜAbd al-Qādir and begged Mawlay ᶜAbd al-Raḥmān to mobilise the south.[135] The sultan at last responded: in letters to his son he criticised him for sending al-Aḥmar into the Rif without sufficient backing but promised that he would come north to direct the expected Rif campaign.[136] The Makhzan jihad against ᶜAbd al-Qādir's *fasād* was about to begin.

In the Rif the distinction between Makhzan and Qādirī supporters became clearer as ᶜAbd al-Qādir raided the tribes who had supported al-Aḥmar, the Banū Tūzīn, Temsamān and Qalᶜaya, triggering the latter's mobilisation against the Dā'ira.[137] ᶜAbd al-Qādir speedily moved the Dā'ira eastwards and prepared to attack the Qalᶜaya who appealed to Sīdī Muḥammad for *niẓāmī* reinforcements, an indication that the *niẓām-i cedīd* was becoming an accepted form of military organisation.[138] The Qalᶜaya averted attack by making ᶜAbd al-Qādir an *ᶜār* sacrifice of eight bulls and agreeing to pay a large fine, tactics usually employed in confrontations between tribes and the Makhzan.[139] These raids helped provision the Dā'ira, but also added to the growing impression in the Rif that ᶜAbd al-Qādir was a political rather than religious figure and that the choice between him and the sultan was not one between the ideal and its degradation but between two manifestations of power.

Further south Makhzan forces managed to clear the way to Taza and several tribes who had pillaged the Makhzan camp after the defeat of al-Aḥmar surrendered their booty.[140] When Mawlay ᶜAbd al-Raḥmān arrived in Rabat in July, Sīdī Muḥammad advised an immediate strike against ᶜAbd al-Qādir. At this juncture, the Makhzan and ᶜAbd al-Qādir reconsidered enlisting European help in the struggle, an indication that the European factor had become a recognised part of domestic politics.[141] On the Makhzan side, the governor of the Rif, Muḥammad b. ᶜAbd al-Ṣādiq, asked De Chasteau if the French would land a small force near Melilla to intimidate local tribes into supporting the Makhzan.[142] Meanwhile, ᶜAbd al-Qādir renewed contact with Melilla in August 1847 with the aim, so the French suspected, of gaining access to munitions from European powers.[143] He also tried to persuade the Makhzan of his good intentions by surrendering the citadel of Tafarsit and the booty seized in his clash with al-Aḥmar.[144]

The next stage in hostilities involved resettled Algerian tribes, the Banū ᶜAmir, Ḥashem and Jaᶜāfra, whose position in the sultanate became steadily more untenable as tensions between ᶜAbd al-Qādir and the Makhzan rose.[145] The situation of the tribes had first become awkward in September 1846 when the Makhzan had begun to suspect that they were in contact with ᶜAbd al-Qādir. Although they had protested their loyalty, they again came under suspicion in February 1847 when Sīdī Muḥammad feared that ᶜAbd al-Qādir was about to march on Fes. Then, after the clash with al-Aḥmar, they were put under the surveillance of the ᶜAbīd Pasha of Fes, al-Faragī.[146] Caught between the Makhzan and ᶜAbd al-Qādir, the tribes made several approaches to the French consulate in Tanger asking for repatriation to Algeria but the military in Algiers refused to countenance their return. The situation came to a head in August 1847 when the tribes received word from ᶜAbd al-Qādir that he had signed a treaty with the French which would allow them to return to Algeria.[147] No such treaty existed but the tribes agreed to meet ᶜAbd al-Qādir near Taza to return to Algeria together, or so they later claimed.[148]

The Makhzan got wind of the planned rendezvous and interpreted it as an indication that ᶜAbd al-Qādir planned to stage a general insurrection involving the Algerian tribes, his Rif allies and Mawlay ᶜAbd al-Raḥmān b. Sulaymān.[149] Sīdī Muḥammad immediately commanded the largest Algerian tribe, the Banū ᶜAmir, to leave for Marrakesh under Makhzan escort to prevent them joining ᶜAbd al-Qādir.[150] The cavalcade set off southwards but the Banū ᶜAmir turned east in defiance of their escort. The Pasha of Fes called for reinforcements and a *maḥalla* of Sharāga and auxiliaries pursued the Banū ᶜAmir into the Rif.[151] They caught up with them at a narrow defile called Rasifa or Hajrat al-Kuhayla near ᶜAyn Madyuna northeast of Fes and attacked.[152] The two sides fought for several days during which many of the Banū ᶜAmir were killed. The rest melted away into the Rif and made their way across the border into Algeria or to Tanger to put themselves under French protection. ᶜAbd al-Qādir, who had come westwards for the rendezvous, retreated towards the Muluwiya as news of the debacle spread through the Rif.

The fate of the Ḥashem and Jaᶜāfra tribes was even worse. At approximately the same time as Sīdī Muḥammad ordered the Banū ᶜAmir to move south the sultan demanded hostages from the Ḥashem and Jaᶜāfra as guarantees that they would not join ᶜAbd al-Qādir. They refused and sought refuge in one of the shrines of the Gharb. When Sīdī Muḥammad heard that the Banū ᶜAmir were on their way to join ᶜAbd al-Qādir, he ordered the governor of the Gharb to attack the Ḥashem and Jaᶜāfra, regardless of the fact that they had put themselves under the protection of a holy man. Makhzan forces duly encircled the shrine and in violation of its *ḥurm* (sacred precincts) attacked the Ḥashem and Jaᶜāfra within. Fighting lasted for twenty four hours during which the tribes were 'overpowered, pillaged and butchered'.[153] Some were said to have killed their women and children, then finally themselves, to avoid capture by the Makhzan fighters.[154] Those who escaped fled to the Wazzāniyya *zāwiya* in the Jbala before continuing to Tanger and the protection of the consuls. Over a thousand refugees from the three tribes arrived in Tanger during the autumn putting an enormous strain on the urban infrastructure.[155] Makhzan authorities, however, refused to allow their repatriation as long as ᶜAbd al-Qādir remained at large in the Rif.[156]

Sīdī Muḥammad celebrated his victory by parading the captive tribesmen through Fes and ordering that the markets of Taza be decorated in thanksgiving for the Makhzan's victorious holy war against rebellion.[157] He also permitted Makhzan corps and tribes who had participated in the attacks to enslave women and children from the shattered tribes.[158] The unusual violence of the Makhzan onslaught reflected the changing complexion of politics in the sultanate. The tribes had arrived as Muslim brethren seeking refuge from the infidel but after 1845 a distinction between migrants and indigenous inhabitants had developed and attitudes towards the infidel had become more complex. These changes were due to a number of factors: the demarcation of the ᶜAlawī–Algerian border in

1845, the pressure put on limited resources by the presence of 'Algerians' in the northern sultanate and the ideological conflict between the Makhzan and ᶜAbd al-Qādir. As a result territorially bounded concepts of the *umma* had begun to emerge and the resettled tribes had become strangers and even enemies: Banū ᶜAmir survivors said that their attackers had accused them of being 'easterners' and 'Christian-lovers'.[159] Such differentiation forced not only the remnants of resettled tribes but also some prominent individuals resident in Fes to seek repatriation to a land which was their own, even if ruled by the French.[160]

Changing attitudes were also evident in the public response to the incidents. When informed of what Sīdī Muḥammad had done, Mawlay ᶜAbd al-Raḥmān was deeply concerned about the ideological mileage ᶜAbd al-Qādir might gain by accusing the Makhzan of betraying its Islamic duty to care for migrants from infidel territory.[161] ᶜAbd al-Qādir did indeed portray the attacks as the illegitimate slaughter of Muslims who had put themselves under the protection of the sultan. In the words of his son, Muḥammad:

> [The attackers] rendered it permissible to shed the blood of a believing people who had struggling in the way of God and spent their wealth to elevate religion, who were under their protection and had not entered the domains of the sultan until he had given them permission and guaranteed their safety.[162]

There was, however, no public outcry and instead a general shift among the Rif tribes in favour of the Makhzan. Whether the northern tribes accepted the Makhzan claim that the resettled tribes had colluded with ᶜAbd al-Qādir in a seditious attempt to overthrow the ᶜAlawī Makhzan or not, it had become clear that from the state's perspective ᶜAbd al-Qādir was the enemy against whom the jihad was directed. As late as 1846 the Rif tribes would not have accepted such an interpretation but by August 1847 they were willing to acknowledge its possible validity. ᶜAbd al-Qādir was guilty of attacking many of them, stealing their livestock for the Dā'ira, and, worse, his attack on al-Aḥmar and attempt to join the resettled tribes had made a Makhzan offensive into the Rif directed by the sultan himself a strong possibility. The Rif tribes possessed the same ambivalence to central authority that had made it impossible for ᶜAbd al-Qādir to maintain an indigenous state in Algeria. Now that a final show-down between the two men appeared inevitable Mawlay ᶜAbd al-Raḥmān's claim that ᶜAbd al-Qādir was a *mufsid*, a splitter of the distaff of Islam, seemed true, and the sultan's huge army and historical legitimacy seemed more important than ᶜAbd al-Qādir's declining popularity as a *mujāhid* and marabout. In al-Nāṣirī's words:

> Respect between ᶜAbd al-Qādir and the *amīr al-mu'minīn* Abu Zayd [Mawlay ᶜAbd al-Raḥmān] ceased, their enmity became apparent and the people began to fear ᶜAbd al-Qādir.[163]

This shift in Rif affiliations became apparent as ᶜAbd al-Qādir retreated towards the Muluwiya and found that tribes who had given him their allegiance had transferred it back to the Makhzan. The Banū Tūzīn, the Tsūl and the Brānis all refused him passage through their territory.[164] Meanwhile a Qalᶜaya raiding party attacked the Dā'ira, seizing cattle and grain in the process.[165] ᶜAbd al-Qādir launched a violent counter-raid in which he destroyed the raiding party's village, killing many of the defenders and capturing their women and children.[166] The violence of ᶜAbd al-Qādir's attack suggested that for him as much as for the Makhzan righteous war was no longer an issue of fighting the French but of fighting those who were guilty of betraying the faith, the godless within society. The parameters of jihad had thus moved to a classic conflict between a sultan and a challenger who each claimed to be waging jihad against *fasād*.

In the case of the Qalᶜaya raid, ᶜAbd al-Qādir achieved his immediate objective: the clan involved relinquished their plunder and agreed to pay a large fine but his ideological position was not widely accepted.[167] A marabout of the nearby Banū Saᶜīd described the attack as a demonstration of 'unbelievable cruelty', implicitly unbecoming to a religious figure and ᶜAbd al-Qādir and the Dā'ira found themselves increasingly isolated.[168] To break the hostile encirclement of the Dā'ira, ᶜAbd al-Qādir applied to Wuld Sīdī Ramaḍān, a marabout of the Banū Yznāsen, for permission to camp on the Rif coast. Although ᶜAbd al-Qādir no longer enjoyed full Banū Yznāsen support, Wuld Sīdī Ramaḍān gave his permission, but warned him that the coast's proximity to Spanish Melilla made it unsafe. However, proximity to non-ᶜAlawī territory was exactly what ᶜAbd al-Qādir wanted and during September he moved the Dā'ira to Qasbat Salwan twelve miles south of Melilla.[169] From Salwan he contacted the Spanish whom he asked to mediate with the French on his behalf.[170] He also asked to purchase gunpowder and the French suspected that he was awaiting English munitions, a suspicion reinforced by a private British initiative to contact ᶜAbd al-Qādir from Melilla.[171] Nonetheless the French did make ᶜAbd al-Qādir an offer: an annual stipend of one million francs if he would accept permanent exile from the Maghrib to either the Levant or the Hijaz.[172]

While ᶜAbd al-Qādir renewed contact with European powers, the Makhzan prepared for its Rif campaign. By late September 1847 the sultan and several of his sons were in the north. Mawlay ᶜAbd al-Raḥmān was in Rabat, Sīdī Muḥammad and Mawlay Sulaymān were preparing a large army in Fes and Mawlay Aḥmad was campaigning against the Hayayna and Ghiyāta outside Taza. A fourth son, Mawlay Idrīs, sporadically mentioned in the sources, seems to have also been in Taza and another ᶜAlawī *sharīf*, Mawlay Ibrāhīm, held Tafarsit. Preparations for war continued apace in a mobilisation which was greater than any of the mobilisations which had destabilised the sultanate between 1840 and 1844. Not only were the sultan and his elder sons all involved but the Makhzan chose this moment to recall to service the Udāyā corps, marginalised since their revolt in 1831. Udāyā from Laraish, Rabat and Wad Nafis outside Marrakesh were all called up, as were the precious *niẓāmī* units from the main cities.[173]

Mawlay ᶜAbd al-Raḥmān himself took an unprecedented interest in the campaign, warning Sīdī Muḥammad repeatedly to personally involve himself in routine organisation and planning and take an interest in his men to avoid a repetition of the mistakes at Isly.[174] In early October the sultan travelled from Rabat to Meknes and authorised the departure of Sīdī Muḥammad, Mawlay Sulaymān and the main *maḥalla* for Taza where the number of fighters had already reached an estimated 33,000 men.[175] After their departure Mawlay ᶜAbd al-Raḥmān travelled to Fes to take their place. He arrived on 17 October 1847 and issued an ultimatum to ᶜAbd al-Qādir that if he did not leave the sultanate with the Dā'ira, he would be attacked.[176] The sultan and his sons planned a two-pronged attack: Mawlay Aḥmad was to travel from Taza to Tafarsit where he would meet the central Rif *maḥalla* commanded by Mawlay Ibrāhīm and Muḥammad b. ᶜAbd al-Ṣādiq before advancing on the Dā'ira at Salwan. Sīdī Muḥammad and the main *maḥalla* would follow the more direct easterly route towards Salwan via ᶜAyn Zura. Mawlay ᶜAbd al-Raḥmān would remain in Fes.

The impending Rif campaign undoubtedly reminded him of Mawlay Sulaymān's disastrous campaign into the Middle Atlas in the last years of his life, and the subsequent collapse of his Makhzan which had triggered years of civil war in which Mawlay ᶜAbd al-Raḥmān had himself played a key part. Now elderly and in a poor state of health he had no desire to see a repeat of those years with himself playing Mawlay Sulaymān's role. The stakes were actually higher than they had been twenty-five years before: Mawlay Sulaymān had faced a powerful Darqāwa–Berber coalition but it had lacked a figurehead of ᶜAbd al-Qādir's stature. The only man who could compete with ᶜAbd al-Qādir for the loyalty of the inhabitants of the sultanate was in fact Mawlay ᶜAbd al-Raḥmān who, for all his flaws, possessed the prestige reserved for the ruling sultan.[177] He was also better liked than Sīdī Muḥammad who had made himself extremely unpopular in Fes by heavy handed treatment of ᶜAbd al-Qādir's supporters and was reputedly vain and obsessed with avenging the honour he had lost at Isly in 1844.[178]

As Sīdī Muḥammad's *maḥalla* moved towards Taza a growing number of Rif tribes renewed their loyalty to the Makhzan or were beaten into submission. After considerable effort on the part of Mawlay Aḥmad and Sīdī Muḥammad the Hayayna and Ghiyāta capitulated. The Tsūl and Brānis made a symbolic *ᶜār* sacrifice of five black bullocks and five white heifers, thereby placing themselves under Makhzan protection, and tribes further afield sent deputations with their oaths of allegiance.[179] Sīdī Muḥammad responded that the only proof of loyalty he would accept was assistance in provisioning the *maḥalla*. He accompanied his words with judicious distribution of money among the border tribes still beyond his reach, notably the Aḥlāf and Banū Yznāsen.[180] In November shortly before *ᶜīd al-aḍḥā* Sīdī Muḥammad and Mawlay Aḥmad left Taza for ᶜAyn Zura and Tafarsit respectively.

The arrival of the sultan in Fes and the departure of the princes from Taza convinced ᶜAbd al-Qādir that after years of prevarication the Makhzan finally intended to attack him. The inhabitants of the Dā'ira wanted to leave the sultanate as the sultan demanded, either by travelling directly east into Algeria or by moving southeast into the Sahara.[181] ᶜAbd al-Qādir, however, preferred to seek the intercession of the *shurafā'* of Wazzan which the sultan rejected on the grounds that ᶜAbd al-Qādir had disobeyed his master and betrayed his host and could therefore no longer be considered a Muslim.[182] ᶜAbd al-Qādir then appealed to Mawlay Aḥmad and Sīdī Muḥammad to settle the conflict using the Sharīᶜa as a basis for negotiation rather than by force but neither prince responded.

The time for words had passed and as the central Rif *maḥalla* advanced towards Salwan, ᶜAbd al-Qādir and the Dā'ira retreated east towards Banū Yznāsen territory.[183] Muḥammad b. ᶜAbd al-Ṣādiq and Mawlay Ibrāhīm occupied Salwan shortly afterwards and set up camp to await the armies of Mawlay Aḥmad and Sīdī Muḥammad. The huge Makhzan presence at Salwan persuaded the Mtalsa, Qalᶜaya and Banū Yznāsen to declare for the Makhzan.[184] The Qalᶜaya and Mtalsa greeted the princes arrival with ostentatious gunpowder play and the Banū Yznāsen blocked the Dā'ira's escape route into the Sahara.[185] ᶜAbd al-Qādir's problems were compounded by the arrival of a French column at Lalla Maghnia with instructions to prevent him crossing the border into Algeria.[186]

At this critical juncture ᶜAbd al-Qādir's position was suddenly improved by news that Mawlay ᶜAbd al-Raḥmān was mortally ill. It was generally assumed that if the sultan died before Sīdī Muḥammad had won a victory he would not be able to keep the loyalty of the Makhzan armies and they would desert *en masse* to ᶜAbd al-Qādir. The untimely death of the sultan could upset everything and plunge the country into chaos with Mawlay ᶜAbd al-Raḥmān's own sons, the sons of Mawlay Sulaymān, other ᶜAlawī *shurafā'* in Tafilalt and an Idrīsī party headed by ᶜAbd al-Qādir, all fighting for supremacy.[187] Sīdī Muḥammad, however, did not dare order an attack with his father at death's door and the Makhzan armies remained in a state of suspense at Salwan. ᶜAbd al-Qādir seized the opportunity to institute another round of feverish negotiations. On the one hand, he persuaded the ᶜAlawī *niẓāmī* corps to defect to his side if the sultan were to die. On the other, he persuaded Sīdī Muḥammad to delay his attack so he could sent a Rif notable to Fes to ask Mawlay ᶜAbd al-Raḥmān to receive Bū Ḥamīdī to negotiate a settlement.[188] Another envoy went to Tlemsen to discuss the possibility of a settlement with the French, while Leon Roches in Tanger repeated his earlier opportunistic suggestion that the French would support ᶜAbd al-Qādir's bid for power in the sultanate on condition that he would not disrupt *l'Algérie française* in any way and would sever the sultanate's relations with Britain.[189]

Mawlay ᶜAbd al-Raḥmān made an unexpected recovery but nevertheless welcomed ᶜAbd al-Qādir's go-between Muḥammad b. ᶜAbd Allah al-Aḥlāfī and agreed to see Bū Ḥamīdī. As a token of his good faith he was said to have sent his prayer beads to ᶜAbd al-Qādir.[190] However, his inclination to conciliation was sorely tried by his chance discovery of correspondence detailing the *niẓāmī* conspiracy to defect to ᶜAbd al-Qādir in the event of his death.[191] At the same time the French in Algeria demanded that he refuse to negotiate with ᶜAbd al-Qādir's envoys.[192] When Bū Ḥamīdī's delegation arrived in late November the sultan therefore received them coldly and kept Bū Ḥamīdī waiting several days before giving him an audience. When the audience finally took place Mawlay ᶜAbd al-Raḥmān reiterated his earlier ultimatum that ᶜAbd al-Qādir and the Dā'ira must retire to Fes or leave the sultanate. If he failed to take one of these two options, he would be attacked by the *maḥalla*.[193] Envoys left Fes on 6 or 7 December to take the Makhzan ultimatum to ᶜAbd al-Qādir and inform Sīdī Muḥammad at Salwan of the outcome of the negotiations.[194]

News of the sultan's ultimatum reached ᶜAbd al-Qādir first. He neither trusted the sultan's promise that he and his family would be allowed to live safely in Fes, nor trusted the Makhzan army to allow his safe departure for the Sahara, he therefore decided to launch a surprise night attack on the Makhzan camp. He hoped that this would create enough time for the Dā'ira to retreat eastwards across the Muluwiya and then cross into Algeria. He and his fighters could then decide whether to surrender – either to the Makhzan or the French – or retreat into the Sahara. The inequality between the size of ᶜAbd al-Qādir's forces and those of the tripartite Makhzan army camped at Salwan was huge, his strategy of attack was therefore calculated to generate maximum surprise and fear among the Makhzan troops.

He ordered his men to load two camels with bundles of brushwood dipped in pitch and led them to the edge of Mawlay Aḥmad's camp. They then lit the bundles and drove the camels into the camp. The terrified screaming animals charged through overturning and setting fire to tents. Behind them came ᶜAbd al-Qādir and his men firing at the troops as they rushed out of their tents and tried to grab their weapons.[195] A witness from the camp of the Rif *maḥalla* which was located across a small stream later told the French consul that ᶜAbd al-Qādir had spread 'terror, disorder and death' through the camp.[196] From Mawlay Aḥmad's camp the camels plunged on into the adjacent camp of Sīdī Muḥammad. The second camp, however, was forewarned of their approach by the commotion from Mawlay Aḥmad's camp and Sīdī Muḥammad directed his cannon against the attackers. ᶜAbd al-Qādir and his men swerved out of the line of fire which landed in Mawlay Aḥmad's camp causing additional casualties.

At dawn ᶜAbd al-Qādir retreated, stopping only to gather the corpses of his comrades and bury them hastily in a communal grave. He was pursued for a short distance by Sīdī Muḥammad but beat him off and headed east to protect the Dā'ira which was already moving towards the Muluwiya and the border into Algeria beyond. Sīdī Muḥammad returned to Salwan to assess the situation. The discovery of the bodies of around thirty of ᶜAbd al-Qādir's men enabled him to send a complement of heads to Fes and claim a victory, but in reality many more of the Makhzan's fighters had died and ᶜAbd al-Qādir was still at large.[197] The inconclusive nature of the battle gave Sīdī Muḥammad little option but to continue the campaign.

The Makhzan army therefore advanced towards the Muluwiya catching up with ᶜAbd al-Qādir a short distance from the river. As in other parts of the Rif the arrival of the Makhzan army elicited support and provisions from tribes who had previously backed cAbd al-Qādir.[198] The Makhzan renewed its gunpowder supplies from a French ship fortuitously anchored in the bay near Melilla. Despite superior forces, local support and fresh gunpowder, French sources suggest that Sīdī Muḥammad hesitated to attack cAbd al-Qādir and would have let him cross the Muluwiya unharmed. However, Mawlay Aḥmad and Muḥammad b. cAbd al-Ṣadiq attacked and Sīdī Muḥammad joined them.[199] Sīdī Muḥammad later told Mawlay cAbd al-Raḥmān that he had insisted on the attack but his hesitancy was natural since he, as future sultan, had the most to lose from a defeat.[200] cAbd al-Qādir and the Dā'ira had crossed the Muluwiya by the time the cAlawī attack started and his aim was to hold the Makhzan forces at the river long enough to allow the Dā'ira to cross into Algeria.[201] When he judged his aim to have been achieved he and a handful of men retreated into the Banū Yznāsen mountains. Approximately one third of his men had been killed and another third captured enabling Sīdī Muḥammad to send sixty six prisoners and a complement of heads to Fes to announce his victory.[202]

This battle was the last in the Makhzan campaign against cAbd al-Qādir. The Dā'ira crossed safely into Algeria and cAbd al-Qādir and his band decided that their best option was surrender to the French. They contacted the French garrison at Jamicat al-Ghazwat and after three days of negotiations they marched into the fort and formally surrendered to the Duc d'Aumale and General Lamoricière on 23 December 1847.[203] In return for his surrender, the Duc d'Aumale had promised cAbd al-Qādir that he, his family and those of his followers who so wished would be given passage to the Arab east and that those who wished to remain in Algeria would be allowed to return to their homes without harassment.[204] These promises were broken: cAbd al-Qādir and his entourage were taken to Algiers by ship and then conveyed to France and imprisoned. After five years they were allowed to retire to Bursa in Anatolia on a pension and only after an earthquake did they finally gain permission to move to Damascus where they spent the rest of their lives.

Sīdī Muḥammad was jubilant when news of cAbd al-Qādir's surrender reached the Makhzan camp, confirming that he had indeed won his victory against him. The Makhzan troops returned to Fes and Sīdī Muḥammad wrote to his father informing him that the *mufsid* cAbd al-Qādir had surrendered to the infidel, thereby proving the falsity of his claim to have been a fighter for the faith.[205] In the ensuing weeks the Makhzan capitalised on cAbd al-Qādir's surrender to the French, using it as an indication that he was neither the man of religion nor the enemy of the French he had claimed to be. Indeed the whole conflict was quickly tailored to fit Makhzan religio-political requirements. A letter from a Rif notable and Makhzan *qā'id*, Wuld Ab(u) Muḥammad, to the sultan's chief minister indicates how the Makhzan interpreted events: jihad against the infidel was erased from the schema and the conflict presented as a classic case of Makhzan jihad against societal *fasād* directed by cAbd al-Qādir, a rebel and insurgent (*al-fāsid al-fattān*) who had been tempted to leave the path of God by his greed for power.

God had punished him by making him the victim of his own rebellion and he had ended up generally despised, the perennial reward of those 'who spread corruption in the earth and unsheath the sword of rebellion'. The letter interpreted the sultan's fear of challenging a recognised *mujāhid* as a sign of his magnanimity and hope that the wayward ᶜAbd al-Qādir would abandon his search for temporal power and return to the true faith.[206] Mawlay ᶜAbd al-Raḥmān's own exposé of the conflict followed a similar line:

> That rebel and insurrectionary, the henchman of the devil, went far in recklessness. He mounted the beast of destruction and travelled a willful road, straying from the path of reason. His ambition, which was stronger than he, spoke and seduced him with the idea that he was marked out to become a ruler. He then desired to split the distaff of Islam and confuse the minds of men. He promoted evil and brought the good into doubt and was profoundly versed in duplicity and deceit .... He spread his harmful and pernicious message through the land in a guise which attracted the ignorant, the blind and the misguided and we despaired of guiding him. We realised his true aim and prepared an army marked for victory, with banners flying, commanded by our most revered son, Sīdī Muḥammad ... but we demanded that he exert every effort to avert the spilling of blood ... and only use force as a last resort.[207]

The story of ᶜAbd al-Qādir thus turned full circle; he and his followers who had scorned the Makhzan and claimed to be the true *mujāhidīn* were brought low and became the objects of derision and a Makhzan jihad. Mawlay ᶜAbd al-Raḥmān avoided describing the Rif campaign as a jihad, but he evidently conceptualised himself as a righteous ruler who had endeavoured to guide ᶜAbd al-Qādir along the path which his religion demanded, but had been compelled to use force against him in a dualistic conflict between the positive forces of Islamic order, represented by the Makhzan, and the evil forces of unrest and sedition, represented by ᶜAbd al-Qādir. This schema was constantly reiterated in sultanic letters read out in great mosques and tribal markets with all the usual panoply of victory: gun salutes, celebrations and decoration of the markets with banners and ribbons.[208] Governors and notables repeated the Makhzan formulation in the replies they sent back to the sultan and it was picked up with minor variations by contemporary Makhzan historians and their pre-colonial successors.[209]

7

ISLAMIC STATEHOOD AND JIHAD IN NINETEENTH CENTURY MOROCCO

^{c}Abd al-Qādir's departure from North Africa marked the end of his long and complex relationship with Mawlay ^{c}Abd al-Raḥmān and a divergence in their respective historiographies. ^{c}Abd al-Qādir became an archetypal hero, characterised as a noble warrior in European historiography, as a mystic in the Levant and as a national figurehead in Algerian nationalist discourse. Mawlay ^{c}Abd al-Raḥmān remained sultan until his death in 1859 when he was duly succeeded by Sīdī Muḥammad. He came to be celebrated in ^{c}Alawī historical literature as a sultan of the stature of Mawlay Ismā^{c}īl and Sīdī Muḥammad b. ^{c}Abd Allah. Later ^{c}Alawī historians laid the responsibility for the conflict which had rocked his Makhzan for so many years squarely at the door of ^{c}Abd al-Qādir, a holy warrior who fought the French in Algeria on behalf of Islam and its earthly representative, the ^{c}Alawī imam, only to become their *de facto* ally by challenging the imam and acting as a vehicle for the forces of fragmentation. Although many historians exhibited sympathy for ^{c}Abd al-Qādir and acknowledged that he fought a true jihad in the 1830s, they consistently presented his later activities as *fasād*.[1]

The drama of Mawlay ^{c}Abd al-Raḥmān and ^{c}Abd al-Qādir played itself out in the context of the establishment of French colonial rule in Algeria but it was equally part of longer term processes of state formation in the sultanate which was one variation on a theme familiar throughout the Islamic world. From the establishment of the ^{c}Alawī sultanate in the seventeeth century the sultans had worked steadily to transform themselves from tribal chiefs into theocratic rulers. They had also striven to accrue the material and ideological means to extend central government out from the cities and plains to the mountain fringe and to push ^{c}Alawī borders east beyond Tlemsen, an area claimed by the Turks of Algiers but perceived as part of the sultanate in an ideal past age.

They used two key concepts – sharifism and jihad – both of which tapped into pre-existing religious and socio-political patterns and provided rulers with a status which was readily comprehensible to the tribes. The Marīnid and Sa^{c}dī periods had established the concept of a religio-political state headed by a *sharīf* but societal acknowledgement of the right to rule of the *shurafā'* still left a multiplicity of sharifian lineages who could theoretically make a bid for power. The sharifian dynasties therefore had to persuade their subjects of the legitimacy of their particular blood line. They achieved this by suggesting that the head of state ought to be a warrior capable of leading his subjects in the jihad as well as a *sharīf.* On the western Islamic frontier jihad was a particularly important obligation as a result of the Reconquista and the expansion of the Portuguese and Spanish into North Africa during the fifteenth and sixteenth centuries. The state's responsibility to lead the community in this particular jihad not only enabled rulers to prove themselves militarily and secure the legitimation which warrior prowess bestowed upon tribal chieftains, but did so in an arena where their religio-political credentials were dramatically affirmed.

The concepts of sharifism and jihad underlay both the structure and ideology of government in Morocco before the colonial period, and by applying and manipulating them the sultans recognised – and sought to surmount – constraints on the extension of their power over tribal society. In common with more powerful Islamic regimes of the time such as the Ottomans they harboured absolutist pretensions and envisaged the development of a more efficient governmental structure. To realise these objectives the sharifian sultans had to create a military absolutist state of the type identified by Marshall Hodgson as a 'gunpowder empire', a state run by a professional elite who performed both political and military functions.[2] State initiatives constantly pushed in this direction under the influence of Ottoman models but the inability of the sultans to fully secure their power over the tribes, or their authority over the *ᶜulamā'* and rural religious lineages, prevented the transformation from taking place.

Instead this struggle engendered an ongoing ideological exchange between rulers and ruled and a series of religious and political challenges to the dynasty from the tribal fringe. Differing interpretations of the meaning of jihad by the sultans and their subjects stood at the heart of this exchange which was informed by two basic premises: that the sharifian state was theocratic in nature and that it existed to defend Morocco from the infidel by means of jihad. What this meant in practice, however, varied considerably. The idiom of jihad was inherently vague: its religio-legal definition was exertion/struggle in the service of God of which military action was only the 'lesser' or 'smaller' part.[3]

This vagueness enabled the ᶜAlawī sultans to apply the term 'jihad' to a wide range of activities. On the one hand, they extended the meaning of jihad against the infidel from direct military confrontations to corsairing, known as the maritime jihad, ransoming of Muslims in Christian captivity and handouts to the Rif 'holy warriors' who monitored the Spanish enclaves of Ceuta and Melilla. On the other hand, they identified opposition to the state as a religious as well as political challenge based on the sultan's theocratic identity as God's representative on Earth. This enabled the sultans to describe military action against their own subjects as a jihad against *fasād* or corruption of the body politic. The concept of *fasād* was as flexible as the concept of jihad but, from the perspective of the state, its basic range of meanings was endemic dissidence, rebellion, or an armed challenge for power.

However, manipulation of the idiom of holy war and interpretation of rebellion in religious terms proved to be a double-edged sword. Having accepted sharifian rule society did not reject the state's ideology but maintained that sharifian theocracy had to be constantly validated by jihad against the infidel. If a sultan failed to prove his *baraka* in this arena the jihad against *fasād* had no legitimacy and rebellion or a challenge for power from the tribal periphery could be legitimised as a societal jihad against dynastic *fasād*. This religious and political dialogue gave the sultanate a crucial role, first, in the development of the ideology of eighteenth century religious renewal and, second, in nineteenth century Maghribi resistence to colonialism whether directly by the sultan or other sharifian holy warriors such as ᶜAbd al-Qādir.

The process began with Mawlay Ismāᶜīl's formation of the ᶜAbīd slave army which he legitimised as an instrument for state jihad against the Iberian coastal enclaves. His grandson, Sīdī Muḥammad b. ᶜAbd Allah, continued the task by launching a bid for theocratic power in the doctrinal sphere. His 'proto-Salafi' religious reforms were opposed not by the tribes but by the urban *ᶜulamā'* who saw his religious and economic policies as a threat to their hegemony. They challenged his centralising 'jihad' in the decades after his death by supporting sultanic claimants who would legitimise their theocratic pretensions in warfare rather than doctrinal disputation.

The fears of a new European crusade against the Islamic world aroused by the Napoleonic Wars strengthened society's right to demand a warrior sultan, by rebellion if necessary, and forced the dynasty to develop an ideological answer. The answer started to emerge during the troubled last years of Mawlay Sulaymān when he asserted that rebellion was contrary to religion in a theocratic state and that state action against rebels was therefore a form of jihad – jihad against *fasād* – holy war against corruption of the body politic. His nascent theory of jihad against *fasād* exploited the multiple meanings of 'endeavor in the service of God' to extend jihad from the well-established obligation of the state to fight against the infidel to military action against domestic threats to the Islamic state. The theory matured during the pivotal reign of Mawlay ᶜAbd al-Raḥmān who realised that the jihad against *fasād* was only a valid tool for state centralisation when accompanied by successful state jihad against the infidel. His efforts to restart the maritime jihad and reimpose the Islamic bounds in the 1820s were thus two sides of the same coin designed to achieve an equilibrium between jihad against the infidel and jihad against *fasād*.

The moment of equilibrium was, however, brief as the French conquest of Algiers in 1830 opened a new chapter in the politics of holy war and rebellion. As the historian of Moroccan nationalism, Abdellah Laroui, points out, it was the fall of Algiers in 1830 which signalled the beginning of the 'prelude to protectorate' period in the sultanate, rather than later events such as the much-cited Anglo–Moroccan trade treaty (1856) or the Tetuan War of 1859–60:

> Une lecture même rapide de la documentation contemporaine de l'événement … ne laisse aucun doute que la chute du pouvoir turc en Algérie a eu un immense retentissement à la cour marocaine et dans les

> provinces limitrophes. Le sultan eut dès le début à faire un choix: accepter ou non la bay'a de Tlemcen. Plus tard, le déroulement des événements aboutit à une crise de conscience dans la classe cléricale et à une crise politique à l'intérieur du Makhzen qui changèrent la nature même du régime politique marocain. Bien sûr, cela ne devint clair qu'en 1844 après la bataille d'Isly.[4]

Initially the demise of the Turks appeared to offer the ^{c}Alawī sultan an opportunity to realise the dynasty's ambition to rule west Algeria. Mawlay ^{c}Abd al-Raḥmān took the opportunity by accepting the *bay^{c}a* of Tlemsen. His actions amounted to a public statement that he was responsible for the jihad in all its forms not only within his traditional domains but also in neighbouring regions bereft of Islamic leadership. His universalist ideological aspirations were unachievable in view of his limited resources, tribal dissidence and French territorial imperialism, but they were adopted by ^{c}Abd al-Qādir who further evolved the theory of jihad against *fasād* within a new colonial context.

As a product of the sharifian maraboutic milieu, ^{c}Abd al-Qādir placed the discourse of Islamic revival, itself influenced by ^{c}Alawī ideology, at the service of the state and asserted that its responsibilities included both renewing the faith and expelling the infidel. The jihad against *fasād* thereby took its place as a precondition for jihad against the infidel. The fact that his vision of statehood owed a considerable religio-political debt to the ^{c}Alawī sultanate and that he felt obliged to pay homage to the sultan made his ideological initiatives as relevent to ^{c}Alawī religio-political discourse as to his own. In particular, the Fāsī *fatwa* permitting him to define rebels as non-Muslims in the context of an infidel threat and to insist that jihad leadership was the prerogative of the state became crucial to Makhzan discourse in the 1840s.

Mawlay ^{c}Abd al-Raḥmān and ^{c}Abd al-Qādir acted as mirrors recognising and empowering each other even as they competed for power because both ultimately subscribed to the statist view that jihad leadership was the prerogative of a qualified Islamic ruler. Throughout the 1830s ^{c}Abd al-Qādir maintained that jihad leadership was the right as well as the duty of the ruler and that independently organised jihad, however well-meaning, was *fasād* because it disrupted the balance within society essential to its well-being. In the 1840s, Mawlay ^{c}Abd al-Raḥmān adopted exactly the same ideological stance to combat ^{c}Abd al-Qādir, who challenged him after Isly, not by threatening the system but by insisting that he had failed to fulfil his self-proclaimed obligation to defend the *umma* and that his subjects should therefore join a regional jihad, irrespective of his wishes.

At this time of crisis, Mawlay ^{c}Abd al-Raḥmān took the jihad against *fasād* construct a step further and denounced ^{c}Abd al-Qādir as a rebel rather than a holy warrior on the grounds that independent action, even against the infidel, was an act of rebellion against the divinely appointed state. This was a significant ideological step forward and became part of the Makhzan's moral armoury against a population made restive by the changes taking place in the region as a result of its engagement with European imperialism. Jihad against the infidel needed no justification but the Makhzan now asserted that when and how it was to be waged needed both consideration and explanation. Subsequent Makhzan discourse claimed that the imperfections of the *umma* rendered military modernisation, economic reform and strengthening of the Islamic state essential preconditions for a successful jihad. To contradict the sultan's policies by word or deed constituted opposition to the vital task of religious and political renewal, and suppression of such opposition was one of his most important tasks in a world politically and culturally threatened by modern Europe.[5]

The theory of jihad against *fasād* thus became the ideological corollary to modernisation and anti-colonial resistance in the sultanate until the imposition of the French and Spanish protectorates in 1912. The success of the theory was, however, also its weakness in the context of French colonialism in Algeria and European economic and political penetration of the sultanate. For the remainder of the pre-colonial period domestic politics were characterised by tension between a Makhzan trying to expand its reach into society in order to rally the resources to wage the jihad and a society which increasingly responded to peripheral or oppositional jihad movements and rejected the initiatives of ruling sultans, compromised by their capitulations to European pressure. ᶜAbd al-Qādir had become a serious threat because he could secure societal backing for his own jihad against the perceived *fasād* of the Makhzan when the enemy was at the door. His strength lay in his Idrīsī sharifian ancestry, his performance as a warrior and his maintenance of a traditional, non-territorial concept of jihad which retained and nurtured the long historical connection between the Rif and Tlemsen, despite French efforts to draw a border between the sultanate and *l'Algérie française*.

As the nineteenth century progressed the sultan's subjects remained resistant to the Makhzan's acceptance of a spatially-bounded concept of jihad which encompassed accommodation as well as resistance, and saw in Makhzan policies signs of *fasād* which they challenged using the ideological framework of jihad. When Mawlay ᶜAbd al-Raḥmān died his martial cousin, Mawlay ᶜAbd al-Raḥmān b. Sulayman, who had consistently supported ᶜAbd al-Qādir, contested the accession of Sīdī Muḥammad.[6] A year later a *sharīf* from the Jbala region, al-Jilānī al-Rūgī, harangued the tribes to fight the Spanish who had occupied Tetuan rather than allow Sīdī Muḥammad's Makhzan to make irreligious concessions to them. Between 1873 and 1894 the Makhzan regained control under the direction of Mawlay al-Ḥasan and his modern *niẓāmī* army but his inability to use it to decrease European political and commercial privileges within the sultanate generated resentment.

When he was succeeded by his son, Mawlay ᶜAbd al-ᶜAzīz, a minor under the influence of his chief minister and various European representatives, the country rose again in revolt. In 1902, al-Jilānī b. ᶜAbd al-Salām, better known as Bū Ḥimāra, established a counter-sultanate at Taza in the Rif. Posing as Mawlay Muḥammad, the elder brother of Mawlay ᶜAbd al-ᶜAzīz, he claimed that he would overthrow the corrupt and traitorous sultan who had sold the country to the French and lead the jihad against the infidel.[7] His following which stretched into west Algeria consisted largely of the same tribes as those who had supported ᶜAbd al-Qādir sixty years before.[8] The rise of Mawlay al-Hafīẓ, governor of Marrakesh, against his brother, Mawlay ᶜAbd al-ᶜAzīz, in 1907 used the same language of jihad against *fasād* and was ultimately recognised as a jihad when the former became sultan in place of his discredited brother. However Mawlay al-Hafīẓ relied on French help to achieve power and his assertion that he would rid the sultanate of infidel influence proved impossible to fulfil. The cycle of jihad against *fasād* therefore continued with the Saharan challenges of Mā' al-ᶜAynayn in 1910 and his son, al-Hiba, in 1912, challenges crushed not by the Makhzan but by the French who took over the perennial task of restoring order against *fasād*.[9]

The French interpreted the widespread dissidence and revolt they encountered within the sultanate as proof of permanent political dysfunction, a chronic division between tax-paying lands obedient to the state, the *bilād al-makhzan*, and non-tax-paying lands of dissidence, the *bilād al-sība*. Certainly large sections of the subject population in the pre-colonial sultanate did exhibit permanent or recurrent opposition to the gathering of their resources by the state, creating a *bilād al-sība*, or 'land running to waste' beyond the reach of the '*makhzan*' or treasury. However, to translate *sība* as dissidence suggests a division of the Moroccan body politic into two separate geo-political zones which would have been unrecognisable to the population. It also necessitates an untenable distinction between the sultan's political and religious powers rather than between his power and authority. The sultan's power was doubtlessly limited by his military capacity at any given time, but his authority as imam and 'Shadow of God on Earth' was theoretically unlimited and had political implications throughout his domains, into Algeria and down into the Sahara.[10]

Islamic statehood in nineteenth century Morocco cannot therefore be satisfactorily described using solely the categories of *makhzan* and *sība*. Nor can it be fully explained by Khaldunian or Ottoman paradigms, which Gellner combined in his vision of a state based on God-given shepherding of a passive flock of subjects repeatedly menaced by tribal 'wolves' on the periphery. The concept of jihad against *fasād* adds dynamism and reciprocity to the relationship between the state and all its subjects. The placing of *fasād* alongside *sība* and jihad alongside tax collection does not deny the reality of societal opposition to the state but locates it within a shared political discourse whose terms were ambiguous and therefore allowed the constant renegotiation of political boundaries and relationships.

The discourse of jihad against *fasād* enabled popular involvement in a political system whose head was perpetually on trial, ideologically and militarily, for failure to fulfil his duty as defender of the faith at home and abroad. It became particularly important during times of crisis like the 1840s when it involved the entire population in 'national' politics. Subsequent opposition movements all adopted similar ideologies of jihad. Such struggles could not prevent political and economic fragmentation under the pressures exerted by European colonialism and, in fact, tore the sultanate apart. However, contrary to the colonial French interpretation, they simultaneously suggested the existence of a distinct Muslim political community which provided the subjects of the sultanate with a sense of cohesion upon which they based their later Moroccan national identity.

The formation of a proto-national Moroccan community was a unique process but it was also a variation on theme common to other Islamic societies as they came into economic, political and intellectual contact with Europe during the nineteenth century. Other states and their subjects also had to adapt traditional religious and political ideas to handle the tensions generated by imperialism. For the Ottomans governing in the nineteenth century was an equally complex matter involving the assertion of the state over its subjects, a renegotiation of the traditional political contract and a search for authenticity to preserve Muslim autonomy. Iran and Khedival Egypt faced similar challenges. The need to legitimise modernisation varied according to the power of the regimes involved but where it was necessary, jihad as the military defence of Muslim territory and the strengthening of Muslim society was frequently given as its justification. From this perspective, Moroccan jihad discourse stands at one end of the complex spectrum of Islamic ideological perspectives which emerged during the nineteenth century.

In the Ottoman sphere the ethics of *ghazā*, jihad's eastern synonym, informed Maḥmud II's decision to legitimise his *niẓām-i cedīd* force by calling it the Victorious Muhammadan Army. The Tanzimat reforms, designed to secularise and modernise Ottoman government, were presented by their draftsmen as a means of strengthening the Ottoman empire by introducing a new type of social justice. They were, in effect, a secular version of the circle of equity and the just Islamic order championed by the religious reformers of the period 1750–1830. Tanzimat secularism, however, presented a disjuncture with the past avoided by the Islamic vision upheld by ᶜAbd al-Qādir and the ᶜAlawī sultans. As a result, it destroyed the social contract represented by the *bayᶜa* and the *dhimma* and facilitated the development of secular national ideologies in opposition to Ottoman imperialism.

The Islamic voice re-emerged in the late nineteenth century in both state and society discourses. On the one hand, Abdülḥamīd II asserted his status as caliph of the *umma*, thereby bolstered his position with theocratic symbols in a move comparable to the steps of the ᶜAlawī sultans earlier in the century. On the other hand, eastern Muslim subjects reassessed Islam for themselves and developed their own visions of the jihad necessary to establish a new modern Islamic order capable of surviving the colonial onslaught. The fruits of this reassessment were Pan-Islamism and Islamic Modernism. These eastern Islamic movements were perhaps more sophisticated than Moroccan society's jihad against sultanic *fasād*, but their underlying principles were the same and they also helped to create proto-national communities out of the more or less passive subject 'flocks' of the past.

The difference lay primarily in the fact that the coincidence between territorial, religious and political identities which developed in Morocco was rarely replicated elsewhere. The late Ottoman universal Islamic order clashed with alternative ethno-linguistic and 'national' orders, rather than fusing with them, generating opposition to the Ottoman order in its entirety rather than its particular representatives. However, the ultimate breakdown of the pre-colonial Ottoman order did not indicate a complete Islamic political failure any more than it did in the ᶜAlawī sultanate. Rather, the Moroccan example examined here suggests that pre-colonial political fragmentation actually nourished the development of political discourses within society which retained Islamic components. These discourses were submerged by the alternative secular national paradigms upheld by post-independence governments and western educated elites. However, as in the pre-colonial era, the perceived political, economic and social failures of such governments have triggered the re-emergence of Muslim society's ever-present demand for the implementation of the just social and political order first promised by Muḥammad to the *umma*.

GLOSSARY OF FOREIGN TERMS

^{c}Abīd al-Bukhārī slaves of al-Bukhari, Mawlay Ismā^{c}īl's black slave army.

^{c}adū allah, a^{c}dā' allah enemy of God, i.e. foreign aggressors or rebels.

^{c}adū'l-dīn, a^{c}dā'al-dīn enemy of religion, i.e. foreign aggressors or rebels.

ahl al-fasād people of corruption, i.e. rebels.

ahl al-ḥall wa'l-^{c}aqd those with the power to loose and bind, i.e. people of authority.

ajwād tribal/military chiefs in western Algeria.

akhwāl maternal relatives.

^{c}āmil provincial governor.

amīn a makhzan official usually employed to administer collection of customs duties.

amīr military leader.

amīr al-mu'minīn Commander of the Faithful.

^{c}ār sacrifice of shame/compulsion. In order to secure protection or pardon, a person enters a forbidden zone possessed by the man whose pardon/protection he seeks and makes a sacrifice before him.

^{c}aṣabiyya group solidarity generated by real or fictional blood relations.

askerī (Turkish) military, the ruling military elite.

^{c}aṣyān see ma^{c}ṣiya.

awbāsh rabble.

bāghī, būghāt rebel.

baraka the ability to channel divine beneficence, charisma, blessing.

bay^{c}a oath of allegiance.

bilād al-makhzan 'lands of the Makhzan', territories which paid taxes to the sultan and provided military auxiliaries on a regular basis.

bilād al-sība 'lands of dissidence', mountainous regions which rarely paid taxes or provided military auxiliaries.

dā'ira, duwār tribal encampment.

al-dajjāl the false saviour.

dār al-ḥarb 'the land of war', i.e. non-Muslim territory.

dār al-islām 'the land of Islam', i.e. Muslim-ruled territory.

dār al-sulṭān the sultan's palace.

farḍ ᶜayn a religious duty incumbent on every Muslim.

farḍ kifāya a communal religious duty.

fasād lit. corruption/corruption of the body politic, hence, dissidence, rebellion, politico-military challenges to the sultan.

fāsid, fussād one who spreads fasād (corruption/rebellion), a rebel. See also: fattān, mufsid.

fattān one who causes fitna (civil strife), a rebel.

fatwa a legal ruling or decision.

fitna civil strife, revolt, rebellion.

ḥaḍar townspeople, sedentarists.

ḥadd, ḥudūd the Qur'anic bounds, the transgression of which merited harsh punishment.

ḥajj the annual pilgrimage to Mecca in the month of Dhū'l-Ḥijja.

ḥājj a person who has performed the ḥajj.

ḥarka, ḥarakāt Makhzan military campaign or progress, tax-gathering expedition. See also: maḥalla.

hijra migration from non-Muslim territory to Muslim territory, often in preparation for jihad.

ḥurm a sanctuary and its environs where violence is prohibited.

ᶜibād allah servants/worshippers of God, i.e. good Muslims and, in the Moroccan context, loyal subjects.

ᶜīd al-aḍḥā the annual feast of the sacrifice to commemorate Abraham's sacrifice of Ishaq which occurs at the end of the ḥajj.

ᶜīd al-fiṭr the annual feast celebrating the end of the fast month of Ramadan.

ijtihād independent religio-legal reasoning using the Qur'ān and Hadīth.

imām prayer leader, religious head of the Muslim community.

al-imāma the imamate, theocratic rule. See also: khilāfa.

iṣlāḥ reform.

jāh nobility.

jamāᶜat al-muslimīn the Muslim community. See also: milla, umma.

jaysh army, a military tribe.

jihād religious endeavour, religiously justifiable warfare, war against Christians and rebels.

jihād al-baḥr the maritime jihad, corsairing.

al-jihād fī sabīl'illah religious endeavour in the service of God.

kāfir, kuffār apostate, unbeliever, infidel.

kātib, kuttāb clerk, Makhzan scribe.

khalīfa (a) caliph, (b) the deputies of the sultan in the key areas of Fes, Marrakesh and Tafilalt, generally chosen from the ᶜAlawī lineage, (c) deputies of provincial governors and other Makhzan personnel.

al-khulafā' al-rāshidūn the 'rightly guided' caliphs, i.e. the first four caliphs after Muḥammad.

khāriji, khawārij 'seceders', members of an early breakaway Muslim sect, rebels and dissidents in nineteenth century Morocco.

al-khilāfa the caliphate, theocratic rule.
khirqa Sufi robe of investiture.
kulogullari (Turkish) the sons of Janissaries and indigenous women in Algeria.
kulughlī, kulughlān Arabic form of kulogullari.
madrasa, madāris theological college.
maḥalla, maḥallāt expeditionary force, a military progress or campaign. See also: ḥarka.
mahdī saviour, the Muslim equivalent of the Messiah.
al-mahdī al-muntaẓar the saviour expected to appear at the end of time to inaugurate a final era of justice.
majlis meeting of notables.
makhzan a treasury/storage place, the apparatus of government.
maks, mukūs customs, tolls, market taxes regarded as non-canonical taxation.
ma^{c}ṣīya rebellion, often against God.
ma^{c}ūna extraordinary tax which could only be levied legally in times of war, or threat of war.
mawlid al-nabī a festival celebrating the Prophet's birthday.
al-milla al-muḥammadiyya the Muslim (Muhammadan) community.
mīzān scales, equilibrium, societal balance.
mufsid, mufsidūn a spreader of corruption, a dissident/rebel.
muhājir, muhājirūn migrants, Muslims who migrate from territory under infidel rule to the dār al-islām.
mujāhid, mujāhidūn fighter in the jihad.
mujtahid, mujtahidūn a scholar qualified to use independent reasoning (ijtihād).
mukhtaṣar a commentary.
murābiṭ, murābiṭūn a holy man, marabout.
murtadd, murtaddūn apostate.
naqīb al-ashrāf administrative head of a community of shurafā'.
naṣīḥa advice, usually of a religious nature.
Nāṣir al-Dīn Champion of Religion.
niẓām organisation/order, used in the nineteenth century for European-style military and governmental organisation.
Niẓām-i cedīd (Turkish) the New Order in military organisation introduced to the Muslim Mediterranean from Europe in the nineteenth century.
niẓāmī adjective used for soldiers trained in the niẓām-i cedīd.
qabīla, qabā'il tribe.
qāḍī Sharī^{c}a judge.
qā'id, quwwād military commander, military governor.
qaṣr, qṣūr a fortified village in the pre-Sahara.
ra^{c}āyā flocks, subjects. See also: reaya.
reaya (Turkish) flock, subjects.
ṣaff a row, military formation in orderly lines, a tribal confederation.
Sharī^{c}a Islamic law.

sharīf, shurafā'/ashrāf a descendant of the Prophet in the line of ^{c}Ali and Fatima.

shirk polytheism.

shayṭān a devil.

shūrā consultation.

sība dissidence, non-payment of taxes.

siyāsa policy, political means.

ṭarīqa, ṭuruq religious brotherhood.

tujjār al-sulṭān 'Merchants of the Sultan', a cartel of privileged merchants who traded for the Makhzan and gained various tax breaks and benefits as a result.

Udāyā a Saharan cavalry corps founded by Mawlay Ismā^{c}īl from pre-Saharan Arab tribes from the Ma^{c}qīl confederation and nomads from the oasis of Tuat.

^{c}ulamā' religious scholars, the religious establishment.

umma the universal Muslim community, also used for regional Muslim political communities.

zāwiya, zawāyā a shrine, an independent Sufi lodge, a lodge of a religious brotherhood.

ẓillu'llahi fī'l-arḍ 'Shadow of God on Earth', a theocratic title used by the ^{c}Alawi sultans.

NOTES

1 INTRODUCTION

1 Rex O'Fahey, *Enigmatic Saint: Ahmad b. Idris and the Idrisi Tradition*, London, 1990, 27–33.
2 Cornell Vincent, *Realm of the Saint: Power and Authority in Moroccan Sufism*, Austin, 1998, xxiv, 31.
3 One significant non-tribal group were agriculturalists of sub-Saharan African origin who resided in the pre-Saharan oases and depended on patron tribes for protection.
4 Richard Pennell, 'The geography of piracy: northern Morocco in the mid-nineteenth century', *Journal of Historical Geography* 20, 3, (1994), 272–82.
5 Ross Dunn, *Resistance in the Desert: Moroccan responses to French Imperialism 1881-1912*, Madison, 1977, 106–34.
6 Houari Touati, 'En relisant les Nawāzil Mazouna, marabouts et chorfa au Maghreb centrale au XVe siècle', *Studia Islamica* LXIX (1989), 77.
7 Aziz al-Azmeh, *Muslim Kingship: Power and the Sacred in Muslim, Christian and Pagan Polities*, London & New York, 1997, 128–30.
8 Kinalizade Ali Çelebi's, 'Ahlak-i 'Ala'i' quoted in Fleischer, Cornell, 'Royal authority, dynastic cyclism and "Ibn Khaldunism" ', Bruce Lawrence (ed.), *Ibn Khaldun and Islamic Ideology*, Leiden, 1984, 49.
9 For a concise overview of Ottoman political theory see, Virginia Aksan, 'Ottoman Political Writing, 1768–1808', *International Journal of Middle Eastern Studies* 25, (1993), 53–69.
10 Ernest Gellner, 'Tribalism and the state in the Middle East', P. Khoury and J. Kostiner (eds), *Tribes and State Formation in the Middle East*, Berkeley, 1990, 113.
11 Ibn Khaldun, *The Muqaddimah: An Introduction to History*, translated by F. Rosenthal, edited and abridged by N. J. Dawud, Princeton, 1969 edn, 91–142.
12 Andrew Hess explores this issue in *The Forgotten Frontier: a history of the sixteenth century Ibero-African frontier*, Chicago, 1978.
13 A classic description of rural socio-political organisation in Morocco. Montagne (1930).
14 Although the Ottoman claim to caliphate became explicit in the eighteenth and nineteenth centuries, it was present in sultanic honorifics from the sixteenth century. Colin Imber, *Ebu's-su'ud: the Islamic Legal Tradition*, Edinburgh, 1997, 103–6.
15 Ibn Khaldun, *Muqaddimah*, 155.
16 al-Ḍuᶜayyif al-Ribāṭī, *Tārīkh al-dawla al-ᶜAlawīyya al-saᶜīda*, Casablanca, 1988 edn, 155.
17 Murray Last, 'Reform in West Africa: the jihad movements of the nineteenth century', In J. Ajayi & M. Crowder (eds), *History of West Africa*, vol two, 1987 edn.
18 See O'Fahey, *Enigmatic Saint*; Knut Vikør, *Sufi and Scholar on the Desert Edge: Muhammad b. 'Ali Sanusi and his brotherhood*, London, 1995.
19 Alexandre Bellemare, *Abd el-Kader: sa vie politique et militaire*, Paris, 1863.

20 Wilfred Blunt, *Desert Hawk – Abd al-Kader and the French Conquest of Algeria*, London, 1947; Charles Henry Churchill, *The Life of Abdel Kader ex-Sultan of the Arabs of Algeria*, London, 1867.
21 For example, Philipe Estailleur-Chanteraine, *Abd el-Kader: l'Europe et l'Islam au XIX siecle*, Paris, 1947 and *L'Emir Magnanime: Abd el-Kader le Croyant*, Paris, 1959; Bruno Etienne, *Abdelkader*, Paris, 1994.
22 See Edmund Burke, 'The Image of the Moroccan state in French historical literature', Ernest Gellner and Charles Micaud (eds), *Arabs and Berbers,* London, 1973, 175–99.
23 Edmund Burke, "The Sociology of Islam: the French tradition", Malcolm Kerr (ed.), *Islamic Studies: a tradition and its problems*, Malibu, 1980, 77.
24 An example of this genre is Henri Terrasse, *Histoire du Maroc*, Casablanca, 1950.
25 Rahma Bourquia & Susan Gilson Miller (eds), *In the Shadow of the Sultan: Culture, Power and Politics in Morocco*, Cambridge MA, 1999.
26 Abdellah Hammoudi, *Master and Disciple: The cultural foundations of Moroccan authoritarianism*, Chicago, 1997.

2 THE EVOLUTION OF THE SHARIFIAN JIHAD STATE OF MOROCCO

1 Herman Beck, *l'Image d'Idris II ses descendants de Fas et la politique sharifienne des sultans Marinides*, Leiden, 1989, 91–3.
2 Maya Shatzmiller presents a new assessment of Marīnid religious policies in her recent book, *The Berbers and the Islamic State: The Marinid Experience in pre-Protectorate Morocco*, Princeton, 2000, 45–54.
3 Cornell, *Realm of the Saint*, 119–20.
4 A. Sebti, 'Au Maroc: Sharifisme citadin, charisme et historiographie', *Annales Economies Sociétés Civilisations* 41, 2, (1986), 436–7.
5 Beck, *l'Image d'Idris*, 82, 95.
6 Touati, 'Les *Nawāzil* Mazouna', 84.
7 Touati, 'Les *Nawāzil* Mazouna', 84–5.
8 Mercedes García-Arenal, 'The revolution of Fas in 869/1465 and the death of Sultan 'Abd al-Haqq al-Marini', *Bulletin of the School of Oriental and African Studies* XLI, 1 (1978), 43–66.
9 F. Weston Cook, *The Hundred Years War for Morocco: Gunpowder and the Military Revolution in the Early Modern Muslim World*, Oxford, 1994, 94.
10 Cornell, *Realm of the Saint*, 155–95.
11 Cornell, *Realm of the Saint*, 240–63.
12 Dahiru Yahya, *Morocco in the Sixteenth Century*, London, 1981, 145–64.
13 Ralph Willis, 'Morocco and the Western Sudan: Fin de Siècle-Fin du Temps. Some aspects of Religion and Culture to 1600', *Maghreb Review* 14, 1–2 (1989), 91–3.
14 For accounts of the history of Dila' see Jacques Berque, *Ulémas, fondateurs, insurgés du Maghreb*, Paris, 1982, 81–123, and Muhammad Hajji, *al-Zāwiya al-dilā'iyya*, Rabat, 1983.
15 Patricia Mercer describes the material and moral foundations of Mawlay Ismāʿīl's sultanate in her article, "Palace and jihad: the early 'Alawi state in Morocco", *Journal of African History* 18, 4, (1977), 531–53.
16 Mercer, 'Palace and Jihad', 549–51.
17 Mawlay Ismāʿīl's initiative led to an efflorescence of sharifian genealogical literature (*ansāb*). Sebti, 'Sharifisme citadin', 437–9.
18 Abdelouahid Ben Talha, *Moulay-Idriss du Zerhoun*, Rabat, 1965, 13.
19 Patricia Mercer, 'Political and Military Developments within Morocco during the early 'Alawi period (1659-1727)', Unpublished doctoral thesis, University of London, 1974, 236, 321–7.

20 Houari Touati, "Prestige ancestral et système symbolique sharifien dans le Maghreb centrale du XVIIème siècle", *Arabica* XXXIX (1992), 7.

21 Abū'l-Qāsim al-Zayyānī recounts his travels in his history, *al-Turjumāna al-kubrā fi akhbār al-ma'mūr barran wa baḥran*, Rabat, 1967.

22 Daniel Schroeter, *Merchants of Essaouira: Urban Society and Imperialism in Southwestern Morocco 1844-1886*, Cambridge, 1988, 8.

23 Fatima Harrak, 'State and Religion in Eighteenth Century Morocco: The Religious Policy of Sidi Muhammad Ibn 'Abd Allah', Unpublished doctoral thesis, University of London, 1989, 28.

24 Aḥmad al-Ghazzāl, 'Natījat al-ijtihād fī'l-muhādana wa'l-jihād', D107, Bibliotheque Generale, Rabat, 1–10; al-Zayyānī, *Turjumāna*, 131–2.

25 The often harsh treatment of foreign representatives by the sultans was designed to demonstrate their subservient status. See George Høst, *Histoire de l'Empereur du Maroc Mohamed Ben Abdallah*, translated from Danish by F. Damgaard and P. Gailhanou, Rabat, 1998.

26 M'hammed Benaboud, 'Authority and Power in the Ottoman State in the Eighteenth century', Caesar Farah (ed.), *Decision Making and Change in the Ottoman Empire*, Northeast Missouri State University, 1993, 67–79.

27 al-Ḍu^{c}ayyif, *Tārīkh* I, 379, 382, 393, 411.

28 Aḥmad b. Khālid al-Nāṣirī, *Kitāb al-istiqṣā' l'akhbār al-duwal al-Maghrib al-Aqṣā*, Casablanca, 1956, VIII, 81.

29 al-Ḍu^{c}ayyif, *Tārīkh* I, 387.

30 *al-Istiqṣā'* VIII, 83, al-Ḍu^{c}ayyif, *Tārīkh* I, 423.

31 al-Ḍu^{c}ayyif, *Tārīkh* I, 427.

32 al-Ḍu^{c}ayyif, *Tārīkh* I, 429.

33 al-Ḍu^{c}ayyif, *Tārīkh* II, 449–51.

34 al-Ḍu^{c}ayyif, *Tārīkh* II, 449.

35 Mohamed El Mansour, *Morocco in the Reign of Mawlay Sulaymān*, Outwell, Wisbech UK, 1990, 102.

36 Maghribi concerns were reflected in their vehement opposition to the French occupation of Cairo and leadership of popular resistance. ^{c}Abd al-Raḥmān al-Jabartī, *Tārīkh ^{c}ajā'ib al-āthār fi'l-tarājim wa'l-akhbār* II, Beirut, n.d., 186.

37 al-Ḍu^{c}ayyif, *Tārīkh* II, 636, 640.

38 al-Ḍu^{c}ayyif, *Tārīkh* II, 575–7.

39 El Mansour, *Morocco*, 107.

40 El Mansour, *Morocco*, 189.

41 DAR: Tetuan I: Mawlay Sulaymān to ^{c}Abd al-Raḥmān Ash^{c}āsh, 2 Muḥarram 1235 (21/10/1819).

42 El Mansour, *Morocco*, 197.

43 El Mansour, *Morocco*, 160.

44 al-Ḍu^{c}ayyif, *Tārīkh* II, 751.

45 *al-Istiqṣā'* IX, 11; al-Zayyānī, '^{c}Aqd al-jumān fi shamā'il al-sulṭān sayyidnā wa mawlānā ^{c}Abd al-Raḥmān', H40 Bibliotheque Generale & 126 Bibliotheque Royale, Rabat, 18.

46 Nacer al-Fassi, 'Mohamed Ibn Idrīs, vizir et poète de la cour de Moulay Abderrahman', *Hesperis* III, 1 (1962), 50.

47 Muḥammad Akansūs, *al-Jaysh al-^{c}aramram al-khumāsī fi dawlat awlād mawlānā ^{c}Alī al-Sijilmāsī* II, Fes, 1336/1918, 4–5.

48 al-Zayyānī, '^{c}Aqd al-jumān', 18–19; *al-Jaysh* II, 5 & *al-Istiqṣā'* IX, 8–9.

49 *al-Istiqṣā'* IX, 6 and *al-Jaysh* II, 52.

50 al-Zayyānī, '^{c}Aqd al-jumān', 19–22.

51 FO52/24: Douglas to Bathurst, 13/2/1823.

52 *al-Jaysh* II, 8; *al-Istiqṣā'* IX, 8–10; al-Zayyānī, '^{c}Aqd al-jumān', 23–4.

53 FO52/25: Douglas to Bathurst, 5/2/1824.
54 The story of Ibn al-Ghāzī's downfall is given in *al-Jaysh* II, 52–3 and *al-Istiqṣā'* IX, 11.
55 FO52/26: Douglas to Norton, 3/5/1825.
56 Abu'l-^{c}Alā Idrīs, 'al-Ibtisām fī dawlat Ibn Hishām', 12490, Bibliotheque Royale, Rabat, 70–3.
57 al-Zayyānī, '^{c}Aqd al-jumān', 18.
58 Jocelyne Dakhlia explores the symbolic meaning of monarchical progresses across the Maghrib in her article, "Dans la mouvance du prince: la symbolique du pouvoir itinérant au Maghreb", *Annales Economies Sociétés Civilisations* 43, 3 (1988), 735–60.
59 al-Zayyānī, '^{c}Aqd al-Jumān', 21–2.
60 al-Zayyānī, '^{c}Aqd al-Jumān', 28.
61 al-Zayyānī, '^{c}Aqd al-Jumān', 29.
62 al-Zayyānī, '^{c}Aqd al-Jumān', 23–4, 27.
63 FO52/23: Consular translation of the Sultan's circular to the foreign consuls, 25/12/1822; J.-L. Miège, *Le Maroc et l'Europe* II, Paris, 1963, 39–41; 'al-Ibtisām', 71–2.
64 FO52/25: Douglas to Chatham, 3/12/1824 and 27/12/1824.
65 FO52/26: Douglas to Bathurst, 2/1/1825 and 30/10/1825.
66 FO52/28: Douglas to Bathurst, 24/9/1827.
67 FO52/27: Douglas to Bathurst, 17/3/1826.
68 FO52/28: Douglas to Bathurst, 23/3/1827.
69 FO52/29: Douglas to Macpherson, 10/2/1828.
70 FO52/31: Précis of correspondence … respecting the detention of two British vessels by Moorish cruisers; Diary of the proceedings of the British vice-consulate in Tetuan, 10/8/1828.
71 al-Zayyānī, '^{c}Aqd al-jumān', 29–30; 'al-Ibtisām', 74; *al-Jaysh* II, 11–13; *al-Istiqṣā'* IX, 18–21.
72 FO52/29: Douglas to Murray, 11/8/1828.
73 al-Zayyānī, '^{c}Aqd al-jumān', 30; *al-Istiqṣā'* IX, 21.
74 *al-Istiqṣā'* IX, 20.
75 FO52/31: Webster to Douglas, 16/6/1829; FO52/31: Hay to R. W. Hay, 14/8/1829.
76 FO52/32: Hay to Murray, 23/4/1830.
77 CPM3: Delaporte à Solignac, 12/4/1830.
78 DAR: Iḥtilāl al-Jazā'ir: Sultan to Muḥammad Ash^{c}āsh, 27 Shawwal 1245 (26/4/1830); CPM3: Delaporte à Solignac, 12/4/1830.
79 CPM3: Delaporte à Solignac, 7/5/1830.
80 CPM3: Delaporte à Solignac, 12/4/1830.

3 FRENCH COLONIALISM AND SHARIFIAN JIHAD IN ALGERIA, 1830–2

1 Touati, 'Prestige ancestral', 15–19.
2 Touati, 'Prestige ancestral', 7.
3 Muḥammad b. ^{c}Abd al-Qādir, *Tuḥfat al-zā'ir fī tārīkh al-Jazā'ir wa'l-amīr ^{c}Abd al-Qādir*, Beirut, 1964, 928.
4 *Tuḥfat al-zā'ir* 929.
5 Marcel Emérit, *L'Algérie à l'epoque d'Abd-el-Kader*, Paris, 1951, 202.
6 *Tuḥfat al-zā'ir*, 115 & al-Sulaymānī, 'Zubdat al-tārīkh wa-zuhrat al-shamārīkh', D3657 Bibliotheque Generale, Rabat, III, 124.
7 *Tuḥfat al-zā'ir*, 125.
8 Ann Thomson, 'Arguments for the conquest of Algiers in the late eighteenth and early nineteenth centuries', *Maghreb Review* 14, 1–2 (1989), 108–18.

9 FO3/32: St John to R. W. Hay, 4/4/1830 and Diary of the Consulate, January–June 1830.
10 *Tuḥfat al-zā'ir*, 131.
11 *Tuḥfat al-zā'ir*, 133.
12 *Tuḥfat al-zā'ir*, 146.
13 CPM3: Delaporte à Solignac, 13/7/1830 and 24/7/1830.
14 DAR: Iḥtilāl al-Jazā'ir: Sultan to Ash^{c}āsh, 10 Ṣafar 1246 (30/7/1830).
15 CPM3: Copies des pièces mentionnées dans la dépêche du 19/11/1830.
16 DAR: Iḥtilāl al-Jazā'ir: Sultan to Ash^{c}āsh, 22 Rabī^{c} I 1246 (10/9/1830).
17 DAR: Iḥtilāl al-Jazā'ir: Sultan to Ash^{c}āsh, 23 Jumāda I 1246 (9/11/1830).
18 DAR: TA: Sultan to Ash^{c}āsh, 22 Rabī^{c} I 1246 (10/9/1830).
19 *Tuḥfat al-zā'ir*, 45, 47.
20 Ibrahim Yasin, 'Mawqif al-dawla al-maghribiyya min iḥtilāl Faransā li'l-Jazā'ir mā bayna 1830 wa 1847', Thèse de Diplōme, Université Mohamed V, Rabat, 1987, 53.
21 CPM3: Delaporte au Secretaire des Affaires Etrangères, 30/9/1830.
22 CPM3: Delaporte au Secretaire des Affaires Etrangères, 30/9/1830.
23 *al-Istiqṣā'* IX, 27–9 & Muḥammad al-Mashrafī, 'al-Ḥulal al-bāhiyya fī tārīkh mulūk al-dawla al-^{c}Alawiyya', D1463, Bibliotheque Generale, Rabat: 204–5.
24 'al-Ibtisām', 78.
25 *al-Jaysh* II, 16–17.
26 'al-Ibtisām', 78.
27 DAR: al-Jazā'ir: Sultan to the Western Tribes, 17 Rabī^{c} II 1246 (5/10/1830).
28 DAR: al-Jazā'ir: Sultan to Mawlay ^{c}Alī and Idrīs al-Jirārī, 7 Jumāda II 1246 (23/11/1830).
29 'al-Ibtisām', 77. The garrison in Tlemsen consisted of between 100 and 150 Turks and 4,500 Kulughlān. Emérit (1951: 11).
30 'al-Ibtisām', 78-79; P. De Cossé-Brissac, *Les Rapports de la France et du Maroc*, Paris, 1931, 16.
31 DAR: al-Jazā'ir: Sultan to the Kulughlān, 26 Jumāda II 1246 (12/12/1830).
32 CPM3: Delaporte à Sebastiani, 13/1/1831 & 27/1/1831; Yasin, 'al-Dawla al-maghribiyya', 65–7.
33 DAR: Wajda: Sultan to Idrīs al-Jirārī, 10 Jumāda I 1246 (27/10/1830); al-Jazā'ir: Sultan to Mawlay ^{c}Alī and Idrīs al-Jirārī, 16 Jumāda I 1246 (2/11/1830) and 18 Jumāda II 1246 (4/12/1830).
34 CPM3: Delaporte à Sebastiani, 10/1/1831; DAR: TA: Sultan to Mawlay ^{c}Alī and Idrīs al-Jirārī, 18 Jumāda II 1246 (4/12/1830).
35 DAR: al-Jazā'ir: Sultan to Mawlay ^{c}Alī and Idrīs al-Jirārī, 4 Jumāda II 1246 (20/11/1830).
36 CPM3: Copie d'une dépêche au Duc de Dalmatie, 26/2/1831.
37 FO3/32: St John to Murray, 24/9/1830; FO3/33: Diary of the Consulate July–December 1830, 6/12/1830.
38 CPM3: Delaporte au Secretaire des Affaires Etrangères, 1/11/1830 and 6/12/1830.
39 FO52/34: Hay to R. W. Hay, 15/1/1831.
40 DAR: Tetuan I: Bin Idrīs to Ash^{c}āsh, 12 Rajab 1246 (27/12/1830).
41 CPM3: Delaporte à Sebastiani, 10/1/1831; FO52/34: Hay to R. W. Hay, 15/1/1831.
42 DAR: al-Jazā'ir: Sultan to Mawlay ^{c}Alī and Idrīs al-Jirārī, 9 Sha^{c}bān 1246 (23/1/1831).
43 FO52/34: Hay to R. W. Hay, 15/1/1831.
44 FO3/33: Diary of the Consulate January–June 1831, 26/1/1831.
45 FO3/33: St John to R. W. Hay, 25/3/1831.
46 CPM3: Delaporte à Sebastiani, 25/2/1831.
47 DAR: al-Jazā'ir: Sultan to Mawlay ^{c}Alī and Idrīs al-Jirārī, 12 Ramaḍān 1246 (24/2/1831); DAR: TA: Bin Idrīs to Ash^{c}āsh, 17 Ramaḍān 1246 (1/3/1831).
48 CPM3: Delaporte au Secretaire de Affaires Etrangères, 25/5/1831.
49 DAR: TA: Sultan to Mawlay ^{c}Alī and Idrīs al-Jirārī, 24 Ramaḍān 1246 (8/3/1831).

50 FO52/34: Hay to R. W. Hay, 9/4/1831.
51 Yasin, 'al-Dawla al-maghribiyya', 108.
52 'al-Ibtisām', 79. Al-Mashrafī claims that the *maḥalla* left Tlemsen without the permission of the sultan. al-Mashrafī, 'Ḥulal', 206.
53 *al-Istiqṣā'* IX, 33.
54 al-Fassi, *Mohamed Ibn Idris*, 49.
55 Although al-Nāṣirī does not mention the presence of Muḥammad b. Idrīs with al-Bukhārī, earlier sources attest that he did go out to meet the *maḥalla*. FO52/34: Hay to R. W. Hay, 3/6/1831.
56 FO52/34: Hay to R. W. Hay, 3/6/1831.
57 *al-Istiqṣā'* IX, 33.
58 'al-Jaysh', 374.
59 *al-Istiqṣā'* IX, 33–4.
60 'al-Ibtisām', 80.
61 *al-Istiqṣā'* IX, 34.
62 'al-Ibtisām', 80–1; 'al-Jaysh', 375; *al-Istiqṣā'* IX, 34.
63 *al-Istiqṣā'* IX, 32; FO52/34: Hay to R. W. Hay, 3/6/1831.
64 'al-Jaysh', 375.
65 FO52/34: Report upon the accompanying abstract of opinions of Sir Sidney Smith by Consul Hay, 29/4/1831.
66 'al-Ibtisām', 81.
67 FO52/34: Hay to R. W. Hay, postscript to 3/6/1831.
68 DAR: TA: Sultan to Ash[c]āsh, 19 Dhū'l-Ḥijja 1246 (31/5/1831).
69 FO52/34: Hay to R. W. Hay, 5/6/1831 postscript to 3/6/1831. Fāsī outrage at the appointment of al-Wadīnī al-Bukhārī as governor of Fes is recorded in al-Zayyānī's account. al-Zayyānī, 'Takmīl al-turjumāna', 32, 35–54.
70 FO52/34: Hay to R. W. Hay, 5/6/1831 postscript to 3/6/1831.
71 Henry Munson, *Religion and Power in Morocco*, New Haven & London, 1993, 35–55.
72 *al-Istiqṣā'* IX, 35.
73 FO52/35: Hay to Vice-Admiral Horsham, 9/7/1831.
74 'al-Ibtisām', 83.
75 FO52/35: Hay to Vice-Admiral Horsham, 9/7/1831.
76 FO52/35: Hay to R. W. Hay, 22/8/1831.
77 FO52/34: Hay to R. W. Hay, 26/6/1831.
78 FO52/35: Hay to Sultan: 21/9/1831.
79 FO52/35: Hay to Goderich: 4/9/1831; CPM3: Delaporte au Secretaire de Affaires Etrangères, 9/12/1831.
80 DAR: TA: Sultan to al-Slāwī, 12 Muḥarram 1247 (22/6/1831).
81 Al-Nāṣirī suggests that Idrīs was particularly concerned for the [c]Alawī captives in Fes because his lover, Lalla Fāṭima bint Mawlay Sulaymān, was among their number. *al-Istiqṣā'* IX, 35–6.
82 DAR: TA: Sultan to Ash[c]āsh, 13 Muḥarram 1247 (23/6/1831).
83 'al-Ibtisām', 84 and *al-Istiqṣā'* IX, 36.
84 FO52/35: Hay to R. W. Hay, 22/8/1831.
85 DAR: TA: Sultan to Ash[c]āsh, 10 Ṣafar 1247 (22/7/1831).
86 'al-Ibtisām', 85.
87 *al-Jaysh* II, 16.
88 'al-Jaysh', 377.
89 *al-Istiqṣā'* IX, 37.
90 'al-Jaysh', 377.
91 *al-Istiqṣā'* IX, 37; FO52/35: Hay to R. W. Hay, 25/11/1831.
92 al-Ḥajwī, 'Ikhtiṣār', 33.

93 FO52/36: Hay to R. W. Hay, 14/1/1832.
94 FO3/33: St John to R. W. Hay, 20/10/1831.
95 Yasin, 'al-Dawla al-maghribiyya' , 125.
96 CPM3: Delaporte au Secretaire des Affaires Etrangères, 5/11/1831.
97 Yasin, 'al-Dawla al-maghribiyya', 126–9.
98 CPM3: Delaporte au Secretaire des Affaires Etrangères, 26/12/1831 and 2/1/1832; De Mornay à Sebastiani, 26/2/1832.
99 FO52/35: Hay to R. W. Hay, 9/12/1831.
100 FO52/36: Hay to R. W. Hay, 6/2/1832.
101 FO52/36: Hay to R. W. Hay, 6/2/1832 and CPM3: De Mornay à Sebastiani, 12/2/1832.
102 DAR: TA: Sultan to al-Slāwī, 1 Ramaḍān 1247 (3/2/1832).
103 FO52/36: Hay to R. W. Hay, 5/3/1832.
104 CPM3: De Mornay à Sebastiani, 23/3/1832.
105 CPM3: De Mornay à Sebastiani, 23/3/1832.
106 CPM3: De Mornay à Sebastiani, 4/4/1832.
107 CPM3: Delaporte à Sebastiani, 2/6/1832.
108 *al-Istiqṣā'* IX, 38–40.
109 FO52/36: Hay to R. W. Hay, 3/6/1832 and CPM3: Delaporte à Sebastiani, 2/6/1832.
110 al-Ḥajwī, 'Ikhtiṣār', 33.
111 FO52/36: Hay to R. W. Hay, 16/9/1832.
112 *al-Istiqṣā'* IX, 40.
113 CPM3: Delaporte à Sebastiani, 7/9/1832.
114 CPM4: Delaporte au Duc de Broglie, 20/1/1833; DAR:TA: Sultan to al-Slāwī, 19 Rabī^{c} II 1249 (5/9/1833) and Sultan to al-Slāwī, 6 Jumāda II 1249 (21/10/1833).
115 FO52/36: Hay to R. W. Hay, 3/6/1832.

4 AN AMBIVALENT ALLIANCE: MOROCCO AND ^{c}ABD AL-QĀDIR'S JIHAD, 1832–9

1 CPM3: Extrait d'un dépêche du Géneral Boyer au Ministre de la Guerre, 10/4/1832.
2 De Cossé-Brissac, *Rapports*, 30, Raphael Danziger, *Abd al-Qadir and the Algerians*, London and New York, 1977, 60. Yasin asserts that Muḥyī al-Dīn's position as ^{c}Alawī representative was informal rather than an official appointment as deputy. Yasin, 'al-Dawla al-maghribiyya', 170–1.
3 CPM3: Delaporte à Sebastiani, 2/6/1832.
4 *Tuḥfat al-zā'ir*, 156.
5 *Tuḥfat al-zā'ir*, 156.
6 *Tuḥfat al-zā'ir*, 159; Churchill, *Abdel Kader*, 32–3.
7 Aḥmad b. Ṭuwayr al-Janna recounts that in spiritual communion with dead Muslim holy men, they informed him that they had allowed Algeria to fall into infidel hands because her people had 'transgressed the limits of God's law'. H. Norris, *The Pilgrimage of Ahmad - son of the little bird of Paradise*, Warminster, 1977, 84.
8 Ruwayla, Muḥammad 'Wushāt al-makātib wa zīnat al-jaysh al-muḥammadī al-ghālib', D1542, Bibliotheque Generale, Rabat, 6–7. Shinar also takes this view. Shinar, P., ''Abd al-Qadir & 'Abd al-Krim: religious influences on their thought and action'. *Asian and African Studies* 1, (1965), 139–74.
9 The title '*khalīfa*' was not used for Moroccan rulers because it designated a Makhzan deputy or governor. The theocratic possibilities which the title originally conveyed were contained in the ^{c}Alawī title, 'Shadow of God on Earth'.
10 Zebadia, A. 'The career and correspondence of Ahmad al-Bakkay', unpublished doctoral thesis, University of London, 1974, 181.

11 Zebadia, 'Ahmad al-Bakkay', 196. French reports corroborate this view. AHG: H227: La puissance d'Abd el-Kader étant detruite, marche à suivre pour gouverner les arabes.
12 *Tuḥfat al-zā'ir*, 156.
13 *Tuḥfat al-zā'ir*, 164.
14 The Desmichels treaty of 1834 described ^{c}Abd al-Qādir as *amīr al-mu'minīn* and he also used the title in his 1836 approaches to the British and American consuls in Tanger.
15 *Tuḥfat al-zā'ir*, 166.
16 *Tuḥfat al-zā'ir*, 191–212; 'Wushāt al-makātib'.
17 *Tuḥfat al-zā'ir*, 161–2.
18 CPM4: Delaporte au Duc de Broglie, 20/1/1833; CPM4: Méchain au Duc de Broglie, 5/3/1833.
19 Danziger, *Abd al-Qadir*, 78; CPM4: Méchain au Duc de Broglie, 23/4/1833.
20 DAR: TA: Sultan to Méchain, 19 Dhū'l-Qa^{c}da 1248 (9/4/1833).
21 Yasin, 'al-Dawla al-maghribiyya', 190–1.
22 DAR: TA: Sultan to Muṣṭafā b. Ismā^{c}īl, 1 Muḥarram 1250 (10/5/1834).
23 CPM4: Méchain au Duc de Broglie, 16/10/1833.
24 CPM4: Méchain au Duc de Broglie, 31/12/1833.
25 FO52/38: Hay to R. W. Hay, 14/4/1834.
26 CPM4: Copie du dépeche du Géneral Desmichels au Ministre de la Guerre, 10/1/1834.
27 CPM4: Méchain au Duc de Broglie, 31/12/1833.
28 The text of the Desmichels treaty is given in Danziger, *Abd al-Qadir*, 241–5.
29 Danziger, *Abd al-Qadir*, 94–5.
30 *Tuḥfat al-zā'ir*, 191.
31 Churchill, *Abdel Kader*, 62; Emérit, *l'Algérie*, 205.
32 *Tuḥfat al-zā'ir*, 215.
33 Danziger, *Abd al-Qadir*, 116.
34 FO52/39: Hay to R. W. Hay, 15/7/1835.
35 FO52/39: Hay to R.W. Hay, 12/8/1835; Yasin, 'al-Dawla al-maghribiyya', 215.
36 FO52/39: Hay to R. W. Hay, 12/8/1835.
37 CPM4: Méchain au Duc de Broglie, 2/12/1835. Méchain erroneously believed that Bin Idrīs was opposed to the jihad.
38 CPM4: Extrait d'une dépêche de Méchain, 20/8/1835; FO52/39: Hay to R. W. Hay, 10/10/1835; Esquer, G., *Correspondance du Maréchal Clauzel* I, Paris, 1948: Clauzel au Ministre de la Guerre, 8/10/1835.
39 It is possible that the author was the Udāyā commander, Abū'l-^{c}Alā Idrīs al-Jirārī. The letter is undated but its place in the 'Ibtisām' and its content suggest a date before the disastrous Muslim defeat at the Battle of the Sikkak in 1836. 'al-Ibtisām', 213–17.
40 'al-Ibtisām', 213.
41 Hammoudi, *Master and Disciple*.
42 CPM4: Méchain au Duc de Broglie, 2/12/1835.
43 Esquer, *Correspondance* I: Clauzel au Ministre de la Guerre, 23/1/1836.
44 Full details of the campaign are contained in Clauzel's correspondence in Esquer, *Correspondance* I.
45 Esquer, *Correspondance* I: Clauzel au Ministre de la Guerre, 16/1/1836.
46 FO52/40: Hay to Glenelg, 12/2/1836.
47 FO52/40: Hay to Glenelg, 17/2/1836 and 31/3/1836.
48 FO52/40: Hay to Glenelg, 13/1/1836; Esquer, *Correspondance* I: Clauzel au Ministre de la Guerre, 13/2/1836.
49 Esquer, *Correspondance* I: Clauzel au Ministre de la Guerre, 13/2/1836.
50 Esquer, *Correspondance* I: Clauzel au Ministre de la Guerre, 25/2/1836.
51 Esquer, *Correspondance* I: General d'Arlanges au General Rapatel, 27/4/1836 (two letters); General d'Arlanges au General Rapatel, 28/4/1836.
52 CPM4: Méchain à Thiers, 4/4/1836.

53 DAR: TA: Sultan to Méchain, 27 Muḥarram 1252 (14/5/1836).
54 DAR: TA: al-Bayyāz to Méchain, 10 Ṣafar 1252 (27/5/1836).
55 Hay's translation of a letter sent from the sultan to the governor of Tanger. FO52/40: Hay to Palmerston, 14/5/1836.
56 Danziger, *Abd al-Qadir*, 124.
57 Esquer, *Correspondance* II, appendix 1: De la Rue au Ministre des Affaires Etrangères, 14/7/1836.
58 DAR: TA: Sultan to ^{c}Abd al-Salām al-Slāwī, 23 Rabī^{c} I 1252 (8/7/1836).
59 FO52/41: Hay to Palmerston, 13/7/1836.
60 DAR: TA: al-Bayyāz to Baron de la Rue, 22 Rabī^{c} II 1252 (6/8/1836); Esquer, *Correspondance* II, appendix 1: De la Rue au Ministre des Affaires Etrangères, 17/8/1836.
61 Esquer, *Correspondance* II, appendix 1: De la Rue au Ministre des Affaires Etrangères, 29/7/1836.
62 Esquer, *Correspondance* II, appendix 1: De la Rue au Ministre des Affaires Etrangères, 8/7/1836.
63 Esquer, *Correspondance* II, appendix 1: De la Rue au Ministre des Affaires Etrangères, 29/7/1836.
64 FO52/41: Hay to Palmerston, 15/8/1836.
65 Danziger, *Abd al-Qadir*, 128.
66 *Tuḥfat al-zā'ir*, 316–17.
67 *Tuḥfat al-zā'ir*, 329.
68 *Tuḥfat al-zā'ir*, 317.
69 FO52/39: Hay to R. W. Hay, 10/10/1835.
70 For the full text of the treaty, see Danziger, *Abd al-Qadir*, 248–56.
71 CPM5: Delaporte au Comte Mole, 16/8/1837; Méchain au Comte Mole, 23/7/1837.
72 CPM5: Méchain au Comte Mole, 23/7/1837.
73 CPM5: Méchain au Comte Mole, 21/11/1837.
74 DAR: TA: Sultan to al-Slāwī, 20 Dhū'l-Ḥijja 1252 (28/3/1837).
75 DAR: TA: Sultan to al-Slāwī, 9 Muḥarram 1253 (15/4/1837).
76 Churchill, *Abdel Kader*, 151; *Tuḥfat al-zā'ir*, 339–42.
77 Danziger, *Abd al-Qadir*, 156.
78 *Tuḥfat al-zā'ir*, 339–42.
79 Danziger, *Abd al-Qadir*, 169; CPM5: Méchain au Comte Mole, 6/3/1839.
80 Danziger, *Abd al-Qadir*, 155.
81 Danziger, *Abd al-Qadir*, 163–4.
82 CPM5: Delaporte au Duc de Dalmatie, 19/7/1839.
83 *Tuḥfat al-zā'ir*, 387–9.
84 CPM5: Delaporte au Duc de Dalmatie, 19/7/1839.
85 CPM5: Méchain au Duc de Dalmatie, 1/8/1839.
86 CPM5: Méchain au Comte Mole, 6/3/1839.
87 DAR: ^{c}Abd al-Qādir: ^{c}Abd al-Qādir to Sīdī Muḥammad, 16 Ramaḍān 1255 (23/11/1839).

5 THE ^{c}ALAWĪ JIHAD DURING THE FRENCH WAR TO CONQUER ALGERIA, 1839–45

1 CPM5: De Nion au Duc de Dalmatie, 28/12/1839 and 8/1/1840.
2 CPM5: De Nion au Duc de Dalmatie, 4/1/1840; CPM6: De Nion au Thiers, 16/5/1840 and Notes remises par Marius Garcin, 26/7/1840.
3 DAR: ^{c}Abd al-Qādir: Sultan to Muḥammad Ash^{c}āsh, 1 Muḥarram 1256 (5/3/1840).
4 FO99/5: Hay to Palmerston, 7/6/1840; CPM6: De Nion à Thiers, 27/7/1840 and 18/6/1840; DAR: Iḥtilāl al-Jazā'ir, Sultan to Muḥammad Ash^{c}āsh, 6 Jumāda II 1256 (5/8/1840).

5 FO99/5: Hay to Palmerston, 5/2/1840.

6 DAR: TA: Sultan to De Nion, 19 Dhū'l-Qa^{c}da 1255 (24/1/1840).

7 FO99/5: Hay to Palmerston, 19/2/1840; CPM5: De Nion au Duc de Dalmatie, 19/2/1840.

8 CPM6: De Nion à Thiers, 28/3/1840.

9 FO99/6: Hay to Woodford, 3/5/1840.

10 CPM6: De Nion au Duc de Dalmatie, 22/3/1840; DAR: TA: Sultan to Ash^{c}āsh, 2 Ṣafar 1256 (5/4/1840); CPM6: De Nion à Thiers, 4/5/1840; DAR: TA: Sultan to ^{c}Abd al-Salām al-Slāwī, 3 Jumāda II 1256 (2/8/1840).

11 DAR: TA: Sultan to Ash^{c}āsh, 7 Ṣafar 1256 (10/4/1840); FO99/5: Hay to Palmerston, 5/5/1840.

12 CPM6: De Nion à Thiers, 6/6/1840.

13 DAR: TA: Sultan to Ash^{c}āsh, 25 Ṣafar 1256 (28/4/1840); FO99/5: Hay to Palmerston, 16/6/1840.

14 FO99/5: Palmerston to Hay, 12/2/1840.

15 CPM6: De Nion à Thiers, 16/4/1840.

16 FO99/5: Hay to Palmerston, 8/6/1840 and CPM6: De Nion à Thiers, 6/6/1840.

17 CPM6: De Nion à Thiers, 24/7/1840, 7/8/1840 and 24/8/1840.

18 CPM6: De Nion à Thiers, 5/9/1840.

19 CPM6: De Nion à Thiers, 20/12/1840.

20 FO99/5: Willshire to Hay, 21/10/1840.

21 DAR: TA: De Nion to the Sultan, 14 Shawwal 1256 (9/12/1840).

22 FO99/7: Hay to Palmerston, 11/1/1841.

23 FO99/7: Hay to Palmerston, 5/2/1841.

24 CPM7: De Nion à Guizot, 3/2/1841; DAR: TA: Sultan to Bū Silhām, 20 Dhū'l-Qa^{c}da 1256 (13/1/1841).

25 FO99/7: Hay to Palmerston, 11 /1/1841; CPM7: De Nion à Guizot, 1/1/1841.

26 FO99/7: Hay to Palmerston, 5/2/1841.

27 FO99/7: Hay to Palmerston, 11/1/841.

28 FO99/7: Palmerston to Hay, 12/2/1841. Palmerston unguardedly said that the British would use their 'good offices' to prevent any European power invading Morocco. The Makhzan took this to mean that Britain would militarily prevent a French attack. F. Flournoy, *British Foreign Policy towards Morocco*, Baltimore, 1935, 63–5.

29 FO99/7: Hay to Palmerston, 31/3/1841.

30 James Scott, *A Journal of a Residence in the Esmailla of Abd el-Kader*, London, 1842, 4–6.

31 Scott, *Journal*, 66.

32 Scott, *Journal*, 52.

33 Scott, *Journal*, 76–7.

34 Scott, *Journal*, xiii.

35 DAR: Iḥtilāl al-Jazā'ir: Sultan to Ash^{c}āsh, end of Muḥarram 1257 (24/3/1841).

36 FO99/7: Hay to Palmerston, 30/3/1841.

37 DAR: TA: Sharifian Ḍāhir, 29 Ṣafar 1257 (22/4/1841).

38 DAR: TA: Sultan to Muḥammad Ash^{c}āsh, end of Rabī^{c} I 1257 (22/5/1841).

39 FO99/7: Hay to Palmerston, 16/3/1841.

40 FO99/7: Hay to Palmerston, 29/4/1841.

41 CPM7: De Nion à Guizot, 18/5/1841.

42 CPM7: Beuscher à Guizot, 14/7/1841.

43 CPM7: De Nion à Guizot, 17/8/1841.

44 DAR: Iḥtilāl al-Jazā'ir: Sultan to Muḥammad Ash^{c}āsh, 18 Jumāda II 1257 (7/8/1841); Scott (1842: 180, 188); CPM7: De Nion à Guizot, 4/9/1841.

45 DAR: TA: Sultan to Bu Silhām, 21 Jumāda I 1257 (11/7/1841); Sharifian Ḍāhir to Captain Aḥmad U al-Ḥājj, 2 Jumāda II 1257 (22/7/1841).

46 DAR: TA: Sultan to Muḥammad Ash^{c}āsh, 1 Ṣafar 1258 (14/3/1842).
47 CPM7: De Nion à Guizot, 5/10/1841 and 24/12/1841.
48 CPM8: De Nion à Guizot, 6/2/1842.
49 CPM8: De Nion à Guizot, 10/4/1842.
50 CPM8: De Nion à Guizot, 21/1/1842 and 23/2/1842.
51 CPM8: De Nion à Guizot, 23/2/1842 and 1/3/1842; DAR: TA: Bū Silhām to De Nion, 25 Muḥarram 1258 (8/3/1842).
52 FO99/9: Hay to Aberdeen, 4/4/1842.
53 CPM8: Bedeau à Bugeaud, 22/3/1842.
54 FO99/9: Hay to Aberdeen, 4/4/1842 and 3/5/1842.
55 CPM8: De Nion à Guizot, 6/2/1842.
56 DAR: TA: De Nion to the Sultan, 3 Rabī^{c} I 1258 (14/4/1842).
57 DAR: TA: Sultan to De Nion, 21 Rabī^{c} I 1258 (2/5/1842).
58 FO99/9: Hay to Aberdeen, 1/6/1842.
59 CPM8: De Nion à Guizot, 6/5/1842.
60 CPM8: Lamoricière à Debar (Algiers), 25/4/1842; FO99/9: Hay to Aberdeen, 19/7/1842.
61 CPM8: De Nion au Sultan, 14/5/1842: DAR: TA: De Nion to the Sultan, 4 Jumāda I 1258 (13/6/1842).
62 CPM8: De Nion à Guizot, 6/5/1842.
63 DAR: TA: Sultan to Muḥammad Ash^{c}āsh, 4 Rabī^{c} II 1258 (15/5/1842).
64 FO99/9: Hay to Aberdeen, 2/6/1842.
65 CPM8: De Nion à Guizot, 30/5/1842.
66 FO99/9: Hay to Aberdeen, 12/7/1842.
67 FO99/9: Hay to Aberdeen, 12/7/1842.
68 FO99/9: Hay to Aberdeen, 19/7/1842; CPM8: De Nion à Guizot, 22/7/1842.
69 CPM8: Duc de Dalmatie à Guizot, 19/7/1842.
70 CPM8: De Nion à Guizot, 22/8/1842.
71 DAR: TA: Sultan to Muḥammad Ash^{c}āsh, 29 Jumāda II 1258 (7/8/1842).
72 DAR: TA: De Nion to the Sultan, end of Rajab 1258 (6/9/1842).
73 CPM9: De Nion to Guizot, 6/3/1843.
74 CPM8: De Nion à Guizot, 12/9/1842.
75 CPM8: De Nion à Guizot, 27/9/1842.
76 CPM8: De Nion à Guizot, 15/11/1842.
77 CPM8: De Nion à Guizot, 24/12/1842.
78 CPM9: De Nion à Guizot, 11/1/1843.
79 CPM9: Bugeaud au Ministre de la Guerre, 9/4/1843; De Nion à Guizot, 14/4/1843; FO99/11: Hay to Aberdeen, 27/5/1843.
80 CPM9: De Nion à Guizot, 14/4/1843 and 2/5/1843; De Nion à Lamoricière, 14/4/1843.
81 CPM9: De Nion à Guizot, 22/4/1843 and 22/5/1843.
82 CPM9: Capitaine du 'Turpin' au Ministre de la Marine, 9/6/1843.
83 CPM9: De Nion à Guizot, 13/6/1843.
84 FO99/11: Hay to Aberdeen, 14/6/1843.
85 CPM9: De Nion à Guizot, 15/7/1843.
86 FO99/11: Hay to Aberdeen, 17/8/1843.
87 CPM9: De Nion à Guizot, 10/8/1843.
88 FO99/11: Hay to Aberdeen, 17/8/1843.
89 CPM9: De Nion à Guizot, 4/10/1843; Bugeaud au Ministre de la Guerre, 30/10/1843.
90 CPM9: De Nion à Guizot, 4/10/1843; DAR: Iḥtilāl al-Jazā'ir: Sultan to Bū Silhām, 24 Ramaḍān 1259 (18/10/1843).
91 CPM9: De Nion à Guizot, 6/9/1843.
92 CPM9: De Nion à Guizot, 6/9/1843.
93 CPM9: De Nion à Guizot, 20/9/1843.

94 CPM9: De Nion à Guizot, 29/11/1843.
95 CPM9: De Nion à Guizot, 27/12/1843.
96 AHG:H235: Warnier, Affaires du Maroc – preliminaires–hostilités–traité de paix. According to De Nion, the Sultan did give Bin [c]Arrāsh and Muḥammad al-Sa[c]īd the weapons and supplies they requested. CPM10: De Nion à Guizot, 6/2/1844.
97 CPM10: De Nion à Guizot, 20/1/1844.
98 CPM9: De Nion à Guizot, 27/12/1843.
99 AHG:H229: Rapport de Bugeaud, 15/1/1844.
100 CPM10: De Nion à Bū Silhām, 6/1/1844.
101 CPM10: De Nion à Guizot, 6/2/1844; DAR: TA: Sultan to Bū Silhām, 28 Ṣafar 1260 (19/3/1844).
102 DAR: Tetuan I: Sultan to Muḥammad Ash[c]āsh, 23 Ṣafar 1260 (14/3/1844).
103 FO99/14: Willshire to Hay, 22/3/1844.
104 CPM10: De Nion à Guizot, 23/2/1844.
105 CPM10: De Nion à Guizot, 13/5/1844.
106 AHG:H212: Journal de la division d'Oran, 1844.
107 'al-Ibtisām', 218; FO99/14: Hay to Aberdeen, 6/4/1844.
108 See several letters in CPM10: April–May 1844.
109 DAR: TA: Sultan to Ash[c]āsh, 6 Rabī[c] II 1260 (25/4/1844) and 8 Jumāda I 1260 (26/5/1844).
110 FO99/14: Hay to Aberdeen, 28/3/1844; DAR: TA: Sultan to Bū Silhām, 1 Rabī[c] I 1260 (21/3/1844).
111 DAR: TA: Sultan to Bū Silhām, 10 Rabī[c] I 1260 (30/3/1844).
112 CPM10: De Nion à Guizot, 17/5/1844.
113 FO99/15: Redman to Hay, 1/6/1844.
114 FO99/14: Hay to Vice-Admiral Edward Owen, 6/5/1844.
115 CPM10: De Nion à Guizot, 24/5/1844.
116 FO99/15: Redman to Hay, 1/6/1844.
117 CPM10: De Nion à Guizot, 10/4/1844.
118 CPM10: De Nion à Guizot, 28/4/1844.
119 DAR: Iḥtilāl al-Jazā'ir: Sultan to Bū Silhām, 1 Jumāda II, 1260 (18/6/1844).
120 CPM10: De Nion à Guizot, 4/6/1844.
121 CPM11: De Nion à Guizot, 21/6/1844.
122 DAR: TA: Sultan to Bū Silhām, 11 Rajab 1260 (27/7/1844).
123 CPM10: Extrait de plusieurs dépêches de Bugeaud, 5/6/1844.
124 DAR: TA: Bin Idrīs to De Nion, 7 Jumāda II 1260 (24/6/1844).
125 CPM10: De Nion à Guizot, 9/6/1844.
126 CPM10: Bugeaud à Bedeau, 14/6/1844.
127 AHG:H235: Correspondance de Maréchal Bugeaud au Prince de Joinville, 26/6/1844.
128 CPM10: Bedeau à Bugeaud, 15/6/1844.
129 CPM10: General Thiery au Commandant de la station navale, 17/6/1844; AHG:H212: Journal des operations du corps expeditionnaire de l'ouest, 28/5/1844–30/8/1844.
130 CPM11: De Nion à Guizot, 2/7/1844.
131 CPM11: De Nion à Guizot, 9/7/1844.
132 FO99/13: Aberdeen to Hay, 15/6/1844 and 19/6/1844.
133 CPM10: De Nion à Guizot, 28/6/1844.
134 DAR: TA: Sultan to Bu Silhām, 13 Jumāda II 1260 (30/6/1844).
135 FO99/15: Hay to Bulwer, 27/6/1844; DAR: TA: Sīdī Muḥammad to the Sultan, 4 Jumāda II 1260 (21/6/1844).
136 DAR: Iḥtilāl al-Jazā'ir: Sultan to Bū Silhām, 1 Jumāda II 1260 (18/6/1844) and DAR: TA: Sultan to Bū Silhām, 5 Rajab 1260 (21/7/1844).
137 CPM11: De Nion à Guizot, 7/7/1844.

138 DAR: TA: Sultan to Bū Silhām, 11 Rajab 1260 (27/7/1844) and 13 Jumāda II 1260 (30/6/1844).
139 CPM11: De Nion à Guizot, 19/7/1844; al-Ḥajwī (H114: 68–9).
140 FO99/16: Report on the renegade Jules Mayer, 8/1844. A considerable number of fighters were already in the border area. Rough estimates suggest around 7,000 Makhzan and tribal cavalrymen, ^{c}Abd al-Qādir's *niẓāmī* corps of 200 or so men, and about 2,000 Algerian cavalry.
141 FO99/15: Hay to Aberdeen, 1/7/1844.
142 DAR: TA: Sultan to Bū Silhām, 11 Rajab 1260 (27/7/1844).
143 CPM11: De Nion à Guizot, 25/7/1844.
144 FO99/15: Murray to Aberdeen, 26/7/1844.
145 FO99/16: Murray to Aberdeen, 1/8/1844.
146 DAR: TA: Sultan to the People of the Rif, 12 Rajab 1260 (28/7/1844); Sultan to Bū Silhām, 12 Rajab 1260 (28/7/1844).
147 DAR: Tanger I: Bū Silhām to the Sultan, 14 Rajab 1260 (30/7/1844).
148 al-Ḥajwī, 'Ikhtiṣār', 69.
149 DAR: Tanger I: Aḥmad al-Razīnī to the Sultan, 21 Rajab 1260 (7/8/1844).
150 al-Ḥajwī, 'Ikhtiṣār', 69.
151 AHG:H235: Correspondance de Maréchal Bugeaud au Prince de Joinville, 1/8/1844.
152 FO99/16: Hay to Aberdeen, 10/8/1844.
153 FO99/16: Report on the renegade Jules Mayer, 8/1844.
154 AHG:H235: Correspondance de Maréchal Bugeaud au Prince de Joinville, 17/8/1844.
155 *al-Istiqṣā'* IX, 51.
156 *al-Jaysh* II, 28.
157 al-Mashrafī, 'Ḥulal', 212.
158 *al-Jaysh* II, 29.
159 AHG:H235: Correspondance de Maréchal Bugeaud au Prince de Joinville, 17/8/1844
160 *al-Istiqṣā'* IX, 51–3.
161 AHG:H235: Correspondance de Maréchal Bugeaud au Prince de Joinville, 17/8/1844.
162 *al-Istiqṣā'* IX, 53.
163 DAR: TA: Muḥammad Ash^{c}āsh to the Sultan, 23 Rajab 1260 (8/8/1844); 'al-Ibtisām', 220.
164 CPM12: De Nion à Guizot, 18/8/1844.
165 CPM12: Gucksberg to Guizot, 28/8/1844.
166 Flournoy, *British Policy*, 98.
167 FO99/17: Hay to Bulwer, 4 /9/1844.
168 FO99/17: Hay to Aberdeen, 10/9/1844.
169 FO99/17: Hay to Aberdeen, 20/9/1844; FO99/18: Hay to Aberdeen, 28/10/1844.
170 FO99/17: Bulwer to Hay, 9/9/1844.
171 FO99/17: Hay to Aberdeen, 8/9/1844. The European consuls began to press the Makhzan to draft new treaties with Sweden and Denmark in February 1845. The sultan stalled, but the threat of Scandinavian bombardment forced him to draft new conventions in March 1845.
172 DAR: TA: Sultan to the People of Essawira, 16 Sha^{c}bān 1260 (31/8/1844).
173 DAR: TA: Sultan to Bu Silhām, 8 Sha^{c}ban 1260 (23/8/1844).
174 al-Mashrafī, 'Ḥulal', 213; 'al-Ibtisām', 220.
175 DAR: Tetuan I: Sultan to Ash^{c}āsh, 19 Sha^{c}bān 1260 (3/9/1844).
176 DAR: TA: Sultan to Bū Silhām, 8 Ramaḍān 1260 (21/9/1844).
177 DAR: TA: Sultan to Bū Silhām, 17 Sha^{c}bān 1260 (1/9/1844).
178 'al-Ibtisām', 220.

179 CPM13: Rapport de Daumas, 25/2/1844.
180 CPM12: Mauboussin à Guizot, 24/9/1844.
181 FO99/18: Hay to Wilson, 1/10/1844.
182 FO99/18: Redman to Hay, 3/10/1844.
183 FO99/18: Hay to Aberdeen, 31/10/1844.
184 CPM13: Rapport de Daumas, 25/2/1845.
185 DAR: al-Jazā'ir: ᶜAbd al-Qādir to Muḥammad b. al-Mukhtār, 25 Shaᶜbān 1260 (9/9/1844).
186 CPM12: Mauboussin à Guizot, 10/10/1844; CPM13: Rapport de Daumas, 25/2/1845.
187 *Tuḥfat al-zā'ir*, 292.
188 Churchill, *Abdel Kader*, 237.
189 Churchill, *Abdel Kader*, 237.
190 FO99/18: Hay to Aberdeen, 31/10/1844.
191 FO99/18: Hay to Aberdeen, 14/12/1844; CPM13: Rapport de Daumas, 25/2/1845.
192 DAR: ᶜAbd al-Qādir: Sultan to Bū Silhām, 22 Muḥarram 1261 (31/1/1845).
193 CPM13: De Chasteau à Guizot, 8/1/1845 and 14/2/1845.
194 FO99/25: Hay to Aberdeen, 6/3/1845.
195 Leon Roches was the son of a French colonist who learnt Arabic and joined ᶜAbd al-Qādir during the period when he was at peace with the French. Roches converted to Islam and married a Muslim woman but then left ᶜAbd al-Qādir when war broke out in 1839. He then used his knowledge of Arabic and ᶜAbd al-Qādir to aid the French military, becoming in time General Bugeaud's translator. After serving as a member of the border demarcation team he became secretary of the French legation in Tanger and married Consul De Chasteau's daughter. However, despite his facility in Arabic and his personal charm, Roches' frequent 'about-turns' created distrust among his own associates in Tanger, the Makhzan and the government in Paris.
196 FO99/18: Hay to Aberdeen, 1/12/1844.
197 CPM13: Mauboussin à Bū Silhām, 15/2/1845.
198 DAR: TA: Count de la Rue to the Sultan, 15 Ṣafar 1261 (23/2/1845).
199 FO99/25: Hay to Aberdeen, 6/3/1845 and 26/3/1845.
200 CPM13: Lamoricière au Duc de Dalmatie, 25/2/1844.
201 AHG:H212: Journal de la Division d'Oran, 1844; AHG:H235: Correspondance de Maréchal Bugeaud au Prince de Joinville, 26/6/1844.
202 AHG:H235: Correspondance de Bugeaud au Prince de Joinville, 1/8/1844.
203 F. Trout, *Morocco's Saharan Frontiers*, Geneva, 1969, 19–23.
204 CPM13: De la Rue au Duc de Dalmatie, 12/3/1844; Considerations sur le traité de commerce conclu entre la France et le Maroc au camp de Lalla Maghnia le 18 Mars 1845.
205 FO99/25: Hay to Aberdeen, 16/4/1845.
206 DAR: TA: Bin Idrīs to Bū Silhām, 11 Jumāda II 1261 (9/6/1845).
207 FO99/26: Hay to Aberdeen, 4/5/1845.
208 De Cossé-Brissac, *Rapports*, 111.
209 CPM13: De la Rue au Duc de Dalmatie, 15/3/1845.
210 DAR: TA: Sultan to Bū Silhām, 9 Rabīᶜ II 1261 (17/4/1845).
211 DAR: TA: Bin Idrīs to Bū Silhām, 22 Jumāda I 1261 (29/5/1845).
212 DAR: TA: Sultan to Sīdī Muḥammad, 6 Rabīᶜ II 1261 (14/4/1845).
213 DAR: TA: Bin Idrīs to Bū Silhām, 22 Jumāda I 1261 (29/5/1845).
214 DAR: TA: Bin Idrīs to Bū Silhām, 11 Jumāda II 1261 (17/6/1845).
215 DAR: TA: Notables of the Banū Yznāsen to the Sultan, 14 Rabīᶜ II 1261 (22/4/1845).
216 DAR: TA: Sultan to Bū Silhām, 10 Jumāda II 1261 (16/6/1845) and 1 Rajab 1261 (5/7/1845).
217 FO99/26: Hay to Aberdeen, 2/7/1845.
218 FO99/26: Hay to Aberdeen, 18/6/1845.

6 THE ^{c}ALAWĪ JIHAD AGAINST ^{c}ABD AL-QĀDIR, 1845–7

1 FO99/18: Hay to Aberdeen, 16/10/1844.
2 FO99/18: Hay to Aberdeen, 17/12/1844.
3 FO99/26: Hay to Aberdeen, 13/5/1845 and 26/6/1845.
4 DAR: TA: Bin Idrīs to Bū Silhām, 21 Rajab 1261 (17/4/1845).
5 DAR: TA: Muṣṭafā al-Dukkālī to Muḥammad b. Idrīs, 1 Rabī^{c} II 1261 (9/4/1845).
6 DAR: TA: Sultan to ^{c}Abd al-Qādir Ash^{c}āsh, 19 Rabī^{c} II 1261 (27/4/1845).
7 DAR: TA: Sultan to Aḥmad al-Razīnī, 19 Rabī^{c} II 1261 (27/4/1845).
8 CPM14: De Chasteau à Guizot, 16/7/1845; FO99:26: Hay to Aberdeen, 26/7/1845 and 31/7/1845.
9 FO99/26: Hay to Aberdeen, 13/5/1845.
10 CPM14: De Chasteau à Guizot, 16/7/1845; DAR: Tanger I: Bū Silhām to the Sultan, 16 Rabī^{c} I 1261 (25/3/1845); DAR: TA: Bin Idrīs to Muḥammad al-Razīnī, 24 Jumāda I 1261 (31/5/1845); DAR: ^{c}Abd al-Qādir Ash^{c}āsh I: Sultan to ^{c}Abd al-Qādir Ash^{c}āsh, 25 Jumāda I 1261 (1/6/1845); DAR: Tanger I: Bin Idrīs to Bū Silhām, 14 Rajab 1261 (10/4/1845).
11 FO99/26: Hay to Aberdeen, 13/5/1845.
12 CPM14: De Chasteau à Guizot, 26/9/1845.
13 DAR: TA: Bin Idrīs to Muḥammad al-Razīnī, 27 Jumāda I 1261 (3/6/1845); CPM14: De Chasteau à Guizot, 26/9/1845.
14 For instance, Muḥammad al-Khūja's, 'Risāla fī tanẓīm al-jaysh', K2733, Bibliotheque Generale, Rabat.
15 Muḥammad al-Kardūdī, 'Kashf al-ghumma bi-bayān inna ḥarb al-niẓām ḥaqq ^{c}ala al-umma', D1281, Bibliotheque Generale, Rabat, 10.
16 CPM13: Rapport de Tlemcen, 14/6/1845; FO99/26: Hay to Aberdeen, 6/8/1845; DAR: TA: Bin Idrīs to Bū Silhām, 13 Sha^{c}bān 1261 (17/8/1845).
17 FO99/26: Hay to Aberdeen, 13/5/1845.
18 CPM14: Roches à Bin Idrīs, 19/9/1845.
19 DAR: al-Jazā'ir: Ḥamīda b. ^{c}Alī to the Sultan, 21 Ramaḍān 1261 (23/9/1845).
20 DAR: al-Jazā'ir: Ḥamīda b. ^{c}Alī to the Sultan, 27 Ramaḍān 1261 (29/9/1845); CPM15: resumé des renseignements fournis (1) par un habitant de la Mecque venant d'Oran (2) par un ancien habitant de Mascara refugié a Fes, 11/1845.
21 CPM14: Guizot à De Chasteau, 13/10/1845; DAR: ^{c}Abd al-Qādir: Sultan to Bū Silhām, 25 Shawwāl 1261 (27/10/1845).
22 CPM15: De Chasteau à Guizot, 27/10/1845; FO 99/26: Hay to Aberdeen, 28/10/1845 and CPM14: De Chasteau à Bugeaud, 23/10/1845.
23 FO99/26: Hay to Aberdeen, 17/11/1845; DAR: ^{c}Abd al-Qādir: Bū Silhām to Bin Idrīs, 25 Shawwāl 1261 (27/10/1845).
24 CPM14: De Chasteau à Guizot, 6/10/1845.
25 FO99/26: Hay to Aberdeen, 11/10/1845.
26 'al-Ibtisām', 245–6.
27 CPM15: Bin Idrīs à Roches, 2/11/1845.
28 DAR: cAbd al-Qādir: Sultan to Bū Silhām, 25 Shawwāl 1261 (27/10/1845).
29 DAR: TA: Sultan to Bū Silhām, 2 Shawwāl 1261 (4/10/1845).
30 CPM18: De Chasteau à Guizot, 15/5/1847.
31 CPM15: Roches à De Chasteau, 20/11/1845.
32 CPM14: Roches à Guizot, 20/10/1845.
33 CPM15: De Chasteau à Guizot, 12/12/1845 and 16/12/1845.
34 DAR: al-Jazā'ir: ^{c}Abd al-Qādir Ash^{c}āsh to the French, 7 Muḥarram 1262 (5/1/1846).
35 DAR: Tetuan II: ^{c}Abd al-Qādir Ash^{c}āsh to ^{c}Abd Allah Ash^{c}āsh, 1 Muḥarram 1262 (30/12/1845).

36 DAR: TA: ^{c}Abd al-Qādir Ash^{c}āsh to Guizot, 26 Muḥarram 1262 (24/1/1845).
37 See, Susan Miller, *Disorienting Encounters: Travels of a Moroccan Scholar in France in 1845-1846*, Berkeley, 1991.
38 DAR: al-Jazā'ir: Sultan to Bū Silhām, 8 Jumāda II 1263 (24/5/1847); Tetuan II: Sultan to Bū Silhām; Sultan to ^{c}Abd al-Qādir Ash^{c}āsh, 18 Sha^{c}bān 1263 (1/8/1847).
39 CPM15: De Chasteau à Guizot, 26/2/1846.
40 FO99/31: Hay to Aberdeen, 3/2/1846.
41 FO99/31: Hay to Aberdeen, 3/2/1846.
42 CPM16: Bugeaud à Guizot, 10/4/1846.
43 CPM15: Rapport de Roches' sur son mission à Rabat, 5/12/1845; CPM16: Roches à Bin Idrīs, 30/3/1846.
44 CPM16: De Chasteau à Guizot, 30/3/1846.
45 DAR: al-Jazā'ir: Ḥamīda b. ^{c}Alī to Bin Idrīs, 15 Dhū'l-Qa^{c}da 1261 (15/11/1845) and Ḥamīda b. ^{c}Alī to the Sultan, 27 Ramaḍān 1261 (29/9/1845).
46 Raymond Jamous, *Honneur et Baraka: les structures sociales traditionnelles dans le Rif*, Cambridge, 1981, 213–214; David Hart, *The Ait Waryaghar of the Moroccan Rif*, Tucson, 1976, 306.
47 DAR: TA: Muhammad b. ^{c}Abd al-Malik to Bin Idrīs, 7 Ṣafar 1262 (4/2/1846).
48 CPM16: De Chasteau à Guizot, 10/3/1846.
49 CPM16: De Chasteau à Guizot, 4/1/1846.
50 CPM15: De Chasteau à Guizot, 27/11/1845; FO99/26: Hay to Aberdeen, 28/11/1845; DAR: TA: Bū Zayyān to the Sultan, 11 Muḥarram 1262 (9/1/1846).
51 DAR: ^{c}Abd al-Qādir: Bū Zayyān to Bin Idrīs, 11 Muḥarram 1262 (9/1/1846).
52 CPM16: De Chasteau à Guizot, 8/3/1846.
53 CPM17: De Chasteau à Guizot, 20/7/1846.
54 CPM16: De Chasteau à Guizot, 30/3/1846.
55 FO99/31: Hay to Aberdeen, 3/5/1846; DAR: Fes: Sultan to Sīdī Muḥammad, 13 Jumāda I 1262 (9/5/1846).
56 al-Sulaymānī, 'Zubda' III, 208.
57 DAR: Meknes: al-^{c}Amir b. Idrīs to the Sultan, 11 Ṣafar 1262 (8/2/1846).
58 DAR: Meknes: al-Jilānī b. Bū ^{c}Izza to the Sultan, 16 Ṣafar 1262 (13/2/1846).
59 DAR: Meknes: al-Ṭālib Ḥusayn to the Sultan, 24 Rabī ^{c} II 1262 (21/4/1846).
60 DAR: TA: Sultan to Bū Silhām, 8 Jumāda I 1262 (4/5/1846); Meknes: al-Ṭālib Ḥusayn to the Sultan, 24 Rabī^{c} II 1262 (21/4/1846); Tetuan II: ^{c}Abd Allah Ash^{c}āsh to Bin Idrīs, 28 Rabī^{c} II 1262 (24/4/1846).
61 DAR: al-Jazā'ir: Bū Zayyān to the Sultan, 2 Jumāda I 1262 (28/4/1846).
62 CPM16: Guizot à De Chasteau, 12/3/1846.
63 CPM16: Bugeaud à Guizot, 10/4/1846; De Chasteau à Guizot, 14/4/1846; De Chasteau à Bin Idrīs, 14/4/1846 and Bugeaud au Ministre de la Guerre 23/4/1846.
64 DAR: TA: Sīdī Muḥammad to Bin Idrīs, 13 Jumāda I 1262 (9/5/1846).
65 FO99/31: Hay to Aberdeen, 3/5/1846; DAR: TA: Sīdī Muḥammad to Bin Idrīs, 13 Jumāda I 1262 (9/5/1846); CPM16: De Chasteau à Guizot, 9/5/1846; De Chasteau à Bugeaud, 20/5/1846.
66 DAR: Tanger I: Muḥammad b. ^{c}Abd al-Malik to the Sultan, 24 Jumāda I 1262 (20/5/1846) and CPM16: De Chasteau à Guizot, 21/5/1846.
67 CPM17: De Chasteau à Guizot, 4/7/1846.
68 DAR: TA: Anon to local shaykhs, 7 Jumāda II 1262 (2/6/1846).
69 CPM16: De Chasteau à Guizot, 1/6/1846.
70 DAR: TA: Sultan to Sīdī Muḥammad, 23 Jumāda II 1262 (18/6/1846).
71 DAR: TA: Sīdī Muḥammad to Bū Silhām, 23 Jumāda II 1262 (18/6/1846).
72 CPM17: De Chasteau à Guizot, 4/7/1846.
73 CPM17: De Chasteau à Guizot, 6/10/1846.
74 CPM17: De Chasteau à Guizot, 4/7/1846.

75 FO99/31: Hay to Addington, 21/8/1846; DAR: al-Jazā'ir: Anon to Sīdī Aḥmad al-Zammūrī, end of Rajab 1262 (24/7/1846).
76 DAR: al-Jazā'ir: Anon to Sīdī Aḥmad al-Zammūrī, end of Rajab 1262 (24/7/1846).
77 CPM17: De Chasteau à Guizot, 4/7/1846.
78 CPM17: Roches à De Chasteau, 3/8/1846.
79 CPM17: De Chasteau à Guizot, 29/7/1846 and 6/8/1846.
80 CPM17: De Chasteau à Guizot, 20/7/1846.
81 CPM17: De Chasteau à Bū Silhām, 11/8/1846.
82 DAR: TA: Sīdī Muḥammad to the Sultan, 26 Sha^{c}bān 1262 (19/8/1846).
83 FO99/31 Hay to Palmerston, 31/8/1846.
84 CPM17: De Chasteau à Guizot, 20/8/1846.
85 CPM17: De Chasteau à Guizot, 18/8/1846.
86 FO99/31: Hay to Addington, 21/8/1846; CPM17: De Chasteau à Guizot, 20/8/1846.
87 FO99/31: Hay to Addington, 21/8/1846.
88 FO99/31: Hay to Palmerston, 31/8/1846.
89 FO99/31: Hay to Addington, 21/8/1846; CPM17: De Chasteau à Guizot, 20/8/1846.
90 CPM17: De Chasteau à Guizot, 23/8/1846.
91 CPM17: De Chasteau à Guizot, 5/9/1846.
92 FO99/31: Hay to Palmerston, 31/8/1846.
93 CPM17: De Chasteau à Guizot, 5/9/1846; FO99/31: Hay to Palmerston, 16/9/1846.
94 CPM17: De Chasteau à Guizot, 21/9/1846.
95 FO99/31: Hay to Palmerston, 1/9/1846; DAR: TA: Sultan to Sīdī Muhammad, 2 Shawwāl 1262 (23/9/1846).
96 CPM17: De Chasteau à Guizot, 21/9/1846; DAR: TA: Sultan to Sīdī Muḥammad, 27 Shawwāl 1262 (18/10/1846).
97 DAR: TA: The jurist Ismā^{c}īl al-^{c}Amirī to the Sultan, 9 Shawwāl 1262 (30/9/1846).
98 DAR: al-Jazā'ir: Sultan to Sīdī Muḥammad, Dhū'l-Qa^{c}da 1262 (Nov 1846).
99 CPM17: De Chasteau à Guizot, 6/10/1846 and 4/11/1846; FO99/31: Hay to Palmerston, 2/11/1846.
100 DAR: ^{c}Abd al-Qādir: Ḥammād b. al-^{c}Abbās to Sīdī Muḥammad, 5 Shawwāl 1262 (26/9/1846); TA: Bū Zayyān to the Sultan, 3 Dhū'l-Qa^{c}da 1262 (23/10/1846); al-Jazā'ir: Bū Zayyān to Bin Idrīs, 19 Dhū'l-Qa^{c}da 1262 (8/11/1846).
101 DAR: TA: Sultan to Sīdī Muḥammad, 19 Dhū'l-Ḥijja 1262 (8/12/1846).
102 DAR: al-Jazā'ir: Ibrāhīm b. ^{c}Abd al-Malik to Sīdī Muḥammad, 19 Dhū'l-Qa^{c}da 1262 (8/11/1846).
103 CPM17: Roches à De Chasteau, 3/8/1846; De Chasteau à Guizot, 4/11/1846; DAR: al-Jazā'ir: ^{c}Abd al-Qādir to De Chasteau, 4 Dhū'l-Ḥijja 1262 (23/11/1846); Muḥammad b. al-Ḥājj to Sīdī Muḥammad, 7 Dhū'l-Ḥijja 1262 (26/11/1846).
104 CPM18: Reports by De Chasteau and Roches on the mission to Marrakesh and its aims, 2/1847; FO99/31: Hay to Palmerston, 2/10/1846.
105 FO99/31: Hay to Addington, 4/11/1846.
106 CPM18: De Chasteau à Bugeaud, 22/3/1847; Bugeaud à De Chasteau, 2/2/1847 and 8/4/1847.
107 DAR: TA: Sultan to Sīdī Muḥammad, 2 Shawwāl 1262 (23/9/1846); ^{c}Allāl al-Tuzīnī to Sīdī Muḥammad, 10 Rabī^{c} I 1263 (1/3/1847); Sultan to Sīdī Muḥammad, 4 Rajab 1263 *et al.* (21/6/1847).
108 DAR: TA: ^{c}Alī b. Aḥmad al-Tasūlī and Aḥmad b. ^{c}Abd Allah al-Tasūlī to the Sultan, 9 Ramaḍān 1263 (24/8/1847).
109 DAR: TA: Sultan to Sīdī Muḥammad, 4 Rajab 1263 (21/6/1847) and 21 Rajab 1263 (18/7/1847).
110 CPM18: A. Beaumier, 'Note sur l'influence des marabouts dans les contrées meridionales du Maroc et sur les pays de Draa'.

111 CPM18: De Chasteau à Guizot, 26/3/1847.
112 DAR: TA: Wuld Ab(u) Muḥammad to Sīdī Muḥammad, 26 Ṣafar 1263 (16/2/1847); CPM18: De Chasteau à Guizot, 16/5/1847.
113 FO99/35: Hay to Palmerston, 2/3/1847; CPM18: De Chasteau à Bugeaud, 22/3/1847; De Chasteau à Guizot, 16/5/1847.
114 FO99/35: Hay to Palmerston, 13/3/1847; CPM18: De Chasteau à Guizot, 26/3/1847; DAR: al-Jazā'ir: Ismā[c]īl al-[c]Amirī to Sīdī Muḥammad, 9 Rabī[c] II 1263 (30/3/1847).
115 CPM18: De Chasteau à Guizot, 16/3/1847.
116 CPM18: De Chasteau à Guizot, 23/3/1847; FO99/35: Hay to Addington, 27/3/1847; DAR: Tetuan II: Sultan to Bū Silhām, 8 Jumāda II 1263 (27/5/1847).
117 FO99/35: Hay to Palmerston, 2/3/1847; CPM18: De Chasteau à Guizot, 26/3/1847.
118 FO99/35: Hay to Addington, 17/4/1847 and CPM18: De Chasteau à Guizot, 20/4/1847.
119 FO99/35: Hay to Addington, 17/4/1847. De Chasteau informed Paris that he had paid Bin Abū 18,000 francs for his services. CPM18: De Chasteau à Guizot, 25/4/1847.
120 CPM18: De Chasteau à Bugeaud, 25/4/1847.
121 FO99/35: Hay to Palmerston, 19/4/1847.
122 DAR: TA: Sīdī Muḥammad to the Sultan, 6 Jumāda II 1263 (25/5/1847); CPM18: De Chasteau à Bugeaud, 25/4/1847.
123 *Tuḥfat al-zā'ir*, 489.
124 CPM18: De Chasteau à Guizot, 16/5/1847 and 24/5/1847.
125 CPM18: De Chasteau à Guizot, 24/5/1847.
126 CPM18: De Chasteau à Guizot, 10/6/1847.
127 FO99/35: Hay to Palmerston, 4/5/1847.
128 CPM18: De Chasteau à Guizot, 15/5/1847.
129 CPM18: De Chasteau à Guizot, 16/5/1847.
130 DAR: TA: Sīdī Muḥammad to the Sultan, 6 Jumāda II 1263 (25/5/1847).
131 DAR: TA: Sultan to Sīdī Muḥammad, 29 Jumāda II 1263 (17/6/1847).
132 This account is based on [c]Alawī, French and British reports of the battle. DAR: TA: Sīdī Muḥammad to Sultan, 28 Jumāda II 1263 (16/6/1847); Muḥammad al-Walyashkī to Sīdī Muḥammad, 1 Rajab 1263 (18/6/1847); CPM18: De Chasteau à Guizot, 21/6/1847 and 22/6/1847; FO99/34: Hay to Addington, 17/6/1847.
133 FO99/35: Hay to Palmerston, 4/6/1847; Hay to Addington, 17/6/1847.
134 FO99/35: Hay to Palmerston, 21/6/1847.
135 FO99/35: Hay to Addington, 17/6/1847; DAR: TA Sīdī Muḥammad to the Sultan, 3 Rajab 1263 (20/6/1847).
136 DAR: al-Jazā'ir: Sultan to Sīdī Muḥammad, 2 Rajab 1263 (19/6/1847); TA: Sultan to Sīdī Muḥammad, 4 Rajab 1263 (21/6/1847).
137 DAR: TA: Muḥammad al-Walyashkī to Sīdī Muḥammad, 1 Rajab 1263 (18/6/1847); Sultan to Sīdī Muḥammad, 21 Rajab 1263 (18/7/1847).
138 DAR: TA: Muḥammad al-Walyashkī to Sīdī Muḥammad, 1 Rajab 1263 (18/6/1847); Muḥammad al-Tuzīnī to Sīdī Muḥammad, 12 Rajab 1263 (9/7/1847).
139 CPM19: De Chasteau à Guizot, 20/7/1847.
140 DAR: TA: Muḥammad b. [c]Abd al-Wahhāb to Sīdī Muḥammad, 14 Rajab 1263 (11/7/1847).
141 DAR: TA: Sultan to Sīdī Muḥammad, 21 Rajab 1263 (18/7/1847).
142 CPM19: De Chasteau à Guizot, 5/7/1847.
143 CPM19: Depêche de D'Arbourville, temporary commander in Oran, 14/8/1847; CPM19: De Chasteau à Guizot, 20/8/1847.
144 DAR: TA: Sīdī Muḥammad to the Sultan, 3 Rajab 1263 (20/6/1847); CPM19: De Chasteau à Guizot, 10/8/1847.
145 A. K. Bennison, 'The 1847 revolt of 'Abd al-Qādir and the Algerians against Mawlay 'Abd al-Rahmān, Sultan of Morocco'. *Maghreb Review* 22, 1–2, (1997), 109–123.
146 AHG:H122: MacMahon to Rénault, 1/9/1847.

147 AHG:H122: Interrogatoire de Mokhtar ben Kabou, 17/9/1847.
148 CPM19: De Chasteau à Guizot, 4/9/1847; *Tuḥfat al-zā'ir*, 491; 'al-Ibtisām', 230.
149 FO99/35: Murray to Palmerston, 14/8/1847; AHG:H122: Bedeau au Ministre de la Guerre, 2/9/1847; CPM19: Ministre de la Guerre à Guizot, 21/9/1847.
150 AHG:H122: Depêche de Bazaine sur l'emigration du Banu Amir, 8/9/1847.
151 'al-Ibtisām', 221.
152 AHG:H122: Depêche de Bazaine sur l'emigration du Banu Amir, 8/9/1847.
153 FO99/35: Murray to Palmerston, 1/9/1847.
154 *al-Istiqṣa'* IX, 56.
155 CPM19: De Chasteau à Guizot, 4/9/1847; FO99/35: Murray to Palmerston, 25/10/1847; Hay to Palmerston, 5/11/1847.
156 CPM19: De Chasteau à Guizot, 24/9/1847; DAR: Tanger I: Bin Idrīs to Bū Silhām, 27 Dhū'l-Qa^{c}da 1263 (9/11/1847).
157 DAR: al-Jazā'ir: Wuld Ab(u) Muḥammad to Sīdī Muḥammad, 25 Ramaḍān 1263 (9/9/1847).
158 'al-Ibtisām', 222; CPM19: De Chasteau à Guizot, 4/9/1847.
159 AHG:H122: Depêche de Bazaine sur l'emigration du Banu Amir, 8/9/1847.
160 AHG:H122: Depêche de Bazaine sur l'emigration du Banu Amir, 8/9/1847; CPM19: De Chasteau à Guizot, 3/10/1847.
161 DAR: al-Jazā'ir: Sultan to Sīdī Muḥammad, 12 Shawwāl 1263 (26/9/1847).
162 *Tuḥfat al-zā'ir*, 492.
163 al-Ḥajwī, 'Ikhtiṣar', 73.
164 DAR: TA: ^{c}Alī b. Aḥmad al-Tasūlī and Aḥmad b. ^{c}Abd Allah al-Tasūlī to Sīdī Muḥammad, 9 Ramaḍān 1263 (24/8/1847); Wajda: Muḥammad al-Tuzīnī to Muḥammad b. ^{c}Abd al-Karīm, 22 Ramaḍān 1263 (6/9/1847); CPM19: De Chasteau à Guizot, 25/9/1847.
165 CPM19: De Chasteau à Guizot, 4/9/1847; FO99/35: Murray to Palmerston, 5/10/1847.
166 CPM19: De Chasteau à Guizot, 25/9/1847.
167 FO99/35: Murray to Palmerston, 5/10/1847.
168 CPM19: Marabout of the Banū Sa^{c}īd to De Chasteau, 10/1847.
169 DAR: TA: Anon to Muḥammad b. Muḥammad b. ^{c}Abd al-Karīm, 29 Ramaḍān 1263 (12/9/1847).
170 DAR: al-Jazā'ir: ^{c}Abd al-Qādir to the Queen of Spain, 12 Shawwāl 1263 (26/9/1847) and FO99/35: Murray to Palmerston, 20/10/1847.
171 CPM19: Béchameil au Ministre de la Marine, 14/9/1847; De Chasteau à Guizot, 4/9/1847 and 25/9/1847.
172 FO99/35: Hay to Palmerston, 31/10/1847 and 20/11/1847.
173 DAR: Tanger I: Sultan to Bū Silhām, 21 Shawwāl 1263 (5/10/1847).
174 DAR: TA: Sultan to Sīdī Muḥammad, 22 Shawwāl 1263 (6/10/1847).
175 DAR: TA: Sultan to Sīdī Muḥammad, 21 Shawwāl 1263 (5/10/1847); DAR: TA: Sultan to Sīdī Muḥammad, 29 Shawwāl 1263 (13/10/1847); FO99/35: Murray to Palmerston, 23/9/1847 and CPM19: De Chasteau à Guizot, 25/9/1847.
176 FO99/35: Murray to Palmerston, 25/10/1847.
177 FO99/35: Murray to Palmerston, 20/10/1847.
178 CPM19: De Chasteau à Guizot, 3/10/1847.
179 CPM19: De Chasteau à Guizot, 7/11/1847.
180 DAR: Wajda: Sultan to Sīdī Muḥammad, 26 Shawwāl 1263 (10/10/1847) and end of Shawwāl 1263 (13/10/1847).
181 CPM19: Marabout of the Banū Sa^{c}īd to De Chasteau, 10/1847.
182 CPM19: De Chasteau à Guizot, 7/11/1847.
183 CPM19: De Chasteau à Guizot, 19/11/1847.
184 CPM19: De Chasteau à Guizot, 6/1/1848.
185 DAR: TA: Sīdī Muḥammad to the Sultan, end of Dhū'l-Ḥijja 1263 (11/12/1847).

186 CPM19: Lamoricière au Ministre de la Guerre, 24/11/1847.
187 CPM19: De Chasteau à Guizot, 19/11/1847.
188 CPM19: De Chasteau à Guizot, 25/11/1847.
189 CPM19: De Chasteau à Guizot, 24/11/1847; FO99/35: Hay to Palmerston, 20/11/1847.
190 CPM19: De Chasteau à Guizot, 26/11/1847.
191 FO99/35: Hay to Palmerston, 26/11/1847.
192 CPM19: De Chasteau à Guizot, 4/12/1847.
193 'al-Ibtisām', 222.
194 CPM19: De Chasteau à Guizot, 12/12/1847.
195 DAR: TA: Sīdī Muḥammad to the Sultan, 5 Muḥarram 1264 (13/12/1847).
196 CPM19: De Chasteau à Guizot, 6/1/1848.
197 DAR: TA: Sīdī Muḥammad to the Sultan, 3 Muḥarram 1264 (11/12/1847); CPM19: De Chasteau à Guizot, 6/1/1847.
198 DAR: TA: Sīdī Muḥammad to the Sultan, 8 Muḥarram 1264 (16/12/1847).
199 CPM19: De Chasteau à Guizot, 6/1/1847.
200 DAR: Wajda: Sīdī Muḥammad to the Sultan, 9 Muḥarram 1264 (17/12/1847).
201 *Tuḥfat al-zā'ir*, 495–6.
202 DAR: al-Jazā'ir: Sīdī Muḥammad to the Sultan, Muḥarram 1264 (December 1847) and Sīdī Muḥammad to Sīdī al-ᶜArabī b. al-Mukhtār, 15 Muḥarram 1264 (23/12/1847).
203 Churchill, *Abdel Kader*, 265 and *Tuḥfat al-zā'ir*, 499.
204 *Tuḥfat al-zā'ir*, 500.
205 DAR: TA: Sīdī Muḥammad to the Sultan, 21 Muḥarram 1264 (29/12/1847).
206 DAR: TA: Wuld Ab(u) Muḥammad to Sīdī al-ᶜArabī al-Mukhtār, 16 Muharram 1264 (24/12/1847).
207 DAR: TA: Sultan to ᶜAbd al-Qādir Ashᶜāsh, 22 Muḥarram 1264 (30/12/1847).
208 Makhzan correspondence refers to celebrations in Tetuan, Tanger, Meknes and Salé.
209 DAR: al-Jazā'ir: Muḥammad b. Ibrāhīm. b. al-Ṭālib to the Sultan, 15 Ṣafar 1264 (22/1/1848).

7 ISLAMIC STATEHOOD AND JIHAD IN NINETEENTH CENTURY MOROCCO

1 'al-Ibtisām' 221–2; *al-Jaysh* II, 21; *al-Istiqṣā'* IX, 56.
2 Marshall Hodgson, *The Venture of Islam 3: The Gunpowder Empires and Modern Times*, Chicago, 1974 edn, 16–27.
3 Rudolph Peters, *Jihad in Classical and Modern Islam*, Princeton, 1996, 1–8.
4 Abdallah Laroui, *Les origines sociales et culturelles du nationalisme marocain*, Paris, 1977, 19.
5 al-Kardūdī, 'Kashf al-ghumma', 4; Muḥammad al-Ghālī, 'Maqmaᶜ al-Kufr'.
6 al-Saqāt, Muḥammad b. al-Tawdī, 'Muqayyada hawla ḥādithatayn', 12348, Bibliotheque Royale, Rabat.
7 Louis Arnaud, *Au temps des "Mehallas"*, Casablanca, 1952, 157.
8 Mohammed al-Khalloufi, *Bouhmara: du Jihad à la compromission: le Maroc oriental et le Rif de 1900 à 1909*, Rabat, 1993.
9 Burke, *Moroccan State*, 183.
10 Dunn, *Resistance in the Desert*, 46–8.

SELECTED BIBLIOGRAPHY

Archives

Direction des Archives Royales, Rabat, Morocco

General Correspondence (*al-tartīb al-^{c}āmm*), 1245–64 (1829–47).
Subject Files (*al-tartīb al-khāṣṣ*), 1238–76 (1822–59).

Public Record Office, London, UK

Morocco General Correspondence, 1822–37: FO52/23–45.
Morocco General Correspondence, 1838–47: FO99/1–35.
Morocco Confidential Print: FO413/1–3.
Algiers General Correspondence: FO3/32–6.

Les Archives Historiques de la Guerre, Chateau de Vincennes, France

Correspondance Generale, l'Algérie: H64–5, 122.
Journaux des Marches: H212, 213.
L'Algérie – Memoires Divers: H227, 229.
Documents pour servir a l'histoire d'Algérie: H235, 236.

Les Archives des Affaires Etrangères, Paris, France

Correspondance Politique – Maroc 1842–7: CP8–19.

Unpublished primary sources

Abū'l-Imlāq, ^{c}Abd al-Qādir, *al-Khabr ^{c}an al-faqīh al-^{c}Ayyāshī bi-hādhihi 'l-bilād wa dhikr sabab qiyāmihi bi-waẓīfat al-jihād*, D91, Bibliotheque Generale, Rabat.

Akansūs, Muḥammad, *al-Jaysh al-^{c}aramram al-khumāsī fī dawlat awlād mawlānā ^{c}Alī al-Sijilmāsī*, D965, Bibliotheque Generale, Rabat.

Anonymous, *Kitāb al-qawānīn al-dākhiliyya al-muta^{c}allaqa li-mushāt al-^{c}asākir al-jihādiyya fī sabīl Allah*, 57, Bibliotheque Royale, Rabat.

al-Darqāwī, al-Madghirī, *Risāla li-taḥdhīr ^{c}alā al-jihād*, D3355, Bibliotheque Generale, Rabat.

al-Dukkālī, Muḥammad, *Itḥāf al-wajīz bi-akhbār al-^{c}adwatayn lī mawlānā ^{c}Abd al-^{c}Azīz*, D42, Bibliotheque Generale, Rabat.

al-Ghālī, Muḥammad, *Maqma^{c} al-kufr bi'l-sinān wa'l-ḥusām fī bayān iyjāb al-isti^{c}dād wa ḥarb al-niẓām*, 965, Bibliotheque Royale, Rabat.

al-Ghazzāl, Aḥmad, *Natījat al-ijtihād fi'l-muhādana wa'l-jihād*, D107, Bibliotheque Generale, Rabat.
al-Ḥajwī, Muḥammad, *Ikhtiṣār al-Ibtisām*, H114, Bibliotheque Generale, Rabat.
—— *al-Nafs al-nafīs fī tarjamat al-wazīr Ibn Idrīs*, H139, Bibliotheque Generale, Rabat.
Idrīs, Abū'l-ᶜAlā, *al-Ibtisām fī dawlat Ibn Hishām*, 12490, Bibliotheque Royale, Rabat.
Ibn ᶜAzzūz, *Risālat al-ᶜabd al-ḍaᶜīf illa'l-sulṭān al-aᶜzam al-sharīf*, D1623, Bibliotheque Generale, Rabat.
al-Kardūdī, Aḥmad, *Kashf al-ghumma bi bayān inna ḥarb al-niẓām ḥaqq ᶜalā al-umma*, D1281, Bibliotheque Generale, Rabat.
al-Khūjā, Muḥammad, *Risāla fī tanẓīm al-jaysh*, K2733, Bibliotheque Generale, Rabat.
al-Maghīlī, Muḥammad, *Jawāb ᶜalā su'āl fī mā yajib ᶜala al-muslimīn min ijtināb al-kuffār*, D2013, Bibliotheque Generale, Rabat.
al-Mashrafī, Muḥammad, *al-Ḥulal al-bāhiyya fī tārīkh mulūk al-dawla al-ᶜAlawiyya*, D1463, Bibliotheque Generale, Rabat.
Ruwayla, Qaddūr b. Muḥammad, *Wushāt al-makātib wa zīnat al-jaysh al-muḥammadī al-ghālib*, D1542, Bibliotheque Generale, Rabat.
al-Saqāt, Muḥammad al-Tawdī, *Muqayyada ḥawla ḥādithatayn*, 12348, Bibliotheque Royale, Rabat.
al-Sulaymānī, Muḥammad, *Zubdat al-tārīkh wa zuhrat al-shamārīkh*, D3657, Bibliotheque Generale, Rabat.
al-Zayyānī, Abū'l-Qāsim, *ᶜAqd al-jumān fī shamā'il al-sulṭan sayyidnā wa mawlānā ᶜAbd al-Raḥmān*, H40, Bibliotheque Generale & 126, Bibliotheque Royale, Rabat.
—— *Takmīl al-turjumāna fī khilāfat Mawlay ᶜAbd al-Raḥmān*, 126, Bibliotheque Royale, Rabat.

Unpublished theses

Harrak, Fatima, *State and Religion in Eighteenth Century Morocco: The Religious Policy of Sidi Muhammad Ibn Abdallah*, Doctoral thesis, University of London, 1989.
Issawi, Fatima, *Jawānib min ᶜalāqat al-makhzan bi'l-ḥiraf 1822–1894*, Thèse de Diplôme, Université Mohamed V, Rabat, 1989.
Mercer, Patricia, *Political and Military Developments within Morocco During the Early 'Alawi Period (1659–1727)*, Doctoral thesis, University of London, 1974.
Yasin, Ibrahim, *Mawqif al-dawla al-maghribiyya min iḥtilāl Faransā li'l-Jazā'ir mā bayna 1830 wa 1847*, Thèse de Diplôme, Université Mohamed V, 1987.
Zebadia, Abdelkader, *The Career and Correspondence of Ahmad al-Bakkay of Timbuctoo: A Historical Study of His Political and Religious Role from 1847–1866*, Doctoral thesis, University of London, 1974.

Published works (primary and secondary)

ᶜAbd al-Qādir, Muḥammad b., *Tuḥfat al-zā'ir fī tārīkh al-Jazā'ir wa'l-amīr ᶜAbd al-Qādir*, Mamduh al-Haqqi (ed.), Beirut, 1964.
Abou El Fadl, Khaled, 'Ahkam al-Bughat: irregular warfare and the law of rebellion in Islam', J. Johnson and J. Kelsay (eds), *Cross, Crescent and Sword*, Westport, 1990.
Abun Nasr, Jamil, *A History of the Maghrib in the Islamic Period*, Cambridge, 1987.
—— *The Tijaniyya: A Sufi Order in the Modern World*, Oxford and London, 1965.

Abū Ṭālib, Muḥammed, 'Mawāqif Briṭānyā min al-Maghrib al-qarn al-tāsi^{c} ^{c}ashar', *al-Iṣlāḥ wa'l-mujtama^{c} al-maghribī fī 'l-qarn al-tāsi^{c} ^{c}ashar*, Rabat, 1986, 295–314.

Ageron, Charles-Robert, 'Abd el-Kader et la première résistance algérienne', C.-R. Ageron *et al.* (eds), *Les Africains*, Paris, 1977.

—— 'Abd el-Kader, souverain d'un royaume Arabe d'Orient', *Revue de l'Occident Musulman Méditerranée*, (1970), 15–30.

Akansūs, Muḥammad, *al-Jaysh al-^{c}aramram al-khumāsī fī dawlat awlād mawlānā ^{c}Alī al-Sijilmāsī*, Fes, 1336/1918.

Aksan, Virginia, 'Ottoman political writing, 1768–1808', *International Journal of Middle Eastern Studies* 25 (1993), 53–69.

Arnaud, Louis, *Au temps du 'Mehallas' ou le Maroc de 1860 à 1912*, Casablanca, 1952.

—— 'Le seige d'Ain-Madi par el-Hadj Abd el-Kader ben Mohi ed-Din', *Revue Africaine* 8 (1864), 354–71 and 435–53.

Azan, Paul, *L'Emir Abd el-Kader 1808–1883 – du fanatisme musulman au patriotisme française*, Paris, 1925.

al-Azmeh, Aziz, *Muslim Kingship: Power and the Sacred in Muslim, Christian and Pagan Polities*, London and New York, 1997.

Beck, Herman, *L'image d'Idris II, ses descendants de Fas et la politique sharifienne des sultans marinides (656–869/1258–1465)*, Leiden, 1989.

Bel, Alfred, *La Religion Musulman en Berberie*, Paris, 1938.

Bellemare, Alexandre, *Abd el-Kader: sa vie politique et militaire*, Paris, 1863.

Ben Talha, Abdelouahed, *Moulay-Idriss du Zerhoun*, Rabat, 1965.

Benaboud, M'hammed, 'Authority and power in the Ottoman state in the eighteenth century', Caesar Farah (ed.), *Decision Making and Change in the Ottoman Empire*, Northeast Missouri State University, 1993, 67–79.

Bennison, Amira. K., 'The 1847 revolt of 'Abd al-Qadir and the Algerians against Mawlay 'Abd al-Rahman, Sultan of Morocco', *Maghreb Review* 22, 1–2 (1997), 109–23.

Berbrugger, Louis, 'Les Frontières de l'Algérie', *Revue Africaine* 4 (1860), 401–17.

—— 'Itinéraires et Renseignements sur le pays de Sous et les autres pays méridionales du Maroc', *Description Geographique de l'Empire du Maroc*, Renou, 1846.

—— *Relation de l'Expédition de Mascara*, Paris, 1836.

Berque, Jacques, *Ulémas, Fondateurs, Insurgés du Maghreb*, Paris, 1982.

—— *L'Interieur du Maghreb XV–XIX siècles*, Paris, 1978.

Blunt, Wilfred, *Desert Hawk – Abd al-Kader and the French Conquest of Algeria*, London, 1947.

Bourqia, Rahma, 'Vol, pillage et banditisme dans le Maroc du XIXe siècle', *Hesperis Tamuda* XXIX, 2 (1991), 191–226.

Bourquia, Rahma and Susan Gilson Miller (eds), *In the Shadow of the Sultan: Culture, Power and Politics in Morocco*, Cambridge MA, 1999.

Brett, Michael, 'On the historical links between Morocco and Europe', George Joffé (ed.), *Morocco and Europe*, SOAS Occasional Papers 7, 1989.

—— 'Continuity and change: Egypt and North Africa in the nineteenth century', *Journal of African History* 27 (1986), 149–62.

—— 'Morocco and the Ottomans: the sixteenth century in North Africa', *Journal of African History* 25 (1984), 331–41.

—— 'Modernisation in nineteenth century North Africa', *Maghreb Review* 7, 1–2 (1982), 16–22.

Brett, Michael and Fentress, Elizabeth, *The Berbers*, Oxford, 1996.

Brown, Kenneth, 'Profile of a nineteenth century Moroccan scholar', Nikki Keddie (ed.), *Scholars, Saints and Sufis: Muslim Religious Institutions Since 1500*, Berkeley, 1981, 127–48.
—— *People of Salé: Continuity and Change in a Moroccan City 1830–1930*, Manchester, 1976.
Bu ^{c}Aziz, Yahya, *al-Jadīd fī ^{c}alāqat al-amīr ^{c}Abd al-Qādir ma^{c}a Asbāniya wa ḥukāmiha al-^{c}askariyyīn bi-Malīlyā*, Algiers, 1982.
Burke, Edmund III, 'The sociology of Islam: the French tradition', Malcolm Kerr (ed.), *Islamic Studies: A Tradition and its Problems*, Malibu, 1980, 73–88.
—— *Prelude to Protectorate in Morocco: Precolonial Protest and Resistance 1860–1912*, Chicago, 1976.
—— 'The image of the Moroccan state in French historical literature: new light on the origins of Lyautey's Berber policy', Ernest Gellner and Charles Micaud (eds), *Arabs and Berbers*, London, 1973, 175–99.
—— 'Pan-Islam and Moroccan resistance', *Journal of African History* 13, 1 (1972), 97–118.
Caillé, Jacques, 'Un Français a Marrakesh en 1851', *Hesperis* XLIII, 3–4 (1956), 437–47.
—— *Une Mission de Léon Roches à Rabat*, l'Institut des Hautes Etudes Marocaines, 1947.
—— 'La France et le Maroc en 1849', Hesperis XXXIII, 1–2 (1946), 123–55.
Churchill, Charles Henry, *The Life of Abdel Kader ex-Sultan of the Arabs of Algeria*, London, 1867.
Cigar, Norman, *Muhammad al-Qadiri's Nashr al-Mathani: The Chronicles*, Oxford and London, 1981.
—— 'Société et vie politique a Fes sous les premiers Alawites', *Hesperis Tamuda* XVIII (1978–9), 93–172.
—— 'Conflict and Community in an urban milieu: under the Alawis (ca 1666–1830)' *Maghreb Review* 3, 10 (1978) 3–13.
Clancy-Smith, Julia, *Rebel and Saint: Muslim Notables, Populist Protest, Colonial Encounters*, Berkeley, 1994.
—— 'Saints, Mahdis and Arms: religion and resistance in 19th century North Africa', Edmund Burke and Ira Lapidus (eds), *Islam, Politics and Social Movements*, Berkeley, 1988, 60–80.
Cook, Weston F., *The Hundred Years War for Morocco: Gunpowder and the Military Revolution in the Early Modern Muslim World*, Boulder, San Francisco and Oxford, 1994.
Cornell, Vincent J., 'Socioeconomic dimensions of reconquista and jihad in Morocco: Portuguese Dukkala and the Sadid Sus, 1450–1557', *International Journal of Middle Eastern Studies* 22 (1990), 379–418.
Cour, Auguste, 'L'Occupation Marocaine de Tlemcen', *Revue Africaine* 52 (1908), 29–73.
Dakhlia, Jocelyne, 'Dans le mouvance du prince: la symbolique du pouvoir itinérant au Maghreb', *Annales Economies Sociétés Civilisations* 43, 3 (1988), 735–60.
Danziger, Raphael, 'The attitudes of Morocco's sultan Abd al-Rahman toward the French as reflected in his internal correspondance 1844–1847', *Revue de l'Occident Musulman et Méditerranée* 36, 2 (1983).
—— 'Abd al-Qadir and Abd al-Rahman: religious and political aspects of their confrontation 1843–1847', *Maghreb Review* 6, 1–2 (1981), 27–35.

Danziger, Raphael, 'From alliance to belligerency: Abd al-Qadir in Morocco 1843–1847', *Maghreb Review* 5, 2–4 (1980), 63–73.

—— 'Diplomatic deception as a last resort: Abd al-Qadir's oblique pleas to the French and the British 1846–1847', *Maghreb Review* 14, 4–6 (1979), 126–8.

—— *Abd al-Qadir and the Algerians*, New York and London, 1977.

—— 'Abd al-Qadir's first overtures to the British and the Americans (1835–1836)', *Revue de l'Occident Musulman et Méditerranée* 18, 2 (1974), 45–64.

De Cossé Brissac, P., *Les rapports de la France et du Maroc*, Paris, 1931.

Delpech, Adrien, 'Resumé historique sur le soulevement des Derkaoua d'apres la chronique d'el Mossellem ben Mohammed Bach Deftar du Bey Hassan de 1800 a 1813 (1215–1228 AH)', *Revue Africaine* 18 (1874), 38–58.

Donner, Fred, 'The sources of Islamic conceptions of war', J. Kelsay and J. Johnson (eds), *Just War and Jihad*, 1988, 31–70.

Drague, Georges, *Esquisse d'Histoire Religieuse du Maroc: Confreries et Zaouias*, Paris, 1951.

al-Ḍu^{c}ayyif al-Ribāṭī, *Tārīkh al-dawla al-^{c}alawiyya al-sa^{c}īda min nashātihā illa awākhir ^{c}ahd Mawlay Sulaymān* 1043–1238/1633–1812, 2 vols, Casablanca, 1988.

Dugat, Gustave, *Le livre de Abd el-Kader intitulé: Rappel a l'Intelligent avis a l'Indifferant*, Paris, 1858.

Dunn, Ross, *Resistance in the Desert: Moroccan Responses to French Imperialism 1881–1912*, Madison, 1977.

Emerit, Marcel, *L'Algèrie à l'Epoque d'Abd-el-Kader*, Paris, 1951.

—— 'Hadj Ahmad Bey et la résistance constantinoise a la conquēte française', C.-R. Ageron *et al.* (eds), *Les Africains*, Paris, 1977.

Ennaji, Mohamed, *Expansion europèene et changement social au Maroc*, Casablanca, 1996.

Esquer, Gabriel, *Correspondance du Maréchal Clauzel*, Vols I and II, Paris, 1948.

Estailleur-Chanteraine, Philipe, *L'Emir Magnanime: Abd el-Kader le Croyant*, Paris, 1959.

—— *Abd el-Kader: l'Europe et l'Islam au XIX siecle*, Paris, 1947.

Etienne, Bruno, *Abdelkader*, Paris, 1994.

Farouk, Ahmed, 'Les forces Marocaines pouvaient-elles inquieter la France lors de la prise d'Alger?', *Hesperis Tamuda* XXVIII (1990), 47–63.

el-Fassi, Nacer, 'Mohammed Ibn Idris, vizir et poete de la cour de Moulay Abderrahman', *Hesperis Tamuda* III, 1 (1962), 43–62.

Fleischer, Cornell, 'Royal authority, dynastic cyclism and "Ibn Khaldunism"', Bruce Lawrence (ed.), *Ibn Khaldun and Islamic Ideology*, Leiden, 1984, 46–67.

Flournoy, Francis R., *British Policy towards Morocco in the Age of Palmerston (1830–1865)*, Baltimore, 1935.

Fournier, P., 'L'Etat d'Abd el-Kader et sa puissance en 1841', *Revue d'Histoire Moderne et Contemporaine* 14 (1967), 123–57.

Gallissot, René, 'La guerre d'Abd el Kader ou la ruine de la nationalité Algérienne (1839–1847)', *Hesperis Tamuda* V (1964), 119–14.

García-Arenal, Mercedes, 'The revolution of Fas in 869/1465 and the death of Sultan 'Abd al-Haqq al-Marini', *Bulletin of the School of Oriental and African Studies* XLI, 1 (1978), 43–66.

Gellner, Ernest, 'Tribalism and state in the Middle East', P. Khoury and J. Kostiner (eds), *Tribes and State Formation in the Middle East*, Berkeley, 1990, 109–26.

—— *Muslim Society*, Cambridge, 1983.

Green, Arnold, *The Tunisian Ulama 1873–1915: Social Structure and Response to Ideological Currents*, Leiden, 1978.

al-Hajji, Mohamed, *al-Zāwiya al-dilā'iyya*, Rabat, 1983.

Hammoudi, Abdellah, *Master and Disciple: The Cultural Foundations of Moroccan Authoritarianism*, Chicago and London, 1997.

Hamdan Khoja, *Le Miroir: Aperçu historique et statistique sur le Regence d'Alger*, Paris, 1985.

Hart, David, *The Ait Waryaghar of the Moroccan Rif*, Tucson, 1976.

Hess, Andrew, *The Forgotten Frontier: A History of the Sixteenth Century Ibero-African Frontier*, Chicago and London, 1978.

Hodgson, Marshall, *The Venture of Islam, Conscience and History in a World Civilisation 3: The Gunpowder Empires and Modern Times*, Chicago, 1974.

George Høst, *Histoire de l'Empereur du Maroc Mohamed Ben Abdallah*, translated from Danish by F. Damgaard and P. Gailhanou, Rabat, 1998.

Ibn Fūdī, ᶜUthmān (Usuman Dan Fodio), *Bayān wujūb al-hijra*, edited and translated by F.H. al-Masri, 1975.

Ibn Khaldun, *The Muqaddimah: An Introduction to History*, translated by F. Rosenthal, edited and abridged by N. J. Dawud, Princeton, 1989.

Ibn Sūdā, ᶜAbd al-Salām, *Dalīl mu'arrikh al-Maghrib al-Aqṣā*, Tetuan, 1950/1369 AH.

Imber, Colin, *Ebu's-su'ud: the Islamic Legal Tradition*, Edinburgh, 1997.

al-Jabartī, ᶜAbd al-Raḥmān, *Tārikh ᶜajā'ib al-āthār fī'l-tarājim wa'l-akhbār*, 3 vols, Beirut, n.d.

Jackson-Grey, James, *An Account of the Empire of Morocco*, 3rd edn, London, 1968.

Jamous, Raymond, *Honneur et Baraka: Les structures sociales traditionnelles dans le Rif*, Cambridge, 1981.

Jenkins, R. G., 'The evolution of religious brotherhoods in north and northwest Africa 1523–1900', John Ralph Willis (ed.), *The Cultivators of Islam*, London, 1979, 40–77.

Joffé, George, '*The Zawiya of Wazzan: relations between the Shurafa' and tribe up to 1860*', George Joffé and Richard Pennell (eds), *Tribe and State: Essays in Honour of David Montgomery Hart*, Outwell, Wisbech UK, 1991, 84–118.

—— (ed.) *Morocco and Europe*, London, SOAS, Centre for Middle Eastern Studies Occasional Papers 7, 1989.

Kelsay, John, *Islam and War*, Louisville, Kentucky, 1993.

—— and Johnson, J. (eds), *Cross, Crescent and Sword: The Justification and Limitation of War in Western and Islamic Tradition*, Westport, Connecticut, 1990.

—— and Johnson, J. (eds), *Just War and Jihad: Historical and Theoretical Perspectives on War and Peace in Western and Islamic Traditions*, London and New York, 1988.

Kenbib, Mohamed, 'The impact of the French Conquest of Algeria on Morocco', *Hesperis Tamuda* XXIX, 1 (1991), 47–60.

—— 'Changing aspects of state and society in nineteenth century Morocco', Abdelali Doumou (ed.), *The Moroccan State in Historical Perspective 1850–1985*, Dakar, 1990, 11–28.

al-Khalloufi, Mohammed Essaghir, *Bouhmara du jihad à la compromission: Le Maroc oriental et le Rif de 1900 à 1909*, Rabat, 1993.

King, John, 'Abd el-Kader and Arab nationalism', John Spagnolo (ed.), *Problems of the Modern Middle East in Historical Perspective: Essays in Honour of Albert Hourani*, Reading, 1992, 133–50.

Laroui, Abdallah, *The History of the Maghrib: An Interpretative Essay*, translated from the French by Ralph Manheim, Princeton, 1977.

—— *Les Origines Sociales et Culturelles du Nationalisme Marocain (1830–1912)*, Paris, 1977.

Last, D. Murray, 'Reform in West Africa: the jihad movements of the nineteenth century', J. Ajayi and M. Crowder (eds), *History of West Africa*, vol II, 1987.

Lawrence, Bruce, 'Holy war (jihad) in Islamic religion and nation-state ideologies', J. Kelsay and J. Johnson (eds), *Just War and Jihad*, London and New York, 1988, 141–60.

—— (ed.), *Ibn Khaldun and Islamic Ideology*, Leiden, 1984.

Levi-Provençal, Evariste, *Les Historiens des Chorfa*, Paris, 1922.

Levtzion, Nehemia and John Voll (eds), *Eighteenth Century Renewal and Reform in Islam*, Syracuse, 1987.

Lewis, Bernard, *Political Language of Islam*, Chicago and London, 1988.

El Mansour, Mohamed, *Morocco in the Reign of Mawlay Sulayman*, Outwell, Wisbech UK, 1990.

—— 'Sharifian Sufism: the religious and social practice of the Wazzani Zawiya', George Joffé and Richard Pennell (eds), *Tribe and State: Essays in Honour of David Montgomery Hart*, Outwell, Wisbech UK, 1991, 69–83.

—— 'Le commerce maritime du Maroc pendant le régne de Moulay Slimane (1792–1822)', *Maghreb Review* 12, 3–4 (1987) 90–3.

—— 'al-Haraka al-wahhābiyya wa'l-radd fa^{c}l al-maghribī fī bidāyat al-qarn al-tāsi^{c} ^{c}ashar', *al-Iṣlāḥ wa'l-mujtama^{c} al-maghribī*, Rabat, 1986, 175–89.

al-Manouni, Mohamed, *al-Maṣādir al-^{c}arabīyya li'tārīkh al-Maghrib: al-fatra al-mu^{c}āṣ ṣara* 1790–1930, Casablanca, 1989.

—— 'Namādhij min tafattuḥ Maghrib al-qarn al-tāsi^{c} ^{c}ashar ^{c}ala mu^{c}ṭiyāt nahda Uruba wa'l-Sharq al-islāmī', *al-Iṣlāḥ wa'l-mujtama^{c} al-maghribī*, Rabat, 1986, 193–205.

—— *Maẓāhir al-yaqẓa al-maghribī al-ḥadīth*, 2 vols, Rabat, 1985.

Martin, B. G., *Muslim Brotherhoods in Nineteenth Century Africa*, Cambridge, 1976.

Martin, Richard C., 'The religious foundations of war, peace and statecraft in Islam', J. Kelsay and J. Johnson (eds), *Just War and Jihad*, London and New York, 1988, 91–118.

Meakin, Budgett, *The Moorish Empire*, London, 1899.

Mercer, Patricia, 'Palace and jihad in the early 'Alawi state in Morocco', *Journal of African History* 18, 4 (1977), 531–53.

Michaux-Bellaire, Edouard, 'Le souveraineté et le califat au Maroc', *Revue du Monde Musulman* 59, 1 (1925), 117–46.

—— 'La legende Idrisite et le cherifisme au Maroc', *Revue du Monde Musulman* 35 (1917–1918), 57–73.

Miege, J. L., *Le Maroc et l'Europe*, 4 vols, Paris, 1963.

Miller, Susan Gilson, *Disorienting Encounters: Travels of a Moroccan Scholar in France in 1845–1846*, Berkeley, 1992.

Mojuetan, B. A., 'Legitimacy in a power state: Moroccan politics in the seventeenth century during the interregnum', *International Journal of Middle Eastern Studies* 13 (1981), 347–60.

—— 'Myth and legend as functional instruments in politics: the establishment of the Alawi dynasty in Morocco', *Journal of African History* 16, 1 (1975), 17–27.

Montagne, Robert, *Les Berbères et le makhzen dans le sud du Maroc*, Paris, 1930.

El Moudden, Abderrahman, 'Etat et Société rurale a travers la harka au Maroc du XIXième siècle', *Maghreb Review* 8, 5–6 (1983), 141–5.

Munson, Henry Jnr, *Religion and Power in Morocco*, New Haven, 1993.

al-Nāṣirī, Aḥmad b. Khālid, *Kitāb al-istiqṣā' li'akhbār al-duwal al-Maghrib al-Aqṣā*, 9 vols, Casablanca, 1956.

Norris, H. T., *The Pilgrimage of Ahmad – Son of the Little Bird of Paradise*, Warminster, England, 1977.

O'Fahey, Rex, *Enigmatic Saint: Ahmad b. Idris and the Idrisi Tradition*, London, 1990.

Pennell, C. Richard, 'The geography of piracy: northern Morocco in the mid-nineteenth century', *Journal of Historical Geography* 20, 3 (1994), 272–82.

—— 'Tyranny, just rule and Moroccan political thought', *Morocco: Occasional Papers* 1 (1994), 13–42.

—— 'Makhzan and Siba in Morocco: an examination of early modern attitudes', George Joffé and Richard Pennell (eds), *Tribe and State: Essays in Honour of David Montgomery Hart*, Outwell, Wisbech UK, 1991, 159–81.

Peters, Rudolph, *Jihad in Classical and Modern Islam*, Princeton, 1996.

—— *Islam and Colonialism: the Doctrine of Jihad in Modern History*, The Hague, 1979.

Pichon, Jules, *Abd el-Kader, sa jeunesse, son rōle politique et religieux, son rōle militaire, sa captivité, sa mort*, Paris, 1899.

Rassam, Amal and Susan Miller, 'Moroccan reaction to European penetration during the late nineteenth century: the view from the court', *Revue de l'Occident Musulman Méditerranée* 36, 2 (1983), 51–64.

Redouane, Joelle, 'British attitudes to the French conquest of Algeria', *Maghreb Review* 15, 1–2 (1990), 2–15.

Roches, Leon, *Trente deux ans a travers l'Islam 1832–1864*, Paris, 1884.

Rogers, P. G., *A History of Anglo–Moroccan Relations to 1900*, London, 1970.

Rohlfs, Gérard, 'Voyage au Maroc', *Revue Africaine* 7 (1863), 205–26.

Sahli, Mohammad Cherif, *Abd el-Kader: Chevalier de la Foi*, Paris, 1968.

al-Ṣaghīr, ᶜAbd al-Majīd, *Ishkāliyyāt iṣlāḥ al-fikr al-ṣūfī fī'l-qarnayn 18–19*, al-Jadida, 1988.

—— 'al-Mawqif al-siyāsī wa dūruhu fi-takyīf mahmat al-iṣlāḥ ᶜand Muḥammad al-Ḥarrāq 1188–1260/1774–1845', *al-Iṣlāḥ wa'l-mujtamaᶜ al-maghribi*, Rabat, 1986, 389–414.

Schroeter, Daniel, *Merchants of Essaouira: Urban society and Imperialism in Southwestern Morocco 1844–1886*, Cambridge, 1988.

Scott, James, *A Journal of Residence in the Esmailla of Abd el-Kader, and of Travels in Morocco and Algiers*, London, 1842.

Sebti, A., 'Au Maroc: sharifisme citadin, charisme et historiographie', *Annales Economies Sociétés Civilisations* 41, 2 (1986), 433–57.

Shatzmiller, Maya, *The Berbers and the Islamic State: The Marinid Experience in pre-Protectorate Morocco*, Princeton, 2000.

Shinar, P., 'Abd al-Qadir and 'Abd al-Krim: religious influences on their thought and action', *African and Asian Studies* 1 (1965), 139–74.

von Sivers, P., 'Rural uprisings as political movements in colonial Algeria', Edmund Burke and Ira Lapidus (eds), *Islam, Politics and Social Movements*, Berkeley, 1988, 39–59.

—— 'Arms and Alms: the combatative saintliness of the Awlad Sidi al-Shaykh in the Algerian Sahara, 16th–19th centuries', *Maghreb Review* 8, 5–6 (1983), 113–23.

Taliadoros, Georges, *La Culture Politique Arabo-Islamique et la naissance du Nationalisme Algerien 1830–1962*, Algiers, 1985.

Terrasse, Henri, *Histoire du Maroc*, Casablanca, 1950.

Thomson, Ann, 'Arguments for the Conquest of Algiers in the late eighteenth and early nineteenth centuries', *Maghreb Review* 14, 1–2 (1989), 108–18.

—— *Barbary and Enlightenment: European Attitudes towards the Maghreb in the 18th Century*, Leiden, 1987.

Touati, Houari, 'Prestige ancestral et système symbolique sharifien dans le Maghreb centrale du XVIIème siècle', *Arabica* XXXIX (1992), 1–24.

—— 'En relisant les *Nawāzil* de Mazouna: Marabouts et Chorfa au Maghreb centrale au XVe siècle', *Studia Islamica* LXIX (1989), 75–94.

Trout, Frank, *Morocco's Saharan Frontiers*, Geneva, 1969.

Vikør, Knut, *Sufi and Scholar on the Desert Edge: Muhammad b. 'Ali Sanusi and his Brotherhood*, London, 1995.

al-Wazzānī, al-Mahdī, *al-Mi^cyār al-Jadīd*, vols III and IV, Fes, 1900.

Willis, John Ralph (ed.), 'Morocco and the Western Sudan: Fin de Siècle–Fin du Temps. Some aspects of religion and culture to 1600', *Maghreb Review* 14, 1–2 (1989), 91–3.

—— 'Jihad fi Sabil Allah – its doctrinal base in Islam and some aspects of its evolution in nineteenth century North Africa', *Journal of African History* 8 (1967), 395.

Yacono, Xavier, 'Les prisonniers de la smala d'Abd el-Kader', *Revue de l'Occident Musulman Méditerranée* 15–16, 2 (1973), 415–34.

Yahya, Dahiru, *Morocco in the Sixteenth Century: Problems and Patterns in African Foreign Policy*, London, 1981.

al-Zayyānī, Abū'l-Qāsim, *al-Turjumāna al-kubrā fī akhbār al-ma'mūr barran wa baḥran*, ^cAbd al-Karīm al-Filālī (ed.), 1967.

INDEX